The Strategic Triangle

The Strategic Triangle

France, Germany, and the United States
in the Shaping of the New Europe

Edited by
Helga Haftendorn, Georges-Henri Soutou,
Stephen F. Szabo, and Samuel F. Wells Jr.

Woodrow Wilson Center Press
Washington, D.C.

The Johns Hopkins University Press
Baltimore

EDITORIAL OFFICES
Woodrow Wilson Center Press
Woodrow Wilson International Center for Scholars
One Woodrow Wilson Plaza
1300 Pennsylvania Avenue, N.W.
Washington, D.C. 20004-3027
Telephone: 202-691-4010
www.wilsoncenter.org

ORDER FROM

The Johns Hopkins University Press
Hampden Station
P.O. Box 50370
Baltimore, Maryland 21211
Telephone: 1-800-537-5487
www.press.jhu.edu/books/

© 2006 by Woodrow Wilson International Center for Scholars
All rights reserved
Printed in the United States of America on acid-free paper ∞

2 4 6 8 9 7 5 3 1

Library of Congress Cataloging-in-Publication Data

The strategic triangle : France, Germany, and the United States in the shaping of the new Europe / edited by Helga Haftendorn ... [et al.].
   p. cm.
  Includes index.
  Papers from a conference organized by the Center for Transatlantic Foreign Policy and Security Studies at the Free University of Berlin and held May 31–June 4, 2000, in Potsdam.
   ISBN-13: 978-0-8018-8563-1 (hbk. : alk. paper)
   ISBN-10: 0-8018-8563-9 (hbk. : alk. paper)
   ISBN-13: 978-0-8018-8564-8 (pbk.)
   ISBN-10: 0-8018-8564-7 (pbk.)
  1. Europe—Politics and government—1945—Congresses. 2. France—Foreign relations—1945—Congresses. 3. Germany—Foreign relations—1945—Congresses. 4. United States—Foreign relations—20th century—Congresses. I. Haftendorn, Helga. II. Freie Universität Berlin. Arbeitsstelle Transatlantische Aussen- und Sicherheitspolitik.
  D1058.S77 2006
  327.4—dc22

2006031689

 Woodrow Wilson International Center for Scholars

The Woodrow Wilson International Center for Scholars, established by Congress in 1968 and headquartered in Washington, D.C., is a living national memorial to President Wilson. The Center's mission is to commemorate the ideals and concerns of Woodrow Wilson by providing a link between the worlds of ideas and policy, while fostering research, study, discussion and collaboration among a broad spectrum of individuals concerned with policy and scholarship in national and international affairs. Supported by public and private funds, the Center is a nonpartisan institution engaged in the study of national and world affairs. It establishes and maintains a neutral forum for free, open and informed dialogue. Conclusions or opinions expressed in Center publications and programs are those of the authors and speakers and do not necessarily reflect the views of the Center staff, fellows, trustees, advisory groups, or any individuals or organizations that provide financial support to the Center.

The Center is the publisher of *The Wilson Quarterly* and home of Woodrow Wilson Center Press, *dialogue* radio and television, and the monthly newsletter "Centerpoint." For more information about the Center's activities and publications, please visit us on the Web at www.wilsoncenter.org.

Lee H. Hamilton, President and Director

Board of Trustees
Joseph B. Gildenhorn, Chair
David A. Metzner, Vice Chair

Public members: James H. Billington, Librarian of Congress; Bruce Cole, Chairman, National Endowment for the Humanities; Michael O. Leavitt, Secretary of Health and Human Services; Condoleezza Rice, Secretary of State; Lawrence M. Small, Secretary of the Smithsonian Institution; Margaret Spellings, Secretary of Education; Allen Weinstein, Archivist of the United States. Designated Appointee of the President from within the federal government: Tami Longaberger

Private citizen members: Robin Cook, Donald E. Garcia, Bruce S. Gelb, Sander R. Gerber, Charles L. Glazer, Susan Hutchinson, Ignacio E. Sanchez

Contents

Acknowledgments	xi
Introduction: Relations in a Strategic Triangle—Bonn/Berlin, Paris, and Washington	1

Part I The European Community at the Crossroads

1	Building Europe: The European Community and the Bonn-Paris-Washington Relationship, 1958–1963 *Desmond Dinan*	29
2	Germany and the Discord of Its Allies: The Case of the European Political Union *Martin Koopmann*	55

Part II The NATO Crisis of the 1960s and the Maturation of the Strategic Triangle

3   The NATO Crisis of 1966–1967: Confronting Germany with a Conflict of Priorities   77
    Helga Haftendorn

4   The NATO Crisis of 1966–1967: A French Point of View   103
    Frédéric Bozo

5   The De Gaulle Challenge: The Johnson Administration and the NATO Crisis of 1966–1967   127
    Thomas A. Schwartz

Part III Dealing with the Collapse of Bretton Woods

6   The Search for a New Monetary System: Germany's Balancing Act   149
    Michael Kreile

7   France, European Monetary Cooperation, and the International Monetary System Crisis, 1968–1973   171
    Eric Bussière

8   The United States and the Search for a New Economic and Monetary System in the 1970s   189
    William H. Becker

Part IV *Ostpolitik* and Détente

9   German *Ostpolitik* in a Multilateral Setting   209
    Helga Haftendorn

10 President Pompidou, *Ostpolitik,* and the Strategy of Détente   229
    Georges-Henri Soutou

Part V Testing Détente and Relaunching Europe

11 The United States Tests Détente   261
    Gale A. Mattox

12 From Euromissiles to Maastricht: The Policies of Reagan-Bush and Mitterrand   287
    Samuel F. Wells Jr.

13	Germany and Relaunching Europe *Markus Jachtenfuchs*	309

Part VI NATO and Post–Cold War Challenges

14	Enlarging NATO: The German-American Design for a New Alliance *Stephen F. Szabo*	327
15	NATO and the Balkan Challenge: An American Perspective *Kori Schake*	351

Epilogue: A New Geometry?	371
Contributors	389
Index	393

Acknowledgments

The planning and the execution of this project have been a truly international endeavor. Following a German-American project on the role of security institutions over time and space, Helga Haftendorn (in Berlin) discussed the idea of a follow-on project with Georges-Henri Soutou (in Paris) and Stephen F. Szabo and Samuel F. Wells Jr. (both in Washington) back in 1998. (See *Imperfect Unions: Security Institutions over Time and Space,* edited by Helga Haftendorn, Robert O. Keohane, and Celeste A. Wallander; Oxford University Press, 1999.) The four coordinators, representing three countries and two disciplines—contemporary history and political science—invited a group of scholars from the same fields and countries to write studies on specific cases that were considered to be most pertinent to shed light on the strategic triangle. These papers, which reflect a diversity of national and disciplinary approaches, were discussed—and criticized!—at a conference, held from May 31 to June 4, 2000, in Potsdam, and organized by the Center for Transatlantic Foreign Policy and Security Studies at the Free University of Berlin. In this context, the editors wish to thank all the conference participants, who added to the conference's success by presenting papers, chairing panels, and contributing to the discussion. Special thanks also go to Cornelius Friesendorf, Sebastian Mayer, Christine Meissler, Olivier Minkwitz, and Heidi Strecker, who helped organize this conference and were always cheerful aides when the conference was in session.

For the final editorial decisions, the coordinators met on several occasions in Washington, Paris, and Berlin. They wish to thank all the authors who took time to revise their papers according to quite demanding suggestions from the editors. Special thanks go to Jane Mutnick, who managed several revisions of the manuscript, and to Christina Balis, Patrick Cohrs, David Norris, Susan Walke, and Stephanie Willmann, who worked on the research and editing as interns at the Woodrow Wilson International Center for Scholars.

The whole project would not have been possible without the academic encouragement and the financial support of the Alexander von Humboldt Stiftung and the Max Planck Society through the award of its 1995 research prize for international cooperation to Helga Haftendorn. The complete freedom to organize the project—and to spend the prize money!—made it possible to overcome the difficulties usually associated with international and interdisciplinary projects. The result is now presented to the critical reader.

Helga Haftendorn, Georges-Henri Soutou,
Stephen F. Szabo, and Samuel F. Wells Jr.

Washington, D.C., September 2006

The Strategic Triangle

Introduction:
Relations in a Strategic Triangle—
Bonn/Berlin, Paris, and Washington

This book proceeds from the assumption that the strategic triangle of Bonn/Berlin, Paris, and Washington has great relevance for the foreign policies of the three countries. For each of them, it provides opportunities and limits options. The triangle has been most relevant for a divided Federal Republic and for a unified Germany, because Bonn as well as Berlin has always depended on intensive cooperation with both France and the United States. France is Germany's most important partner in Europe because the process of European integration relies on an intimate rapport between the two countries. Equally significant has been the close coupling between Germany and the United States. During the East-West conflict, America was the guardian of Germany's security and freedom; today the United States is balancing Germany's power in Europe, considered potentially too overwhelming by some of its neighbors. Historic legacies, geopolitical situation, and political wisdom prohibit Berlin from returning to a nationalistic, unilateral policy and instead dictate a policy of bilateral or multilateral cooperation with its partners. The German-French as well as the

German-American relationships—and in a different way, also the French-American relationship—are thus of great significance for German foreign policy.

There are also other triangles that have been important in the period since the end of World War II. Before the Federal Republic became an international player, the United States, the United Kingdom, and France cooperated closely to establish a new European order in which a "tamed" Germany was to be securely anchored. When French president Charles de Gaulle wanted to extend this relationship to the Atlantic alliance, and proposed establishing a trilateral "directoire" within NATO, both Washington and London balked. They neither wanted to accord to France, still a non-nuclear state, equal status at this time, nor did they want to limit their options vis-à-vis an ascendant Federal Republic. Being rebuffed by the Anglo-Saxon powers, France turned to West Germany. The two nations' "grand old men," de Gaulle and German chancellor Konrad Adenauer, in 1963 concluded a special treaty of friendship and cooperation, known as the Elysée Treaty. Without this treaty and the latent rivalries between the three, the German-French-American triangle would not have come into existence. During German *Ostpolitik* and the process of German reunification, a German-American-Soviet triangle came into being. Any move on the German question required close cooperation between Washington and Moscow. Due to the skill of Chancellor Willy Brandt and his closest adviser, Egon Bahr, Germany became a full partner in the 1970s and thus assured that—unlike in the immediate postwar period or the two Berlin crises—actions were taken not in spite of, but in accordance with, its interests. A third relevant triangle is the one between Germany, France, and Britain. It has become most pronounced since Prime Minister Tony Blair in 1998 proposed closer cooperation between London and Paris on European security. Together with Germany, the three countries are now the most active proponents of the establishment of a common European security and defense policy—not always to the pleasure of the United States, which tries to balance this emerging European power.

Questions and Puzzles

During the period 1965–95, the German-French-American strategic triangle was a significant dimension of the foreign policy of all three countries. Therefore, the essays in this volume examine the hypothesis that the strategic triangle has had, and continues to have, great relevance for the foreign policies of Germany, France, and the United States. If the triangle is seen as a set of three binary relationships, how do these relationships interact with each other, and what kind of dynamic drives them? What impact has the triangle, and the interactions within it, had on the three states?

The triangle is not even-sided. For the past fifty years, the French-German as well as the German-American relationships have been much more intensive than the French-American connection. Far from being irrelevant, the state of French-American relations—whether they are good or bad—has had a strong impact on the two other relationships; it enlarges or limits Germany's options. But how and under what conditions is this the case? When do relations within the strategic triangle offer new possibilities, and when do they circumscribe a country's room for political maneuvering? Does the triangle provide equal opportunities for each country, and in what ways does it limit the options of each?

Because of their different identities and interests, the three states each react in a specific way to the strategic triangle. Germany tends to see it as an opportunity to interact with its two closest partners. Nevertheless, the triangle is a burden if French and American strategic priorities vary widely, and the Federal Republic is forced to side with either one of them. Because Germany is greatly affected by the strategic triangle, it usually tries to act as a balancer between conflicting interests. However, Germany is successful only if its partners are interested in a compromise solution. In the past, Germany could assume that its partners' concern about losing influence over the Federal Republic obliged them not let a conflict get out of control. Obviously this need for compromise and balancing did not apply to any of the three governments in the run-up to the Iraq war in 2002–3.

Paris, for its part, perceives the strategic triangle as a challenge and as a constraint on its room for maneuvering. It can try to secure some kind of special relationship with Washington to enhance its status vis-à-vis the other European powers and be able to put pressure on Bonn/Berlin; or it can ally with the Federal Republic and put pressure on Washington. But the triangle also limits France's control over Germany and limits its ability to drive the United States out of Europe. Recently, in the 1998 Saint Malo initiative, France tried to reduce the negative effects of the triangle on its political options by strengthening cooperation with Britain.

The strategic triangle has the least affect on American policy. The triangle occasionally obliges the United States to consider the interests and priorities of one or the other of its partners, but does not significantly circumscribe American options. The United States therefore has little reason to work for compromise solutions within the triangle, especially not with a France it does not need as a strategic partner on this special occasion. Further, the most important European partners for Washington are London and Berlin, not Paris. This different degree of dependence on the strategic triangle explains why there are fewer conflicts in German-American and in French-German relations than between Washington and Paris.

The Search for Explanations

Because neither a dominant partner—such as the United States—nor a balance-of-power system between America and a uniting Europe had a strong impact on the strategic triangle, we can conclude that realist or neorealist explanations, focusing on power and interest, have only limited explanatory power. To make this argument, we can rely on the empirical evidence available and need not rehash the abundant literature on realism and neorealism.[1] We rather will look for alternative explanations.

Could not the strategic triangle be considered an informal institution, a pluralistic security community, as some authors have suggested?[2] If this were the case, cooperation could be facilitated, transaction costs reduced, and the accountability of member states' behavior increased, although conflicts would not fully disappear. In our case, however, the assumption that institutions further cooperation[3] does not fully explain the dynamics of the triangle. Especially in the NATO crisis in the 1960s, one would assume that membership of all three states in a common institution had facilitated the search for and the achievement of compromise solutions. This was true only in the case of the Federal Republic and the United States, which—for different reasons—were strongly interested in the unencumbered maintenance of the Atlantic alliance. France, conversely, was not convinced that its security depended on its continued participation in an integrated military alliance. With its *force de frappe* (nuclear strike force), the German territory as an eastward *glacis* (buffer zone), and the American nuclear guarantee, Paris estimated that the political costs of an autonomous defense were lower than continued membership in an integrated and American-dominated NATO.

Although, France in the 1960s was apprehensive about the constraints of international institutions, in the 1970s, during the first oil crisis, it furthered their emergence, especially within the framework of European integration when they served its interests. An example is the Euro-Arab dialogue, which enabled Paris and its European partners to develop a position of their own, different from that of the United States. For its part, France tried instead to involve the Europeans to a greater degree in the International Energy Agency, which Washington controlled. Currently, we again observe a competition between institutions, one American led, the other European: NATO and the European Union, with the latter's Common Foreign and Security Policy (CFSP). Because of the U.S. interest in using the Atlantic alliance as an instrument of global alliance strategy, NATO could not sufficiently adapt to the French desire that it should grant the Europeans a larger measure of autonomy within this organization. The EU members, therefore, decided to enlarge the union vertically to encompass a security and defense element. This task went much beyond its original design as an economic and political union. The result has been a competition between NATO and the CFSP for influence.

The existing institutions neither encompass all three corners of the strategic triangle in any regular pattern nor provide solutions for their problems in general. Moreover, common rules and norms are weak, and the common institutional framework does not favor cooperation specifically.

Thomas Risse, in his paper for the Potsdam conference,[4] interprets the strategic triangle as a "pluralistic security community," a concept originally developed by Karl Deutsch[5] and now used in a constructivist sense. Such a community, however, presupposes a set of shared norms and rules as well as a common concept of security. Germany's security concept has changed since the Cold War from a focus on defense against a specific enemy and on deterring an immediate military threat to a notion of common security. Germany incorporates into this new concept its experience that its security is only guaranteed if the potential enemy does not feel threatened either. The French concept of security includes the assumption that the status (*"le rang"*) of the *grande nation* must not be impaired. And the French also insist that the permanent roots of insecurity, such as social and economic tensions and ethnic problems, should be addressed systematically in advance of crises. For the United States, national security involves above all the protection of its territory and its people, but also the unrestricted use of its political, economic, and military options as a global power. Instead of a common concept, we thus observe three different notions of security.

Because the identities of the states in the strategic triangle diverge, they not only perceive the intentions and interests of their partners differently but also react differently to them. Above all, they try to harmonize other actors' output with their own interests and identities. Further, their political as well as social system, and the specific processes legitimizing political action, have an impact on a state's national identity; they influence the perception and performance of political actors. To understand states' actions, studying their interests and perceptions provides important clues. In contrast to neorealists' theoretical assumptions, constructivist thinkers assume that interests do not primarily depend on the power and position of a state in the international system, nor do they result from the need to cooperate, as neoinstitutionalists maintain. Foreign policy interests result from the way states perceive specific challenges and available options. The combination of historical experience, cultural tradition, beliefs, and norms forms a state's identity.

Historical legacies and geopolitical situation motivate Germany to avoid international isolation. The "trademark" of its foreign policy is a strategy of multilateralism. It has proven its value in the process of European integration. Internally, it has led to the evolution of a rudimentary European identity in the Federal Republic when Germany was still divided. For a long period, this European identity served as an ersatz for the one burdened by the Holocaust and lost during division. The country's division and its situation at the dividing line of the East-West conflict have together produced in its society a strong orientation toward security. It is thus not surprising that Germany regularly supports European positions as long as they do not squarely conflict with American policies. If they do, Germany tries to muddle through, for it continues to regard the United States as an essential guarantor of its security.

In contrast to Germany, France can look back to an unbroken national identity—at least in its own understanding. France's national grandeur has been cultivated with care by its political leaders, above all President de Gaulle, to shield French society from the fissures of the twentieth century—twice occupied by German troops, its colonial empire lost, and its economic predominance diminished. In contrast to its eastern neighbor, France cannot expect to improve its status through international integration; it can only hope to exchange some amount of national sovereignty for access to European instruments of control. It has therefore used the European idea as a means to safeguard its aspiration for great power status. The result has been measured steps in the direction of closer European integration, whereby each sacrifice of autonomy is carefully balanced by an increase in influence. Because of the dominant American position in the Atlantic alliance, France cannot count on additional opportunities for control in NATO. French policy therefore wishes to build the EU's CFSP into a counterweight to U.S. power and to limit Washington's influence within the alliance generally, and on Germany specifically. With this policy, France continuously encounters conflicts with the United States, which will endure as long as it is engaged in Europe.

The engagement of the United States in Europe originates in a specific American brand of multilateralism. In the Wilsonian and Rooseveltian tradition, the United States strives to create a liberal and open international system that gives equal opportunities to all members and discriminates against none. Within this system, and in the period under discussion, Europe has been an important military, economic, and financial partner. U.S. policy toward Europe coincides with both the country's concrete interests and with its predominant societal beliefs. It nicely blends the worldly liberalism of a civic nation with the missionary exceptionalism and the vision of a "shining city upon the hill" of the nation's founders. Because this exceptionalism complements the weight of a superpower, the United States feels that it can claim a moral and political leadership role. This does not, however, imply that the United States tries to enforce its interests with all means available; rather, the United States can afford a concession or compromise—as in the NATO crisis of the 1960s—provided that this does not directly clash with its national interests. However, the United States demands —successfully it seems—to set the agenda and control the negotiating process. Thus, it is no surprise that Europe's aspiration to develop its own security and defense policy has led to sustained transatlantic conflicts.

The Strategic Triangle as an Analytical Construct

The structure and impact of the strategic triangle can best be explained when viewed from the perspective of the political actors. Indeed, the triangle is not an independent variable with quasi-objective, causal consequences for the states. It is primarily an analytical construct existing only in the perception of the actors, and thus it results in outputs particular to them. Each actor sees the triangle differently and reacts in a specific way to its challenges and to the other states' inputs. As a rational actor, a decisionmaker will first try to blend its impact with his country's identities and interests. The interaction with the partners has consequences for the structure of the relations among them; it can produce an increased interest in cooperation, or it can exacerbate existing cleavages. States as actors thus create structures that, in turn, have an impact on actors; both are interdependent.[6] The result is historically contingent, dynamic patterns of interaction that change with alterations in the behavior of the actors. Likewise, the specific impact on the actors changes according to the issue area and internal as well as external challenges.

Thus, we need to revise the assumption that the triangle has an equally strong impact on all three states concerned, as well as the belief that both very close and very difficult relations between two partners necessarily produce conflicts with the third, whereas positive relations between all three members of the triangle are an exception. According to their different identities and interests, all three states thus have differing perceptions of the relations within the triangle Bonn/Berlin-Paris-Washington and their relevance.

A German Perspective

The strategic triangle has been most relevant for a divided Federal Republic and for a unified Germany, because Bonn as well as Berlin have depended on intensive cooperation with both France and the United States. Germany's most important partner in Europe has been France, for European integration relied on intimate cooperation between these two states. Equally significant was the close coupling between Germany and the United States in security affairs. During the East-West conflict, America was the guardian of Germany's security and freedom; today, the United States is balancing Germany's power in Europe, considered potentially too overwhelming by some of its neighbors. Because only rarely have the three pairs of bilateral relationships within the triangle been positive, Germany has often been faced with a difficult conflict of priorities.

Both very intimate and very ruffled relations among two partners have caused conflicts with the third. Particularly, tensions between Paris and Washington—not a rare phenomenon—have restricted Bonn's, or Berlin's, foreign policy options, and have forced hard choices among priorities. In 1963, when Adenauer and de Gaulle concluded the Elysée Treaty between their two countries, they were pursuing a hidden agenda of their own. France wished to limit American influence on Germany and to establish itself as the predominant power in Europe, whereas the Federal Republic wanted to open up alternative options to its heavy reliance on the United States.

In Washington, the Elysée Treaty was viewed with great alarm because policymakers were concerned that Germany might follow the French example and distance itself from the Atlantic alliance. To prevent NATO from disintegrating, the United States tried to accommodate German points of view regarding alliance strategy and nuclear sharing and to blend them into the compromise reached in NATO. Presented with a difficult choice between Paris and Washington, Bonn tried to please both governments as much as possible. France became the preferred partner in the process of European integration—at the cost of equally close relations with the United Kingdom—while the United States remained the primary military and economic partner in world affairs. To bridge the uneasy gap between Paris and Washington, Bonn tried to act as an interpreter between the two partners, to blend what was unblendable: France's and America's competing claims to a unique mission in international affairs, and both countries' determination to be second to none.

Also, a very friendly relationship between Paris and Washington burdened French-German as well as German-American relations. Very close French-American cooperation restricted Bonn's room for maneuvering and held the risk that France and the United States might agree among themselves at Germany's expense, thereby marginalizing Germany. Adenauer has referred to such a situation as his Potsdam *cauchemar:* a situation in which Germany would fall between two stools and become a docile subject of the great powers. This danger was greatest when one partner—or both—was concerned that it might lose its influence on German policy. Such situations arose, for example, during *Ostpolitik* in the early 1970s and reunification in the years 1989–90. Then, Paris and Washington quickly buried their disagreements and cooperated to prevent losing control over developments in Germany. Since its founding, the Federal Republic of Germany has always tried to avoid isolation by means of a strategy of multilateralism.

During the Cold War, the triangle had a built-in mechanism that prevented conflicts that could have led to unmendable damage to the trilateral relationship. On the one side, the German factor hindered France from letting disagreements with the United States get out of control. On the other, France's concern with its status and role prevented it from becoming "America's poodle," as Flora Lewis once referred to the United Kingdom's role vis-à-vis America.[7] In the strategic triangle, conflict and cooperation thus balanced each other nicely.

In the early stages of the East-West conflict, the United States as a regional hegemon used the trilateral relationship at its pleasure to further its interests in Europe. Because West Germany depended on American protection as well as on access to world markets, Bonn would bow to Washington's preferences even if its own priorities diverged. Under de Gaulle's leadership, France challenged America's dominant strategic position and its role as international economic gatekeeper, which gave Washington a capacity for rule setting and for enforcing compliance with these rules. To regain a greater say over its own security, France first proposed to share control of the alliance with the United States and Britain; and second, after Washington declined, it set out to restore its autonomy by withdrawing from NATO's military integration. This competition for influence and power lay at the bottom of the French-American conflict. In contrast to France, the Federal Republic did not have the option to develop its own alternatives to heeding U.S. authority.

It is surprising that the U.S. hegemon did very little to quell conflicts in the strategic triangle. In fact, many of the conflicts originated in the troubled French-American relationship. They have not been offset since the European Union has gained influence and power and thus has tried to balance American power. During the early period—for example, the NATO crisis of the 1960s—when the United States largely determined the outcome of conflicts in the triangle, it had, however, to accommodate some German interests when a solution was not possible without Bonn's concurrence. France, in contrast, tried with some success to withdraw from American control.

Later on, especially when economic affairs or the process of European integration were affected, Washington was much less able to impose its interests on its partners. Though Britain, because of its voluntary arm's-length relationship with the continent, could in the past only marginally influence the process of European integration, with Blair's Saint Malo initiative it has now become a competitive European player, thus adding a new element to French-German cooperation. With the creation of the European Security and Defense Policy, a political balance of power system has been created between Europe and the United States that so far does not suggest solutions to the struggle for predominance between the two.

In German eyes, the conflict is about whether the Europeans will be able to build a counterweight to the United States while at the same time continuing to cooperate with the United States on global security and defense. Because Germany highly values good relations with both France and the United States, it will try to achieve a compromise. Germany will influence the structure of the triangle in such a way that its constraints are of lesser relevance and the cooperative aspects of the interaction patterns are instead strengthened. German initiatives aim to enlarge the overlap of common interests between France and the United States. Regarding the European Security and Defense Policy, this will be the case if the European Union and Atlantic alliance do not compete with each other for influence but rather agree on burden sharing and on complementing each other.

In recent years, one can observe a new competitiveness in the strategic triangle that goes beyond the rivalry between EU and NATO for a primary role. Unified Germany was able to shed most of the restrictions that bound the Federal Republic: the division of the country, its sovereignty circumscribed by allied rights and responsibilities concerning Germany as a whole and Berlin, and West Germany's security threatened by a potentially hostile Soviet Union. Thus, Berlin's dependence on the United States and (to a lesser degree) on France in the German question and in security affairs has shrunken, while its confidence in its own abilities has grown. Germany's participation in the Stabilization Force, known as SFOR, and the Kosovo Force, known as KFOR, in the Balkans on an equal footing with its partners has further strengthened its self-esteem. Now Berlin openly competes with Paris for a decisive say on the European Union's final form and function. At the same time, Germany, together with France and Britain, contests the United States' vision of transatlantic cooperation and burden sharing. If able to act jointly, these European nations would be today's only credible contender to American global power—a view to which Washington has not yet adjusted. It tends to consider European power either a paper tiger, or it displays an alarmist attitude not helpful for working toward a constructive relationship.

The German view of the triangle in 2006 is quite different. The bold, if not reckless, U.S. response to the attacks of September 11, 2001, reshaped international political relationships. Europe is less important for the United States, even as Europeans take the threat of terrorism seriously. The events leading up to the Iraq war and their consequences further altered the triangle, as is discussed in the epilogue to this volume. Though the triangle will not function again as it did in the Cold War years, elements of the triangular relationships will survive and form part of a new structure that is still taking shape.

A French Perspective

Concerning France, political and scientific attention has been mainly focused on the so-called Franco-German couple, its emergence in the 1950s, its blossoming in the 1960s and until the end of the Cold War, and its problems since then. The perceived and also actual importance of the couple derived from the fact that it was seen as instrumental in the development of a first reconciled, then more and more closely united, Western Europe. In this respect, the couple is better called in the academic literature "the Franco-German engine of Europe." Conversely, marital problems between Paris and Berlin, or the sputtering of the Franco-German engine since reunification, are seen as one of the major question marks in the current crisis of the European Union, and also of its relationship with the United States.

However, the perception of an all-important Franco-German relationship, after the destructive consequences for Europe of three Franco-German wars since 1870, does not fully explain French foreign policy since 1945. One has to think in terms of a complex triangle between France, Germany, and the United States. Washington was of paramount importance to France, for only Washington could provide it in the 1940s and 1950s with security—economic security, but also geostrategic security against the two perceived threats, the Soviet Union, and also Germany (because the German problem and the need of an American counterweight and reinsurance in that case, even after the onset of the Cold War, were never absent from French minds; the perception of a German problem certainly diminished respective to the Soviet one after 1950 but never completely disappeared).

The undisputed importance of the Franco-German relationship and the tenets of de Gaulle's *"indépendance nationale"* have obscured the fact that until 1963 and again from 1969 onward with Presidents Georges Pompidou and Valery Giscard d'Estaing (less so with President François Mitterrand after 1981, but again with President Jacques Chirac after 1995), the Franco-American relationship was more important for the French than the Franco-German one in several vital sectors—for new technologies (electronics, air and space, nuclear energy), for weapons (particularly nuclear weapons),[8] and for the flow of investments from the United States to France and vice versa. Even de Gaulle, until the end of 1962, was very eager to get access to American technologies. The French aerospace, electronic, and nuclear industries owed a lot to their links with American firms. The same did not apply to their much less important links with Germany. And when de Gaulle broke with Washington in 1963, it was not to escape from a triangle of which he was well aware and which he very much intended to use extensively to France's benefit, but to reorder it in a fashion more suited to French interests, at least in his eyes. The frequently held view that Germany was more concerned with the United States than France was too simplistic. There was in fact a triangle, also for the French, at least during most of the period from the beginning of the Cold War.

The triangle of France–United States–Germany worked basically in the same way for all French leaders starting in 1947, despite their deep differences in other respects. France wished to enjoy the same kind of relationship with Washington as London did, that is, a kind of special relationship (with its very practical benefits in economics, armaments, and modern technologies). Thus reinforced, Paris would be able to take the lead in Western continental Europe and retain its ascendancy over Germany, which was anyway divided, still under the pall cast by its recent past, and prohibited from access to nuclear weapons.

Conversely, the leadership of continental Europe and the mastery of the Franco-German couple would give more weight to France in its dealings with the United States. France would stand at the apex of the triangle and develop its world role far beyond its actual strength. This notion of a continued world role was very important for most leaders of the Fourth and Fifth Republics; it rested on history; on the universality of "French republican values"; and on the former Empire, called the Union Française after 1946 and the Communauté Franco-Africaine after 1958 and still lingering after the practical demise of the Communauté. The notion of a world role, or at least of an international role beyond Europe, was closely linked and is still today closely linked, in French eyes, with the transatlantic triangle.

On this point, there was more continuity from the Fourth Republic to the Fifth Republic than is commonly realized. From 1948 onward, all French leaders agreed that France's international role could no longer be decisive by itself but needed to be supported by strong links with both America and Western Europe, and that it was in the interest of Paris to nurture and manage this triangle and as far as possible to stand at its apex. But there were of course differences about the way the triangle should function. Was the Franco-American relationship the most important link, giving Paris a means to balance renewed German power and to control Germany? Or was the priority a strong Franco-German axis, allowing Paris to gain more weight in the eyes of Washington and to push its agenda more forcefully with the Americans? Under the Fourth Republic, the majority view was that relations with Washington were more important, that a direct tie to the United States, akin to the Anglo-American "special relationship," was the best way to enable France to go on playing a world role. The minority view (most notably expressed by Robert Schuman and Jean Monnet) was that France could no longer seek a world role by itself, that it could now do so only through a strong Western Europe led by Paris, and that it was through this strong Western Europe, resting on Franco-German reconciliation and cooperation, that Paris could make itself heard in Washington.[9]

When de Gaulle returned to power in 1958, he first tried to establish a special relationship with Washington, through a transformation of the Atlantic alliance, which in his eyes did not give France enough authority in strategic and world affairs. This is the meaning of his well-known September 1958 memorandum, asking for a kind of British-American-French directorate within the alliance, the gist of which had already been on the agenda of French leaders since 1953 or 1954. Because he failed (it could be argued that with more patience he could have achieved success), he decided in 1961–63 to activate the other leg of the triangle, that is, the European and Franco-German one. Hence the (failed) Fouchet Plan for a European Union in 1961–62 and the Elysée Treaty concluded with Germany in January 1963, which, however, remained limited in its practical effects because of American pressure on Germany.

Yet de Gaulle did not abandon the triangle—he wanted to reshape it, exerting pressure on Washington to force a transformation of the Atlantic alliance that would give more weight to France. When de Gaulle left the integrated NATO command in 1966, it was not because he no longer believed in the triangle but because he wanted to suppress integration within NATO, which in his view nullified an independent French role in the world. France should instead take the lead in Western Europe and reach a new arrangement with Washington, which would be a bilateral alliance more congenial to French interests than an integrated NATO. France would then stand at the apex of what remained very much a triangle.[10]

As we know, de Gaulle failed, basically because he confronted Germany with a choice between France and the United States. Germany, for obvious reasons, could only choose Washington. Then France remained isolated inside the Atlantic alliance, and Germany replaced France as the major ally of the United States on the continent. And Bonn put itself, in a subtle way, at the apex of the triangle and began to mediate quietly between Paris and Washington, a discreet role that continued until the end of the Cold War and even afterward.[11]

Presidents Pompidou (1969–74) and Giscard d'Estaing (1974–81) realized the deadlock of French foreign policy and, without heralding it (in order not to antagonize the still powerful Gaullist constituency), restored some balance to the triangle and achieved better relations with the United States. For Pompidou, however, it was a restricted triangle; there was no real French-German-American triangle about détente or strategic matters. On those two key elements of the Cold War, Pompidou wanted a bilateral French-American relationship, largely because he distrusted the ulterior motives of the *Ostpolitik,* which he feared might lead to some sort of German-Soviet condominium over Europe. It was only for European affairs and the development of the European Community (EC) that a triangle between Paris, Bonn, and Washington was very much in evidence—with the Americans trying to control the EC through an extension of the scope of the Atlantic alliance, the French resisting that trend, and the Germans trying to mediate between Paris and Washington or aligning themselves with one or the other capital, for instance, ultimately with Paris about the international monetary system, which led in 1973 to the European monetary "snake," a system of fixed parities among European currencies floating together against the dollar.

President Giscard d'Estaing practiced an extended kind of triangle: He tried to solve the economic and monetary problems of the Western world in close agreement with the major Western countries, especially Germany and the United States, in the Group of Seven, which he created together with German chancellor Helmut Schmidt. In strategic matters, he played an important role in the double-track decision of NATO in 1979, working closely with the Germans and the Americans. But after the Soviet invasion of Afghanistan, he partially reverted to a privileged Franco-German relationship, because both he and Schmidt feared that the Americans were overreacting and thus endangering détente. In 1979, they also made the momentous decision to form the European Monetary System, making the Franco-German relationship once again the engine of Europe, and in the end cooling both their attitudes toward the United States.

President Mitterrand, elected in 1981, accentuated this tendency. In 1982 and again in 1988, the Franco-German treaty of 1963 was revitalized, developing into a truly strategic dimension. Meanwhile Paris' relationship with Washington became generally difficult, with disagreements on monetary, economic, and strategic matters (like the Strategic Defense Initiative), as well as on policy toward the Soviet Union. Actually, Mitterrand reverted to a kind of Gaullism, including discreet reassurances to Moscow, at least after Mikhail Gorbachev came to power. The Soviet Union was seen by Mitterrand as a useful counterweight against both Germany and the United States (as he wrote in a book published in 1986[12]). But he was not the first French leader since the war to look at Moscow in that way and to seek in the USSR a kind of reinsurance against German power and American prepotency, or against a perceived German-American special relationship detrimental to French interests.[13] The triangle then became a more complex geometric figure.

That the French-American-German triangle was very fragile became evident at the time of German reunification. France was isolated, in front of a very close American-German relationship during that crisis, with the Soviet Union practically surrendering to Washington and Bonn. In this heated process, Gorbachev was not convinced by Mitterrand's plea at Kiev on December 6, 1989, to cooperate with Paris in slowing down reunification, in cooperation with a grumpy but ineffective United Kingdom.[14] But Mitterrand then successfully restored the French-German relationship with the Maastricht Treaty of 1992, which was one of the major accomplishments of the French-German European engine. But on that occasion he wanted to develop a European foreign policy and defense identity apart from and outside NATO, which the partners, including the Germans, did not want. The language of the Maastricht Treaty obfuscated the issue. French policy in the triangle was once again severely deadlocked when Mitterrand left the presidency in 1995.

In 1995–96, President Chirac tried to find a way out of the deadlock and suggested a compromise: France would rejoin the integrated command structure of NATO it left in 1966, but the United States would accept the emergence of a European defense identity within NATO (and not outside NATO, as previously wished by France). The compromise apparently failed on technicalities (e.g., the French request that the Mediterranean command at Naples should go to a European), but in fact it failed because both Washington and Berlin understood and could not accept the still very present French ulterior motives: to restore a special link with the United States in order to play a more important role in European security and beyond than Germany, a role at least equal to that of the British.[15]

The strategic triangle is today still deadlocked on a range of issues: In trade, defense, and cultural matters, Paris defends the concept of a European identity, Washington remains strictly Atlantic, and Germany tries to mediate between the two. Most other European partners, even if they have misgivings about some aspects of American policies, are not willing to follow the French lead. The Iraq war thoroughly disrupted the functioning of the triangle. Parts of it are showing signs of recovery, especially along the German-American side. It is of course possible that the triangle will further deteriorate and that the European Union and the United States will drift away from each other, due to growing divergences on major issues and also perhaps because of growing differences in their societal and cultural evolution. But if one accepts that the common interest of the West—despite the end of the Cold War, and in face of a series of difficult international problems ranging from the Middle East to Asia through the Balkans and Eastern Europe—mandates a balanced European-American relationship, and within that relationship a working American-German-French triangle, what should and could be done?

In the light of the present study, it appears that the American-German-French triangle is one (but not the only one) of the very major factors of the transatlantic relationship: Its smooth working enhances the efficiency of the Atlantic alliance; its problems hamper the alliance. The best combination is a balanced, equilateral triangle, where Washington, Paris, and Bonn/Berlin agree or compromise on major issues. Since 1947, all other combinations inside the triangle have been tested. They clearly have been ineffectual.

A Franco-American axis (which the French tried to push much more frequently than has been realized, the last time in 1996) does not help to build Europe. To the contrary, it is usually promoted by Euroskeptic French, wanting to retain an international role for France independent from the construction of Europe, which began in 1950. Further, a Franco-American axis smacks of ulterior motives against (or at least about) Germany. This was the case with many strong Atlanticists in France during the 1950s; and it applied to de Gaulle in 1958 and Chirac in 1995–96. Apart from short-term tactical considerations, in the long run it cannot be in the American interest, and is not conducive to a further building of Europe, to support a privileged Franco-American axis bypassing Germany.

Another possible combination, the Franco-German axis, which has been repeatedly tried by Paris (the last time during the Iraq war in 2003) is not always supported by the Germans, who understand quite well French ulterior motives. The end of the Cold War has suppressed the only reason that at times convinced the Germans to follow the French (albeit prudently) along this line: the fear that Paris might otherwise be tempted to seek reinsurances in Moscow. And the Franco-German axis of course disquieted the United States, which also understands French ulterior motive: to profoundly alter the balance inside NATO (which is also resented by the other European partners).

From the point of view of Paris, it would seem that a balanced, equilateral strategic triangle is in the best French interest. A rift between Paris and Washington has put Bonn/Berlin in a mediating position, allowing Bonn/Berlin to further its own ulterior motives. Bonn profited mightily, in fact, from the French decision to leave the integrated NATO command in 1966. Anyway, France cannot win over Germany permanently to a Franco-German axis, because the Federal Republic of Germany during the Cold War could not, and now does not want, to estrange itself from the United States. And even if Paris could construct such an axis, and further the aim of a *"l'Europe-puissance"* potentially rivaling the United States, if Berlin were really willing to assist France in achieving its more ambitious plans about Europe, the French beyond a certain point would have to realize that their economic, scientific, technological, and strategic interests do not allow them to drift too far away from the United States. Already in 1969 (perhaps even under de Gaulle after the domestic crisis of 1968), this was quietly understood in Paris, notwithstanding all the rhetoric about national independence.

What is said here about the need for a balanced, equilateral triangle applies also to the United States, which has a long-term interest in neither privileging an American-German axis nor an American-French one at the expense of the third partner. Washington should resist the temptation to look for a "privileged partner" in Europe—previously, Britain; and since the end of the Cold War, Germany (one thinks here of the "partners in leadership" with Germany, proclaimed by President George H. W. Bush in May 1989 at Mayence). Washington must also resist the temptation to manipulate the French-German relationship, as it did at times (particularly under John Kennedy), from which it cannot reap any real benefit if one agrees that America in the twenty-first century will need a strong Europe as an effective ally.

In the interest of all countries concerned, the triangle should be balanced, equilateral and not isolated, and not warped in the direction of French, German, or American ulterior motives. In practical terms, for all the current issues (trade, European defense, relations with Russia, the Balkans, the Middle East), it means that Washington should recognize and accept the evolution of a common foreign and defense policy for the European Union's member states as well as the growth of a European economic and political identity, and that it should not try to block these developments, either directly by refusing any adaptation of NATO or indirectly by exploiting differences among European countries on those issues. Washington should particularly realize that the times are past when Germany would block French initiatives to develop a European defense identity. In that respect, the triangle is now much more complex and open.

To keep the triangle functioning and beneficial for all the partners, the

EU (and particularly the French and the Germans) should accept that the United States intends to remain fully engaged in European affairs. There is a particular need for compromises in trade matters, and in the relationship between a European defense policy and NATO. And they can be reached, because it is not possible to imagine a major issue on the agenda of this new century (in trade matters or in international or strategic relations) on which vital American and European interests would diverge radically. This compromise is the difficult but inescapable task of the immediate and near future. But it requires serious transatlantic rethinking of all issues.

U.S. Perspectives

As a global power, the United States has interests in all regions of the world. In recent decades, Europe was a major theater of U.S. interest, at times the primary area of concern, but not always so. At some points in the period from 1960 to 2006, the United States had its concern focused on Southeast and Northeast Asia, on South or Central America, or on the Middle East and the Gulf. Asian, Latin American, and Middle Eastern issues always competed with European concerns for the attention of top policymakers in Washington.

Within Europe, the United States has had a traditional relationship with Britain. This dates from the period before World War I, when almost all the outstanding issues between Britain and the United States were resolved. This relationship was absolutely essential to the conduct of U.S. foreign policy during the period of neutrality in World War I, remained important throughout the interwar period, was central during World War II, and continued in importance through the 1950s. By 1963, with the Cuban Missile Crisis and the start of U.S. involvement in Vietnam, the relationship with London began to decline in importance.

As the 1960s progressed, Germany became the primary U.S. partner in Europe, and this was apparent in the diplomacy surrounding the French withdrawal from NATO's integrated command and the response to *Ostpolitik*. Germany was the key partner in NATO and in almost all U.S. policies toward the Soviet Union. Since 1970, the United States' relationship with the Federal Republic of Germany has been its most important political and military tie. Although everyday exchanges may not be as easy and familiar as they are with Britain, American understandings with Germany are at the core of every element of U.S. policy for Europe. They permeate political, economic, scientific, and cultural relations with Europe. Though Britain remained a key NATO partner, it remained a marginal player in Europe and therefore became less central to U.S. European policy. Conversely, Germany was a key player in both NATO and the EU and kept a pan-European role as well, enhancing its importance to the United States.

France was throughout this period less important to the United States, in large part because American leaders viewed Europe primarily in geostrategic terms as an arena of contention and competition with the Soviet Union. When President Charles de Gaulle chose to withdraw France from the NATO military structure, he placed France in self-imposed isolation on the sidelines of what was for Washington the main game. NATO was and, at some considerable cost, remains the primary U.S. instrument for action and influence in Europe. The United States had continuing and expanding economic and cultural ties with France, and we now know that there were even important technological relationships, including the sharing of extensive data on the construction and operation of nuclear weapons. But these ties never matched and could not compete with the relationship established between Washington and Bonn.

In the period under review in this volume, there was rarely a series of instances when the strategic triangle functioned in a balanced way between Washington, Bonn, and Paris. From the American perspective, normally two of three players either took the lead in shaping Western policy or combined to blunt or modify an approach taken by the third partner. The isolated power generally tried to modify the policy outcome and then adjusted to it. *Ostpolitik* was a case when Franco-American relations were closer, at some cost to relations between the United States and Germany. But by 1972, these issues had been largely resolved, and the triangle continued to function until the end of the decade on issues of détente. New monetary coordination and the replacement of the Bretton Woods institutions was another area of cooperation, although Washington's handling of these issues led France and Germany to develop the European Monetary System later in the 1970s. In the following decade of the 1980s, the question of responding to the Soviet challenge of intermediate-range nuclear missiles placed in Central Europe led to extensive collaboration and conflict among the triangular partners in implementing NATO's dual-track decision dealing with Euromissiles. At certain times, the United States and France shared a concern over German neutralism or pacifism; at others, France and Germany worried about what was seen as Ronald Reagan's adventurist, or even reckless, policy on Euromissiles and arms control.

The post–Cold War period found the U.S.-German axis of the triangle to be the key once again. German unification and NATO enlargement were both driven by Germany and the United States against the resistance of both London and Paris. As Europe became more fluid with the end of Soviet control of Eastern and Central Europe and the Baltic republics, Germany reassumed its position as the principal power in both Western and Central Europe. This kept it at the center of American policy toward Europe during this period of the transformation of European security. Yet the European chess board expanded with NATO's enlargement and the addition of ten new members to the European Union, adding Poland as a key player. The return of Britain to Europe under the Blair government also increased options for all three members of the triangle. Extra-European priorities also began to increase in importance, with the rise of China becoming a strategic challenge to the United States.

The Franco-German relationship remained central to both Paris and Berlin as European integration accelerated in the 1990s. Germany became committed to a European Security and Defense Identity and was less willing or able to play a balancing role between Paris and Washington.

For most issues, the strategic triangle was less important to the United States than it was to Germany or France. The United States had many more issues in play, and it negotiated with many more partners in differing combinations. Depending on the issue, other triangles were more significant for Washington. For example, on most NATO issues, Washington operated in a triangle that included London and Bonn; likewise, on strategic negotiations and arms control, Washington would work with Bonn and Moscow in much the same kind of triangle. On broad Asian issues, Washington operated in a triangle with Tokyo and Beijing. On global security issues, a triangle often functioned among Washington, Moscow, and Beijing. On issues of international economics and finance, Washington after the mid-1970s often worked closely in a rough pentagon with four partners, London, Bonn, Paris, and Tokyo.

As the twenty-first century began, the United States faced the question of whether it was in its interest to continue to regard Germany as its privileged partner in Europe. Germany was no longer semisovereign and became more willing to resist U.S. leadership than when it was a divided and vulnerable country. A new generation of German and American leaders was less bound to the close partnership of the Cold War as well. German and American interests regarding Russia also appear to be diverging. In some aspects, France and the United States had more of an interest in working together because they both had an interest in channeling German power in the new Europe. France remained a serious military power in Europe and had interests and a vision that went beyond the continent, while Germany remained a civilian power with a strong regional focus. The strain in the Franco-German relationship under the Gerhard Schröder and Jacques Chirac governments also offered opportunities for closer cooperation between Paris and Washington.

The United States may wish to consider reviving the triangular relationship with Britain and France, particularly if Germany remains reluctant to enhance its military role. Kosovo showed that France and Britain were willing to be reliable security partners in the new types of crises confronting post-Cold War Europe. The United States also has important other partners in Europe, including Italy, the Netherlands, and Poland. As the European Union expands and becomes more fluid, the centrality of Germany to U.S. policy may become too inhibiting and ill suited for the new Europe of the new century.

The Organization of the Book

This book's authors started out with the assumption that the strategic triangle had a significant impact on the foreign policy behavior of the three states concerned. Each participant was asked to analyze this impact in a specific issue area from the perspective of his or her own country. Thus, each problem was viewed from a French, a German, and an American perspective. The author whose country played a dominant role in the case concerned was asked to present a lead paper, with the two other authors writing supporting papers. All twenty-one papers were then discussed at a conference held in Potsdam in early June 2000. From these, the editors selected twelve to be included in the book after revision. Rather than striving for full coverage of the subject, the editors wanted to present to the reader a series of exemplary cases from different time periods and from varying national perspectives.

Part I of the book consists of two chapters dealing with the situation of the EC in the late 1950s and early 1960s. In chapter 1, Desmond Dinan details the emerging U.S. position on the process of European integration, emphasizing how the competing French and American concepts of European integration were used in the battle over the British application for EC membership. In chapter 2, Martin Koopmann looks at the unsuccessful French and German efforts to build a European political union. He attributes the failure of these early efforts on political cooperation to the diverging concepts on Europe entertained by France and Germany. Though Paris wanted to overcome American hegemony on the European continent by building separate institutions, the German political class wanted a politically stable Europe embedded in NATO. Although Adenauer put high emphasis on strengthening relations with France, he had to accommodate the concerns of his aides, who wanted a balance of French-German and German-American relations. These arguments were a prelude to the domestic debate in Germany on the 1963 Elysée Treaty.

Part II presents three chapters on the NATO crisis of the 1960s. In chapter 3, Helga Haftendorn explains why the crisis started and how it contributed to the emergence of the strategic triangle. In chapter 4, Frédéric Bozo deals with the bête noir of this crisis, General de Gaulle's France; and in chapter 5, Thomas Schwartz gives an original analysis of the crisis from an American historian's perspective, based on new U.S. and NATO documents. Both authors also touch on the country most affected by this crisis, the Federal Republic of Germany. For Germany, having to accommodate both French and American interests, the triangle became a heavy liability that confronted it with a serious conflict of priorities.

The collapse of the Bretton Woods monetary system in the wake of the Vietnam War provides the backbone of part III. In chapter 6, Michael Kreile describes how Germany—which as a major trading nation was seriously affected by the collapse of the dollar—searched for a new monetary system. Above all, it fought reevaluation of the deutsche mark, which would have disadvantaged its exports and endangered price stability at home. One option open to Bonn was cooperating with France to build a European monetary system; the other was following the U.S. lead to restore the international monetary institutions and the dollar standard. The first was explored with the Pierre Werner plan. In chapter 7, Eric Bussière tells the story of this plan's evolution and its collapse due to diverging economic and monetary priorities among EC member states, above all between France and Germany. In chapter 8, William Becker recapitulates the U.S. search for a new economic and monetary system after the fixed exchange rate system collapsed in the early 1970s. The result of this search was the short-lived Smithsonian Agreement, which also succumbed to divergent monetary strategies. A second German-French initiative for a continental monetary system at the end of the 1970s, however, was more successful and laid the foundation for the European Monetary System.

Part IV deals with *Ostpolitik* and détente. In this section, the traditional strategic triangle recedes behind other geometric forms, all involving Moscow. Helga Haftendorn's account in chapter 9 of how German *Ostpolitik* was effected is juxtaposed with Georges-Henri Soutou's story in chapter 10 of the French reaction to it, as well as Paris' effort to devise its own strategy of détente. Both chapters chronicle the German and the French effort to shape a new relationship with the Soviet Union. Because the Federal Republic was still subject to allied rights and responsibilities, it needed to cooperate closely with the United States and, to a lesser degree, with France. By taking the initiative in negotiating with Moscow, Bonn to some extent was able to force its partners' hands, while Washington used the lever of Berlin—on which West Germany, because of Four Power rights, had no authority to negotiate—to control Bonn's *Ostpolitik*. French leaders at the same time embarked on a delicate game to balance Germany with the Soviet Union and the Soviet Union with Europe and the United States.

Part V traces the long years in which the United States became increasingly frustrated with détente, while the Europeans after the Soviet invasion of Afghanistan tried to save regional détente from deterioration. This process is described in chapter 11, by Gale Mattox. She also explains the U.S. motives for the NATO dual-track decision of 1979 and the difficult missile debate in Germany, which led to the collapse of the Schmidt government. This is where Samuel Wells picks up the story, explaining U.S. strategic policies from Ronald Reagan to Bill Clinton in chapter 12. He also discusses the American reaction to the European initiatives to develop a European Common Foreign and Security Policy. In chapter 13, Markus Jachtenfuchs complements this account with an analysis of French-German cooperation—and competition—in negotiating the Maastricht and Amsterdam treaties on European political union. The result is a fascinating story of interlocking policies shaping a new, though transient, transatlantic relationship.

The book concludes with a very topical part VI, which deals with the need to reform NATO since the end of the East-West conflict and with the "Balkan challenge." In chapter 14, Stephen Szabo recounts German-American cooperation in adjusting the Atlantic alliance to the new situation, especially by admitting new members that formerly belonged to the opposing Warsaw Pact. And in chapter 15, Kori Schake gives an American interpretation of the deployment of NATO forces in Bosnia and in Kosovo. She concludes by expressing the sober concern that American interests seemed to be no longer sufficiently compatible with European interests for the alliance to be a meaningful tool for jointly managing security.

With the collapse of the strategic triangle in the buildup to the March 2003 invasion of Iraq, the editors of this volume began a discussion about whether the triangle could ever function effectively again. This unresolved debate resulted in an Epilogue built around three national perspectives. The two American editors, Stephen Szabo and Samuel Wells, contend that so many basic factors have changed that the triangle will not likely survive as a policy-shaping concept. It is highly probable that transatlantic relations will be organized through a shifting combination of coalitions of the willing. The French editor, Georges-Henri Soutou, argues that European politics are now dramatically different from the pattern of the Cold War. The strategic triangle no longer serves French national interests and will not likely regain its former role. The German editor, Helga Haftendorn, expects that, while Germany will pursue a more national role in its foreign policy, transatlantic relations will continue to be a significant force in world politics, perhaps through a form of ellipse with European and American nuclei.

Notes

1. See Kenneth N. Waltz, *Theory of International Politics* (Reading, Mass.: Addison-Wesley, 1979); and Robert O. Keohane, ed., *Neorealism and Its Critics* (New York: Columbia University Press, 1986).

2. Christopher Daase shared this observation with me while criticizing a draft of this chapter. Thomas Risse suggested a similar concept in his paper prepared for the Potsdam Conference of May–June 2000; see Thomas Risse, "Testing Détente: Conflict Management and Domestic Politics in the Transatlantic Community during the Early 1980s."

3. See Robert O. Keohane and Joseph S. Nye, *Power and Interdependence* (New York: HarperCollins, 1990); Helga Haftendorn, "Sicherheitsinstitutionen in den internationalen Beziehungen: Eine Einführung," in *Kooperation jenseits von Hegemonie und bedrohung: Sicherheitsinstitutionen in den internationalen Beziehungen*, ed. Helga Haftendorn and Otto Keck (Baden-Baden: Nomos, 1997), 11–33; Helga Haftendorn, Robert O. Keohane, and Celeste Wallander, "Introduction," in *Imperfect Unions: Security Institutions over Time and Space,* by Helga Haftendorn, Robert O. Keohane, and Celeste Wallander (Oxford: Oxford University Press, 1999), 1–18; and Robert O. Keohane and Celeste Wallander, "Risk, Threat, and Security Institutions," in *Imperfect Unions,* 21–47.

4. See Risse, "Testing Détente."

5. Karl W. Deutsch et al., *France, Germany, and the Western Alliances: A Study of Elite Attitudes on European Integration and World Politics* (New York: Charles Scribner's Sons, 1967). On security communities, see also Emanuel Adler and Michael Barnett, eds., *Security Communities* (Cambridge: Cambridge University Press, 1998).

6. Alexander Wendt, "The Agent-Structure Problem in International Relations Theory," *International Organization* 41 (1987): 335–70.

7. Flora Lewis, "The Same Old French-U.S. Row," *International Herald Tribune,* December 13, 1996, 8.

8. For this special but capital aspect, see Georges-Henri Soutou, *L'Alliance incertaine: Les rapports politico-stratégiques franco-allemands, 1954–1996* (Paris: Fayard, 1996); and Soutou, "Le Président Pompidou et les relations entre les Etats-Unis et l'Europe," *Journal of European Integration History / Revue d'histoire de l'intégration européenne* 6, no. 2 (2000): 111–46.

9. Georges-Henri Soutou, "Georges Bidault et la construction européenne 1944–1954," in *Le MRP et la construction européenne,* ed. Serge Berstein, Jean-Marie Mayeur, and Pierre Milza (Brussels: Éditions Complexe, 1993); Soutou, "Frankreich und das atlantische Bündnis, 1949–1956," in *Nationale Aussen- und Bündnispolitik der NATO-Mitgliedstaaten,* ed. Norbert Wiggershaus and Winfried Heinemann (Munich: Oldenbourg, 2000); Maurice Vaïsse, Pierre Mélandri, and Frédéric Bozo, eds., *La France et l'OTAN, 1949–1996* (Brussels: Éditions Complexe, 1996).

10. Soutou, *L'Alliance incertaine;* Georges-Henri Soutou, "La décision française de quitter le commandement intégré de l'OTAN (1966)," in *Von Truman bis Harmel: Die Bundesrepublik Deutschland im Spannungsfeld von NATO und europäischer Integration,* ed. Hans-Joachim Harder (Munich: Oldenbourg, 2000). For different but not contradictory views, see Maurice Vaïsse, *La grandeur: Politique étrangére du général de Gaulle, 1958–1959* (Paris: Fayard, 1998); and Frédéric Bozo, *Deux stratégies pour l'Europe: De Gaulle, les Etats-Unis et l'Alliance atlantique 1958–1969* (Paris: Plon, 1996).

11. Georges-Henri Soutou, "L'exception française," in *L'OTAN 50e anniversaire* (Paris: François-Xavier de Guibert, 2000).

12. François Mitterrand, *Réflexions sur la politique extérieure de la France* (Paris: Fayard, 1986), 47.

13. Georges-Henri Soutou, "La place de l'URSS dans la politique allemande de la France 1943–1969," in *Les tiers dans les relations franco-allemandes,* ed. Christian Baechler and Klaus Jürgen Müller (Munich: Oldenbourg, 1996).

14. Georges-Henri Soutou, *La Guerre de Cinquante Ans: Les relations Est-Ouest 1943–1990* (Paris: Fayard, 2001), 709–12.

15. Georges-Henri Soutou, "Dissuasion élargie, dissuasion concertée, ou dissuasion pour le roi de Prusse," *Géopolitique,* no. 52 (1995–96); Soutou, "L'exception française;" Soutou, "La France et l'Allemagne vont-elles continuer à être le moteur de l'Europe?" *Géopolitique,* no. 65 (1999): 40–49.

Part I

The European Community at the Crossroads

Chapter 1

Building Europe: The European Community and the Bonn-Paris-Washington Relationship, 1958–1963

Desmond Dinan

The launch of the European Economic Community in January 1958 introduced a new element into the emerging triangular relationship between Bonn, Paris, and Washington. France and Germany were the two leading powers in the six-member European Community (EC). In effect, the EC was a bargain struck between them for mutual economic gain. The deal involved the progressive establishment of a common market with a common external tariff and a common commercial policy; provisions to assuage French concerns about liberalizing intra-EC trade; and, at French insistence, a commitment to develop a common agricultural policy.

By strengthening postwar Franco-German ties, the EC also had an important political dimension. Indeed, Germany conceded a lot to France in the negotiations that led to the EC in order to deepen Franco-German solidarity, a key element of Bonn's goal of binding the Federal Republic into the West. The preamble of the Treaty of Rome, the EC's charter, called for an "ever closer union" among the peoples of Europe. This was a vague assertion of the popular aspiration for European unity.

The United States was an avid supporter of European integration and took a keen interest in the emergence of the EC. Economically, the United States hoped to benefit from expanded production, lower costs, and increased efficiency in Western Europe, the anticipated consequences of greater integration. Successful implementation of the Rome Treaty presented an opportunity to increase trade not only among EC member states but also between them and the United States. Trade creation, the Americans thought, would far outweigh trade diversion. Politically, America's view of the EC was consistent with Washington's original perception of European integration. Thus the EC would anchor West Germany in Western Europe, strengthen Western Europe's ability to withstand communist subversion and Soviet pressure, and stand shoulder to shoulder with America in a strong transatlantic community.

This chapter examines the impact of the EC, in the formative years 1958–63, on relations among Bonn, Paris, and Washington. In these years, the strategic triangle had not fully developed. The United States conducted active bilateral relations with the two continental powers as well as with Britain. The events of this period narrowed the policy options for Washington and reduced Britain's influence with U.S. leaders. The crisis over NATO in 1966–67 is the crucible that ultimately shaped the strategic triangle as it functioned into the early 1990s.

Initially, the EC focused on first principles: taking the initial step toward implementation of the industrial common market. Bonn, Paris, and Washington shared a strong economic interest in having that happen. Bonn and Washington were also motivated by strategic concerns; Paris less so. The main challenge to the launch of the common market between 1958 and 1960 came from Britain, which sought to subsume the nascent EC into a proposed free trade area (FTA). Opposition to British efforts to subvert the EC united Bonn, Paris, and Washington in defense of the common market.

By contrast, economic and strategic interests divided Bonn, Paris, and Washington between 1961 and 1963. Two issues proved particularly troublesome. One was the Common Agricultural Policy (CAP), a predominant French objective to which Germany reluctantly subscribed and in which the United States grudgingly acquiesced for overriding political reasons. The other involved American and French designs for Europe. Both called for European unity as the basis of a strong, equitable transatlantic relationship. There the similarity ended. Whereas the Americans wanted to unite Europe around supranational institutions and to maintain hegemony in transatlantic relations under the guise of a new partnership, the French opposed supranationalism, saw the EC primarily in economic terms, and sought to challenge American supremacy in the Atlantic alliance.

Britain's application for EC membership became the main battleground for these competing French and American designs. Washington supported Britain's application; Paris had serious reservations; and Bonn was equivocal. French president Charles de Gaulle's veto of Britain's membership in January 1963, motivated to a considerable extent by concerns about the CAP, represented a setback for President John Kennedy's Grand Design. The failure of the French proposals for European union in 1962, and the German parliament's emasculation of the Elysée Treaty in 1963, represented a similar reversal for de Gaulle's design. Thereafter, Europe continued to integrate economically, and the CAP became a permanent irritant in U.S.-EC relations, but the EC lost its salience as a divisive political issue among Bonn, Paris, and Washington.

First Principles

The Organization for European Economic Cooperation (OEEC) took up Britain's proposal for an FTA at the ministerial level in October 1957, three months before the EC came into existence. Britain wanted an agreement by January 1, 1959, when the EC was due to make the first tariff cuts and quota increases mandated by the Rome Treaty. Without an agreement at that time, Britain claimed, implementation of the common market would discriminate against other OEEC members, with potentially damaging economic and political consequences for Western Europe. Fearful of the impact of the EC on Britain's exports to its members, Britain sought the advantages of free trade without the obligations of joining a deeper common market. Britain hoped that the prospect of a geographically wider FTA would lure the lower-tariff, larger-trading EC member states, notably Germany and the Netherlands, away from France.[1]

Clearly, each side distrusted the other. The French, who had invested heavily in the Rome Treaty, strongly opposed the proposed FTA. France had already rejected an FTA among the six favoring a common market, which included provisions to protect special French interests and the promise of a CAP. Why should France now accept a wider FTA and risk jeopardizing the EC? French objections were well founded; different external tariffs within the FTA (the six would have a common tariff, but each of the other countries would set its own tariff levels) as well as British participation in the

Commonwealth preference system were problematical. An agreement acceptable to France would require broad policy coordination, strong institutions, and common rules. It would also have to include agriculture, which Britain wanted to exclude from any agreement.

The FTA negotiations were limping along in the OEEC when the French political crisis of April and May of 1958 brought them to a halt. De Gaulle's return to power in June raised questions about the future of the EC and of the proposed FTA. One of the biggest questions was whether the new French government would be willing and able to stick to the treaty timetable for tariff reductions and quota increases on January 1, 1959, or, by letting the deadline slip, signal its lack of interest in the EC. De Gaulle's economic and financial reforms soon put France in a position materially to meet the deadline. Indeed, domestic reform and external liberalization (within limits) were inextricable parts of de Gaulle's approach to economic modernization in France. Much to the relief of its EC partners, the French government announced in October 1958 that it would stick to the treaty timetable.[2]

Given de Gaulle's well-known opposition to supranationalism, the other member states were understandably uncertain about his commitment to the Community. The legalistic nature of the French announcement of October 1958 suggested that de Gaulle was merely meeting a treaty obligation, not enthusiastically embracing intra-EC trade liberalization. The true test of de Gaulle's attitude toward the EC would be his approach to the FTA negotiations. Pursuing a larger FTA would give de Gaulle a chance to put the EC in limbo without breaking any treaty obligations. Killing the free trade proposal, by contrast, would allow him to demonstrate a commitment to the EC on more than legal grounds. When they announced their decision to implement the first EC-wide tariff cuts and quota increases, the French also announced that they had yet to reach a decision on the FTA. The future of the fledgling EC would depend to a considerable extent on de Gaulle's choice.

The United States welcomed the establishment of the EC in January 1958. A memorandum by Douglas Dillon, the assistant secretary of state for European affairs, reporting on the first meeting of the EC Council of Ministers, emphasized the political importance of the event.[3] In a letter to the Embassy in London in February 1958, another U.S. official observed that "given . . . the political flux on the continent, the disparity in political stability and economic structure between France and Germany, and other factors about which you are all too familiar, strong institutional ties of the sort implicit in the . . . Common Market appear to us to be of infinitely greater importance today than in past years."⁴ The United States also looked forward to the dynamic economic effects of market integration.

Britain's FTA proposal clashed with Washington's strong political and economic support for the Community. The U.S. representative to the EC and the U.S. ambassador in Paris repeatedly urged Washington to come out against the FTA. The ambassador in London, sympathetic to Britain's plight, made the opposite case. The administration's official position was that "we favor the FTA on condition that it does not relax the impetus toward the Common Market and general liberalization of trade. We will try to be helpful but direct intervention and pressure [for or against] are regarded as counterproductive."⁵ Publicly, Washington sat on the fence; privately, the United States became increasingly irritated with Britain in 1958, fearing that the FTA would undermine the fledgling EC.

The British put their hopes in de Gaulle's presumed aversion to European integration, even after Prime Minister Harold Macmillan's meeting with the new French leader in June 1958. The meeting between de Gaulle and German chancellor Konrad Adenauer in September was more consequential. De Gaulle and Adenauer had a common interest in ending the free trade initiative, de Gaulle for economic reasons and Adenauer for strategic reasons (strengthening Franco-German relations). At the meeting of the Council of Ministers in Venice a few days later, ministers fell in line behind the tougher French negotiating position (an early example in the history of the EC of the Franco-German axis at work).⁶

It was only a matter of time before de Gaulle administered the coup de grace; yet Britain remained hopeful that he would opt for the FTA and that the United States would come out in support of it. Macmillan told Dillon in London on October 23, 1958, that he saw a link between the FTA and de Gaulle's recent proposal for a restructuring of NATO, contained in a letter to President Dwight Eisenhower. It seemed to Macmillan that de Gaulle's "price for accepting the FTA would be UK and US acceptance in some form" of NATO restructuring. Macmillan thought that he would probably have to settle the matter bilaterally with de Gaulle, "possibly with US assistance in view [of the] implications [of the] de Gaulle letter."⁷

There is no evidence that de Gaulle linked the FTA and NATO proposals. Nor had the United States any intention of getting directly involved in the free trade issue. Matters came to a head in November 1958, when Jacques Soustelle, de Gaulle's information minister, announced that "it was not possible to form a free trade area as had been wished by the British, that is to say by having free trade ... without a common external tariff and without harmonization in the social and economic spheres."[8] Far from embracing the FTA, de Gaulle had maintained the previous government's opposition to it and taken the matter to a logical conclusion. Not only was this consistent with de Gaulle's strategy of modernizing the French economy by means of European integration, but supporting the FTA would have been politically risky for him. As Miriam Camps observed at the time, "The opposition of French industry to a free trade area was fierce and articulate. ... Virtually no one in France saw any appreciable economic advantage in the arrangement."[9]

Washington was pleased with the substance, if not the timing or the manner, of Soustelle's announcement. London was furious. Macmillan had told Dillon in October that, rather than accept defeat of the FTA, "the UK would organize a counter movement of their own and would have to reevaluate her position in NATO."[10] Despite the misgivings of Economics Minister Ludwig Erhard, Adenauer went along with de Gaulle's decision (the two leaders met in Germany twelve days after Soustelle's announcement). The Council of Ministers endorsed what had become a Franco-German position at a meeting in Brussels on December 3. Ironically, it was Erhard who went to London to inform the British officially of the EC's decision (Germany was in the council presidency).

Washington was now anxious to mollify London, prevent British retaliation, and ensure that the common market developed along liberal lines. Despite de Gaulle's unequivocal opposition to the FTA, Britain refused to let the issue drop and continued to press for an agreement of some kind. The matter became a major irritant in Anglo-French relations, as was evident in a meeting of the OEEC Council in December 1958, which ended in acrimonious exchanges between the British and French ministers. The U.S. State Department instructed its representative at the meeting (the United States was an associate member of the OEEC) to "avoid specific comment ... which would put US in position of taking sides. Must use utmost care to avoid any impression that US [is] getting out in front of Europeans [on] this issue."[11]

The FTA dispute continued in one form or another for the next two years. In early 1959, Britain and six other non-EC Western European countries started negotiations to establish a rival trade bloc, the European FTA. This would not bring Britain many immediate economic advantages, because Britain's economy dwarfed those of the other prospective members. Its main purpose was to increase pressure on the EC to reopen negotiations for an all-encompassing FTA. Britain hoped that the United States, concerned about a Europe "at Sixes and Sevens," would twist the EC's arm. Seven countries signed the European Free Trade Association (EFTA) convention in Stockholm in November 1959.

From the outset, the United States was "skeptical" about EFTA which, from Washington's point of view, had no redeeming economic or political features.[12] America's representative to the EC urged Washington to come out strongly against it.[13] As the year wore on, Washington's patience with London grew exceedingly thin. Yet Washington remained publicly neutral, refusing either to endorse or condemn the EFTA idea. Privately, however, American officials vented their frustration with Britain and their opposition to EFTA. The United States believed that the adoption of a liberal trade policy by the Community, which seemed to be happening, and a general lowering of trade barriers through the General Agreement on Tariffs and Trade (GATT), about which EFTA seemed unenthusiastic, were the best solution for all concerned. Bonn, Paris, and Washington were in complete agreement. Even Erhard had abandoned his initial opposition to the EC and support for the FTA. This was due not only to pressure from Adenauer, however indirect, but also to satisfaction with the EC's liberal orientation.

By the end of 1959, Washington would no longer stand aside. Domestic pressure from business interests and members of Congress concerned about EFTA's emergence, and about a possible proliferation of regionalism around the world, forced the administration to act. The State Department hatched a plan to transform the OEEC into a broader economic organization that would include the United States, Canada, and possibly Japan. According to Dillon, "the end result would be a group which would have the public task of reorganizing the OEEC, but could also iron out the problems of the Six and the Seven."[14] As Secretary of State Christian Herter wrote more loftily to President Eisenhower in November 1959, this "would constitute an act of creative United States leadership in a recently deteriorating situation. It would greatly increase the opportunity of the United States to influence the makers of European economic policy in two directions—greater European development efforts and actions to compose European trade quarrels on a basis consistent with sound trade relations."[15] This was the genesis of the Organization for Economic Cooperation and Development (OECD), in which the proposal for a Western European-wide FTA was finally buried.

France and Germany readily accepted the American proposal; Britain did so reluctantly. London held fast to the idea that the EC was an illiberal organization, which would open up only in response to pressure from EFTA. As late as October 1959, a senior British official, in a meeting with Dillon, "made it clear that the ultimate relationship sought by Britain was the revival of the original FTA concept." Remarkably, Britain still looked "for United States help in this endeavor."[16] On a trip to Europe in December 1959 to advocate the OECD, Dillon had congenial meetings in Bonn, Brussels, and Paris, but difficult ones with British officials in London.

Washington's relations with London on EC affairs remained strained well into 1960. Britain took strong exception to a joint statement by Adenauer and Eisenhower in March 1960 endorsing the call by the EC Commission for accelerated tariff cuts and global trade liberalization, seeing it as outright American opposition to EFTA. In response, Macmillan warned once again about possible repercussions for NATO and threatened to withdraw British troops from Germany.[17] A telegram from the usually sympathetic Embassy in London lamented the increasing number of "exaggerated and emotional statements" by the prime minister on the EC, EFTA, and NATO.[18] Under the circumstances, Macmillan's U-turn the following year, when Britain applied for EC membership, was all the more remarkable.

In its first two years, the EC had brought Bonn, Paris, and Washington closer together on a range of economic issues. Fears about the impact of de Gaulle's return to power on the EC, and on EC-related issues in the triangular relationship, were unfounded. France had a reputation for economic protectionism, but Washington gave Paris the benefit of the doubt as far as constructing the EC was concerned. Washington's confidence was vindicated by de Gaulle's endorsement of the EC's first tariff cuts and quota increases in 1959, opposition to the FTA, and support for a liberal EC commercial policy. Nor was the amity between Bonn, Paris, and Washington threatened by any EC-related strategic differences, although the late 1950s was a tense time for transatlantic relations.

Erhard, who was *not* inclined to give the French the benefit of the doubt, remarked to the Americans in June 1959 that "the development of the . . . [EC] had been more problematical under previous French governments, which had been under the influence of protectionist elements. Now, however, France was stronger politically and economically, as a result of which the Common Market had developed faster and more effectively than had been expected."[19] The development of the EC along lines congenial to Erhard, his American interlocutors, and the traditionally protectionist French was due to more than political stability in Paris, however. Political stability allowed France to undertake economic and financial reforms but, as the American Embassy noted in January 1959, "Some lever was required to gear internal corrective measures to world conditions and competition. That lever was supplied by the Common Market and its convenient deadline of January 1, 1959, for action on quotas and tariffs." Implementing the common market, seeing off the FTA, and supporting a liberal EC commercial policy, the embassy observed, were clearly in the French national interest, and were "Gaulliste in fullest sense of the word."[20] They were also fully compatible with American and German interests. But the triangular cooperation on economic issues was soon put to the test by new developments in European integration.

Agricultural Policy, Grand Designs, and British Accession

The harmony among Bonn, Paris, and Washington on EC affairs in 1960 gave way to acrimony by early 1963. Two issues soured the relationship. One was the advent of the CAP, which had a far more negative impact on transatlantic trade than most observers had expected. Washington appreciated the importance of the CAP for European political as well as economic integration. Yet negotiating the CAP in the early 1960s caused serious tension between Bonn and Paris, whereas the CAP itself became a standing irritant in U.S.-EC relations. The first major transatlantic trade dispute broke out at the end of 1962. Predictably, it concerned agriculture (the so-called Chicken War).

The other divisive issue was more complex. It had to do, on the one hand, with Britain's application for EC membership and, on the other, with competing American and French designs for Europe, NATO, and transatlantic relations. These issues were related because the United States championed British membership in the EC as part of its "Grand Design" for a new transatlantic partnership. In Kennedy's famous words, the transatlantic partnership would bind the United States and Europe "on a basis of full equality in all the great and burdensome tasks of building and defending a community of free nations."[21] De Gaulle had a different vision of European unity and transatlantic partnership. He envisioned a Europe based on intergovernmentalism rather than supranationalism; a "Europe of the states" rather than a federal Europe; and a Europe genuinely equal to the United States in NATO rather than militarily subservient to Washington.[22] Britain shared de

Gaulle's antipathy toward supranationalism, but GB it acquiesced in Washington's vision of the transatlantic relationship, a vision that sought to hide American hegemony behind a facade of Euro-American equality.[23]

The Common Agricultural Policy

France fought hard during the negotiations that resulted in the Rome Treaty to include agriculture in the prospective common market. A major agricultural producer, France wanted guaranteed access to an EC marketplace that would be protected from cheaper, non-EC imports. Thus, unlike industrial trade policy, agricultural trade policy in the EC would be avowedly protectionist. The Rome Treaty contained only general principles on agriculture; it was up to the member states, with the help of the EC Commission, to develop a specific policy. When he came to power in 1958, de Gaulle made the achievement of a CAP one of his main objectives. It became a key element of his strategy for French economic modernization. As well as spreading the burden of agricultural subsidies among all member states, the CAP would revolutionize the farm sector.

De Gaulle fought tenaciously with the EC Commission and other member states to fashion the CAP unequivocally along French lines. In June 1961, the French government threatened to block transition to the second stage of the common market, due to begin on January 1, 1962, unless member states agreed on a CAP before then. That set the stage for the marathon CAP negotiations of mid-December 1961 to mid-January 1962 (technically, the negotiations ended successfully at midnight on December 31). Equally difficult negotiations about specific product prices and overall financial arrangements preoccupied the EC throughout the early and middle 1960s.

The United States recognized the political importance of the CAP. The CAP was part of the Franco-German bargain that established the EC, to which the United States implicitly subscribed. Its political salience grew in the EC's early years. In December 1959, French prime minister Michel Debré told Dillon bluntly that "there was one problem in connection with the Common Market that had not been emphasized enough. That was the question of the treatment of agricultural products."[24] When de Gaulle threatened to destroy the EC unless the other member states agreed to his demands for the CAP, inevitably the United States wanted de Gaulle to win, despite disliking many of his specific proposals. The undersecretary of state, George Ball, told Adenauer as much in April 1961, and he went so far as to urge Germany to overcome its opposition to current French demands by taking "the longest steps within the Six in overcoming present domestic difficulties impeding a common agricultural policy."[25]

The United States was in a dilemma. Supporting the CAP made political but not economic sense. The CAP discriminated against non-EC producers in a number of ways. For instance, it included a system of variable levies, based on the difference between lower world prices and higher EC prices, which reduced imports into the EC and protected European farmers. U.S. agricultural interests and their political supporters were outraged. Agriculture was the United States' leading exporting sector; market access was imperative for continued growth, which was all the more important given America's current economic problems.

The issue became increasingly acrimonious in the early 1960s. Karl Brandt, of the U.S. president's Council of Economic Advisers, warned in September 1960 that "the [EC] must refrain from agricultural autarky. . . . De Gaulle has given in to the rioting French farm organizations . . . the situation is extremely dangerous because it is politically most difficult to unlodge the agricultural interests from their new protectionist position in the [EC] once they have entrenched themselves in it. . . . The European farm organizations, particularly in France and Germany, are past masters in the riot techniques and all sorts of revolutionary pressure tactics." Brandt wanted the United States to end its "kid-glove tactfulness" and apply all possible pressure on the Europeans to abandon the CAP.[26] Agriculture Secretary Orville Freeman, a bitter foe of the CAP, complained about it to Kennedy after a visit to Europe in November 1962. "The French are intractable," Freeman lamented.[27]

The situation was especially embarrassing for the administration as it promoted the Trade Expansion Act (TEA) in 1962. On the one hand, the administration touted the TEA as a means of dealing with the economic challenge of the EC; on the other, it tacitly went along with the implementation in Europe of a trade-distorting CAP. There was little that Washington could do. The United States had no choice but to sacrifice economic goals for political ends. William Diebold, a trade specialist who observed America's acquiescence in the CAP with considerable dismay, reminisced years later that there might have been "much sweet reason in what American officials said to their European colleagues [about the discriminatory aspects of the CAP], but the situation was thought to be delicate and there were bounds to what the Americans were willing to do as they accepted the argument that a common agricultural policy was essential to the integration of the Community."[28]

The "Chicken War" of 1962–63 set a pattern for transatlantic trade relations in the context of the CAP and allowed the administration to appease some of its domestic critics. The dispute erupted in July 1962, when the EC's import regime for poultry came into effect. Whereas American exporters had previously faced a national tariff equivalent to about $4^{1}/_{2}$ cents per pound, they now faced an import fee of about $13^{1}/_{2}$ cents per pound. This triple rate increase caused an immediate drop in American sales. American farmers and politicians went on the warpath. Although poultry exports to Germany represented a fraction of overall U.S.-EC trade, the dispute generated considerable publicity. Hostilities ended when both sides accepted the opinion of a special GATT panel, delivered in November 1963, which upheld American complaints but recommended less compensation than the United States wanted. The EC tacitly acknowledged that the poultry regime, and the CAP in general, was discriminatory; the United States lost market share but won some compensation; and agricultural disputes became a fact of life in a U.S.-EC relationship driven by broader political and economic interests.[29]

Grand Designs

Agriculture impinged on the issue of British accession to the EC and therefore, indirectly, on the debate about Europe's future. The United States swallowed the CAP because of Washington's overriding political interest in the EC. Britain fought against the EC until deciding to join it in mid-1961. As a nonmember, Britain did not care about the CAP. After all, Britain was not an agricultural exporter and would not be affected by the EC's agricultural protectionism. As a potential member of the EC, Britain thought differently about the CAP which, should Britain join, would cut off British access to cheap food imports, change the nature of farm subsidization, and increase food prices for the consumer. Ball identified agriculture in April 1961 as "the most serious hindrance to [British] association with the Six."[30] Indeed, the CAP became the most contentious issue in Britain's accession negotiations, possibly triggering de Gaulle's veto of British membership in January 1963.[31] If so, the CAP helped to destroy Washington's Grand Design.

The Kennedy administration, like the Eisenhower administration before it, saw the EC as the basis for a united Europe, with the EC Commission as its political core. Unlike the Eisenhower administration, the Kennedy administration, driven in European affairs by Ball, an old friend of Jean Monnet, intended to do something about it. The administration also sought to develop transatlantic relations along apparently more equitable lines, to mollify Europeans' resentment of America's preponderant power and strengthen the alliance's political cohesion. Thus the United States wanted a strong EC to emerge as part of a stronger Western Europe, which in turn would strengthen the Atlantic alliance.[32]

Where did Britain fit in? As America's favored interlocutor in the alliance (because of what the British called the special relationship), Britain was an important element in America's emerging Grand Design. But Britain's non-membership in the EC, which Washington saw as the nucleus of a uniting Europe, was politically awkward. For that reason, the Americans were relieved when Britain signaled in early 1961 that it might apply for EC membership.[33] The decision would have to be Britain's alone. For the United States publicly to urge Britain to join, Ball noted in May 1961, "would be seen as an 'Anglo-Saxon conspiracy.'"[34] A year later, with Britain in the midst of accession negotiations, the State Department sought "to avoid the impression in Paris and Bonn that we are the principal sponsors of British membership in the Common Market," that British and American views on NATO were identical, and that there was "an Anglo-Saxon bloc opposed to continental interests."[35]

The United States wanted Britain to adopt the Rome Treaty unreservedly rather than join the EC halfheartedly. Politically, Britain should accept supranationalism. Economically, it should not try to negotiate concessions for the Commonwealth and EFTA, and it should embrace the CAP. As Kennedy told Adenauer in Washington in April 1961, "It is best for the Atlantic Community if the UK joined the EEC on an unconditional basis."[36] In a triumph of hope over experience, the United States wanted Britain to abandon its long-standing hostility toward political and economic integration.

Washington concluded that British membership in the EC would benefit the United States economically as well as politically. Kennedy asked Ball in August 1961 to study the possible economic consequences for the United States of British accession. Ball's preliminary estimate was positive: British membership would substantially enlarge a dynamic marketplace, which would attract more American industrial exports. Some U.S. trade in industrial goods would be diverted from Britain, but far more would be created in the enlarged EC. The prognosis for agricultural trade was less certain because of the evolving nature of the CAP, although the United States was likely to lose lucrative export markets in Britain.[37] The United States presumed that Britain would help orient the EC's common commercial policy in a liberal direction, a direction in which it appeared to be headed in any case. Despite Washington's and London's concerns about agricultural policy, there is no indication that the United States pushed British membership to try to wreck the CAP from the inside.

The United States linked its landmark TEA generally to the advent of the Common Market and specifically to British accession. The disappointing outcome of the Dillon Round of the GATT in March 1962 demonstrated the limits of negotiating tariff cuts on an item-by-item basis and the administration's inability to adopt a more radical approach under existing trade legislation. The Kennedy administration responded by proposing the TEA to Congress, calling for greater flexibility to negotiate linear tariff reductions of up to 50 percent especially to meet the challenge, and exploit the opportunity, of economic integration in Europe. The TEA also authorized the president to eliminate duties on articles in categories of goods for which the United States and the EC together accounted for 80 percent or more of world trade. This provision presupposed British membership in the EC. As it was, the United States and the six accounted for 80 percent or more of world trade in only a few categories; with the addition of Britain, the United States and the EC would account for 80 percent or more of world trade in a large number of categories.[38]

While advocating the TEA in public speeches and testimony before Congress, members of the administration harped on the importance of the proposed legislation for U.S.-EC relations. Apart from its economic consequences, the TEA and the ensuing Kennedy Round of GATT negotiations would help cement U.S.-EC political relations and build the Atlantic partnership. "It was this idea that captured the imagination of the American public and the Congress and was in part responsible for [the TEA's] enactment," claims a leading scholar of the Kennedy Round.[39]

Despite favorable assessments of the economic consequences of British accession, and related provisions in the TEA, the official American position was that EC enlargement would damage the United States economically, at least temporarily, but was worth it for political reasons. Thus the political rationale for British membership remained uppermost in Washington. American leaders presumed that France and Germany were also motivated primarily by political concerns. On that basis, the United States assumed (as did the British) that de Gaulle would not look favorably on Britain's application. Initially, Washington considered de Gaulle's attitude toward the issue "resolutely obscure."[40] Ostensibly the French were amenable to British membership, but the Americans had their doubts. These were not dispelled when de Gaulle told Kennedy in Paris in June 1961, that "his position towards British membership is either/or; either full, or none."[41] In other words, Britain was welcome to join as long as it accepted the Rome Treaty unconditionally. Belgian foreign minister Paul-Henri Spaak, who carried greater weight in Washington than the size of his country warranted, told Ball in February 1962 that "on balance de Gaulle did not want British in, as it might threaten France's leading role in the Community."[42] Ball concurred.

Indeed, for de Gaulle, as for the Americans, the question of British membership in the EC had an important political dimension. The EC was relevant to de Gaulle's as well as to Kennedy's geopolitical designs. Between 1959 and 1962, de Gaulle advocated various proposals to promote European political union that took the EC as their economic and geographical core. The first of these, in June 1959, was for foreign policy cooperation among the six, supported by a secretariat in Paris. The other member states opposed establishing a secretariat, and the foreign ministers met only twice (in late 1959 and early 1960) to discuss political cooperation before de Gaulle launched a more ambitious initiative. This emerged in the summer of 1960 but was not made public until a press conference in September. It called for regular meetings of the six heads of state and government to direct intergovernmental cooperation on political, economic, cultural, and defense matters. This did not directly threaten the EC, which de Gaulle continued to view as an indispensable economic organization. Yet it challenged the EC's political potential by insisting that political union would take place intergovernmentally, outside the EC's institutional structure. De Gaulle linked his plans for political union with plans for NATO reform.[43]

Member states discussed de Gaulle's ideas at numerous meetings of foreign ministers and national leaders between 1960 and 1962. A committee under Christian Fouchet worked on the proposals at official level. Negotiations at all levels revealed suspicion on the part of the other five about de Gaulle's intentions. The Dutch and the Belgians, in particular, resisted what they saw as potential French, or Franco-German, hegemony. They wanted Britain, a candidate for EC membership, to participate in the talks. They were also worried about the impact of de Gaulle's plans for political union on the EC (specifically on its supranational elements) and on NATO. The talks veered between near agreement on substantive and institutional questions and total collapse, depending on the issue and the delegation. Finally the Dutch refused to participate until the question of Britain's EC membership was resolved. De Gaulle's excessive demands suggest that he did not expect the negotiations to succeed.[44] After their failure, he focused his strategic attention on bilateral relations with Germany and unilateral action in NATO.

The United States was surprisingly sanguine about what became known as the Fouchet plans. Monnet, who remained influential in Washington because of his close friendship with Ball, reassured American officials. He was generally optimistic about the EC's prospects, despite de Gaulle's hostility toward the Commission, and he was sure that Britain would soon join.[45] If Monnet, an arch supranationalist, was not concerned about de Gaulle's policies, then surely Washington need not be either. The French government also reassured the United States about its political union proposals, claiming that they were consistent with Washington's goal of building European unity. The U.S. view, in late 1961, was that "in general . . . the de Gaulle proposals . . . deserve support in the measure that they further genuine integration of the Six on the basis of the concepts of the Rome Treaty but that if they are likely to weaken the integration concept a serious question will arise."[46]

Spaak warned Ball in November 1961 that the United States should not be complacent; that the French proposals were "not a step toward political unification, but [were] actually retrogressive."[47] Ultimately, Washington relied on the good sense of the other five EC member states to keep de Gaulle in check. Indeed, the Dutch and the Belgians finally killed the French scheme. The United States was relieved. After the breakdown of the negotiations, Secretary of State Dean Rusk remarked that "Spaak's objectives, both with the British [to get them into the EC] and the French [to kill the Fouchet plans] are those we share but any overt intervention by the U.S. at this time would only lead to further recriminations."[48]

Most likely, de Gaulle would not have used the EC as a springboard for the Fouchet plans had Atlanticist Britain been a member state. As it was, de Gaulle opposed involving Britain in the negotiations, despite Britain's candidacy for EC membership. Thus the failure of the Fouchet plans removed a possible obstacle to British membership: Because he no longer saw the EC as the foundation for a European union, de Gaulle might not object to Britain, a large country opposed to his political vision for Europe, joining the EC. Yet the fact that the United States based its own vision of European unity on the EC, and therefore supported British membership, meant that de Gaulle still had ample reason politically to keep Britain out.

Bonn's position on the Fouchet plans and Britain's EC application was a source of some disquiet in the United States. Clearly, Adenauer was trying to balance between Paris and Washington.[49] Germany depended on the

United States for its security, but Adenauer doubted America's military commitment to Germany and to Europe. France could not substitute militarily for America, yet de Gaulle resolutely supported Adenauer during the Berlin crises of 1958–62. De Gaulle's return to power dismayed Adenauer, who remembered the general's earlier anti-German outbursts. Instead of confronting Germany in 1958, however, de Gaulle continued the previous regime's policy of Franco-German reconciliation and courted Adenauer assiduously. It was a difficult courtship: Adenauer distrusted de Gaulle for proposing a French-British-American directorate in NATO in late 1958 (a proposal that de Gaulle did not tell Adenauer about) and generally resented de Gaulle's imperiousness. De Gaulle gradually won Adenauer over, lavishing attention and praise on him, bolstering Adenauer's position on Berlin, and stressing the importance of Franco-German friendship.[50]

De Gaulle's support for the EC reassured Adenauer, for whom European integration was a key foreign policy objective. Yet de Gaulle knew that Adenauer was more interested in the process of binding Germany into the West than in developing federal institutions in Europe. Adenauer would go along, therefore, with de Gaulle's efforts to organize Europe politically along intergovernmental rather than supranational lines. Adeanuer's difficulty lay in reconciling such a development with America's Grand Design, and in allaying domestic criticism (in his own party as well as the opposition) that he was alienating Washington by embracing de Gaulle so closely.

The woollier de Gaulle's and Kennedy's designs for Europe, the better for Adenauer; the more precise their shape, the more awkward for him. The collapse of the Fouchet plans in April 1962 got Adenauer off the hook, in Washington and in Bonn. De Gaulle's switch from the six to the two (France and Germany) as the basis for his "European Europe," culminating in the Elysée Treaty of January 1963, sharpened Adenauer's dilemma and provoked an American and domestic German backlash against his embrace of de Gaulle. In the meantime, the question of Britain's EC application made it difficult for Adenauer to walk a fine line between Paris and Washington.

British Accession

Adenauer disliked Macmillan and distrusted the British, especially because of their vacillation during the Berlin crises. Nevertheless, Adenauer purportedly favored British membership in the EC. He knew that the United States wanted Britain to join, but also that de Gaulle was equivocal, to say the least. Erhard strongly supported British membership for both economic (market access) and political (pro-American and anti-de Gaulle) reasons. Adenauer's cabinet colleagues feared that the chancellor was veering too much in de Gaulle's direction. During a visit to Washington with Adenauer in November 1962, German foreign minister Gerhard Schröder complained to Ball that the chancellor was wavering on the question of British accession and asked if Kennedy would have a word with Adenauer about it.[51]

By that time, the accession negotiations had become bogged down in dreary technicalities. Ball was worried about the situation. In a note to Kennedy on November 15, after the Schröder meeting and before the president's meeting with Adenauer, Ball revealed his growing irritation: "Our own reports from London and the European capitals are alarming. All of the captiousness of the French and the monarchical intolerance of de Gaulle are being brought to bear on the other Europeans to render the British position intolerable. A strong lead from the German side is needed if there is not to be a complete *impasse*.... I feel it very important that you underline to Adenauer this afternoon that lamentable results would follow from letting the U.K.-EEC negotiations break down over commercial trivia. If Adenauer wants to be a statesman, now is an opportunity."[52] Kennedy obliged, warning Adenauer of the possible consequences of a collapse of the negotiations: Britain's Conservative government might fall and be replaced by Labour, which would bode ill for NATO and the Atlantic community.[53]

By the end of 1962, the Americans knew only too well that Britain's accession negotiations were in trouble. They hoped that Germany might provide the necessary political impetus to force a breakthrough early in the new year. In the meantime, the Americans directed their aggravation at Adenauer and de Gaulle. But British reservations and American misjudgments were largely at fault for the situation in which the United States now found itself. Washington continuously urged London to drop its long-standing political and economic misgivings and embrace the EC wholeheartedly. The British would not, or could not, do so. They remained skeptical of supranationalism (a skepticism that de Gaulle shared) and attached to the Commonwealth, EFTA, and an agricultural system incompatible with the emerging CAP.

In the course of the accession negotiations, Britain made many concessions on Commonwealth preferences, relations with the remaining EFTA states, and agriculture, but not enough to suit the French or allay the concerns of the other member states. This was true especially of agriculture, the importance of which Ball, in particular, appreciated for the EC politically as well as economically. As he had predicted before the accession negotiations began, agriculture became the most contentious issue between

Britain and the six. It is remarkable, therefore, that Ball dismissed deep-rooted differences over agricultural policy as "commercial trivia." Ball's note to Kennedy on November 15 shows signs of extreme frustration and poor perspective.

In the event, what Ball called "commercial trivia" may indeed have precipitated de Gaulle's veto of Britain's application in January 1963. Specifically, de Gaulle's determination to shape the CAP to suit French interests (member states had agreed on the basic principles of the CAP in December 1961 but had yet to decide particular operational aspects, including a permanent funding mechanism), made it imperative for him to keep Britain out of the Community. Whereas de Gaulle was able to pressure or cajole current member states to accept his agricultural proposals, he could have faced insurmountable internal opposition if Britain, with its radically different agricultural interests and considerable political clout, acceded to the EC. This was the gist of de Gaulle's carefully scripted answer to a carefully scripted question at his famous press conference on January 14, 1963.[54]

Strategic developments reinforced de Gaulle's interest in ending the accession negotiations. Four weeks before the press conference, Kennedy and Macmillan had struck a deal in Nassau to provide Polaris missiles for Britain's nuclear force, a deal that de Gaulle found deeply repugnant. In de Gaulle's view, the Nassau agreement showed that Britain's nuclear deterrent was not independent, as Britain claimed and as de Gaulle believed a country's military capability should be, but dependent on the United States. With France striving to develop a truly independent nuclear deterrent and end America's hegemony in NATO, the agreement further soured de Gaulle on Britain's role in Europe. Nothing in the agreement precluded British membership in the EC, but the Anglo-American deal heightened de Gaulle's awareness of Britain's close relationship with the United States. Given Washington's oft-stated objective of building an Atlantic partnership on the EC, and de Gaulle's opposition to the kind of partnership envisioned by the United States, the Nassau agreement was a timely reminder to de Gaulle of the potential political difficulties that British membership in the EC could pose for France.

Thus, from the perspective of Britain's accession, the timing and nature of the Nassau agreement were highly unfortunate. The negotiations in Brussels were at a critical stage. There were deep differences between Britain and the six (and not just between Britain and France), especially over agriculture. Other delegations, apart from the French, criticized Britain's conduct of the negotiations. The more Atlanticist member states may have been well disposed politically toward British accession, but they did not want Britain to join at any cost. Nevertheless, the situation did not seem hopeless. With sufficient political will, there could have been a breakthrough early in 1963. The possibility of such a development impelled de Gaulle to act. The Nassau agreement was more grist for his mill. What shocked the five was not that the negotiations ended unsuccessfully, but that de Gaulle acted unilaterally and so abruptly. Given de Gaulle's personality and previous behavior, however, they cannot have been too surprised.

For his part, Charles Bohlen, the U.S. ambassador in Paris, was surprised not by de Gaulle's views but "that he should have stated these publicly with such frankness and brutality." Yet Bohlen, like other American officials, presumed that de Gaulle acted entirely for political reasons. In rejecting British membership, Bohlen claimed that "de Gaulle did not dwell on any of the particular points at issue in the negotiations but . . . [emphasized] certain fundamental factors in the British picture which it should be noted are not . . . susceptible to correction in short order, indeed if ever by any British government."[55] This was an extraordinary observation, given that most of de Gaulle's statement about Britain's EC candidacy dealt with specific economic issues, notably agriculture. In a similar misjudgment of de Gaulle's motives, Rusk informed the German foreign minister on January 28 that the accession negotiations had not failed on economic grounds. Instead, "in the very prospect of success, one government is seeking to halt them on grounds which seem to us to be part of a campaign to break up the Atlantic Alliance."[56] Ironically, in view of de Gaulle's preoccupation with the CAP, Ball concluded that the only good thing to come out of the affair was that the CAP "would probably not now go into effect. The agricultural problems . . . would now be greatly eased."[57] The administration's most senior Europeanist could not have been more wrong.

De Gaulle and Adenauer signed the treaty on Franco-German cooperation in the Elysée Palace a week after the notorious press conference. The United States saw a link between the two events. In his press conference, de Gaulle had rejected British membership in the EC, an intrinsic element of Washington's Grand Design. In the Elysée Treaty, he had seemingly bound Germany to a rival French design for Europe. Adenauer tried to reassure the Americans that the Elysée Treaty would not undermine German support for European integration and Atlantic partnership. After all, a treaty of Franco-German friendship was fully in accord with Germany's and America's postwar European policies. When scolded by the Americans for not consulting them about the treaty, Adenauer retorted that Washington had not discussed with Bonn and Paris "the matters which were agreed to [between Britain and the United States] in Nassau."[58]

Adenauer's reassurances were not enough either for the Americans or for the chancellor's domestic critics. The United States took comfort in the Bundestag resolution, affirming Germany's commitments to the EC, NATO, and the GATT, that accompanied the treaty's ratification. The Bundestag's action humiliated Adenauer—leading members of his own party supported it—and infuriated de Gaulle. It emasculated the treaty from the French point of view. Adenauer's resignation later in 1963 and Erhard's assumption of the chancellorship ended the ascendancy of the German Gaullists and brought German-American relations back to an even keel.

Conclusion

The events of January 1963 left a bitter taste in the Americans' mouths. De Gaulle became a bogeyman in Washington. Mention of his name was enough to incite invective in the White House and State Department (not to mention the Pentagon). Ball, an avid Euro-federalist, could barely contain himself. A memorandum by Ball for Kennedy, before the president's visit to Europe in late June and early July 1963, revealed the extent of his hatred of de Gaulle and concern about the future. "Never at any time since the war," Ball wrote, "has Europe been in graver danger of back-sliding into the old destructive habits—the old fragmentation and national rivalries that have twice brought the world to disaster in the past." What was to blame? "The halting, and at least momentary reversal, of the drive toward unity in Europe. This has come about, as the whole world knows, from the abrupt reassertion of old-style competitive nationalism expressed in a new-style rhetoric." Not only had de Gaulle launched "an assault on the structure of European unity," but also "each week de Gaulle's France grows perceptibly more absolutist. . . . As a result, the French Communists . . . have been given a new lease on life."[59]

Ball's fears were unfounded. The Fifth Republic was more stable than any regime in modern French history, and it remained so after de Gaulle's departure. The process of European integration was not thrown irrevocably off track. De Gaulle opposed supranationalism and checked the EC Commission's political pretensions. But even without de Gaulle, it is doubtful that the EC would have moved in an avowedly federal direction. Economically, the EC became increasingly important, despite the crisis of January

1963 and the "Empty Chair Crisis" of 1965–66, which de Gaulle precipitated to secure the CAP, curb the use of qualified majority voting, and put the Commission in its place. Arguably, the emerging EC withstood the crises of 1963 and 1965 better than it would have survived the shock of accession to it of a large country (Britain) that did not subscribe to core EC principles and objectives.

By the end of 1963, the United States regained a better perspective on de Gaulle and the EC's future. Publicly, the United States stuck with the Grand Design and its vision of European political unity and Atlantic partnership. Privately, Washington accepted that the EC was essentially an economic organization. Erhard's efforts to develop the EC politically in the mid-1960s, which the United States supported, were intended to strengthen the organization's legitimacy rather than build a federal structure. After the excitement of the early 1960s, U.S. interest in the EC focused on economic affairs. Just as the development of the CAP preoccupied EC member states throughout the 1960s, it also dominated U.S.-EC relations. The liberalization of trade in industrial goods, at the root of Washington's economic interest in the EC, returned to center stage, especially with the launch of the Kennedy Round. De Gaulle's veto of Britain's membership had a direct impact on the new GATT negotiations. As well as rendering useless the provision of the TEA that anticipated EC enlargement, de Gaulle's veto, according to a leading scholar, "struck a heavy blow at the idea of partnership which seemed to some to have had such a bright future only several months before. That action alone, seen in retrospect, went a long way towards changing the basic objective of the Kennedy Round from a political to an economic one."[60]

De Gaulle's quest for grandeur continued to pit Paris and Washington against each other, notably on NATO and nuclear issues. But the EC was no longer a battleground for competing French and American visions of Europe. In political and strategic terms, the basis was established for the final steps in the development of the strategic triangle. Thus de Gaulle's veto of Britain's second membership effort, in 1967, was largely devoid of strategic significance. In the meantime, Franco-German strains within the EC, which contributed to and were exacerbated by the Empty Chair Crisis, did not especially worry Washington. Despite differences over the EC's decisionmaking system and financial mechanism, France and Germany remained committed to realizing the EC's economic potential. Notwithstanding the Empty Chair Crisis, European economic integration intensified in the 1960s. This was in Washington's interest. But a dark cloud hovered overhead. It was the CAP, a perpetual irritant in U.S.-EC, and later U.S.–European Union, relations.

Notes

1. For an account of the free trade area initiative, see Miriam Camps, "The Free Trade Area Negotiations," Policy Memorandum 18, February 10, 1959, Center of International Studies, Woodrow Wilson School of Public and International Affairs, Princeton University; James Ellison, *Threatening Europe: Britain and the Creation of the European Community, 1955–1958* (London: Macmillan, 2000); and Richard T. Griffiths, "The End of the OEEC and the Birth of the OECD," in *Explorations in OEEC History*, ed. Richard T. Griffiths (Paris: Organization for Economic Cooperation and Development, 1997).

2. See Andrew Moravcsik, *The Choice for Europe: Social Purpose and State Power from Messina to Maastricht* (Ithaca, N.Y.: Cornell University Press, 1998), 179–82.

3. U.S. Department of State, *Foreign Relations of the United States (FRUS), 1958–1960*, vol. 7, part 1, *Western European Integration and Security; Canada* (Washington, D.C.: U.S. Government Printing Office, 1993) (hereafter *FRUS 1958–60*), 2.

4. *FRUS 1958–60*, 11.
5. Ibid., 71.
6. See Camps, "Free Trade Area," 15–16.
7. *FRUS 1958–60*, 67–68.
8. The text of the announcement is in *L'Année Politique*, 1958, 482.
9. Camps, "Free Trade Area," 36.
10. *FRUS 1958–60*, 67–68.
11. Ibid., 41.
12. Ibid., 121.
13. Ibid., 145–46.
14. Ibid., 206.
15. Ibid., 173.
16. Ibid., 162.
17. Ibid., 271–78.
18. Ibid., 281.
19. Ibid., 122.
20. Ibid., 96–100.
21. John F. Kennedy, "Address at Independence Hall, Philadelphia," July 4, 1962, in U.S. Government, *Public Papers of the Presidents of the United States: John F. Kennedy, January 1 to December 31, 1962* (Washington, D.C.: U.S. Government Printing Office, 1963), 537–39; the quotation here is on 538.

22. On de Gaulle's strategic vision and European policies, see Frédéric Bozo, *Two Strategies for Europe: De Gaulle, the United States, and the Atlantic Alliance* (Lanham, Md.: Rowman & Littlefield, 2001); Alain Peyrefitte, *C'était de Gaulle*, vol. 1, *La France redevient la France* (Paris: Fayard, 1994); Peyrefitte, *C'était de Gaulle*, vol. 2, *La France reprend sa place dans le monde* (Paris: Fayard, 1997); and Maurice Vaïsse, *La grandeur: Politique étrangère du général de Gaulle, 1958–1969* (Paris: Fayard, 1998).

23. On Anglo-American relations and the Grand Design, see Stuart Ward, "Kennedy, Britain, and the European Community," in *John F. Kennedy and Europe,* ed. Douglas Brinkley and Richard T. Griffiths (Baton Rouge: Louisiana State University Press, 1999), 317–32.

24. *FRUS 1958–60,* 216.

25. U.S. Department of State, *Foreign Relations of the United States (FRUS), 1961–1963,* vol. 13, *West Europe and Canada* (Washington, D.C.: U.S. Government Printing Office, 1994) (hereafter FRUS 1961–63), 8–9.

26. *FRUS 1958–60,* 275–77.

27. *FRUS 1961–63,* 129.

28. William Diebold Jr., "A Watershed with Some Dry Sides: The Trade Expansion Act of 1962," in *Kennedy and Europe,* ed. Brinkley and Griffiths, 235–60; the quotation here is on 252.

29. See Herman Walker, "Dispute Settlement: The Chicken War," *American Journal of International Law* 58, issue 3 (July 1964): 671–85; and Ynze Alkema, "European-American Trade Policies, 1961–1963," in *Kennedy and Europe,* ed. Brinkley and Griffiths, 212–34; the citation here is on 226–34.

30. *FRUS 1961–63,* 8.

31. Andrew Moravcsik argues that de Gaulle vetoed the United Kingdom's application because "British membership would kill the CAP." Moravcsik, "De Gaulle between Grain and Grandeur: The Political Economy of French EC Policy, 1958–1970 (Part 2)," *Journal of Cold War Studies* 2, no. 3 (Fall 2000): 4–68; the citation here is on 9. If so, de Gaulle's behavior was consistent with what Moravcsik calls the "commercial interpretation" of de Gaulle's European policy. Moravcsik, "Beyond Grain and Grandeur: An Answer to Critics and an Agenda for Future Research," *Journal of Cold War Studies* 2, no. 3 (Fall 2000): 117–42; the citation here is on 117. See also Moravcsik, *Choice for Europe,* 159–237; and Moravcsik, "De Gaulle between Grain and Grandeur: The Political Economy of French EC Policy, 1958–1970 (Part 1)," *Journal of Cold War Studies* 2, no. 2 (Spring 2000): 3–43.

32. See Pascaline Winand, *Eisenhower, Kennedy, and the United States of Europe* (New York: St. Martin's Press, 1993), 245–64.

33. On the United Kingdom's early relationship with the EC and decision to apply for membership, see Wolfram Kaiser, *Using Europe, Abusing the Europeans: Britain and European Integration, 1945–1963* (London: Macmillan, 1996).

34. *FRUS 1961–63,* 11 (quotation marks in the original).

35. Ibid., 106.

36. Ibid., 6.

37. Ibid., 32–38.

38. On the TEA, see Alkema, "European-American Trade Policies," 226–31; and Diebold, "Watershed," 235–60.

39. John B. Rehm, "Developments in the Law and Institutions of International Economic Relations: The Kennedy Round of Trade Negotiations," *American Journal of International Law* 6, issue 2 (April 1968): 403–34; the citation here is on 406.

40. *FRUS 1961–63,* 85.

41. Ibid., 25.

42. Ibid., 66.

43. On the Fouchet plans, see Robert Bloes, *Le "Plan Fouchet" et le Probléme de l'Europe Politique* (Bruges: College of Europe, 1970); and Susanne J. Bodenheimer,

"The 'Political Union' Debate in Europe: A Case Study of Intergovernmental Diplomacy," *International Organization* 21, no. 1 (Winter 1967): 24–54.

44. Moravcsik argues that this was indeed the case. See Moravcsik, "Between Grain and Grandeur (Part 1)," 34–42.

45. Monnet and de Gaulle drew up a secret memorandum in October 1960 in which Monnet agreed to support the Fouchet plans and de Gaulle agreed to maintain the integrity of the Rome Treaty. See Moravcsik, "Between Grain and Grandeur (Part 1)," 39; and Oliver Bange, *The EEC Crisis of 1963: Kennedy, Macmillan, de Gaulle and Adenauer in Conflict* (London: Macmillan, 2000), 27–28.

46. *FRUS 1961–63*, 304.

47. Ibid., 52.

48. Ibid., 83–84.

49. On Adenauer's relations with the Western allies, see Hans-Peter Schwarz, *Konrad Adenauer: A German Politician and Statesman in a Period of War, Revolution, and Reconstruction, Vol. 2, The Statesman, 1952–1967* (Providence: Berghahn, 1997), 513–627. On his relations specifically with de Gaulle, see Hermann Kusterer, *Der Kanzler und der General* (Stuttgart: Neske, 1995).

50. On de Gaulle's policy toward Germany and relations with Adenauer, see Pierre Maillard, *De Gaulle et l'Allemagne: Le rêve inachevé* (Paris: Plon, 1990).

51. *FRUS 1961–63*, 122–23.

52. Ibid., 124.

53. Ibid., 125–26.

54. See Moravcsik, "Between Grain and Grandeur (Part 2)," 10–24; and Bange, *EEC Crisis of 1963*, 108–16. For a transcript of the press conference, see Charles de Gaulle, *Major Addresses: Statements and Press Conferences of General Charles de Gaulle, May 19, 1958–January 31, 1964* (New York: French Embassy Information Service, 1964), 208–22.

55. *FRUS 1961–63*, 141.

56. Ibid., 153–54.

57. Ibid., 161.

58. Ibid., 201.

59. Ibid., 204–9. Ball's reverence for Monnet and loathing for de Gaulle are evident in his memoirs. See George Ball, *The Past Has Another Pattern* (New York: W. W. Norton, 1982), 96–98.

60. Rehm, "Developments," 406–7.

Chapter 2

Germany and the Discord of Its Allies: The Case of the European Political Union

Martin Koopmann

Shortly after the six founder members of the European Coal and Steel Community had signed the Treaty of Rome and thereby taken the second step toward a comprehensive integration of Western Europe, they broadened the European agenda by adding a new perspective: the institutionalization of their political cooperation. The ensuing debate on the establishment of a political union—continuing, in a first stage, until the spring of 1962—was marked by the conflicting interests of the parties involved. In particular, the negotiations were influenced to a considerable degree by the political objectives of the French and U.S. governments with regard to the European agenda. In fact, it was their incompatibility that was responsible for the failure both of the project as such and of the German government's attempts at

This chapter has been published in a slightly different version as "Failed Mediation: Germany and the European Political Union," by Martin Koopmann, *Journal of European Integration History / Revue d'histoire de l'intégration européenne* 12, no. 1 (2006): 9–24.

mediation. Bonn faced the difficult problem of its two most important partners using the European political arena to carry on a conflict that threatened its good bilateral relations with Paris and Washington. On the one hand, the German government depended on the United States with respect to its security policy; on the other hand, there were compelling economic and political reasons that made a lasting reconciliation with France indispensable. This conflict of priorities placed the Federal Republic in a political dilemma. Both France and the United States had distinct ideas concerning the form and the function of a political union. These ideas, which corresponded with their respective concepts of Western cooperation within the international bipolar political system, left Bonn little room to maneuver as a mediator.

The French policy on European affairs was the result of two objectives, which were fundamental to General Charles de Gaulle's foreign policy. He wanted to make sure that France would be able to protect itself against any future act of aggression by its German neighbor, and he was also striving to restore France's status as one of the great political powers. He was convinced that this would be possible only if France broke away from the supremacy of U.S. security policy and developed an independent political strategy vis-à-vis the Soviet Union. The general's long-term objective in this context was the replacement of the existing bipolar bloc system by a multipolar system of nations—the establishment of a balance of power that would be supported by the United States, the Soviet Union, an independent Western Europe, and further regional powers.[1]

De Gaulle's program depended to a large degree on an independent European foreign policy regarding the countries of the Eastern bloc and had as its final aim a pan-European confederation stretching from the Atlantic to the Urals. Assuming that France would not be able to implement such a program on its own, de Gaulle continued the policy of European integration pursued by the governments of the Fourth Republic. Moreover, he tried to work toward institutionalized cooperation with France's European partners to coordinate their security and defense policies. A European Political Union with intergovernmental structures would provide France with a forum outside NATO in which it could try to enlist support for its own strategic interests within a purely European framework. Irrespective of whether France would have been able to get its European partners to agree to its political ideas in each and every case, Western Europe would have developed its own strategic positions and thus strengthened its independence from the United States. In the long term, Europe would have been able to define its own priorities in foreign and international affairs—priorities that, in the eyes of de Gaulle, might have been quite different from those set by Washington.[2]

Since the end of World War II, such an emancipation of Western Europe had been a main concern of U.S. administrations. Washington aimed to politically stabilize its European allies and to integrate them as reliable partners into the Western alliance. A Europe as a "third power," independent of the two great powers, would have challenged U.S. hegemony in Western Europe and thus posed a risk to U.S. security interests. It was clear that any such attempt had to be thwarted. Moreover, Washington had an interest in strengthening the European economies and thereby gaining strong commercial partners—a development that would also make it possible to share the financial burden of Western defense among several partners. The U.S. government believed that promoting European integration was an adequate tool to reach these two goals. In this context, the concept of a political union of the Western European states could potentially play an important role, for such a union could control the particular interests of single states and thereby promote political unity in Western Europe. In addition, it would have made Western Europe a more reliable partner of the United States and defused the "German question" as a possible source of conflict by integrating the Federal Republic into a stable political structure.[3] For the U.S. government, it was beyond question that any political arrangement in Western Europe would have to fulfill three fundamental conditions: (1) NATO had to remain the basis of Western cooperation and the central decisionmaking body with regard to all questions concerning Western security; (2) political agreements should have no detrimental effects on the existing European communities; and (3) sooner or later, Britain had to be integrated as well.[4]

With respect to the debate about a European political union, the first of these conditions was most likely to create considerable tension. It had been repeatedly emphasized, especially by the smaller member states of the European Economic Community (EEC), that priority had to be given to NATO and the whole of the transatlantic alliance, which was regarded as the foundation for security in Western Europe. For these smaller states, the membership of Britain was crucial to the overall direction that the political union would take with regard to its foreign policy. In view of this situation, the United States had an indirect influence on the debate about the union and the political aspects of European integration, because U.S. interests in Europe were effectively represented by the smaller member states as well as by Italy and in Germany by the Foreign Office.

For Bonn, the difficulty was that it needed to develop a political program for Europe that would satisfy the interests of both its allies and still have a chance of succeeding. The virtually irreconcilable interests of France and the United States forced the German government into a balancing act and led to contradictory positions within the Cabinet. How should decisionmaking processes be organized within the union, and what powers should it be given? In other words, what form and what function should the union have? Even more important, what should its position be relative to NATO? The key players in this process—the chancellor and the Foreign Office—adopted different positions, one being oriented toward French, the other toward U.S. interests. The result was that they reproduced the Franco-American conflict within the German foreign policy decisionmaking system. Consequently, the government could no longer serve as a credible mediator between France and the representatives of the transatlantic option. At the same time, the differences of opinion between the parties involved had the effect that Bonn was unable to develop a coherent policy to pursue its own interests with regard to the political organization of Europe.

In this chapter, I discuss this aspect in more detail, using the example of the Franco-German summit in Rambouillet, held in July 1960, and the debate about the Fouchet Plans one year later.

The Summit of Rambouillet

After de Gaulle's initiative to establish a tripartite NATO directorate with the United States and Britain had failed, the French president made a concrete attempt to establish a closer political cooperation among the six. He suggested to the Italian president Giovanni Gronchi to have "an organized European cooperation" including regular meetings of the foreign ministers and a small secretariat.[5]

During the talks that the six governments held in the following months, the policy of the government in Bonn was characterized by a tripartite division of positions within the Cabinet. From early on, the Economics Ministry, led by Ludwig Erhard, was one of the main critics of a political union. It regarded a political institutionalization of the cooperation among the six as an unacceptable limitation of the free development of the community's economies and called for an extended free trade zone, including Britain and additional Organization for European Economic Cooperation member states. Chancellor Konrad Adenauer and the Foreign Office, conversely, agreed in principle to the union but set different priorities with respect to its institutional setup. To achieve Europe's political unity, the chancellor was willing to make concessions regarding the supranational character of the envisaged political cooperation, at least in its initial stages. He was convinced that a unified Europe was only conceivable if Germany and France fully agreed on the fundamental issues, and therefore he showed himself quite willing to compromise with Paris. The Foreign Office, however, put more emphasis on supranational priorities whenever France made an attempt to push through a higher degree of intergovernmental structures. On this point, it could be sure of support from the United States, which under both presidents Dwight Eisenhower and John Kennedy used every opportunity to point out that it was interested in a strong, integrated Europe as a partner.

The outline for a political union drafted by the Political Department in 1959 and sent to Adenauer by Foreign Minister Heinrich von Brentano clearly shows the Foreign Office's emphasis on integration. Deputies, supported by a permanent secretariat, were to meet on a monthly basis to prepare conferences of the foreign ministers to be held every three months. The authorities of the existing communities were granted the right to make proposals for the agendas of these conferences. They were to be involved in regular consultations and, like the European Parliament, were to be informed about the talks.[6] The plan obviously aimed to link the political cooperation with the integration of the EEC and was therefore incompatible with the French point of view. Given the cautious stance of the Benelux countries, Brentano conceded that "the conditions for a deeper European integration are currently less than favorable." He also added, however, that "this should not lead to abandoning [its] further development."[7] Furthermore, it was of utmost importance to the German Foreign Office that the political cooperation of the six did not infringe on the powers of NATO. European cooperation had to be confined "to the specific questions of the relationship between the [European] communities and their environment and to the further promotion of Europe's integration." Consultations, which went beyond this range of topics, should be "brought to the attention of the other allies in NATO and the [Western European Union] and, if necessary, put up for discussion."[8]

The plan that President de Gaulle presented to the chancellor during the Franco-German summit in Rambouillet at the end of July 1960 was incompatible with such a point of view. De Gaulle proposed a political organization for Europe that would encompass foreign affairs, economic issues, and cultural aspects as well as the partners' defense strategies. According to the

French president, such an organization would take the form of intergovernmental cooperation and include quarterly meetings of the heads of state and government and the ministers concerned. The talks should be prepared by national officials in four committees. He pointed out that the new structures of cooperation should be supplemented by a reform of both the existing communities and NATO, and he made clear that he wished to reduce the influence of existing supranational institutions to a bare minimum: "It is up to the governments to cooperate directly. Concerning the Commissions, they must be subordinated."[9] The chancellor did not challenge de Gaulle's ideas, and one day later he agreed to the proposals that de Gaulle presented to him in written form.[10]

In principle, Adenauer was also convinced that it was essential for Western Europe to gain a larger degree of independence within the transatlantic alliance. Unlike de Gaulle, however, he thought it necessary that the EEC member states not only intensify their cooperation with regard to their foreign policies but also strengthen the existing structures for a deeper integration.[11] This was his position only a few weeks before Rambouillet.

The fact that the chancellor failed to push through his point of view at that meeting was in part due to flaws in his negotiation tactics. More important, however, Adenauer did not challenge the French position because he regarded good Franco-German relations as an essential prerequisite for realizing his foreign policy goals: With regard to the Berlin Crisis, the Federal Republic depended on France as its most reliable partner among the allies. This dependence had been strengthened by de Gaulle's firm stance in the run-up to the failed summit of the four in Paris in May 1960. Adenauer in particular benefited from de Gaulle's unyielding position. When he himself refused to make concessions to the U.S. and British governments, which were willing to negotiate, he met with considerable domestic resistance—even from members of his Cabinet—and had to turn to de Gaulle for support.[12]

The situation was further complicated by Adenauer's own European agenda. Although he regarded political union as the logical continuation of the unification process started in the early 1950s, he was more interested in achieving that goal than in the actual process that would lead to it. At the Rambouillet summit, he was even prepared to make surprising concessions regarding the supranational character of the existing communities; he denied that the EEC and Euratom had a supranational character and complained that both organizations nevertheless behaved as if they possessed such powers. In response to the French demand that NATO be completely reorganized, he merely said that such a demand had to be reconsidered to avoid the impression that France and the Federal Republic intended to cut ties with the United States.[13]

The way in which Adenauer led the negotiations in Rambouillet immediately isolated him in his own domestic political system. The chairman of the Christian Democratic Union / Christian Social Union (CDU/CSU) parliamentary party, Heinrich Krone, warned of questioning the European institutions and spoke of a "complete turning away from the policy we have pursued so far with regard to Europe." He said he had "grave doubts" about the French plans for reforming NATO, for these would reinforce isolationist tendencies in the United States and thus lead to "a policy in America [which would be] disastrous for European security."[14] Numerous leading politicians of the CDU and CSU clearly rejected a change of Germany's policy on Europe under the influence of de Gaulle. At this stage, Brentano expressly thought about withdrawing from his office as foreign minister.[15] As early as 1960, the Foreign Office had noted that de Gaulle was apparently laying "claim to continental leadership,"[16] and German ambassador Herbert Blankenhorn came to the conclusion that the chancellor was not aware of "the possible consequences" of the plans proposed by the French president.[17]

In view of the severe criticism he received from members of his government and his own party, Adenauer had to concede. Within a few days, he changed his course and, only one week after the summit in Rambouillet, he transmitted a message to the French foreign minister, Maurice Couve de Murville, demanding that the core of the European treaty remain untouched.[18] Shortly afterward, he informed de Gaulle that the wording of the French proposals needed "refinement" to avoid "incorrect interpretations on the part of the general public."[19] The chancellor had suffered a bitter defeat at home. He had to fall in with the line of the Foreign Office, which made itself advocate of the federalist idea of the Treaty of Rome and did not hesitate to forcefully defend this point of view against French objections, underlining the significance of the transatlantic partnership of Western Europe with the United States.

The sudden volte-face of the chancellor was a setback for his policy vis-à-vis France. Adenauer was right in his conviction that political union could only be accomplished together with France. As he firmly believed in the relevance of union for the security and the stability of the Federal Republic, it was easy for him to link it with another important aim of his foreign policy: the indissoluble Franco-German partnership. However, the substantial concessions he made to Paris for the sake of political union were not supported by the crucial actors of his own government. His own party showed him the limits of his scope of action in foreign affairs.

After the summit in Rambouillet, three years before the debate about the preamble of the Franco-German Treaty, there was much evidence that even a chancellor as strong as Konrad Adenauer had to make sure that he was backed by his own political system. Certainly neither Franco-German relations nor the project of political union would be really damaged by the summit in Rambouillet and its consequences. But Adenauer's defeat left no doubt regarding the future positions of Bonn in the ongoing talks about political union. Certain cornerstones of German foreign policy were not to be called into question—not even for the sake of Franco-German friendship. These were, first of all in the field of security, the partnership with the United States within the Atlantic alliance; and second, economic integration within the European Community. Rambouillet showed for the first time how difficult it was for Bonn to realize a constructive policy between French demands and American claims. But Rambouillet also showed that the agreement of all German actors was a crucial prerequisite for successful German foreign policy in this difficult area of conflict between Paris and Washington in general and for the success of political union in particular.

The Fouchet Plans

During the time between the summit in Rambouillet and the first Fouchet Plan, presented in October and November 1961, the six members of the European Community made some progress in their efforts to form a political union. This success was also due to the fact that after Rambouillet the German government adopted a more consistent position: Without questioning the Franco-German partnership as such—something that Bonn could not have afforded in the light of the Berlin Crisis—the representatives of the Federal Republic were now unanimous and clear in their call for an acknowledgment of the *acquis communautaire* and the priority of NATO in defense issues. In his diary, a senior Foreign Office official expressed his concern that the chancellor had played 'the American card' "so perfectly that I start to worry about Franco-German relations."[20]

Especially in the field of security policy, Adenauer was indeed placing far greater emphasis on close cooperation with the United States. The obligation to cooperate with both the conflicting allies, Paris and Washington, helped him now to take a more distant position vis-à-vis President de Gaulle. Shortly after de Gaulle, who was angry about the failed summit of Rambouillet, had vigorously criticized the structures of NATO and the European Communities in public, Adenauer met General Lauris Norstad, the supreme allied commander of NATO in Europe. Norstad explained to Adenauer his concept of a land-based nuclear force for NATO.[21] The participation of the Western European allies—including the Federal Republic—in the Western nuclear defense seemed to be an answer to Western European politicians and mainly Chancellor Adenauer, who had been talking about a so-called lack of credibility concerning the American nuclear guarantee for Western Europe ever since October 1957, when the Soviets had successfully launched *Sputnik*.

The events of the second half of 1960 clearly show the significance of the Paris-Bonn-Washington triangle for the European policy of the Federal Republic. The position of the United States was of growing importance for the development of the conflict between Paris and Bonn, which could no longer be ignored. Shortly after the Rambouillet summit, Washington still did not worry about French criticism of the structures of the European Communities and NATO. The U.S. government regarded de Gaulle's attacks as exaggerated and counted on the other EEC-members to oppose them. The United States had no reason to react hastily.[22] Nevertheless, in the following weeks, the American government grew uneasy about continuing attacks by the French president on EEC and NATO integration. President Eisenhower took up some central aspects of the Norstad project as well as of another plan initiated by the State Department (the Bowie Report) and informed the chancellor that the United States was going to examine the possibility of a multilateral nuclear defense including NATO. This announcement was made only a day before the meeting of Adenauer with French prime minister Michel Debrè, and it was accompanied by the undisguised threat that Washington would withdraw its troops from Europe in case the integrated structures of the alliance should be weakened.[23]

In view of the opposition in Bonn and the increasing pressure from Washington, de Gaulle tried to alleviate the conflict with the Federal Republic. On the one hand, he stressed that he had thought Adenauer more European than the chancellor really was. On the other hand, by offering tactical concessions, he now tried to convince the chancellor to approach French positions. He instructed Debré not to attack the institutions of the European Communities directly. De Gaulle assumed that, if a political cooperation of the six could be realized one day, "the Communities will be ipso facto put at their place."[24] In contrast to the Rambouillet summit, however, the positions of the German side in the talks with Debré were marked by their unyielding character.[25] The change of the German European policy since Rambouillet was obvious: It was the pressure of domestic politics as well as the influence of Washington on the decisionmaking process in Germany that put an end to the pro-French policy of the chancellor. The consequence was a more balanced German position between Paris and Washington.

Considering the fact that de Gaulle now seemed prepared to compromise, the Foreign Office also showed its goodwill. Instead of insisting on an immediate federalist organization of the political union, it now accepted loose political cooperation as a first step, for it knew that without France it would be impossible to make headway on the road to political union. In this phase, the six members made considerable progress, which was reflected in the Bonn Declaration issued in July 1961: In it, there was no longer talk of reforming NATO or altering the Communities' existing bodies, nor did the declaration mention that the political union should include a defense component—an aspect that had been so important to de Gaulle. Instead, the members emphasized the significance of their alliance with the United States and expressed their conviction that their cooperation would "promote the political unification of Europe and thereby strengthen the Atlantic alliance."[26] This phase, which proved so fruitful for European integration, shows how important it was for the project of political union that Germany had a coherent policy on Europe. However, the Bonn agreement was not to be overestimated. It is true that de Gaulle regarded political union as an important means to strengthen Europe's independence from the United States. But in fact, he only accepted a tactical compromise to keep the negotiations going. There was no change in his fundamental objectives for European and security policies or in his ideas concerning the structures of international cooperation.[27]

The Bonn Declaration was followed, in the summer of 1961, by Britain's application to join the EEC. Apart from the deterioration of Britain's economic situation—starting early in 1961—two other factors played a crucial role in the timing of the application. First, there was pressure from the Kennedy administration, which like its predecessors strongly supported the program of European integration and encouraged both Britain and the EEC to have London join the community.[28] Kennedy left no doubt that the United States supported European integration mainly because it aimed to strengthen Western Europe and integrate Germany firmly within these structures. The second factor was that the six were obviously making good progress in their talks on political union. By joining the EEC, Britain wanted to make sure that it had the option to shape the union according to its own—pro-Atlantic—interests. Now the conditions for further talks were clear: The smaller EEC member states wanted to keep the EEC and the political union from being dominated by France and Germany and thus argued that London should join the EEC as soon as possible. At the same time, it was to be expected that France would not accept a transatlantic bias of the union under British influence. Given the growing pressure on Bonn in this situation, the unity of the German position was again in danger.

At this point, the German delegation presented a paper to the Fouchet Committee—established at the Paris summit of the six in February 1961—which was characterized by an intergovernmental approach and satisfied most of France's wishes. It envisaged regular meetings of the heads of state and government and of the foreign ministers as well as conferences of the ambassadors, which were to be prepared and supported by a "Standing Committee." This committee would be "set up as an intergovernmental steering committee" by the heads of state and government and was to consist of "leading officials of the six foreign ministries." The proposals put forward by the German delegation were almost indistinguishable from those made by France. This applies not only to their ideas about the structures of cooperation but also with respect to the powers to be granted to the committee: "discussion and examination of all questions which are of common interest for the policy of the six or where a Member State considers a consultation necessary."[29] However, the Foreign Office overestimated France's willingness to compromise. De Gaulle now thought that it was time to take advantage of Bonn's seemingly unlimited support and to press ahead with far-reaching plans aimed at restraining Anglo-American influence in a Europe of the six. The first Fouchet Plan, presented by France on November 2, 1961, went beyond the Bonn Declaration on a number of important points. Not only did it mention a "common foreign policy"; it also noted explicitly that "the member states would be safer against any aggressive act by [developing] a common defense policy in cooperation with other free nations." Though making reference to defense issues, the text mentioned neither the United States nor the Atlantic alliance.[30]

The reaction of those concerned with foreign affairs in the Federal Republic's government made clear that there had been no major change in their general outlook since Rambouillet. The chancellor responded by saying that he would "agree in principle" to the French plan. Although it was less European in spirit than "originally intended," he conceded that the political union could also be realized "at a somewhat slower pace."[31] He brushed aside critical questions as to whether de Gaulle's European program was directed against the Atlantic alliance and pointed to France's difficult domestic situation over the Algeria crisis. Adenauer wanted to make progress toward a political union no matter what the costs would be. As in the previous year, he was again willing to compromise and set aside the transatlantic precepts of his own foreign policy. Moreover, he also made concessions to France with regard to a common European agricultural policy.[32] Because the economic cooperation of the six would inevitably lead to political cooperation, Adenauer maintained that a common agricultural policy was "a political question of prime importance."[33] He was convinced that political union could only be achieved in cooperation with, but never against, France.

Although the chancellor's general outlook had not changed since Rambouillet, the events in the aftermath of the 1960 summit had led him to express his views more cautiously. The Foreign Office's response was equally restrained. At the diplomatic level, however, and especially in the negotiations in the Fouchet Committee, it left no doubt about its priorities. In a first analysis of the French plan, the Foreign Office noted that "the idea of integration could, even now, be given more emphasis in the treaty." To achieve this, it suggested that "the position of the envisaged European Parliament [be] strengthened and a closer link forged to the European communities."[34] Due to the pressure exerted by the German delegation, France presented an amended draft to the committee. The German side, however, regarded the revised document only as a first step toward political union, "which in our opinion should eventually take the form of a federation." "In view of NATO's responsibilities in this area," the delegation also saw the need for further discussions about a common defense policy and noted that the French draft would have to be amended with regard to these two issues.[35] After the new foreign minister, Gerhard Schröder, had taken over, the Foreign Office—together with the other four partners—continued to plead the case for a federalist set-up of the union in the Fouchet Committee. With respect to the question of the powers that the union should have, the Foreign Office also gave preferential treatment to the Dutch interests regarding NATO. On the other hand—and in contrast to the Belgian and the Dutch positions—it did not deem it necessary to involve Britain in the negotiations straight away, because London had not asked to be included.[36]

More so than the chancellor, the Foreign Office thought of itself as a mediator between France and the small EEC member states and followed a course that was more pragmatic and geared toward consensus. In this context, it can be noticed that the replacement of Brentano as foreign minister by Schröder had no consequences for the position of the Foreign Office. Schröder put more emphasis on British EEC membership and on the differences between the German and the French conceptions of Western cooperation, but there was no change regarding the main ideas of European and security policy. Under both ministers, the diplomats of the Foreign Office elaborated on concepts of a supranational union without touching the competences of NATO. It is true, however, that Brentano and Schröder had different ideas regarding the German interest in foreign policy. Though Brentano reminded Adenauer that "Franco-German cooperation [was] the basis but not the aim of our European policy,"[37] Schröder, in the same context, would have talked about a transatlantic basis for German foreign policy.

Nevertheless, both Schröder and his predecessor were convinced that the Federal Republic could realize a policy according to its interests in Europe only in agreement with Paris and Washington. Looking at a note of May 1962 from the former confidant of Chancellor Adenauer, Herbert Blankenhorn, one can easily see the coherence and the continuity of the European policy of the Foreign Office. Blankenhorn, in the meantime ambassador in Paris, cautioned against a deterioration of German-British relations and against de Gaulle's attempts to conclude an exclusive bilateral alliance with Bonn. He did not forget to add that his note was only destined for State Secretary Karl Carstens and Foreign Minister Schröder (but not at all for Chancellor Adenauer).[38]

In view of the further development of French policy up to the presentation of the second Fouchet Plan on January 18, 1962, it is obvious why the differing positions of the German Chancellery and the Foreign Office were significant for the project of political union: Together with the other four delegations,[39] Germany was openly criticizing France in the Fouchet Committee. Against the background of this completely isolated position, the Direction d'Europe of the Quai d'Orsay, headed by Jean-Marie Soutou, drew up a new plan. The aim of this draft, which had been authorized by Couve de Murville and was presented to the other five partners on January 13, 1962, was clearly to create the basis for a compromise; it sought a common foreign and defense policy with the explicit goal to strengthen the Atlantic alliance. The communities' existing structures were to be streamlined. At the same time, the draft guaranteed that such a reform would remain within the bounds of the Treaty of Rome. The European Parliament was to gain in status.[40]

In contrast to the Quai d'Orsay, whose diplomats in the Fouchet Committee were faced with a unified front and yielded to enormous pressure, de Gaulle could play his German card, and the course of action taken by the chancellor must have confirmed him in his position. During the Franco-German meeting held in Paris on December 9, 1961, the president and the chancellor were unanimous in their assessment of the European process. Adenauer promised de Gaulle that he would support his position regarding a common EEC agricultural market and refrained from bringing up the delicate question of political union. The fact that Adenauer failed to state his position unambiguously resulted again in de Gaulle's overestimating the chances for a Franco-German alliance within the European process; de Gaulle explained to Adenauer that, if by further reducing customs tariffs toward the end of the year the next phase of the Common Market could be launched, the next step should be the implementation of political union. This would strengthen Europe's position with regard to both the United States and the Soviet Union. If Paris and Bonn agreed on this point, de Gaulle reasoned, Belgian and Dutch resistance would be of no consequence.[41]

It is obvious that de Gaulle did not really want to establish a political union that would have restricted French autonomy on issues of foreign policy and defense. He would not even have accepted such a union if his partners had offered concessions to him, for example on the basis of the Bonn Declaration. Contrary to his own intentions, however, Chancellor Adenauer became a kind of pacemaker in the decline of the project of political union. His European policy was based on the misunderstanding that de Gaulle also regarded political union as an integral part of the process of European integration, as just another step in the process had started with the three communities in the 1950s. In spite of the experiences of Rambouillet, he did not explain to the French president where the Federal Republic set the limits of possible concessions. In this way, he encouraged de Gaulle to believe in the possibility of a common Franco-German front vis-à-vis the transatlantic-oriented smaller EEC-partners.

Because the chancellor again did not contradict de Gaulle, it is not surprising that the president now took the offensive at the level of the six. After the successful conclusion of the EEC negotiations on a common agricultural market, de Gaulle presented an amended version of the draft of January 13 to the other five partners. In his new draft, he returned to the proposals made at Rambouillet: References to the Atlantic alliance had been deleted; the union was also to be responsible for economic issues (a clear attack on the existing communities); and there was no mention of a guarantee of the communities' structures established by the Treaty of Rome.[42]

At this stage, the Foreign Office pressed the chancellor, who was himself surprised by the anti-American and anticommunity tenor of de Gaulle's position,[43] not to follow the line taken by France. The Foreign Office had come to the conclusion that de Gaulle, after all, had not modified his foreign policy since Rambouillet. Adenauer's halfhearted attempts at persuading de Gaulle to give in had proved ineffective. Though Adenauer had shown his willingness to make concessions, the French president had responded with uncompromising proposals in the Fouchet Committee.[44] Therefore, the Foreign Office's policy toward Paris became unyielding again. By rejecting the second Fouchet Plan, the German delegation was instrumental in completely isolating the French delegation in the committee. The Foreign Office held on to the political course that it had followed since the beginning of the debate about political union and that was based on keeping the balance in the cooperation with Paris and Washington.

When the conference of foreign ministers in Luxembourg on April 17, 1962, failed, the project of political union was abandoned. At first glance, it may seem that the hard line of the Netherlands and Belgium led to the failure of the negotiations, for both made the establishment of political union conditional upon London's joining the EEC. In reality, however, the "British question" was merely a welcome excuse to abandon the project of political union altogether. Aside from Belgium and the Netherlands, Italy was also hesitant. All three parties were well aware of de Gaulle's maneuver at the beginning of the year when he revised the second Fouchet Plan, drawn up in his own Foreign Ministry, and returned to the proposals he had made at Rambouillet in the summer of 1960, distancing himself once again from the Atlantic alliance. All things considered, it was the legitimate doubt about de Gaulle's willingness to compromise that led the participants to finally abandon the effort to create a political union.

The Strategic Triangle as Obstacle

The development of the debate on European political union showed that the Federal Republic had failed to fulfill its role as mediator between the two dominant positions on the European process. Because both sides were unwilling to compromise, it was impossible to bridge the gap between the Anglo-American approach of transatlantic cooperation with a politically stable Europe embedded in NATO and the French efforts to overcome American hegemony on the European continent. The conflict between the key players, France and the United States—the latter represented in European debates by the Netherlands, Belgium, Italy and, of course, Britain—had a considerable impact on the Federal Republic's foreign policy decisions, which basically reproduced the conflicting views.

The need to find a balance between the two positions led the Federal Republic to follow an ambiguous policy, and the government's key players in the field of foreign affairs were unable to agree on a common position vis-à-vis their partners. It is true that both the chancellor and the Foreign Office wanted institutionalized political cooperation among the EEC member states. They disagreed, however, on how to achieve it. The differences of opinion resulted from the participants' particular orientation toward one of the two dominant conceptions of how security and economic cooperation should be organized in Europe and were to a large degree reflected in the extent to which they were willing to make concessions to Paris. The conflict between Bonn's two most important partners—mirrored and continued within the German political system—had the effect that the Federal Republic was not able to contribute constructively to the European process.

Furthermore, the Federal Republic's indecisiveness led the government to move away from its goal of a politically strong Europe. Nonetheless, Bonn's weak policy with regard to the European process was not the main reason for the failure of the political union project. In the end, the decisive factor was the incompatibility of ideas about the role of the United States in Europe and, in this context, of the structure of NATO, that is, the power relationships within the alliance. In this case, the strategic triangle functioned as an obstacle to agreement within the EEC. Once France had managed to push through its economic interests by securing a common agricultural market, there was no reason left for de Gaulle to make any concessions to his partners. Moreover, the German chancellor's policy must have made the French president believe that, no matter what happened, he could still hope for preferential treatment from Bonn. Consequently, there was no risk involved, and he simply dropped the project of political union. Given the conflicting interests, the Federal Republic had no means of resolving the conflict between its two most important allies. It therefore failed as mediator and had to accept, at least for the time being, that it would not be able to achieve the goal it had set itself in the European process.

Notes

1. Cf. Maurice Vaïsse, *La grandeur: Politique étrangère du général de Gaulle 1958–1969* (Paris: Fayard, 1998), 38–40; Edward A. Kolodziej, "De Gaulle, l'Allemagne et les superpuissances: L'unification allemande et la fin de la guerre froide," in *L'Europe,* vol. 5 in *De Gaulle en son siècle,* ed. Institut Charles de Gaulle (Paris: La Documentation Française/Plon, 1992), 383.
2. Cf. Stephen A. Kocs, *Autonomy or Power? The Franco-German Relationship and Europe's Strategic Choices, 1955–1995* (Westport, Conn.: Praeger, 1995), 37–38.
3. See, e.g., President Kennedy to Prime Minister Macmillan, May 22, 1961, and Department of State to the Embassy in the United Kingdom, telegram, May 23, 1961, in U.S. Department of State, *Foreign Relations of the United States (FRUS), 1961–1963,* vol. 13 (Washington, D.C.: U.S. Government Printing Office, 1994) (hereafter *FRUS 1961–63),* 20.
4. Cf. Department of State to Certain Missions in Europe, circular telegram, June 14, 1963, in *FRUS 1961–63,* 204.
5. General de Gaulle and Gronchi, conversation in the Italian presidential train, *Documents Diplomatiques Français* (herafter *DDF*) 1959/I, Direction Jean-Baptiste Duroselle (Paris: Government of France, 1994), 874–75.
6. Cf. undated note from the Auswärtiges Amt, attachment to Foreign Minister Brentano to Chancellor Adenauer, September 3, 1959; Bundesarchiv (BA), Nachlaß Brentano, vol. 157, 2–4.
7. Foreign Minister Brentano to Chancellor Adenauer, letter, September 3, 1959, Politisches Archiv des Auswärtigen Amts (PA/AA), Ministerbüro, vol. 49.
8. Note from Legationsrat I. Klasse Obermeyer (Referat 200), 18 September 1959, PA/AA, Referat 201, vol. 369.
9. French-German meetings at Rambouillet, July 29–30, 1960, second meeting between General de Gaulle and Chancellor Adenauer, July 29, 1960, 16h10; *DDF 1960/II,* 171. Two weeks before the summit of Rambouillet already, de Gaulle had left no doubt vis-à-vis his ministers that he aimed at restricting the influence of the supranational institutions of the Communities: "The objective of this initiative will be to make Europe progress to unity by the cooperation of the states and not by delegating power to non responsible political organs. Thus a political secretariat and an economic secretariat could be constituted which would be without doubt very similar to the Commissions but would be organs composed of officials preparing the decisions of the Member States." Quoted by Georges-Henri Soutou, "Le général de Gaulle et le plan Fouchet," in *L'Europe,* 128 (translation by Martin Koopmann).
10. French-German meetings at Rambouillet, July 29–30, 1960, third meeting between General de Gaulle and Chancellor Adenauer, July 30, 1960, 11h15 to 12h30, *DDF 1960/II,* 174–76.
11. More specifically, the chancellor was thinking of a fusion of the executive bodies of the three existing communities and a direct election of the European Parliament. Cf. note from Ambassador Blankenhorn, June 14, 1960, BA, Nachlaß Blankenhorn, vol. 101, sheet 31–35.
12. For the Franco-German relations in the Berlin Crisis, see Martin Koopmann, *Das schwierige Bündnisz: Die deutsch-französischen Beziehungen und die Außenpolitik der Bundesrepublik Deutschland 1958–1965* (Baden-Baden: Nomos, 2000), 45–123.
13. French-German meetings at Rambouillet, July 29–30, 1960, third meeting be-

tween General de Gaulle and Chancellor Adenauer, July 30, 1960, 11h15 to 12h30, *DDF 1960/II,* 174.

14. Heinrich Krone to Chancellor Adenauer, August 2, 1960, Archiv für Christlich-Demokratische Politik, Nachlaß Krone, I-028-006/4.

15. Cf. note from Heinrich Krone, August 1, 1960, in *Tagebücher* 1 (1945–61), by Heinrich Krone (Düsseldorf: Droste, 1995), 439.

16. Note from Wilhelm Hartlieb, January 12, 1960, PA/AA, Referat 201, vol. 370.

17. Note from Blankenhorn, July 29, 1960, in *Verständnis und Verständigung. Blätter eines politischen Tagebuchs 1949 bis 1979,* by Herbert Blankenhorn (Frankfurt: Propyläen, 1980), 383.

18. Cf. note from Permanent Secretary van Scherpenberg about the conversation with Couve de Murville, August 6, 1960, BA, Nachlaß Blankenhorn, vol. 103, sheet 307.

19. Chancellor Adenauer to President de Gaulle, letter, August 15, 1960, Archives Diplomatiques du Ministère des Affaires Etrangères, Série Cabinet du Ministre, Sous-Série Cabinet Couve de Murville, vol. 295.

20. Note from Jansen, February 8, 1961, Archiv für Christlich-Demokratische Politik, Nachlaß Jansen, Tagebuch, I-149-008/-1-5.

21. For the meeting of Chancellor Adenauer with General Norstad at Lake Como, September 9, 1960, see Koopmann, *Das schwierige Bündnisz,* 197–98.

22. On August 22, 1960, the State Department wrote to the Embassy in France: "Dep[artmen]t does not believe that this situation calls for any basic modification in U.S. policies or for any major U.S. intervention at this time. One reason is that de Gaulle's move is so patently in direction of French control on Continent that it has already aroused resistance from other Common Market members." U.S. Department of State, *Foreign Relations of the United States (FRUS), 1958–1960,* vol. 7, part 1, *Western European Integration and Security; Canada* (Washington, D.C.: U.S. Government Printing Office, 1993), 296.

23. Cf. President Eisenhower to Chancellor Adenauer, October 6, 1960, BA, Nachlaß Blankenhorn, vol. 104, sheet 184–87.

24. Directive for Michel Debré, prime minister, September 30, 1960, in *Lettres, notes et carnets,* by Charles de Gaulle (Paris: Plon, 1987), vol. 8, 398–99.

25. For the talks in Bonn, October 7–8, 1960, see DDF 1960/II, 467–86.

26. "Erklärung der Konferenz der Staats- bzw: Regierungschefs der sechs Mitgliedstaaten der EWG in Bonn vom 18 Juli 1961 über die Verstärkung der europäischen Zusammenarbeit (Bonner Erklärung)," Europa-Archiv (hereafter EA) 16 (1961): D 469-70.

27. Cf. Soutou, "Le général de Gaulle et le plan Fouchet," 134–35.

28. In a directive issued on April 20, 1961, the State Department wrote: "The U.S. should make clear its support for the movement toward European integration. The U.K. should not be encouraged to oppose or stay apart from that movement by doubts as to the U.S. attitude or by hopes of a 'special' relation with the U.S. The six should be encouraged to welcome U.K. association with the Community and not to set the price too high for such association, providing that there is to be no weakening of essential ties among the six." FRUS 1961–63, 286–87.

29. "Evaluation of all questions which are of common interest for the six members, or which are of interest for a particular member upon interest." Memorandum of the German Delegation, September 21, 1961, PA/AA, Referat 201, vol. 372.

30. "Erster französischer Entwurf vom 2 November 1961 für einen Vertrag über die Gründung einer union der Europäischen Völker," *EA* 19 (1964): D 466–85.

31. Adenauer on the occasion of the "Tea Talk" held on December 13, 1961, in *Adenauer, Konrad, Teegespräche, 1961–1963*, ed. Rudolf Morsey and Hans-Peter Schwarz (Berlin: Siedler, 1992), 42–43.

32. Cf. Meeting between General de Gaulle and Chancellor Adenauer, December 9, 1961, *DDF* 1961/II, 705–6.

33. Adenauer on the occasion of the 'Tea Talk' held on December 14, 1961, in *Adenauer, Konrad, Teegespräche*, 58.

34. Note from Legationsrat Lang (Referat 200), November 7, 1961, PA/AA, Referat 201, vol. 373.

35. Note from Legationsrat Lang (Referat 200), January 12, 1962, BA, Nachlaß Brentano, vol. 166.

36. For the meeting of the Fouchet Committee on November 10, 1961, see circular telegram from French Foreign Minister Couve de Murville to certain missions in Western Europe, November 14, 1961; *DDF* 1961/II, 587–89.

37. Letter from Von Brentano, the leader of the CDU/CSU in the Bundestag, to Chancellor Adenauer, June 22, 1962, BA, Nachlaß Brentano, vol. 159, 2.

38. Cf. Note from Blankenhorn, May 29, 1962, BA, Nachlaß Blankenhorn, vol. 132a, sheet 3–7.

39. For the discussion in the Fouchet Committee about the first Fouchet Plan, see Soutou, "Le général de Gaulle et le plan Fouchet," 135–36.

40. Cf. Georges-Henri Soutou, *L'alliance incertaine: Les rapports politico-stratégiques franco-allemands, 1954–1996* (Paris: Fayard, 1996), 189.

41. Meeting between General de Gaulle and Chancellor Adenauer, December 9, 1961, 706.

42. Cf. ibid.

43. Cf. note from Ambassador Blankenhorn, February 12, 1962, BA, Nachlaß Blankenhorn, vol. 128b, sheet 13–14.

44. Cf. Koopmann, *Das schwierige Bündnisz*, 170–73.

Part II

The NATO Crisis of the 1960s and the Maturation of the Strategic Triangle

Chapter 3

The NATO Crisis of 1966–1967: Confronting Germany with a Conflict of Priorities

Helga Haftendorn

Stanley Hoffmann wrote in 1981, "The history of the Atlantic Alliance is a history of crises."[1] He added, however, that one had to distinguish between true crises in which the very existence of the alliance was at stake,[2] and the "routine difficulties engendered by Western Europe's dependence on the United States for its security," difficulties that subsided again just as quickly as they had appeared.

In Germany, the NATO crisis of 1966–67 was viewed as a situation in which the survival and future course of the alliance were in jeopardy.[3] This was not NATO's first serious crisis; yet many political leaders feared that unless extraordinary measures were taken to resolve it, the alliance could fall apart after 1969—as of April 1969, the North Atlantic Treaty could be denounced on one year's notice—or else be gradually eroded by divergent interests.

This chapter draws on chapters 1 and 6 of *NATO and the Nuclear Revolution: A Crisis of Credibility, 1966–1967* by Helga Haftendorn (Oxford: Clarendon Press, 1996).

A Precarious German-French Alliance

The NATO crisis, which had been building for years, came into full public view when French president Charles de Gaulle declared on February 21, 1966, that France intended to regain sovereignty over its national territory and armed forces and would therefore review its relations with the Atlantic alliance. Shortly thereafter, the Paris government announced that France would withdraw from the integrated structure of NATO effective July 1, 1966, and that all Allied staffs and military institutions had to be removed from the country by April 1, 1967.[4]

This announcement did not come as a complete surprise. The Fifth Republic had been distancing itself from the alliance by stages,[5] and there had been signals prior to the final step in the spring of 1966, though nothing had been said as to what measures were being contemplated.[6] By pulling out of NATO's integrated military structures, the French president shook the foundations of the alliance and thereby called into question one of the essential elements of the European postwar order. Having failed in 1958 to reform the alliance by establishing a tripartite directorate, which would have given France a more prominent position equal to the two Anglo-Saxon countries and commensurate with its claimed "special status" in world affairs,[7] de Gaulle now called into question the core of the alliance: its integrated military structure. France wanted to reestablish normal conditions of sovereignty, in which all that was France—its soil, sky, sea and its forces, and every foreign element within it—should be subject solely to French authority.[8]

However, de Gaulle made it clear that France would remain a member of the alliance, for the French move would not affect the 1949 Treaty of Washington. Rather, France intended to challenge the dominant position of the United States in NATO, a dominance that denied France an equal role in world affairs. It could not forget the affront of the Anglo-American Nassau Agreement, when Washington had offered nuclear cooperation to Britain but denied it to France.[9] Further, it was greatly disturbed that the United States, despite French opposition, continued to press for its strategic conceptions in the alliance and increasingly found support among its partners. The French government categorically rejected the concept of Flexible Response put forward by U.S. secretary of defense Robert McNamara, for this ran counter to its view that deterrence still had to be based on the threat of a rapid and full use of nuclear weapons ("massive retaliation"). Although French territory was protected in the initial phase of a conflict by the

German military *glacis,* French leaders recognized the danger that it too could become a battlefield if a conventional attack by the Warsaw Pact were countered primarily using non-nuclear means and the United States hesitated to launch a strategic counterstrike.

The French move had significant effects on the Federal Republic of Germany. First of all, it demonstrated publicly that the close entente between the two countries envisioned by German chancellor Konrad Adenauer and the French president, and documented in the Treaty of Friendship and Cooperation, signed January 1963, had lost its binding force. Though German military and political elites shared their neighbor's concern about the security risks involved in the strategic revisions that the U.S. secretary of defense tried to force on NATO, they were reluctant to support policies that could further endanger NATO's cohesion and weaken the ties between America and Western Europe's defense. The talks among the militaries of both countries, which had regularly met between 1961 and 1963 to develop a joint position on strategy, had floundered on these differences.[10] De Gaulle believed that a greater distance from America was essential to realize his ideas of a new European order. His alternative to President John Kennedy's conception of an "Atlantic Partnership"[11] envisioned a core Europe limited to Western Europe, with France as its leading power (and not the growing economic power Germany), cooperating with the United States on an equal basis. On this question, the German political body was deeply split. As the debate on the ratification of the German-French Treaty showed, large parts of the ruling Christian Democratic Union/Christian Social Union (CDU/CSU), and most Social Democratic Party (SPD) and Free Democratic Party (FDP) members, were deeply suspicious of too close a relationship with France out of concern that it would weaken the transatlantic link.

France also claimed to be a spokesman for European interests vis-à-vis the Soviet Union. De Gaulle's aim was to establish a new equilibrium in Europe, with rapprochement and cooperation among European states "from the Atlantic to the Urals" encompassing a settlement of the German question as well.[12] To that end, French policy devised a formula of "détente, entente, and cooperation."[13] Thus, during his visit to Moscow in June 1966, de Gaulle proposed to the Soviet leaders a negotiating package that entailed the creation of a collective European security system and the withdrawal of American troops from Europe together with German reunification.[14] With that, France not only contradicted the position of the Federal Republic but also formulated its own plan for the future order of Europe.

The NATO crisis not only brought these disagreements to the fore but also showed to the Bonn government how limited was its room for maneuvering in international affairs.

Causes of the NATO Crisis

The French withdrawal from military integration, spectacular as it appeared at the time, was really just a symptom, not the cause, of the crisis in NATO. From a German perspective, five basic problems were involved:

- the credibility of nuclear deterrence and the unequal risk faced by European and American NATO allies;
- meeting NATO's force goals, and offsetting costs for U.S. and British troops stationed in Germany;
- control over nuclear weapons and nuclear strategy, and whether some kind of nuclear sharing was possible;
- assessment of the Soviet Union's political and military intentions and the possibilities for East-West détente, as well as a solution to the German question; and
- the role of the United States and its allies, particularly France and West Germany, in a future European political order.

The NATO crisis concerned the question of how the credibility of nuclear deterrence could be maintained under the conditions of nuclear stalemate.[15] Under what conditions would the United States be prepared to wage a nuclear defense of its European allies if in the event of a nuclear conflict it had to contemplate the destruction of its own territory? The American call to reduce NATO's strategic reliance on using nuclear weapons and instead strengthen its conventional capabilities—that is, to replace its prevailing strategy of massive retaliation (known in alliance terminology as MC 14/2) with one of Flexible Response (MC 14/3)[16]—was regarded by the Europeans as an indication that the United States was about to decouple itself from the defense of Western Europe. But from the German standpoint especially, the security of the West was best guaranteed if the alliance had recourse to a continuum of nuclear weapons, in particular nuclear systems stationed in Western Europe and capable of covering targets in Soviet territory.

Related concerns were raised regarding the assumptions or threat scenarios whereby force planning would be guided because the credibility of deterrence depended on a suitable force posture. Would it be possible to agree on common force requirements to handle the most likely conflicts, and could these then be met at the national level? At a time when the threat of war in Europe seemed to have diminished, the United States was embroiled in the Vietnam War and—like Britain for other reasons—had to contend with difficult budgetary problems, there was growing domestic pressure in all countries for a reduction of forces. Yet the strategy of Flexible Response called for a strengthening of conventional combat power. If the trend toward unilateral reductions could not be stopped, there was a danger that, contrary to the Americans' original thinking, the nuclear threshold would necessarily be lowered again. The new strategic concept would thus have lost credibility before the alliance had even adopted it.

NATO's nuclear dilemmas[17] were heightened by the fact that essentially only the United States had the requisite nuclear capabilities for the defense of Europe. Britain depended on the support of the United States to keep its strategic systems operationally ready; the French *force de frappe* was still in the making. Contrary to some earlier hints from de Gaulle to Adenauer and his confidants that France was prepared to share its nuclear force with West Germany,[18] France made no bones about the fact that it was not prepared to allow any other state a say in nuclear planning. Yet a country such as the Federal Republic, which considered itself most threatened by the superior military power of the Warsaw Pact, was excluded from nuclear collaboration. This gave rise to its desire for a greater say in nuclear matters, possibly in the form of a multilateral nuclear force (MLF) under NATO's command. When this ultimately failed in 1966 and the United States began working with the Soviet Union to reach an international agreement on the nonproliferation of nuclear weapons, many West German politicians saw this as further discrimination against the non-nuclear allies. They accused the United States of giving cooperation with Moscow priority over solving the alliance's internal problems.

The Federal Republic and France shared the concern that the United States was reordering its global priorities. President de Gaulle's February 1966 announcement that France would pull out of NATO integration was as much concerned with the political order in Europe as it was a European-American conflict over strategy and the nuclear question at the Atlantic level. Though France insisted on its role as a European nuclear power and challenged the dominance of the United States in the alliance, the latter was intent on maintaining its global leadership in security matters and on exercising control over the further development of East-West relations. To reduce the risk of nuclear confrontation—a lesson of the Cuban missile crisis—while keeping the Soviet Union at bay in Southeast Asia, the United States had started a carefully calculated political dialogue with Moscow, which achieved some initial success with the Test Ban Treaty and the draft Non-Proliferation Treaty (NPT). West German aims were also guided by considerations of the basic political order; in the alliance, Bonn was striving for a greater degree of equality and (nuclear) cooperation, while also trying to ensure that those measures did not hamper European integration. Its goal was to create a European union that would assume more and more the sovereign rights of its member states and would include Britain, Denmark, and Norway. The Atlantic alliance should then one day rest on both a European and an American pillar. The German model thus largely accorded with the American design of an Atlantic partnership.[19] Both, however, conflicted with the French concept of a European confederation that would not circumscribe the sovereign rights of a nation. There was also no prospect of Britain's being admitted, because the French government insisted that it should first emancipate itself from the United States.

The Vietnam War fueled further conflicts within the alliance. In June 1966, the U.S. military presence in Vietnam had risen to 285,000 men, with substantial reinforcements anticipated up to the end of the year. That same month, the United States intensified the air war against North Vietnam and began bombing the capital, Hanoi, and the port city, Haiphong. Arguing that in Indochina it was also defending the freedom of Western Europe, the United States called upon its allies for substantial support. Bonn did regard the U.S. engagement in Southeast Asia as an indication that Washington would also meet its alliance commitments in any conflict over Berlin; yet it confined itself to inconspicuous humanitarian aid and declaratory support.[20] However, many European governments took a skeptical view of the "domino theory." France openly criticized the U.S. position in the Vietnam War and claimed a role in settling the conflict, referring to its prominent position as a member of the UN Security Council and as a nuclear power.[21]

Even more serious was the fact that the war in Southeast Asia began to preoccupy Washington more and more. On Thanksgiving weekend of 1966, a meeting of the president with his closest advisers at his ranch in Texas, where important NATO decisions were to have been made, was instead dominated by the Vietnam problem and related military questions.[22] From this point on, the administration was concerned almost exclusively with the war in Southeast Asia. Furthermore, the United States was making increasing efforts to keep the Soviet Union out of the Vietnam War. Because the only negotiable issues were in the area of arms control—with measures that would neither alter the strategic balance nor hinder the American engagement in Southeast Asia—increasing tensions developed between the United States and its European allies, which felt that their interests were being slighted.

Linked with the first two sets of problems was the question of how the alliance assessed the threat and the future shape of East-West relations, or indeed whether there still was a common assessment. The majority of the allies assumed that because the Berlin Crisis and the Cuban missile crisis had abated, the critical threat had lessened and limited cooperation with the Soviet Union and other Eastern European countries was in the Western interest. Various European countries—for example Belgium, Denmark, and Italy—began to intensify their contacts with the Eastern European countries. In part, they wished to restore the political and cultural relations that had been frozen by the Cold War; in part, they hoped to be able to tap investment opportunities and new markets for their products in Eastern Europe. With his trips to the Soviet Union and Poland, President de Gaulle sought to make himself a spokesman for the Europeans and put forward new initiatives for a European security system. However, the French proposals had not been agreed upon with the allies; they rather called into question the alliance's past position. The Federal Republic maintained that a relaxation of East-West tensions in Europe could come about only in conjunction with a solution of the question of German reunification, and that it would be inconceivable for Bonn to give up its close ties with its Western European partners and the United States to do so. Nor could the Federal Republic accept special discriminatory terms. With its "Peace Note" of March 1966, Bonn made an effort to demonstrate to all sides its readiness for détente.[23] It stuck to its past positions regarding Germany but did propose to the Soviet Union and the other Eastern European countries talks on renunciation of force in mutual relations. Yet in trying to keep open the German question so that a final determination of German borders would have to be part and parcel of a peace treaty, the Federal Republic inevitably found itself increasingly at odds with the détente policy of its partners, with alliance relations strained as a result.[24]

The United States had just initiated a cautious revision of its policy toward Eastern Europe. The new element in President Lyndon Johnson's "bridge building" speech of October 7, 1966, was the offer to constructively reshape East-West relations, although without mention of German reunification.[25] Moreover, the United States was eager to reduce the dangers of confrontation by negotiating arms control agreements with the Soviet Union. Yet the Test Ban Treaty of August 1963 had already led to a crisis in German-American relations, as Bonn saw the German Democratic Republic's international standing enhanced by its signature of the treaty. The NPT generated even more serious strains. But in all its efforts to achieve a controlled détente in East-West relations, the United States wanted to avoid at all costs having the allies relax their defense efforts or distance themselves from the alliance. The problem, then, was to find a common framework wherein a suitable defense policy, including provision of the requisite means to achieve it, was compatible with a careful bilateral as well as multilateral détente policy. If this could not be done, there would be no stopping the centrifugal forces in the alliance.

The development of common positions within NATO was also complicated by the fact that the member countries faced growing discrepancies between domestic political demands and alliance requirements. There were various reasons for this, including the slackening threat and doubts about the credibility of deterrence. In this situation, de Gaulle was not the only one to announce unilateral measures. At roughly the same time, it was reported that American troops would be moved from Europe to Vietnam; the British government declared that it would drastically reduce its Army of the Rhine unless the Federal Republic was prepared to fully offset the foreign exchange costs resulting from the stationing of British forces; and finally, the Bonn government had to concede that because of its own budget problems it was no longer able to fulfill the current offset agreement with the United States. Bonn argued, however, that the allied troops not only guaranteed Germany's security but were also there for the defense of other allies. The size of these forces should be geared to the threat and to the strategic concepts in operation, not to the ability of some countries to pay. The offset crisis ultimately became so explosive that it resulted in the fall of Ludwig Erhard's government in November 1966.

In view of the multitude of problems, one wonders how the allies were able to settle the NATO crisis of 1966–67 without weakening the cohesion and workability of the alliance—apart from France's departure from NATO integration. Moreover, the crisis was overcome without any impetus from a worsening international situation (it was not until August 1968 that the Warsaw Pact intervention in Czechoslovakia occurred, a good half year later), whereas the crucial alliance compromises had been reached in December 1967. However, neither the adoption of the strategy of Flexible Response nor of the Harmel Report provided a real solution to the central problems of the alliance or for the differing conceptions of political order. Rather, the solutions reached were marked by a great deal of ambiguity. Still, by the end of 1967, the malaise and doubt about NATO's workability or its necessity had dissipated; the possibility of a treaty denunciation after 1969 had been removed.

Mending the Crisis of Credibility

The principal objective in devising a new strategic concept was to overcome the discrepancy between a U.S. nuclear doctrine newly adapted to the nuclear stalemate and the alliance strategy of "massive retaliation," which still by and large met European needs but had ceased to be credible. The Western alliance had faced a dilemma ever since the Soviet Union acquired long-range nuclear weapons and thus could threaten the United States with devastating strikes in any military conflict. The United States still had superior strategic nuclear forces; yet under circumstances of the nuclear stalemate, it was not very credible that Washington would use this capability and risk its own destruction if the Soviets were to venture a sudden strike on "just" Hamburg or Frankfurt.

This predicament gave rise to a growing conviction in America that a limited conflict could be reliably deterred only if the West had at its disposal other, more credible military means besides the ultimate option of strategic nuclear weapons. From the U.S. standpoint, this meant primarily conventional forces. If the Warsaw Pact were to launch a military attack without using nuclear weapons, then NATO should confine itself to a conventional defense as long as possible. The European allies, and Germany in particular, were still convinced that the security of Western Europe would be best ensured if NATO could rely on a continuous spectrum of nuclear weapons and particularly if it deployed on the continent medium-range nuclear missiles that could be employed quickly and could cover targets in Soviet territory.

These two positions, which reflected the different ways that America and Western Europe were threatened, were not readily compatible. For a number of reasons, the Federal Republic in the early 1960s ruled out any substantial strengthening of conventional forces. Besides financial and manpower constraints, it rejected above all the idea that there could be a sustained military conflict in Europe, entailing massive destruction, without the United States using its "nuclear sword" to terminate the conflict rapidly. Compared with the Americans, the Germans were, in the words of

Lawrence Freedman, "not so interested in the threshold between conventional and nuclear war and much more preoccupied by the threshold between peace and war.... [Because] any war would be catastrophic for Europe, so war itself, not just nuclear war, had to be deterred."[26]

Thus, the search for a new strategic concept to replace what had become an incredible strategy of massive retaliation involved no less than a redistribution of military risks, which the United States did not wish to assume alone, but the Germans and the other Europeans were not prepared to bear either. Efforts to find a common denominator despite the contrary interests had all the appearances of trying to square the circle. Maximizing one's own interests was not likely to yield a solution. There had to be an added element of willingness on the part of every NATO member to accept risks for the sake of common goals and values if in return some compensation could be expected in other areas.

The compromise was the strategy of Flexible Response, whereby the Europeans—and in particular the Germans, the ally whose geostrategic situation was most exposed—accepted a greater recourse to conventional forces in the event of Warsaw Pact aggression carried out with non-nuclear means. For its part, the United States agreed to a larger role than it had originally intended for tactical nuclear weapons in defense against enemy aggression. The link between conventional defense and the use of nuclear weapons was controlled escalation. Yet for the time being, it remained uncertain when, under what conditions, and in what way nuclear weapons ought to be used. The agreement was thus marked by a high degree of ambiguity.

To achieve this agreement, the allies had to narrow their differences on a number of specific questions. Germany accepted, although with some qualification, the American argument that the danger of a geographically and militarily limited conflict was greater than that of a large-scale surprise attack with nuclear weapons, and that NATO therefore had to prepare for a non-nuclear direct defense at the dividing line between East and West. They also agreed that a conflict would be preceded by a period of tension and warning—though opinions differed as to its length. Regarding the military balance—the supreme allied commander in Europe (SACEUR) and Germany assumed a significant Warsaw Pact superiority in conventional forces, whereas the United States claimed an approximate parity—the Germans conceded that the current level of NATO forces was sufficient but that certain "imbalances" had to be eliminated. Further, reinforcement and mobilization capabilities had to be improved so that NATO could draw on external forces and reservists in the event of military conflict. Conversely, the

United States recognized that there could be situations that called for the use of tactical nuclear weapons and that it was politically imperative to work out with the European members of NATO employment principles to govern such use. This work was subsequently undertaken by the Nuclear Planning Group (NPG).

The narrowing of differences on strategy took place not so much in the multilateral NATO bodies but rather in negotiating forums of more limited purpose and participation. In general, key documents did not get final consideration in NATO's Military Committee, Defense Planning Committee, or the Council until compromises on the critical points had been found in a smaller circle or in bilateral talks. The bilateral German-American contacts and study groups were especially important for building consensus. These provided the opportunity for intensive discussion of threat assessment, the military balance, and the conclusions to be drawn for military policy, but they also worked as a kind of "learning exercise" that allowed the allies to impart information, break down prejudices, and narrow the differences between their positions. These were supplemented by discussions in the NPG and by trilateral accords between the United States, Britain, and Germany. Thus, the essential compromises that opened the way for adoption of a new ministerial guidance in May 1967 and for approval of the new strategic concept of Flexible Response—in alliance terminology, again, MC 14/3—in December 1967 were worked out in the trilateral talks on troop deployments and offset arrangements in November 1966.

Agreement on a new strategy was greatly facilitated by two other developments. On the one hand, France's withdrawal from NATO integration, and thus from the bodies concerned with revising strategy, made it possible finally to carry on a purposive debate on strategy. This increased the pressure on Germany, however. Because the Federal Republic now represented the most important opposition to U.S. views, Bonn became the primary focus of expectations of accommodation. The German government was prepared to compromise because, more so than the other partners, it feared a military decoupling by the United States and wanted to ensure that American (and British) forces remained in Germany without major cutbacks. Essential to the credibility of the Flexible Response strategy was the political commitment of the United States, sustained by the presence of its troops in Europe. A further condition was Washington's promise not to reduce the tactical nuclear weapons deployed in Western Europe.[27]

On the other hand, the United States had to take the Europeans' interests more into account if American leaders wanted to keep them from taking the

French road and distancing themselves from the alliance.[28] There were fears in Washington that the alliance might fall apart after 1969. However, for a variety of reasons, neither the Federal Republic nor the United States wanted to risk a dissolution or weakening of NATO. Despite all its problems, the alliance provided credible protection against military aggression—although the likelihood of this had diminished—and, moreover, it guaranteed America's political and military ties with Western Europe as well as the integration of Germany in an Atlantic context.

Agreement on NATO Force Planning and on Offsetting Costs for Troops Stationed in Germany

NATO's central problem was to raise sufficient and appropriate allied forces to sustain a credible deterrence and, if that should fail, to ensure an effective defense. Since the 1950s, NATO had tried, without signal success, to close the "Lisbon gap,"[29] that is, to overcome the discrepancy between NATO's force goals and the numbers of troops actually made available by its members for the common defense.[30] By the early 1960s, this problem had acquired a new urgency. It became evident that changes in NATO's force posture were necessary if the alliance were to be prepared to meet the contingencies most likely to arise in the event of a conflict. U.S. secretary of defense Robert McNamara sought to convince the allies that a strengthening of the conventional elements of NATO defense was both economically feasible and strategically wise. With NATO secretary general Dirk Stikker initiating studies on force planning ("Stikker Exercise"), the Europeans hoped to reach a consensus with the United States on the requisite allied force goals based on an agreed threat assessment and the financial as well as manpower potentials of the member nations. Whereas the United States saw the solution in major increases in conventional capabilities (and in what it regarded as a more realistic estimation of the military balance between NATO and the Warsaw Pact), the Europeans expected that they could convince the Americans of the European realities of a continued communist threat, a high risk even in a limited conventional conflict, especially with restricted financial and manpower resources.

It was not difficult to agree on procedures and organs to deal with NATO force planning; given the contrary motives of the two sides, it was much harder to come to terms on the substance. U.S. officials wrongly assumed that a pragmatic process of force planning would enable them to circumvent the strategic disagreement, whereas a corresponding configuration of NATO capabilities would help change the strategic conditions for Western defense in terms of American conceptions. Force structure and strategic concept were too closely connected to allow for an artificial separation of the two areas. Force planning therefore reached a dead end whenever basic strategic assumptions came into play. Success was not forthcoming until substantive matters were set aside for the time being. In December 1965, the NATO defense ministers adopted a "rolling five-year plan" as a new process for force planning; and in December 1967, they approved a force plan for 1968–72 based upon it.

Force planning had been effectively decoupled from the development of a new strategic concept, including decisions as to its operational implementation. A substantive connection remained only inasmuch as military stipulations entered into the force goals formulated by the NATO commanders, but the results were largely determined by what the individual states were willing to undertake. Whereas the Flexible Response strategy approved in December 1967 (MC 14/3) and the operational document (MC 48/3) based upon it formulated military missions, the nature and extent of the armed forces provided by the member states were largely dictated by economic and domestic political necessities. The adoption of planning procedures thus altered nothing of the fact that NATO's existing military capabilities would not allow the alliance to accomplish the missions set forth in the strategic concept. But by forgoing a fundamental reform of its force structure and instead taking the approach of a slow adaptation process, NATO accepted this discrepancy.

The new process accorded the NATO member states an increased responsibility for force planning. It therefore remained susceptible to domestic developments. The first force plan devised according to the new process had not yet been adopted when Britain threatened to withdraw parts of the British Army of the Rhine if the Federal Republic were not prepared to provide greater compensation to offset British foreign exchange outflows. For the government in London, the crisis of the pound was more compelling than its alliance commitments. A few months later, the German government found itself compelled to go back on its offset promises and thus risk troop withdrawals, because it saw no other way of plugging the hole in the federal budget. Washington, too, was quick to raise the prospect of reducing its troops in Germany—euphemistically termed a rotation—to augment U.S.

forces in Vietnam and provide some financial relief, while also taking the wind out of the sails of Senator Mike Mansfield (D-Mont.) and his colleagues, who were demanding significant troop withdrawals from Europe.

Finally, President de Gaulle threw the whole of NATO planning into question when he announced in the spring of 1966 that France would withdraw from NATO's integrated structures. Besides the removal of French troops and territory, this raised the question of what arrangements could be made regarding the two French divisions remaining in Germany following France's withdrawal from NATO integration. Efforts to find a solution satisfactory to the alliance as a whole failed in the face of opposition from Paris; the German government had to be content with a bilateral exchange of notes with the French government. Future military cooperation between France and NATO was to be confined to wartime conditions.

One useful vehicle for coordinating a common response to the French move, and in particular for establishing a compromise on troop deployments and offset, was a process of confidential trilateral talks between the three governments principally concerned. The fear that Germany might follow the French step had prompted the United States to send its former high commissioner, John McCloy, to Bonn in April 1966; together with German and British government representatives, McCloy was to work toward a united and unambiguous Western response to de Gaulle's action. His mission and the U.S.-German-British talks then served as an institutional model for resolving the offset crisis in the fall of that year. The success of these talks was in large measure attributable to the American negotiator himself: McCloy was not only exceedingly knowledgeable about Europe and a friend of the Europeans, but he also had direct access to President Johnson, and thus he could act as an honest broker among the parties involved.

Because the Federal Republic had little room for maneuvering on the offset question, Bonn had to make the greatest concessions. Germany agreed to increased foreign exchange adjustments to Britain and monetary measures in favor of the United States; all the same, it had to accept some, although smaller, British and U.S. troop withdrawals. Although Washington was able to set the agenda for the talks, its latitude was also limited, for it did not want to risk either a collapse of the alliance or greater German reliance on France. However, the Franco-German Treaty of 1963 and the suspicions it had aroused in Washington proved to be a bargaining chip for Bonn. To realize their goals and ensure a successful conclusion of the trilateral talks, all the negotiating partners had to make concessions going beyond the subject of the offset negotiations. Though the United States sought to accommodate the strategic concerns of its non-nuclear partners by conceding a larger role for tactical nuclear weapons and by offering these allies a greater say in nuclear affairs Britain was expected to lend greater support for U.S. defense policy and Germany to give up its opposition to the NPT.

The greatest success of the trilateral talks was that the offset question did not, as initially feared, become an explosive issue within the alliance but instead paved the way for its consolidation. The demonstrated ability to reach an acceptable compromise in what appeared in the summer of 1966 to be a hopeless offset crisis had more positive effects than the negative fact that the two Anglo-Saxon powers had set themselves above the newly instituted procedures for force planning—if not by the letter, at least in spirit. In fact the "fourteen" NATO members were shortly thereafter able to agree on a new ministerial guidance for developing force goals and a revised strategic concept. On the question of the continued allied military presence, the German arguments were now turned around: Whereas the German government had in the past always argued for a rapid nuclear strike, it now stressed that because a lowering of the nuclear threshold was undesirable, any redeployment of American or British forces would undermine the credibility of the new NATO strategy.[31]

Overcoming the Nuclear Dilemmas of the Alliance

Not only had NATO's strategy and force posture lost much of their credibility, but the nuclear stalemate had also accentuated the geostrategically based unequal distribution of risks between the allies. This asymmetry was further compounded by the uneven opportunities to participate in nuclear affairs. Though the discussion of a new strategic concept was concerned primarily with the role of strategic and tactical nuclear weapons as well as conventional forces in deterrence and with the conditions for the use of nuclear weapons in the event of military conflict, a solution to the nuclear problem was viewed primarily in terms of a greater involvement of NATO's non-nuclear members. Like Germany, they wished to take a greater part in planning and decisionmaking for nuclear weapons employment, and as a result the unequal risk, though not eliminated, should be made more bearable.

A fully satisfactory solution to NATO's nuclear problem was out of the question because neither the geography could be changed nor the fact altered that the United States insisted on the president's sole responsibility for the use of nuclear weapons. For the latter reason, the alliance failed to embrace a collective nuclear solution such as the MLF sought by Germany, Italy, and some of the smaller NATO countries. It would have provided for a jointly financed and manned fleet of surface ships assigned to SACEUR and armed with nuclear missiles.

The MLF also failed to come about because of the European allies' reluctance to support a project that would have entailed considerable costs yet would have changed the asymmetries in NATO only marginally. Because Washington sensed little inclination on the part of the allies to commit themselves to a solution in which they had only a moderate interest but which could have been implemented only over considerable domestic political opposition, the Johnson administration shelved the MLF in December 1964. It had conceived of the MLF as a kind of placebo for the nuclear anxieties and desires of its allies, above all as a way of preventing the emergence of other independent nuclear powers; the Federal Republic, however, had quickly become the project's staunchest proponent. Bonn felt that in this way it would gain a measure of nuclear involvement that was otherwise closed to it. However, with increasing French pressure on Bonn to give up the MLF, by late 1964 members of the CDU/CSU in the Bundestag also began to distance themselves from the project. To avoid sharpening the intraparty rift between "Atlanticists" and "Gaullists" and to keep the MLF out of the 1965 Bundestag election campaign, Chancellor Ludwig Erhard requested that the project be temporarily held back. Officially, however, the German government adhered to the project and felt it could successfully do so because there were still MLF supporters within the U.S. administration, and so the project seemed by no means dead. Finally, in September 1966, Bonn had to recognize that a hardware solution no longer had any chance of being realized.

Subsequently, the failure of the MLF was often ascribed to American officials having given priority to the NPT with the Soviet Union over the project of a NATO nuclear force. This element certainly played a role but was not decisive. The decision to no longer pursue the MLF actively was taken in December 1964, whereas U.S. nonproliferation policy only materialized in the course of 1965, and serious negotiations with the Soviet Union did not begin until a year later. The United States had previously worked toward an intra-alliance solution to the nuclear problem, but with the NPT the problem was raised to the global level, with the Soviet Union gaining a say on NATO's nuclear affairs. The nonproliferation issue sorely strained allied relations, particularly because America's partners felt inadequately consulted. In view of the unequal obligations between nuclear and non-nuclear states, they accused Washington of an "atomic complicity" with Moscow.[32] Other concerns pertained to the absence of guarantees for the non-nuclear states, keeping open the "European option," and maintaining an unhindered peaceful utilization of atomic energy. Not all these fears were allayed by the treaty text or by interpretations of it. However, they lost some of their political urgency over the course of 1967 as agreement on a new NATO strategy as well as improved consultation for the non-nuclear allies began to take shape.

Washington conceived the Nuclear Planning Group—or rather its predecessor, the Special Committee—as a means for the non-nuclear partners' participation in nuclear affairs, especially when the MLF did not materialize. The NPG was a pure planning body, without decisionmaking powers. Its activity was limited to the period before the beginning of a conflict, whereas once a conflict had broken out, the release decision rested with the U.S. president; and although rules and procedures had been developed for this, no one could force the president to observe them. For its effectiveness and for the cohesion of the alliance, it was therefore important to create a climate of trusting cooperation before a crisis emerged and for the allies to make every effort to consider the specific security interests of their partners. It was assumed that this would foster a practice of consensus conflict resolution that would stand the test in a crisis.

In 1966–67, the NPG contributed greatly to facilitating the search for sustainable compromises among the differences of opinion about a new strategic concept. On the one hand, to remove the strongest objections against it, the United States accepted a larger role for tactical nuclear weapons within the framework of controlled escalation. Moreover, it reassured the allies that it planned no reduction in the nuclear weapons deployed in Europe. On the other hand, greater awareness and understanding of American nuclear capabilities and the operational plans for them helped to remove doubts about the credibility of the U.S. nuclear umbrella and thus about the effectiveness of deterrence. The adoption by the NPG in November 1969 of political guidelines for the initial use of tactical nuclear weapons helped to clarify in one critical area the ambivalence of the Flexible Response strategy.

Agreement on a Common Détente Policy

The initiative of Belgian foreign minister Pierre Harmel that resulted in the Harmel Report was designed to resolve NATO's conflict of priorities between security and détente. Some allies took the view that because the Soviet threat had subsided it was time to improve political, economic, and cultural cooperation with the Eastern European states and the Soviet Union, whereas others feared that this might weaken the Atlantic alliance and compromise its security function. With the formation of the Grand Coalition of the CDU/CSU and the SDP in December 1966, the Federal Republic was in a phase of reorientation of its *Ostpolitik* but had yet to reach agreement on its future course. Though some of its partners demanded that Bonn stop dragging its heels on détente, the German government tried to keep the discussion of détente from getting away from the German question.

Driving forces in urging a common Western approach to détente were the Belgian foreign minister, Pierre Harmel, and the ambitious Belgian state minister and former NATO secretary general, Paul-Henri Spaak. Having just agreed to the transfer of NATO's seat and headquarters to Brussels, the Belgians wanted to show a special commitment to détente policy. The United States had given a green light for Harmel's proposed study because it hoped the results would have a positive impact on alliance cohesion, but it did not expect any new departures resulting from it. On the one hand, Washington wanted to avoid having political differences complicate the discussion on strategy that had just resumed in NATO; on the other, it did not want its bilateral arms control dialogue with the Soviet Union diluted by pan-European palaver. Bonn was particularly intent that Paris be included in the exercise from the start. Bonn saw the Harmel study as a way of keeping France in the alliance, especially because it did not participate in the negotiations on the new strategic concept or on force planning.

The preparation of the reports of the four subgroups and of the overall report and its adoption by the North Atlantic Council were accompanied by numerous conflicts and differences of opinion. Bonn was hard put to establish its essentials on the German question. Its demand that there could be no détente in Europe without a solution to the German question met with opposition primarily from the smaller NATO countries, which no longer wanted to see détente blocked in deference to Bonn. The change of government in December 1966, with Willy Brandt heading the Foreign Office, brought greater flexibility in German thinking, although no consensus within the German government on the future course it should take.

Work on the Harmel Report was greatly facilitated by the progress made in working out a new strategic concept and in increasing the involvement of non-nuclear allies in NATO's nuclear planning. This bolstered confidence in the credibility of deterrence and in the adequacy of the means provided for it. The United States had originally endeavored to keep military matters out of the Harmel discussions, but following the adoption of the ministerial guidance and agreement on the draft for the strategic concept in September 1967, the Americans now sought to integrate the newfound compromise into the results reported by subgroup three on security policy.

French opposition prevented formal adoption of the working group reports. Instead, the alliance accepted a very general final report, which many participants criticized as being without substance. For Germany especially, but also for Belgium and Canada, it was politically important both that a common report be passed and that France accept it. Faced with the choice of either accepting what it regarded as an unnecessary declaration that in part also ran counter to its interests or else provoking a new crisis in NATO, the government in Paris opted for the former and accepted the Harmel Report. From the French standpoint, the alliance served above all to integrate Germany firmly in a Western context. To that end, U.S. ties to Europe were also necessary. Moreover, although without conceding as much, France continued to profit from the U.S. nuclear guarantee as well as from the allied troops in the German *glacis* to France's eastern frontier. But because the French government continued to block any enlargement of the European Communities, it did not want to risk putting new strains on relations with its allies, particularly not the Federal Republic. Under the chancellorship of Kurt Georg Kiesinger, the Bonn government worked to revive the Franco-German Treaty, but it was primarily intent on avoiding having to choose between Washington and Paris. For this reason, it strongly supported a compromise on the Harmel Report.

The breakthrough came on the eve of the December 1967 NATO conference, at the traditional "Germany dinner" of the foreign ministers of the Federal Republic and the three nations with special rights and responsibilities regarding Germany as a whole and Berlin. However, the critical groundwork had been done before that in bilateral agreements between the governments concerned as well as in countless ambassadorial breakfasts and other informal meetings. NATO's secretary general, Manlio Brosio, also played an important role in mediating and inventing one compromise formulation after another—although the initiators of the Harmel exercise originally wanted to keep him as well as the ambassadors to NATO as far removed from the studies as possible, for they feared that bringing in NATO's traditional authorities would stifle creativity. But as it turned out, political effectiveness demanded not just creativity but also a willingness to compromise and the possibility of recourse to institutional structures.

To resolve the conflict of priorities, the allies devised the broadly accepted formula that the alliance had two functions, to guarantee military security and to conduct a policy of détente, which were not contradictory but rather complementary. This formula provided a basis both for maintaining the compatibility of new initiatives for East-West détente with a security policy still based on deterrence and defense, and for substantiating and justifying military measures in a period of relaxation of East-West tensions. It was an acceptable compromise between the views of those allies that continued to regard NATO's primary task as deterrence and defense in case of Warsaw Pact aggression and those who—whether from conviction or out of domestic political considerations—wanted to place a greater emphasis on an active détente policy.

The new element in the Harmel Report was not that the alliance claimed to have a political function—it had had this since its founding—but rather that it now explicitly claimed a competence in arms control policy and furthermore provided a multilateral framework for developing détente policy. In the succeeding years, it carried out this claim with its "Reykjavik Signal" (NATO's Declaration on Mutual and Balanced Force Reductions of June 25, 1968) and offered to negotiate with the Warsaw Pact on mutual troop reductions. NATO also served as a framework for informational exchange and coordination for the Conference on Security and Cooperation in Europe. However, alliance involvement in shaping constructive security relations was limited by the continued U.S. claim to conduct the policy of a global power and carry the sole responsibility for strategic nuclear weapons systems. Apart from arms control, the Harmel Report did not say anything substantive regarding what a policy of détente toward the Soviet Union and the Eastern European states should look like. But it was for this very reason that the open Harmel formula remained applicable under changed international conditions.

On the whole, the Harmel exercise and the report's adoption made but a slight contribution to overcoming the NATO crisis of 1966–67. There is much to suggest that this crisis had already passed its peak in December 1966 when the NATO ministers commissioned the report. The nations remaining in the military command structures had found ways and means of managing NATO's expulsion from France. The removal of the seat of NATO from Paris to Brussels and of its headquarters (SHAPE) from

Fontainebleu to Mons-Casteau had presented relatively few political problems and had been concluded on September 30, 1967, as scheduled. However, the alliance did not rest content with a transfer of NATO institutions, but undertook at the same time an organizational reform. This reform, chiefly the disbanding of the Standing Group and the creation of the NPG, contributed greatly to reducing the asymmetries in the alliance and increasing the influence of the non-nuclear members. Most important, of course, was the adoption of the new strategic concept of Flexible Response (MC 14/3) by NATO in December 1967. Still, it was not possible to establish an integral connection between the military goal of deterrence and the goal of détente to overcome the conflict politically. But the credibility of the new strategy was enhanced by the fact that the danger of miscalculation was lessened by a dialogue between the adversaries, as provided for in the Harmel Report.[33]

The NATO Crisis and Relations in the Strategic Triangle

The country with the biggest stakes in the NATO crisis of 1966–67 was the Federal Republic of Germany. Its relations with France were seriously strained when President de Gaulle announced the withdrawal of its forces from NATO integration. Bonn was not in a position to induce France to reconsider this step; nor could it follow suit. The German-French Treaty of 1963, agreed by Chancellor Adenauer and President de Gaulle in January 1963, but later put on the back burner by the Erhard government, had completely lost its binding force when Paris neither consulted nor informed Bonn before the public announcement of its new NATO policy. Although shocked, Germany could not risk further deterioration of its relations with its European neighbor. It therefore used the Harmel exercise to get France back into an alliance context. It was successful in this endeavor, although it ran the risk that its effort would be falsely interpreted as if Bonn wished to change sides.

The doubts about the credibility of the United States' resolve to risk its survival for the defense of its European allies burdened German-American relations to a degree not experienced before. Still, for the Federal Republic there was no alternative to an effective and coherent NATO alliance and to close relations with the United States, on which its own security in the face of a still-existing Soviet threat depended. A primary concern for German policy was thus to abstain from any move that could further endanger

NATO's cohesion. Nevertheless, working for compromise solutions, Bonn tried to save as many of its own interests as possible. This effort was partially successful, because Washington sought reconciliation, being that it was concerned that Bonn might follow the French example of a more independent defense policy.

The greatest adjustments the Federal Republic had to make did not concern NATO proper, but with the Harmel Report it agreed to a policy of détente without insisting that German reunification be achieved simultaneously. Given the conflictual relationship between the United States and France in NATO matters, Bonn could further its own interests by balancing both partners' requests on German policies. Because both—for very different reasons—wished to improve their relations with the Soviet Union and the countries of Central and Eastern Europe, Bonn could not afford to drag its feet on détente without risking international isolation.

Though the Federal Republic profited from the French-American disagreements on NATO and their countries' role in world affairs, it did not find itself in an entirely happy situation. The conflict of priorities on whether to cooperate more closely with Paris—its partner in the European Communities—or with the United States—its indispensable NATO ally—strained its foreign as well as its domestic policy. In foreign affairs, the conflict highlighted the limited room for maneuvering for German policy. Domestically, it was torn by the controversy between "Gaullists" and "Atlanticists." To some extent, this conflict contributed to the downfall of Erhard and the demise of Adenauer's party as the leading political force in German politics. More than the CDU/CSU, the SDP recognized the overriding interest of its two major allies in a policy of détente. When Willy Brandt and Walter Scheel embarked on an active *Ostpolitik* that had a bearing on the German question and the Federal Republic's relations with the Soviet Union, Washington and Paris would quickly shelve their bilateral conflict in the concern that they might lose control over developments in Germany.

Although it is just a limited case study, the NATO crisis exemplifies an interesting pattern of international relations reaching beyond that particular time frame. First, at no time were all three pairs of binary relations smooth. Second, the particularly difficult as well as exceptionally intimate relations between Paris and Washington had negative repercussions for German foreign policy. Both limited Germany's policy options and left its decisionmakers with few choices to affect this phenomenon decisively. Third, until Germany was reunified, this pattern could not be altered by an outside threat—as the 1958–61 Berlin Crisis exemplified—but only by a German move that seemed to threaten its allies' control over developments in the center of Europe.[34] Because the Federal Republic could neither afford to risk its close relations with France nor endanger its security links to the United States, this option was not open to German policymakers.

Notes

1. Stanley Hoffmann, "NATO and Nuclear Weapons: Reason and Unreason," *Foreign Affairs* 60 (1981–82): 327.

2. Hoffmann is referring here to intra-alliance crises, the subject of this study, and not to external crises involving political controversy or military confrontation with an adversary such as in the Berlin Crisis. On this distinction, see Gerd Schmückle, *Crisis Management in an Alliance of Sovereign States,* Working Paper 56 (Washington, D.C.: International Security Studies Program, Woodrow Wilson International Center for Scholars, 1984).

3. See Henry A. Kissinger, "Strains on the Alliance," *Foreign Affairs* 41 (1963): 261–85; and Alastair Buchan, "'NATO-Krise' und die europäische Entspannung," *Europa-Archiv* 22 (1967): 301–12.

4. See the press conference of French president Charles de Gaulle on February 21, 1966, in *Discours et Messages* by Charles de Gaulle (Paris: Plon, 1970), vol. 5, 6–23; also, Statement of the French government spokesman Yvon Bourges on the decisions of the Council of Ministers of March 9, 1966, in *Europa-Archiv* 21 (1966): D141–47; letter from President Charles de Gaulle to President Lyndon B. Johnson, March 7, 1966, in *Documents on American Foreign Relations, 1966,* ed. Richard B. Stebbins (New York: Harper & Row, 1967) (hereafter *American Foreign Relations*), 107–8; "French Memorandum Delivered to the Fourteen Representatives of the Governments of the Atlantic Alliance on March 8 and 10, 1966," and "Second French Memorandum of March 29 and 30, 1966," in *American Foreign Relations,* 109–12, 120–22.

5. France had withdrawn its Mediterranean fleet from NATO assignment in 1959 and its Atlantic fleet in 1963. It also rejected arming its air force with American nuclear weapons if the decision to use them rested with the U.S. president, and it prohibited the storage of U.S. nuclear weapons on its soil. The United States thereupon removed its nuclear-capable aircraft to the United Kingdom. However, French armed forces stationed in Germany still had nuclear weapons of the Honest John and Nike-Ajax type. Though these remained outside French territory, they allowed France to gain initial experience in dealing with nuclear systems.

6. At a press conference on September 9, 1965, President de Gaulle had announced that France would "remain an ally of its allies, but as initial treaty terms are concluded, that is in 1969 at the latest . . . the subordination known as 'integration' which is provided for by NATO and which delivers our fate to foreign authority will cease"; quoted in *Major Addresses, Statements and Press Conferences of General Charles de Gaulle, March 17, 1964–May 16, 1967,* ed. Ambassade de France (New York: Service de Presse et d'Information, 1967), 98. Defense Minister Pierre Messmer is said to have given his Ameri-

can counterpart a similar indication back in May 1965. See Militärisches Tagebuch, Defense Minister Kai-Uwe von Hassel, May 31, 1965, private papers of von Hassel.

7. See Wilfried Loth, *Geschichte Frankreichs im 20 Jahrhundert* (Stuttgart: Kohlhammer, 1987), 209; and Peter Schmidt, *Thesen zu den generellen Hintergrundmotivationen aktueller französischer Sicherheits- und Verteidigungspolitik in der Allianz und Westeuropa* (Ebenhausen: Stiftung Wissenschaft und Politk, 1992).

8. See press conference of the French President on February 21, 1966, in de Gaulle, *Discours et Messages,* 5, 6–23.

9. See "Joint Communiqué on the talks between Prime Minister Harold Macmillan and President John F. Kennedy, in Nassau, the Bahamas," December 18–21, 1962, as well as "Joint Statement on Nuclear Defense Systems (Nassau Agreement)," *Department of State Bulletin* 48 (1963): 43–45. Washington subsequently offered to provide France with Polaris missiles as well, though at that point France, unlike Britain, did not yet have nuclear-capable submarines or the requisite warheads for these systems.

10. See Georges-Henri Soutou, "De Gaulle, Adenauer und die gemeinsame Front gegen die amerikanische Nuklearstrategie," in *Politischer Wandel, organisierte Gewalt und nationale Sicherheit: Beiträge zur neueren Geschichte Deutschlands und Frankreichs,* Festschrift für Klaus-Jürgen Müller, hrsg. von Ernst Willi Hansen, Georg Schreiber und Bernd Wagner (Munich: R. Oldenbourg, 1995), 491–518.

11. See speech by President John F. Kennedy on July 4, 1962, on the Goal of an Atlantic Partnership, *Department of State Bulletin* 47 (1962): 131–33; also Harold van B. Cleveland, "Die Zukunft der atlantischen Idee: Die Spannungen zwischen dem atlantischen und dem europäischen Gedanken," *Europa-Archiv* 22 (1967): 313–22.

12. See press conference of President Charles de Gaulle on February 4, 1965, in *Major Addresses,* ed. Ambassade de France.

13. See Centre d'Etudes de Politque Etrangère, "Modèles de securité europèene," *Politique Etrangère* 32 (1967): 519–41.

14. Georges-Henri Soutou, conversation with the author, Paris, July 1991.

15. See Albert Wohlstetter, "The Delicate Balance of Terror," *Foreign Affairs* 37 (1959): 211–34.

16. See Secretary Robert S. McNamara, Speech to NATO Council, Athens, May 5, 1962, in *U.S. Nuclear Strategy: A Reader,* ed. Phillip Bobbitt, Lawrence Freedman, and Gregory F. Treverton (London: Macmillan, 1989), 205–22.

17. See Uwe Nerlich, "Die nuklearen Dilemmas der Bundesrepublik Deutschland," *Europa-Archiv* 20 (1965): 637–52; Nerlich, *Der NV-Vertrag in der Politik der BRD: Zur Struktur eines aussenpolitischen Prioritätskonflikts* (Ebenhausen: Stiftung Wissenschaft und Politik, 1973), 32–33; and David N. Schwartz, *NATO's Nuclear Dilemmas* (Washington, D.C.: Brookings Institution Press, 1983).

18. See "Gespräche des Staatssekretärs Carstens mit Staatspräsident de Gaulle und dem französischen Außenminister Couve de Murville," July 4, 1964, Document 186, *Akten zur Auswärtigen Politik der Bundesrepublik Deutschland,* hrsg. vom Institut für Zeitgeschichte im Auftrag des Auswärtigen Amtes, 1964, part 2 (Munich: R. Oldenbourg, 1995), 187.

19. See on this Kurt Birrenbach, "Partnerschaft und Konsultation in der NATO: Grundsatzfragen und aktuelle Probleme der amerikanisch-europäischen Partnerschaft," *Europa-Archiv* 18 (1963): 861–70; Harold B. Cleveland, *The Atlantic Idea and Its Ri-*

vals (New York: McGraw-Hill, 1966); and Cleveland, "Die Zukunft der atlantischen Idee," *Europa-Archiv* 22 (1967): 313–32.

20. The Federal Republic granted Vietnam technical and training assistance for a technical school in Thu Duc and the university in Hue, in addition to (up to 1967) development aid credits amounting to 85 million deutsche marks. Furthermore, it sent the hospital ship *Helgoland* to Vietnam and provided two dental clinics and thirty ambulances. See "German Assistance to Viet-Nam," WB/B-8, 1967, National Security Files (NSF), Country File, Germany, box 193, Lyndon B. Johnson Library (LBJL).

21. See press conference of the French President on September 9, 1965, in *Major Addresses*, ed. Ambassade de France.

22. See "Proposed Agenda, NATO Meeting," the Ranch, November 22, 1966; and Rusk, McNamara, and LBJ, "Recommendations at Texas LBJ Ranch," November 22, 1966, NSF, Trilateral Negotiations and NATO, box 50, LBJL.

23. See "Circular Note on German Peace Policy," reprinted in *Department of State Bulletin* 54 (1966): 654–57; on its origins, see Helga Haftendorn, *Sicherheit und Entspannung: Zur Aussenpolitik der Bundesrepublik Deutschland 1955–1982*, 2nd ed. (Baden-Baden: Nomos, 1986), 278–94.

24. See "Aufzeichnung von Staatssekretär Karl Carstens zur Deutschland-Politik," St.S.-2310/66, secret, October 17, 1966, Archives of the Ludwig-Erhard-Stiftung, Bonn. Excerpts published in "Schweigen Ehrensache," *Der Spiegel*, October 24, 1966, 27. The German government entered onto its allies' course of détente only with great reluctance. Bonn found itself in the unfortunate situation where Moscow's position still gave it every reason to distrust the Soviet Union, yet at the same time it could no longer count on its allies to support its position on the German question.

25. See the speech by the president to the National Editorial Writers Conference, New York, October 7, 1966, reprinted in *American Foreign Relations*, 73–80; on the German reaction to this, see Bundesministerium für Innerdeutsche Beziehungen, ed., *Dokumente zur Deutschlandpolitik*, 4th ser., vol. 12, bk. 2 (Frankfurt: Alfred Metzner, 1981), 1478.

26. Lawrence Freedman, "The Wilderness Years," in *The Nuclear Confrontation in Europe*, ed. Jeffrey D. Boutwell, Paul Doty, and Gregory F. Treverton (London: Croom Helm, 1985), 47.

27. See Remarks, January 12, 1968, Stromseth papers, Washington; also, personal papers of General Ulrich de Maizière (ret.), Bonn; McCloy to the President, November 21, 1966, Trilateral Negotiations, box 50, LBJL.

28. See John J. McCloy to the President, "Conclusions and Recommendations," report, November 21, 1966, NSF, Trilateral Negotiations and NATO, box 50, LBJL.

29. In Lisbon in February 1952, NATO had decided to raise by the end of 1954 a force of 90 divisions (including 52 in the Central Region of Europe), 9,000 aircraft, and 950 larger ships. Of the 90 divisions, 42 were to be active-duty and immediately combat ready (including 35 in the Central Region). These intentions, however, were never realized. See Christian Greiner, "Das miliärstrategisches Konzept der NATO von 1952–1957," in *Zwischen Kaltem Krieg und Entspannung: Sicherheits- und Deutschlandpolitik der Bundesrepublik im Mächtesystem der Jahre 1953–1956*, ed. Bruno Thross and Hans-Erich Volkmann, Militärgeschichte seit 1945 (Boppard: Harald Boldt Verlag for the Militärgeschichtliches Forschungsamt, 1988), 213.

30. In December 1961, NATO had approved document MC 26/4, thus committing

the allies to deploy twenty-nine 2/3 divisions in NATO's Central Region by the end of 1966. In the first half of the 1960s, the alliance fell far short of meeting this goal both in terms of numbers and with regard to the equipping and training of NATO forces. See Christian Tuschhoff, *Die MC 70 und die Einführung nuklearer Trägersysteme in die Bundeswehr 1956–1959* (Nuclear History Program) (Ebenhausen: Stiftung Wissenschaft und Politik, 1990), 19.

31. Federal Minister of Defense, ed., *Weissbuch 1970: Zur Sicherheit der Bundesrepublik Deutschland und zur Lage der Bundeswehr* (Bonn: Press and Information Office of the German Government, 1970), 28; similarly, the British Defence White Paper, 1970.

32. Thus Chancellor Kurt Georg Kiesinger speaking to the Union press in Bonn in late February 1967; see Dieter Oberdörfer, ed., *Die Grosse Koalition: Reden und Erklärungen des Bundeskanzlers* (Stuttgart: Deutsche Verlagsanstalt, 1979), 36–38.

33. See Ivo H. Daalder, *The Nature and Practice of Flexible Response: NATO Strategy and Theater Nuclear Forces since 1967* (New York: Columbia University Press, 1991), 10.

34. German *Ostpolitik,* 1969–70, and the events leading to German unification, 1989–90, are such examples.

Chapter 4

The NATO Crisis of 1966–1967: A French Point of View

Frédéric Bozo

Most scholars and political analysts have interpreted the NATO crisis of 1966–67 mainly through the prism of General Charles de Gaulle's March 1966 decision to withdraw French forces from NATO integration. Yet this is only one aspect of a more complex story. Indeed, while France's semi-withdrawal was undoubtedly a catalyst of the crisis, it was by no means its only agent. Moreover, though dominant interpretations have long emphasized—on both sides—the idea of a major military rupture between France and NATO, recent evidence shows that France's military estrangement was only a relative one. Finally, though it is true that de Gaulle's decision marked in many ways the apogee of Atlantic discord, it also, and more important, served as a springboard from which the Americans would reestablish their leadership in NATO while rebuilding a consensus among allies.

This chapter first addresses the origins of the crisis of 1966–67, which steadily built up against a backdrop of change in the overall international system, and, in particular, in the West-West as well as East-West distribution of power. These profound evolutions represented challenges as well for the alliance and for the transatlantic relationship in that period; and de Gaulle's pre-1966 Atlantic policies were, essentially, France's response to these challenges. The chapter then focuses on the crisis at its peak in 1966–67: France's progressive disengagement from NATO integration and the moderate U.S. response to de Gaulle's March 1966 decision are key to understanding the process of Franco-American negotiations after March 1966, which provided the framework for renewed French participation in Western defense. Finally, the chapter looks at the short-, mid-, and long-term consequences of the crisis: whether in military, strategic, or political terms, France's withdrawal paradoxically led to a strengthening of NATO and of U.S. leadership, as well as to a much-needed adaptation of the alliance. In retrospect, the 1966–67 crisis may be seen as pivotal in the alliance's Cold War history, the second part of which—during the period of the European status quo—was shaped by decisions made in these critical years.

The Origins of the NATO Crisis and French Policy

As with all crises, the NATO crisis took place against the backdrop of a profound evolution in the international system, which the events of 1966–67 would reveal, crystallize, and precipitate. In the early 1960s, transatlantic relations were conditioned by changes on three levels: national, West-West, and East-West.

The Strategic Context

The national level was obviously the most significant from a French point of view. De Gaulle made it clear to the Americans as soon as he had returned to power: "France is there. It reassumes its means. It is a considerable element in the world and the proof is that you and I are both here," he told John Foster Dulles in July 1958.[1] This would remain the key assumption behind France's Atlantic policy: Though France "was no longer a great power and had no ambitions to become one again" at the time NATO was created, "today she has again some ambition as a nation," the general told President John F. Kennedy in June 1961.[2] Surely, for de Gaulle, only France had regained both economic strength *and* political status, which naturally entitled it to a leadership role in Europe; but he was ready to acknowledge the recovery of the other Western Europeans: "Germany is now very productive and economically strong," and Italy "has also made great progress."[3] So, whereas a decade earlier "the important nations of Europe" were "in decline," it was a fact that "now the situation had changed."[4]

Hence the evolution on the West-West level: The most significant change bearing on the overall Atlantic context in the period leading up to the NATO crisis was clearly the changing Euro-American distribution of power. In retrospect, it is easy to forget that the background of the transatlantic misunderstandings in the 1960s was fundamentally an emerging new balance between Europe and the United States. In fact, it took people at the time a while to realize the implications of the new situation: "Basically, the difficulty of our policy in regard to Europe is that we have not fully adjusted to the fact of European recovery, . . . not only the economic and financial recovery, but also the moral and spiritual vigor that seems to have accompanied the process."[5] Charles Bohlen (then the U.S. ambassador to France) wrote to McGeorge Bundy, Kennedy's national security adviser, at the height of the European and Atlantic crisis of the first months of 1963. The new Euro-American balance, to be sure, stemmed primarily from the continent's postwar recovery and from the dynamics of European integration. But it also, arguably, reflected another reality: the relative erosion of the foundations of American power—notably economic—which had become obviously less preponderant than in the postwar years, as evidenced, inter alia, by the Kennedy administration's obsession with balance of payments problems.

Finally, there was the changing balance of power on the East-West level. In retrospect, the NATO crisis can hardly be dissociated from the consequences of the launching of *Sputnik* and from the profound transformation of the international system that it entailed. First, in strategic terms: When de Gaulle told Kennedy in June 1961 that "the Soviets and the Americans are more or less equal and each can destroy the other,"[6] he may have been anticipating future Soviet capabilities, but he was not much ahead of U.S. perceptions; in December of that same year, Kennedy himself would indeed point out that "in two or three years" the Soviet-U.S. balance of terror would become an irreversible reality.[7] Thus, starting early in the decade, strategic parity had emerged as a key perception, a change fraught with vast implications, not least for the alliance. And beyond the strategic equilibrium, there emerged the perception of an overall equilibrium: Though Nikita Khrushchev's post-*Sputnik* claim that the Soviet Union and the communist system could compete in all domains on a real parity basis with the United States and the capitalist system quickly proved fanciful, the notion that Soviet power had by and large come to balance America's became widespread in the 1960s, and no one was more ready to acknowledge this than de Gaulle. He told Leonid Brezhnev in June 1966: "We see no inconvenience in [Soviet] power, for, without it, we would be exposed to the U.S.'s irresistible hegemony," immediately adding that "similarly, we see no inconvenience in U.S. power, without which we would probably be exposed to Soviet hegemony."[8]

The Looming Atlantic Crisis

Such trends in the distribution of power and in the international system were the background for a malaise that was already looming large in the Western alliance by the time de Gaulle returned to power: "It has become customary to speak of an Atlantic crisis," wrote a French analyst in June 1958.[9] And though the nuclear issue was then the central problem, it was by no means the only one: As the 1950s—and the Dwight D. Eisenhower administration—drew to a close, the "Western political system as a whole was in disarray," and the problems were growing, Marc Trachtenberg rightly remarks.[10] In fact, the NATO crisis, as it developed in the early 1960s, had three, often intertwined, dimensions: It was a crisis of leadership; it was a crisis of credibility; and it was a crisis of legitimacy.

The crisis of leadership in NATO was, obviously, a crisis of American leadership. To be sure, this was a phenomenon to some extent contingent on the internal situation in the United States—whether, for example, at the end of the Eisenhower presidency in 1958–60, when "everything was very much up in the air" and the world "had the sense of an administration at loose ends";[11] or, for very different reasons, in 1965–68 against the backdrop of the escalation of the war in Vietnam and the growing antiwar protest in the United States and Europe. But it was also, and more important, a structural phenomenon stemming from the systemic changes described above; the recovery of America's allies, the dynamics of European unification, the changing East-West balance of power could hardly have no effect on U.S. leadership of the alliance. Hence, in the early 1960s, the recurrent and indeed monotonous longing for a more assertive leadership role appeared in many U.S. policy documents pertaining to NATO; as one paper of December 1962 stated: "Perhaps more than at any time in recent years, the United States will be expected to provide leadership and guidance."[12] This kind of formula, in substance, had become a leitmotiv by the time of the 1966–67 crisis.

The crisis of credibility—which mainly pertained to the nuclear question—was, as Helga Haftendorn has rightly argued, the most existential dimension of the overall Atlantic malaise in the years leading up to the 1966–67 NATO crisis.[13] To be sure, the credibility problem had been around well before the perceived emergence of the balance of terror in the late 1950s and early 1960s; in retrospect, it appears as consubstantial with the very logic of extended deterrence from the start. Yet by having the North Atlantic Council discuss the alliance's strategic concept along the lines of the April 1961 Acheson report—in other words, by putting the doctrine of Flexible Response on the NATO agenda—the Kennedy administration, as early as May 1961, was opening a strategic Pandora's box that would not be closed before the end of the 1966–67 crisis. "It is not certain that the U.S. will strike first with atomic weapons," de Gaulle told Kennedy in June 1961. "The raising of the threshold for the use of atomic weapons simply means an attempt at obtaining better control" of such weapons, Kennedy replied.[14] Here again, the first meeting between the two presidents summarized the terms of the new "great debate."[15]

Leadership and credibility, however, were not NATO's sole problems before 1966. The alliance, increasingly, was undergoing a crisis of legitimacy. By the mid-1960s, events in Europe and beyond Europe were indeed raising the question of its scope and raison d'être. First, the growing U.S. military implication in Vietnam was a direct challenge to NATO's solidarity, which the Americans argued "could not be limited to the problems in the North Atlantic area" but had to "cover East-West problems arising anywhere."[16] But whereas the United States was making allied support of its Southeast Asian policies the test of NATO unity, the Europeans were less and less inclined to endorse American military escalation in Vietnam, which they saw as detrimental to the alliance's cohesion.

Second, in the meantime, the emerging pattern of détente in Europe raised another danger for an alliance that had been created in the midst of the Cold War. How could NATO's military effectiveness be preserved at a time when "the threat of direct aggression seem[ed] remote?"[17] And how could the alliance be kept politically cohesive in an era of relaxed East-West relations? Of course, the Americans, starting in 1965, began to provide answers to these queries: Détente was but the consequence of NATO's "full success" as a "credible military deterrent,"[18] and the alliance should therefore be kept strong. Moreover, détente called for an active NATO role in East-West relations, which in itself would strengthen the alliance's cohesion.[19] Yet by the time of the 1966 crisis, a consensus among the allies on NATO's very purpose in an era of détente remained quite elusive.

France's Pre-1966 Atlantic Policies

France's policy toward the alliance in the years leading to the events of 1966–67 must be analyzed against the background of this looming Atlantic crisis. The picture that emerges from such an analysis is a complex one. On the one hand, de Gaulle's policies did not generate the Atlantic crisis—it was already there; in fact, the case can be made that far from aiming at the weakening, let alone at the destruction of the alliance—which de Gaulle considered to be vital as long as there was a threat—his policies aimed to strengthen it by adapting it to the new context. On the other hand, de Gaulle's Atlantic revisionism at the same time tended to accelerate and ultimately precipitate the crisis.[20] From 1958 to 1966, France's policy toward the alliance can be described as de Gaulle's attempt at calling into question the established order in NATO; it may be summarized in three successive phases—each of which may be associated with one particular side of the triangular relationship between France, the United States, and Germany.

The first phase, between 1958 and 1960–61, was dominated by de Gaulle's tripartite diplomacy. The famous September 1958 memorandum, sent to Eisenhower and British prime minister Harold Macmillan, was not—as has been often interpreted—a pretext for justifying France's subsequent progressive withdrawal from NATO military integration. It was a serious attempt to restructure the transatlantic relationship around what de Gaulle, at that time, considered its most reliable backbone: the relationship between France, the United States, and the United Kingdom.[21] Of course, de Gaulle's aim was first and foremost to reestablish France's international status by formalizing its rank as one of the three "great" (or "global") Western powers; in that, the memorandum was very much about emphasizing the French-U.S. side of the triangular relationship—even at the expense of the French-German side, which in this early phase was not yet a priority.[22] And yet, at the same time, de Gaulle earnestly saw such a tripartite organization of Western strategy—from which a reform of NATO would have to follow—as an answer to the perceived crisis of U.S. leadership. Although Eisenhower had responded as early as October 1958 with what amounted to a polite but blunt refusal,[23] French diplomacy kept on trying to convince the Americans. It was not until 1961 that de Gaulle in effect abandoned his tripartite scheme; as his envoy Jacques Chaban-Delmas had warned Kennedy in March, "Such a combination of favorable circumstances may not recur again."[24]

Hence the second phase of de Gaulle's Atlantic policies: Having realized the limits of his tripartite approach, the general, between 1960–61 and 1963, embarked on a continental approach, which essentially consisted of using the promotion of a Western European strategic entity as a lever to bring about change in the transatlantic balance. In this second phase (which evolved against the background of the "great debate" and growing—especially German—doubts over the credibility of the U.S. nuclear guarantee[25]), the French-German side of the triangle was clearly the most determining. All along the backbone of de Gaulle's effort to build up the Europe of Six into a strategic entity along the Fouchet plan of 1961–62 had been the French-German—and, indeed, the de Gaulle–Konrad Adenauer relation—and the January 1963 Elysée Treaty was but a fallback position for the two nations' European ambitions after the failure of the plan in April 1962. Even though —and this quickly became a key U.S. criticism—French diplomacy in that period never actually offered a detailed "blueprint for a reorganization of NATO,"[26] it was clear to the French that "the emergence of a stronger and more independent Europe by no means implie[d] the end of the Atlantic Alliance, but its transformation in order to adapt it to the new situation."[27]

Thus the political and military construction of Europe and alliance reform were the two sides of the same coin; if Europe became a strategic entity, then "another NATO [would be] necessary," de Gaulle argued.[28] But this was exactly what the Americans were not ready to accept: "De Gaulle may be prepared to break up with NATO," an infuriated Kennedy commented after the January 14, 1963, press conference and the signing of the Elysée Treaty a week later, adding that "there is not much we can do against France, but we can exert considerable pressure on the Germans."[29] And so they did, as confirmed by the preamble that the Bundestag added to the Elysée Treaty in May 1963, after months of a fierce "battle" for Germany, which arguably gave rise to the gravest Franco-American crisis in the decade.[30]

However, this in turn only induced de Gaulle to engage in a third phase of his Atlantic policies, during which the main French concern indeed became the third side of the triangle, that is, the German-U.S. relationship. French diplomacy focused on preventing the United States from using its dominance over West German policy to strengthen its NATO leadership and move the alliance in the direction that Washington wanted—and that Paris opposed—thanks, in particular, to the multilateral force.[31] By then— against the backdrop of a rapidly changing East-West environment and of looming interrogations as to NATO's legitimacy and raison d'être in that context—de Gaulle was ready to move from a policy centered on Western European integration and Franco-German reconciliation to one aiming at pan-European cooperation and Franco-Soviet rapprochement. On the one hand, the perspective of "détente, entente, and cooperation" was used as an argument against keeping, let alone reinforcing, the old integrated, United States–dominated NATO; on the other, France's denunciation of NATO integration was used as an argument in favor of the Gaullist vision of détente "beyond blocs."[32] At that point, there was clearly no room left for any kind of compromise between France and the United States on the transformation of NATO.

The Management of the Crisis: France's Withdrawal from NATO, 1966–1967

In retrospect, France's decision to withdraw from NATO's integrated military organization was thus not only the result of purely national considerations; it was also the consequence of the failure of French efforts to call into question the established Atlantic order. Because the allies had all proven to be "advocates of the status quo," France "had to take steps that she believed appropriate."[33] Of course, France's allies would object—as did the secretary general of NATO—that they "never received any plan nor reform proposal,"[34] but this was, in French eyes, an inadmissible objection because Paris, ever since the 1958 memorandum, had ceaselessly asked for such a reform—but to no avail.[35]

Therefore, by 1966, a *concerted* transformation of NATO was no longer on the agenda, and France was led to take unilateral measures. But this was with a view to bringing about the necessary change: "In disengaging ourselves from NATO," de Gaulle said after the French withdrawal, "we have but anticipated a profound transformation of the Alliance which was organized according to the Cold War and therefore calls for an update."[36] Yet by doing so, that is, by "anticipating" change in NATO in the long run, France was also precipitating the NATO crisis, which by March 1966 had become a France-NATO crisis, the management of which was bound to have far-reaching consequences for the future of the alliance as a whole—hence the need to assess the handling of the crisis by its foremost protagonists.

France's Withdrawal

France's handling of the 1966 crisis has long been seen through the prism of de Gaulle's disruptive tactics and rhetoric, thus contributing to an analysis of the French "withdrawal" in terms of a rupture with the alliance and the search for an "option of neutrality." True, de Gaulle's modus operandi, before his final decision on NATO, did involve the search for a surprise effect; he thus deliberately entertained doubts as to the scope and timing of his move.[37] Hence, starting in the spring of 1965, he mentioned the possibility of France withdrawing not only from NATO but also from the alliance altogether—until he made it clear to the Americans in February 1966 that "he would not touch the Treaty itself, but solely the organization."[38] Moreover, he purposefully kept the uncertainty as to the moment of his decision; for example, during his February 21, 1966, press conference, he said that he would continue to change the modalities of France's participation in NATO "until the term provided by the Treaty"[39] (i.e., 1969)—a deliberately vague indication at this stage. Yet, as one of de Gaulle's foremost Atlantic opponents understood, "it was about making the allies fear the worst" so as to have them "heave a sigh of relief" once his decision would be known.[40]

In spite of this abrupt declaratory policy, France's withdrawal from NATO integration was a gradual process. The March 1966 decision, it should not be forgotten, was the last in a series of similar decisions, including the withdrawal from the NATO command of the Mediterranean fleet and the refusal to host U.S. nuclear weapons on French territory (1959), the decision not to reassign to NATO the divisions withdrawn from Algeria (1962), the withdrawal of the Atlantic fleet (1964), and so on. As a result, far from coming out of the blue, the March 1966 decision—in spite of all the suspense that de Gaulle entertained—was to a large extent foreseeable, and foreseen. Starting in 1965, the allies—and the Americans to begin with—perfectly understood that the general's policy would eventually lead to a complete French disengagement from NATO's integrated military bodies. Already in January of that year, Ambassador Bohlen was holding it as likely that de Gaulle would radically change the France-NATO relationship by 1969; and by May 1965, he was advising his superiors in Washington to start studying the issue of relocating U.S. forces stationed in France as well as the necessary arrangements to be concluded in case of a forced departure.[41] So to the extent that the allies were taken by surprise in March 1966, this was mainly due to the *style* of the decision— hence Bohlen's typical overreaction when the French foreign minister, Maurice Couve de Murville, gave him de Gaulle's letter to U.S. president Lyndon Johnson on March 7: "The effect in the U.S. would be considerable," the ambassador said, for France was "violating the 1949 Treaty." To which Couve quietly answered: "The fact is, simply, that the issue has come to maturity."[42]

For the substance of the decision was *not* about France breaking up with NATO, at least in military terms. Behind de Gaulle's harsh rhetoric and his unilateral moves, he by no means intended to cease to participate in Western defense, let alone to leave the alliance: "Everything will be done," he declared shortly before announcing his decision, "in order to avoid disturbing the allies"; "it was not about a rupture, but a necessary adaptation."[43] This was not just rhetoric; it is important to understand that de Gaulle conceived of his decision not so much as the endpoint of a disengagement but as the starting point of a new relationship between France and NATO. Hence his readiness to discuss with the allies the terms of this new relationship. By early June 1966, it was decided that the negotiations would have two objectives: first, to "specify the role of our forces in times of war"—this would be discussed between the supreme allied commander in Europe, General Lyman Lemnitzer, and the French chief of staff, General Charles Ailleret; second, to define the conditions under which U.S. forces could be granted access to facilities in France.[44] And on both scores, de Gaulle was open to wartime cooperation with NATO: In case of a major battle in Europe, he told Ailleret, "France could take part immediately; this would likely mean that our forces would fulfill missions similar to their present ones"; moreover, "one could accept granting the Allies over flight authorization as well as the permission to use our infrastructure."[45]

The United States and the Gaullist Challenge

By 1965, the Americans had little doubt about where de Gaulle's policy was leading. By the summer of that year, their preoccupation had become to prepare the alliance for the possibility of a French withdrawal. In August, the White House issued a directive (National Security Action Memorandum, or NSAM, 36) inviting the State Department, the Pentagon, the Central Intelligence Agency, and the U.S. Information Agency, as well as the Atomic Energy Commission, to undertake the necessary studies with a view to the decisions the United States might have to make in such an eventuality.[46]

By the end of the year, the Americans were ready for all hypotheses, but this does not mean that they were serenely envisioning a French withdrawal. Rather, they faced a dilemma: They could either treat France with firmness in the name of Atlantic solidarity, thus risking a toughening of de Gaulle's policy; or they could negotiate with the general to avoid a major NATO crisis, thus making it easier for him to redefine the France-NATO relationship on his own terms. The Johnson administration was split according to a classical fault line. On the one hand, the State Department, out of political considerations, was inclined to intransigence vis-à-vis Gaullist policy; on the other, the Pentagon and the chiefs of staff proved more pragmatic and willing to avoid a military rupture with France.[47]

The official announcement of the French decision in March 1966 only confirmed these internal cleavages. Secretary of State Dean Rusk—along with, especially, Undersecretary of State George Ball and the former secretary of state, Dean Acheson—thought that the United States should denounce "the serious consequences of de Gaulle's unilateral decision," without which public opinion as well as the U.S. Congress would stop taking the alliance seriously.[48] This attitude was the product of Atlanticist and Europeanist ideologues concerned, like Ball, with the disintegration of the "Atlantic community," but also of those who, like John McCloy, were preoccupied with the evolution of Germany and feared the impact that de Gaulle's decision might have on that important ally.[49]

On the other side, Defense Secretary Robert McNamara and the military leaders advocated a more moderate approach. The Pentagon team wanted to avoid any polemic with de Gaulle in order to continue, as calmly as possible, to strengthen integrated defense—without France but not against France. Though Ball went so far as to suggest that the United States drag its feet in withdrawing from French territory, McNamara saw in the French decision an opportunity to rationalize NATO's structure, improve its efficiency, and cut its costs.[50] The White House entourage occupied an intermediate position: Though a minimum of public debate on the French decision was inevitable, it should be as moderate as possible, the principal objective being to allow NATO to continue functioning without France; this implied avoiding confrontation with Paris while endeavoring to obtain from de Gaulle a minimum necessary for allied defense and effecting the withdrawal of U.S. forces and installations promptly.[51]

Yet what mattered most, of course, was Johnson's personal attitude. And the president was clearly closer to the Pentagon's pragmatic line than to the State Department's punitive one. He saw "no benefit to ourselves or to our allies in debating the position of the French government"; for him, the priority was "to rebuild NATO outside of France as promptly, as economically, and effectively as possible."[52] This approach was formally adopted in a presidential directive on May 4, 1966 (NSAM 345), asking the different departments concerned to issue constructive proposals to strengthen the alliance. Of course, Johnson's attitude was to a large extent instinctive: "When a man asks you to leave his house, you don't argue; you get your hat and go," he is on record as saying.[53] Yet it was a courageous one; as Thomas Schwartz rightly remarks, American public opinion and most allies disapproved of de Gaulle's policy, and Johnson "could have chosen to exploit this issue as a diversion" from his other problems—Vietnam, to begin with.[54] It was, above all, a wise move; the moderate line adopted by the U.S. president was key to keeping open the option to broach in favorable conditions the France-NATO negotiations and, beyond, to giving the new era of relations between France and the rest of the alliance a constructive start.

The France-NATO Negotiations

As Johnson had ordered, the process of NATO's withdrawal from France, involving mainly U.S. forces, went smoothly. As early as May 25, 1966, McNamara could confirm to Johnson that the withdrawal of U.S. troops and installations could begin.[55] Throughout the process, the president, as he underlined during a National Security Council meeting in December 1966, made it a point to abide by the general's deadline; indeed, on April 1, 1967, the U.S. military presence in France had become residual.[56]

The transfer of NATO's infrastructures and commands—especially its headquarters, known as SHAPE; and its Allied Forces Central Europe, known as AFCENT—was almost achieved by that date as well. No doubt this orderly American withdrawal created a favorable context for the shaping of a new France-NATO relationship. "The withdrawal of NATO staffs and troops proceed in dignity," declared the French foreign minister. "The Americans have proved accommodating. The operation will cost them a lot of money. Farewell ceremonies are taking place in a very decent atmosphere. We are leaving each other on friendly terms."[57]

To be sure, all the problems stemming from de Gaulle's decision could not be solved. Hence, though the issue of the use of French airspace gave way to an arrangement that by and large preserved the allies' overflight rights (with France remaining party to the NATO Air Defence Ground Environment, or NADGE, system), the issue of NATO use of facilities on French territory could not—mainly for political reasons on both sides—be settled, thus leading to the only real military discontinuity in France-NATO relations before and after 1966.[58] Yet the central issue of the nature of operational cooperation between French and NATO forces was settled on favorable terms. Whereas Generals Ailleret and Lemnitzer had started their negotiations in late November 1966, by late January 1967 they had already reached an "agreement on substance."[59]

Of course, there were difficulties. On the one hand, the allies and especially the Americans were reluctant to transform the Ailleret-Lemnitzer understanding into a formal agreement for fear of consecrating France's unilateral withdrawal. On the other hand, the French ruled out the possibility of "accepting an agreement without it being mentioned that we do have an agreement."[60] But these political difficulties were eventually overcome by both parties' willingness to reach a military arrangement which, by late August 1967, was formally ratified.[61] Even though the Ailleret-Lemnitzer "agreement" was deliberately kept discrete and, needless to say, secret, its importance for the France-NATO relationship was decisive because it was to be the framework for military "cooperation" after France's withdrawal from "integration." While the details are beyond the scope of this chapter,[62] it is important to understand that far from marking a military rupture between France and NATO, the Ailleret-Lemnitzer agreement only confirmed what the French general had many times told his American counterpart: that, irrespective of nonintegration in peacetime, France, in wartime, would put its forces in a situation little different from that which existed before the withdrawal.[63]

Meanwhile, an arrangement had been reached on the institutional aspects of the French withdrawal. Here also the Americans faced a dilemma. On the one hand, there was a need to avoid sending the "wrong signal" to the rest of the alliance by allowing France to enjoy an "à la carte" membership by participating in some NATO activities while opting out from others. On the other hand, it was equally necessary to avoid France being ostracized from allied bodies in order to allow for the minimum required France-NATO cooperation and, eventually, for its return to the NATO fold.[64] As it turned out, the French themselves carved out an acceptable compromise: France would maintain its participation in the alliance's foremost body, the North Atlantic Council, which would continue to gather with a membership of fifteen to treat issues of political relevance; but it would withdraw from the Defense Planning Committee, which would, from now on, gather with a membership of fourteen to deal with military questions pertaining to integrated defense.[65] Hence the apparent unity of NATO at fifteen was preserved while de facto allowing for its effective functioning at fourteen, thus satisfying both Paris and Washington—even if it implicitly consecrated the French distinction between the alliance and NATO that the Americans refused to acknowledge. As the France-NATO negotiations drew to a close in the spring of 1967, de Gaulle could express his satisfaction: "I note that every one is happy. Therefore we have done what had to be done."[66] "By and large," a little over a year after his decision, "the problems raised by France's withdrawal from the Atlantic military organization" had indeed "been settled."[67]

The Consequences of the 1966–1967 Crisis and the Evolution of the Alliance

Although the scope of the NATO crisis in the 1960s went far beyond the "French problem," by 1966 the latter was identified with the former and vice versa. Thus, even though it was not their only cause, the Americans, by tackling the issue of France-NATO relations, were hoping to be able to solve larger transatlantic difficulties. This proved to be a winning bet: The pragmatic settlement of the modalities of France's new relationship with NATO and the overcoming of the France-NATO crisis opened the way to the solution of the NATO crisis as a whole.

The End of the Crisis

In the short term, the settlement of the France-NATO divorce on mutually acceptable terms indeed represented an opportunity to solve a series of problems that had for some time pervaded the alliance. Since 1963, the risk of a paralysis of the NATO organization had constantly grown as a result of French policy, which the United States interpreted as sheer obstruction; therefore, in the eyes of the Americans, the return to a normal and satisfactory way of functioning constituted a prerequisite for the end of the NATO crisis. The United States could not tolerate France being in a position "to block or delay any progress in fields or activities to which she does not contribute,"[68] as had been increasingly the case in past years. And the France-NATO institutional compromise answered that preoccupation: NATO, the Americans were satisfied, will be able to cooperate with Paris "to the extent that this does not damage essential interests," while at the same time being modernized and adapted by the fourteen members of the Defense Planning Committee to the new political, military, and strategic realities. Thus, by solving the "question of the France-NATO relationship," the alliance had already "met de Gaulle's challenge."[69] Better still, the NATO organization as a consequence of France's withdrawal would find itself "rationalized" as well as "democratized."[70]

In no other domain of alliance activity was the effect of the end of the French institutional deadlock more palpable than in the strategic realm. The France-NATO compromise and the functioning of NATO at "fourteen plus one" indeed made it possible for France's integrated allies to move toward the long-awaited adoption of the alliance's new strategy of Flexible Response, which the Americans had tried to push forward since 1961. By the time of the announcement of de Gaulle's decision, Washington had already stepped up its effort at institutionalizing nuclear consultation in NATO, and the French withdrawal could only facilitate the process because Paris could no longer obstruct the exercise as a result of its de facto "empty chair" policy in the military activities of the alliance.[71]

Accordingly, it was in the Defense Planning Committee, meeting at fourteen for the first time in December 1966, that France's allies decided to establish, on a definitive basis, the alliance's nuclear consulting bodies—the Nuclear Defense Affairs Committee and especially the Nuclear Planning Group.[72] Under these conditions, the adoption of Flexible Response was no more than a formality for the Americans and their allies, and this, by the end of 1967, was essentially done. Because it put a stop to almost ten years of destabilizing debates and to five years of French obstruction, the adoption of Flexible Response not only represented "a major step toward resolving Alliance disagreements on strategy"[73] but also a major political success that contributed to the ending of the NATO crisis.

The relatively smooth settlement of the France-NATO issue and the definition of the country's new status in the alliance also helped assuage some of NATO's military problems. Since the early days of the Kennedy administration, the consolidation of NATO's integrated defense had been a key U.S. objective—one, of course, that was linked with the promotion of Flexible Response. Had de Gaulle's decision led to a total rupture between France and NATO, that objective would have perhaps been fatally endangered. The understanding eventually reached in December 1966—with Washington's blessing—between Couve de Murville and Willy Brandt on the maintenance of French forces in Germany despite France's disengagement from the integrated command, and the subsequent Ailleret-Lemnitzer agreement, were therefore prerequisites to the stabilization of a NATO military apparatus that otherwise would have suffered a serious blow.[74]

Moreover, the French withdrawal from NATO—and NATO's withdrawal from France—as Robert McNamara had anticipated, represented an opportunity to restructure and rationalize the NATO military apparatus as well as the U.S. defense posture in Europe.[75] This was all the more so because the institutional compromise reached between France and NATO deprived Paris of the veto it had used since 1963 to prevent progress in defense planning, as advocated ever since by Washington; by the end of 1967, NATO force planning was again moving ahead.[76]

The Restoration of U.S. Leadership and the Alliance Consensus

Because de Gaulle's decision of March 1966 did not translate into a rupture with the rest of the alliance, while at the same time allowing NATO to function again on a normal basis at fourteen, the relatively smooth settlement of the France-NATO issue was ipso facto a contribution to the solving of the NATO crisis. Yet the impact of France's withdrawal was deeper than that of a quick institutional fix; in many ways, the United States was indeed successful in using de Gaulle's decision as an instrument to reestablish American leadership and restore NATO's cohesion.

The military dimension is a case in point. By the time of France's withdrawal, the risk of a general NATO "disintegration" in many ways exceeded the damaging consequences of French policy itself. The "offset" issue—that is, the problem of financial compensation for the American (and the British) military presence in Germany—had been looming ever since the beginning of the decade; and, by the mid-1960s, it had worsened as a result of America's (and Britain's) deteriorating balance of payments against the backdrop of war in Vietnam and of an ailing British economy. By 1966, the offset problem was threatening to lead to an unraveling of the alliance's military structure as a result of disorderly troop withdrawals;[77] ominous signals were the Mansfield Resolution, in August, proposing U.S. troop withdrawals, and British plans for cutbacks in the British Army of the Rhine. A significant reduction of American troops in Europe, combined with France's withdrawal, could well turn into reality de Gaulle's prophecy about an ineluctable U.S. disengagement from Europe. Thus the trilateral talks between the United States, the United Kingdom, and Germany on the offset problems, launched in the fall of 1966, were of critical importance. Their successful conclusion in the spring of 1967 was a respite for the alliance, which according to the American negotiator, John McCloy, had "come a considerable distance from the unpromising situation we faced last autumn."[78] And French policy had, arguably if paradoxically, contributed to the success: De Gaulle's decision, by crystallizing the problem, had precipitated the solution.

The same logic applies to the strategic dimension, where the United States also used the French dissidence as a lever to restore the alliance's nuclear cohesion and its strategic credibility. The adoption of Flexible Response, indeed, was not only the consequence of France losing its veto power pursuant to its disengagement from NATO bodies; it also reflected, first and foremost, the restoration of a strategic consensus among the fourteen. Whereas in the initial phase of the "great debate," France could claim to speak for Europe,[79] by the time of the withdrawal, this was no longer true. The allies, it was noted in Washington in December 1966, "are moving to give substance to their common interests in the nuclear area—in spite of past French objections."[80]

In the meantime, the Americans had skillfully used the French strategic protest and its radicalization to bring about a middle-ground, centrist answer to NATO's nuclear dilemmas. Not only had France found itself institutionally isolated starting in 1965 as a result of its rejection of McNamara's offer in nuclear planning; Paris was now alone in defending a somewhat doctrinaire deterrence concept at a time when the Americans had considerably softened their own approach to Flexible Response—in essence lowering the nuclear threshold—to meet European concerns and isolate the French.[81] By the time of its adoption in 1967, Flexible Response had become mainstream while the French strategic concept had been marginalized.

Finally, the restoration of the alliance's political legitimacy after the 1966–67 crisis displayed a similar pattern. The key element here—the Harmel Report of December 1967, which put forward a two-way strategy based on the need to combine the maintenance of a strong defense with the quest for détente with the East—was indeed a direct consequence of the French withdrawal. The Belgian proposal of November 1966—immediately endorsed by Washington—was meant to be an answer both to the turmoil created by de Gaulle's March 1966 decision and to the wider challenge of détente—of which the general had heretofore been the foremost champion—which called for a redefinition of the alliance's goals.[82] Just as in the strategic dimension, the American-led tactics of the Harmel exercise aimed at favoring the emergence of a political consensus among allies to marginalize France and its go-it-alone approach to managing East-West relations. This was done by, on the one hand, endorsing the long-term objective of détente and, indeed, overcoming the Cold War—as de Gaulle had long advocated—while, on the other hand, "NATOizing" the détente process by making NATO an active participant therein—contrary to de Gaulle's "antibloc" approach. The success, arguably, went beyond that in the strategic realm; whereas France had rejected Flexible Response, de Gaulle decided—after some hesitation and with much reluctance—to endorse the Harmel Report. Here again, U.S. diplomacy, with the support of key allies, had successfully restored a consensus in the alliance by using French dissent as a lever; in the political, just as in the strategic and the military dimensions, France had been both an agent of the crisis and a catalyst of its solution.

Conclusion

Of course, the 1966–67 crisis was by no means the last in the history of the alliance, which would continue to be the "history of its crises,"[83] and those crises would continue to be about leadership, credibility, and legitimacy— or the recurrent lack thereof. Yet in many ways, the NATO crisis of 1966–67 gave rise if not to solutions to NATO's structural problems, then at least to a durable modus vivendi that allowed the alliance to face the turbulence of the second half of its Cold War history and to meet the crises of the 1970s and 1980s in political, strategic, or military terms. The Harmel concept allowed NATO to take up the challenge of détente and eventually that of the end of the Cold War; Flexible Response helped the allies paper over their divergences and overcome NATO's nuclear dilemmas; burden-sharing arrangements and the streamlining of the integrated structure contributed to keeping U.S. troops in Europe and to the maintenance of a credible defense.

Paradoxically, French policy was thus a major factor in the adaptation of the alliance to the new context at the end of the 1960s. To be sure, NATO was not transformed according to de Gaulle's vision, and his 1966 decision—while representing a manifesto for an inevitable long-term transformation, of which France posed itself as the vanguard—did sanction the failure of his earlier attempts at radically modifying the alliance. But the allies' response to the Gaullist challenge essentially amounted to acknowledging the validity of the general's diagnosis while prescribing different remedies.

So what was the effect of the 1966–67 crisis on the strategic triangle? To be sure, its fundamental geometry did not change: The Washington-Bonn relationship remained the closest; the Paris-Washington relationship remained the most distant; and the Paris-Bonn relationship remained somewhere in between. Yet the triangle became, arguably, more equilateral: Though the U.S.-German partnership was unquestionably confirmed as the backbone of the Atlantic alliance after 1966–67, it had also met its limits during the crisis; meanwhile, the French-German relationship had overcome the strains of that same crisis, and it would henceforth remain the key to the future transformation and especially Europeanization of NATO. Last, the French-U.S. relationship not only recovered from the psychodrama of

France's NATO withdrawal; with hindsight, de Gaulle's decision, by making France a more viable U.S. ally, also paradoxically strengthened that relationship in the long term.[84]

Notes

1. *Documents diplomatiques français* (hereafter DDF), 1958, vol. 2, 22.
2. U.S. Department of State, *Foreign Relations of the United States (FRUS), 1961–1963*, vol. 13 (hereafter *FRUS 1961–63*), 310–11.
3. *FRUS 1961–63*, 310–11.
4. Ibid., 665.
5. Ibid., 767.
6. Ibid., 310.
7. See Marc Trachtenberg, *A Constructed Peace: The Making of the European Settlement 1945–1963* (Princeton, N.J.: Princeton University Press, 1999), 296.
8. Quoted in Alain Peyrefitte, *C'était de Gaulle*, vol. 3, *Tout le monde à besoin d'un France qui marche* (Paris: Fayard, 2000), 200. It is important to understand that this remark by no means suggests a "third way" or a "neutralist" temptation, as the rest of de Gaulle's dealings with Soviet leaders during his June 1966 trip demonstrates; the realist de Gaulle simply recognizes what he believes to be a fact of life in the current distribution of power.
9. Jacques Vernant, "Les deux aspects de la crise atlantique," *Revue de défense nationale*, January 1958, 162–67.
10. Trachtenberg, *Constructed Peace*, 238.
11. Ibid., 244.
12. Scope Paper prepared for the NATO Ministerial Meeting, December 6, 1962, in *FRUS 1961–63*, 454.
13. See Helga Haftendorn, *NATO and the Nuclear Revolution: A Crisis of Credibility, 1966–1967* (Oxford: Clarendon Press, 1996).
14. *FRUS 1961–63*, 312–15.
15. In the words of Raymond Aron, *Le grand débat: Initiation à la stratégie atomique* (Paris: Clamann-Lévy, 1963).
16. "Scope Paper," NATO Ministerial Meeting, The Hague, May 11–14, 1964, Lyndon B. Johnson Library (LBJL), National Security Files (NSF), International Meetings and Travel File (IMTF), box 34.
17. Ibid.
18. Embassy Telegram (EMBTEL) Paris # 3060, December 2, 1965, LBJL, NSF, France, box 172.
19. On this, see Frédéric Bozo, "Détente versus Alliance: France, the United States and the Origins of the Harmel Report," *Contemporary European History* 7, no. 3 (1998): 343–60.
20. This is the main thesis in Frédéric Bozo, *Two Strategies for Europe: De Gaulle, the United States and the Atlantic Alliance* (Lanham, Md.: Rowman & Littlefield, 2001); I draw on this book for the following discussion of Gaullist policy.
21. On the 1958 memorandum, see Bozo, *Two Strategies*, 36–43; and Maurice

Vaïsse, *La Grandeur: Politique étrangère du général de Gaulle* (Paris: Fayard, 1997), 114–25.

22. Adenauer's reaction to the Memorandum was unsurprisingly negative: Not only was the Federal Republic of Germany (FRG) excluded from the "directorate" concept, but de Gaulle, whom he had met at Colombey only a few days before, had told him nothing of his initiative; see Bozo, *Two Strategies*, 20–21; on the France-Germany side of the triangle, see Georges-Henri Soutou, *L'Alliance incertaine: Les rapports politico-stratégiques franco-allemands depuis 1954*, (Paris: Fayard, 1996).

23. Letter, Eisenhower to de Gaulle, October 20, 1958, LBJL, NSF, France, box 172.

24. Memorandum of Conversation, Washington, March 10, 1961, *FRUS 1961–63*, 653.

25. Adenauer's lack of strategic confidence in the United States in that period was an important factor in all this; see Trachtenberg, *Constructed Peace*, 283 ff.

26. See, e.g., the conversation between Dean Rusk and French ambassador Hervé Alphand on February 28, 1963, in *FRUS 1961–63*, 761.

27. Telegram # 3317-30, Washington to Paris, June 9, 1962, Ministère des Affaires Étrangères, Archives diplomatiques (hereafter AD), série Amérique 1952–1963, Etats-Unis.

28. Note au sujet de l'Europe, July 17, 1961, *Lettres, notes et carnets, 1961–1963*, (Paris: Plon, 1986), 107–8. See Georges-Henri Soutou, "Le général de Gaulle et le plan Fouchet," in *De Gaulle en son siècle*, vol. 5, *L'Europe*, ed. Institut Charles de Gaulle (Paris, Plon, 1992).

29. Summary Record of NSC Executive Committee Meeting No. 38 (Part II), Washington, January 25, 1963, in *FRUS 1961–63*, 488–89.

30. According to Maurice Couve de Murville, *Une politique étrangère 1958–1969* (Paris: Plon, 1971), 106; the reading of documents indeed suggests that the clash of the first semester of 1963 was more violent than would be the case in 1966.

31. The German nuclear question was indeed at the center of Gaullist concerns in the years 1964–66. One of the key arguments used by French diplomacy against the multilateral force—which was seen from Paris as Washington's way of turning the FRG into the "satellite" of the United States—was the incompatibility between Germany's (further) nuclearization and its eventual reunification.

32. On the interaction between de Gaulle's détente policy and his challenge to the Atlantic order, see Bozo, *Two Strategies*, 160–62, 175–78.

33. Aide-mémoire of March 11, 1966, quoted in L. Radoux, *La France et l'OTAN*, WEU Assembly, 1967.

34. Note, "Etat de l'Alliance-Rapport du Secrétaire general," June 1, 1966, AD, Pactes 1961–70, box 272.

35. Indeed, Couve de Murville had told Rusk and Kennedy in October 1963 that it had become useless to propose a detailed NATO reform because France's partners were against such a reform. It was better, he added, not to raise the issue any more. Memorandum of Conversation, Couve de Murville–Kennedy, October 7, 1963; and Memorandum of Conversation, Couve de Murville–Rusk, October 8, 1966, John F. Kennedy Library, NSF, France, Box 72 A.

36. Quoted in Peyrefitte, *C'était de Gaulle*, vol. 3, 192.

37. On the following, see Frédéric Bozo, "Chronique d'une décision annoncée: Le retrait de l'organisation militaire (1965–1967)," in *La France et l'OTAN 1949–1996*,

ed. Maurice Vaïsse, Pierre Melandri, and Frédéric Bozo (Brussels: Complexe, 1996), 331–57.

38. Note de Jean de La Granville, February 11, 1966, AD, Pactes 1961–70, box 261.

39. Press Conference, February 21, 1966, *Discours et Messages,* vol. 5 (Paris: Plon, 1970), 6 ff.

40. Paul-Henri Spaak, quoted by Pierre Melandri, *L'Alliance atlantique* (Paris: Gallimard/Julliard, 1979), 187.

41. EMBTEL Paris # 3798, January 5, 1965, LBJL, NSF, France, box 170; EMBTEL Paris # 6238, May 4, 1965, and EMBTEL Paris # 6848, June 3, 1965, LBJL, NSF, box 171.

42. Telegram, Paris to Washington, March 8, 1966, AD, Pactes 1961–70, box 261.

43. Press Conference, February 21, 1966.

44. "Conseil restreint à l'Elysée le 2 juin 1966 (d'après les notes de M. Alphand)," June 3, 1966, AD, Pactes 1961–70, box 265. Separate Franco-German negotiations were also foreseen in order to address the issue of French Forces in Germany.

45. Etat-major des Armées, "Fiche Aide-mémoire," très secret, November 14, 1966, AD, Pactes 1961–70, box 265.

46. DEPTEL Paris # 738, August 14, 1965, LBJL, NSF, France, box 171.

47. Memorandum of Conversation, Ball, Vance, Wheeler, August 26, 1965, LBJL, NSF, France, box 171.

48. Memorandum for the President, "NATO," May 18, 1966, Walt W. Rostow and Francis M. Bator, LBJL, NSF, Memos to the President, box 7.

49. McCloy, sent to Bonn by Johnson in April, seemed to his German hosts extremely virulent about France, imputing to de Gaulle the aim of "destroying NATO" and maintaining the FRG in a state of perpetual inferiority while advocating German intransigence with the General: EMBTEL Bonn #3305, April 15, 1966, LBJL, NSF, Subject File, box 21. On the German-U.S. side of the triangle during the 1966 crisis, see Thomas A. Schwartz, "Lyndon Johnson and Europe: Alliance Politics, Political Economy and 'Growing Out of the Cold War,'" in *The Foreign Policies of Lyndon Johnson: Beyond Vietnam,* ed. H. W. Brands (College Station: Texas A&M University Press, 1999); and Frank Costigliola, "'Not a Normal French Government': La réaction américaine au retrait français de l'OTAN," in *La France et l'OTAN 1949–1996,* ed. Vaïsse, Melandri, and Bozo.

50. Memorandum for the President, "NATO," May 18, 1966.

51. Ibid.

52. Administrative Histories, Department of State, vol. 1, chapter 3, Europe, "France," LBJL, Administrative Histories.

53. Quoted by Schwartz, "Lyndon Johnson and Europe."

54. See Schwartz, "Lyndon Johnson and Europe." It may be argued that Johnson's choice of a "soft" policy on de Gaulle also reflected the limits of U.S. control over the FRG; as Schwartz remarks, the president realized that Acheson's or McCloy's willingness to pressure the Germans on the issue of French forces in Germany (which, they argued, should not be allowed to remain in the FRG if not integrated in the NATO framework) was dangerous and could well backlash into an upsurge of German "Gaullism."

55. Robert S. McNamara, Memorandum for the President, "Disposition of U.S. Facilities and Forces in France," May 25, 1966, LBJL, NSF, France, box 172.

56. Airgram Paris # A-1628, April 15, 1967, LBJL, NSF, France, box 173–74.

57. Couve de Murville during the Council of Ministers of March 22, 1967, quoted in Peyrefitte, *C'était de Gaulle,* vol. 3, 194.

58. In essence, de Gaulle was ready to grant access to facilities in times of war but refused to give any peacetime guarantee of automaticity; as to the Americans, they refused to sign an agreement on the wartime use of facilities absent such a guarantee. Even though Paris and Washington agreed on the use of the Donges-Metz pipeline by the United States, the result of this political intransigence on both sides was that French territory ceased to be NATO's "navel"; see Bozo, *Two Strategies,* 207–10.

59. Letter, Ailleret to Lemnitzer, January 25, 1967, AD, Pactes 1961–70, box 265.

60. Minutes of the Ailleret-Lemnitzer conversation of June 7, 1967, AD, Pactes 1961–70, box 265.

61. Technically, the Ailleret-Lemnitzer "agreement" of August 22, 1967 is but an exchange of letters ratifying "instructions" drafted in common "for wartime cooperation between French forces and NATO forces." See Ailleret's letter dated August 22, 1967, and "Instructions pour la coopération en temps de guerre des forces françaises avec celles de l'OTAN," Secret OTAN, AD, Pactes 1961–70, box 265.

62. For a detailed analysis based on the original document, see especially Bozo, "Chronique d'une décision annoncée"; and Bozo, *La France et l'OTAN: De la guerre froide au nouvel ordre européen* (Paris: Masson, 1991), 99–101.

63. Minutes of the Ailleret-Lemnitzer conversation of June 7. Of course, the arrangement formally excluded any "automatic commitment" of French forces and specified that in case of a government "decision to commit forces alongside NATO forces," they would "operate under national command" and in the framework of "plans agreed in advance"; but there would be a "NATO operational control" of these forces, which would fulfill a "regional reserve" role whose "preparation and coordination" would be undertaken in peacetime.

64. Position Paper, "France/NATO: The Constitutional Issue," December 3, 1966, LBJL, NSF, International Meetings and Travel Files (IMTF), Box 35.

65. Position Paper, "France/NATO"; and Administrative Histories.

66. Quoted in Peyrefitte, *C'était de Gaulle,* vol. 3, 194.

67. Note, "Motifs qui ont justifié la création de l'OTAN," June 17, 1967, AD, Pactes 1961–70, box 264 bis.

68. Position Paper, "France/NATO."

69. Position Paper, "France/NATO"; and Scope Paper, December 7, 1966, LBJL, NSF, IMTF, box 35.

70. The regrouping of SHAPE, the North Atlantic Council, and the Military Committee indeed represented a measure of geographic rationalization; as to the suppression of the Standing Group, also incident to the French withdrawal, it meant the disappearance of the only visible "great power" body in NATO.

71. On this, see Jane E. Stromseth, *The Origins of Flexible Response: NATO's Debate over Strategy in the 1960's* (Oxford: Macmillan, 1988), and Bozo, *Two Strategies.*

72. Fiche d'information, "Problèmes examinés par le comité Spécial ou comité McNamara jusqu'à ce jour," AD, Pactes 1961–70, box 267.

73. NATO Ministerial Meeting, Luxembourg, June 13–15, 1967, Position Paper, June 5, 1967, LBJL, NSF, IMTF, box 35.

74. The Ailleret-Lemnitzer agreement also revealed the limits of the influence of the "Germany firsters" in the administration as well as the continuing significance of the France-Germany strategic triangle for Western security; see above, note 54.

75. See Michael Harrison, *The Reluctant Ally: France and Atlantic Security* (Baltimore: Johns Hopkins University Press, 1091), 146.

76. Administrative Histories, State Department, vol. 1, chap. 3, "Europe," The Troop Problem and Burden Sharing, n.d., 1968, LBJL.

77. On this, see Schwartz, "Lyndon Johnson and Europe."

78. Administrative Histories, State Department, vol. 1, chap. 3, "Europe."

79. E.g., in December 1963, the Americans still noted that "the French, British and German points of view are closer to one another than to the American point of view"; "NATO Force Planning" (n.d.), LBJL, NSF, IMTF, box 34, "NATO Defense Planning Conference," December 2, 1963.

80. Scope Paper, December 7, 1966, LBJL, NSF, IMTF, box 35.

81. See Bozo, *Two Strategies,* 201–3.

82. On the Harmel Report, see Bozo, "Détente versus Alliance"; and Haftendorn, *NATO and the Nuclear Revolution.*

83. Josef Joffe, *The Limited Partnership: Europe, the United States and the Burdens of Alliance* (Cambridge, Mass.: Ballinger, 1987), xiii.

84. See my concluding chapter in *Two Strategies.*

Chapter 5

The De Gaulle Challenge: The Johnson Administration and the NATO Crisis of 1966–1967

Thomas A. Schwartz

In a recent issue of *The Wilson Quarterly,* the historian Lewis L. Gould argues that "in the academy and the political arena alike, there is renewed interest in the large visions that drove Lyndon Johnson and a fresh desire to modify the historical picture of his presidency."[1] Vietnam still overshadows any interpretation of Johnson's foreign policy, but there has been renewed interest in other areas of the world where the Johnson administration took initiatives.[2] Western Europe, where vital American interests were at stake and the United States faced important challenges, should serve as an important part of any reconsideration of Johnson's impact.

Rethinking Lyndon Johnson

Almost every analyst of Johnson's foreign policy begins with the quotation from Eric Goldman, the Princeton historian who wanted to be the Arthur Schlesinger of the Johnson years. Goldman wrote: "Lyndon Johnson entered the White House not only little concerned with the outer world but leery of it. 'Foreigners are not like the folks I am used to,' he remarked, and he was only half-joking."[3] Lyndon Baines Johnson's larger-than-life personality, along with his flamboyant Texas style and occasional crudeness, have contributed to this picture of the "quintessential provincial" in foreign affairs, "a handicap he could not overcome."[4] French president Charles de Gaulle seems to have seen LBJ as something of an ignorant and parochial American politician, remarking once that he was a "cowboy-radical" and a "sergeant who's been crowned."[5] The dramatic contrast with the martyred President John Kennedy, who was pictured by the London *Times* journalist Henry Brandon as a "living fusion of the American and European cultures," only intensified this negative portrayal of Johnson.[6]

However, as Johnson's biographer, Robert Dallek, recently put it, "To date, commentators on LBJ's foreign policies have been more guilty of superficial analysis than Johnson was." With the opening of the archives of the Johnson Library, and most important the records of his telephone conversations, historians are increasingly recognizing that Johnson was "a forceful foreign policy leader who consulted, listened to differing opinions, made up his own mind, and acted upon his conclusions with confidence that, all things considered, he was doing the best he could for the national interest."[7] Although Johnson's priorities in his first years in office were focused on his domestic legislation, he was too smart and experienced—many historians forget his role as Senate majority leader during the Dwight Eisenhower years—to neglect the fundamental importance to any American president of international affairs. And although it might be tempting on European issues to credit the "best and the brightest" advisers, it was Johnson who made the decisions. Only a few months before his death, McGeorge Bundy, in uncharacteristic language, told an interviewer, "It is total baloney that we, Rusk, McNamara, and Bundy were running the government. . . . We understood we were working for a president . . . who insisted on making his own decisions."[8]

In making his decisions, Johnson wanted to maintain control of the policy process. Although he came to recognize how much events in foreign relations could be beyond his control, this did not keep him from attempting to exercise his own prerogatives as president to guide the process of setting U.S. policy. But he also liked to keep his intentions hidden—and options open—until he was ready to act. His obsessive secrecy and concern with leaks to the press—other than the ones he would initiate—is well known, and to some extent accounts for the famous "credibility gap," which undermined domestic support for his Vietnam policy. But it also makes the task of the historian difficult, for Johnson was rarely explicit about the direction of his policy or his own sense of the respective trade-offs in making decisions. Nevertheless, by studying his pattern of decisionmaking, it is possible to recognize a coherent view, one that built on that of his more illustrious predecessor Kennedy and also paved the way for the détente for which his more articulate—at least on foreign policy matters—successor, Richard Nixon, always claimed credit.

U.S., French, and German Relations before 1966

From the tragic beginning of his administration in November 1963, Lyndon Johnson approached de Gaulle's France with caution. Though confident, as he often put it, that when a crisis hit, "we will be able to rely upon our French friends to be at our side," LBJ realized that those times would be few and far between.[9] De Gaulle's continuing attack on American policy in Vietnam and his advocacy of the "neutralization" of Southeast Asia, no matter how prescient that might have been, also complicated relations between the two countries. As *Time* magazine editorialized in July 1964, "From NATO to the U.N., Latin America to Red China, there is hardly an issue or an area in world politics on which France has not taken a stance at variance with U.S. policy."[10]

By contrast, Johnson felt a certain affinity for the Germans and the newly appointed chancellor, the firmly pro-American Ludwig Erhard. He invited Erhard to spend the Christmas holidays in December 1963. In wide-ranging talks, Johnson made clear his own commitment to reducing East-West tensions, but he was careful to try to build up Erhard's prestige in Germany by treating him as a uniquely important ally. He gave the German a Texas-size cowboy hat, took him deer hunting, and brought Erhard to a number of German American communities near the ranch. At the end of the love fest, he announced to the press that "I like simply everything about him," while the German responded, "I love President Johnson, and he loves me."[11]

As important as these contrasting alliance relationships were, Johnson's number one foreign policy issue was the threat of nuclear war. He took very seriously his responsibility to reduce the danger of a nuclear apocalypse. At the first National Security Council meeting after Kennedy's assassination, Johnson read a Bundy-prepared statement stating that "the greatest single requirement is that we find a way to ensure the survival of civilization in the nuclear age. A nuclear war would be the death of all our hopes and it is our task to see that it does not happen."[12] Like his hero-politician Franklin Roosevelt, Johnson was also determined to improve relations with the Soviet Union, a direction that would, incidentally, steal some of the thunder from de Gaulle's own efforts at détente. Throughout his campaign for the presidency in 1964, Johnson affirmed himself as the "peace candidate" against the strident anticommunism of his Republican rival Barry Goldwater, who had suggested giving NATO's supreme commander the authority to use nuclear weapons.

However, for most of his first two years in office, Johnson was not deeply engaged in alliance issues. He did make key decisions in December 1964 that ended the U.S. pressure for a Multilateral Force (MLF), a nuclear-sharing scheme designed to give Germany the appearance of control over nuclear weapons. To substitute for the MLF, the administration created a "software solution," the Nuclear Planning Group in NATO, to allow for German participation in nuclear strategic planning.[13] He also intensified U.S. efforts to negotiate a nuclear Non-Proliferation Treaty (NPT) with the Soviet Union, a move that worried German officials. Movement on a possible NPT also reinforced de Gaulle's fears of superpower hegemony, increasing the American suspicion that the general would act soon against NATO. The elections in France, scheduled for December 1965, further encouraged this belief, and led to the first contingency planning.

In October 1965, the Johnson administration had one of its first high-level meetings to consider a French move against the alliance. The subject was a State Department draft of a National Security Action memorandum titled "France and NATO." The department's draft took a very hard-line approach, threatening that "the United States would withdraw Article V protection" from France if the country "ceased to participate constructively in the alliance." Johnson's White House advisers objected strongly, led by Bundy, who called the statement an "empty threat" and argued with an air of resignation that the United States "might as well face the fact" that the French assumed they had U.S. protection regardless of what Washington might leak to the newspapers.[14] George Ball, the undersecretary of state and a strong opponent of de Gaulle, fired back that the Article V threat was one of the few ways Washington had to pressure the French. Ball may have hoped that it might influence French public opinion away from de Gaulle in the upcoming elections in December. The secretary of defense, Robert McNamara, jumped into the argument as well, stressing that a France that did not contribute troops or support facilities was not entitled to U.S. protection. Ambassador David Bruce intervened in the debate to suggest a compromise formulation, which papered over this division within the administration and simply asserted that "the U.S. security commitment given in Article V will obviously have to be re-examined by the president, so far as it relates to France."[15]

This argument between White House staff members and the representatives of the State and Defense departments reflected the different priorities and agendas of each group. State was determined to protect that pillar of American diplomacy, the NATO alliance, and to punish the French for undermining it. State was also afraid of the example that the French might set, especially with the Germans. Secretary of State Dean Rusk reprimanded the U.S. ambassador in Germany, George McGhee, for taking a position that Rusk felt encouraged good relations between the French and the Germans "at any cost." In language similar to that which he used when discussing the communist world, Rusk told McGhee that "the present French leadership responds to firmness and exploits any whisper of weakness. . . . We should not display any lack of confidence in our own positions or any willingness to compromise them in the interests of transient amity between France and Germany—and this applies to nuclear and offset arrangements, as well as other elements of policy."[16]

McNamara's and the Defense Department's position was a more complicated one. On the one hand, he complained that the Gaullist challenge would "force us to adjust to a peacetime arrangement which would endanger our wartime capability" and weaken the possibility of a truly effective policy of Flexible Response. But the U.S. perception of what was needed for Flexible Response was already changing, affected by the demands of Vietnam and the sense of a reduced threat in Europe. De Gaulle's defiant position opened up backdoor opportunities for the secretary of defense to reduce the conventional American military presence in Europe. In talks with the British, McNamara had already complained bitterly of the "inadequate German force contribution" and the need for a substantial increase. McNamara was stymied by what he saw as a German overreaction "if we withdraw a battalion," yet an unwillingness to face up to their responsibilities.[17] De Gaulle's behavior might create opportunities for a reduction in U.S. troop presence in Europe, an objective McNamara increasingly championed, especially as offset negotiations with the Germans became more difficult and congressional pressure intensified.

For their part, both Bundy and his deputy Francis Bator recognized that Johnson was "determined that France should not be allowed to push the

U.S. around," but that Johnson would "want to play the large cards with France himself; particularly he will want to control what is said to the French and when." Johnson's determination reflected his awareness that his Cabinet secretaries did want a much tougher line toward the French, aware that de Gaulle's behavior complicated their relations with other allies as well as the all-important Congress. Nevertheless, Johnson was determined to maintain his own grip on policy, a grip that would allow him to connect his response to the French with other U.S. priorities. Bundy hinted at one of those in the meeting, when he discussed the possibility of trilateral arrangements with the Germans and British, and that these might be particularly helpful in moving forward on the "nuclear problem." By this he meant not only the doomed MLF or the Atlantic Nuclear Force, but also the possibility of connecting U.S. responses to movement on bridge building with the Soviets and nonproliferation, objectives that had risen in the list of U.S. priorities, and that could serve as effective responses to aspects of de Gaulle's policies.[18]

De Gaulle's March 1966 Letter

De Gaulle's letter of March 7, 1966, began with the assurance that France would remain an active member of the Western alliance, "determined even as today to fight at the side of her allies in case one of them will be the object of unprovoked aggression." However, France was now determined "to recover the entire exercise of her sovereignty over her territory," a sovereignty that was "impaired" by the presence of foreign military forces and France's participation in "integrated" commands.[19] De Gaulle's distinction between France's treaty obligations and the peacetime organizational arrangements of the alliance presented the Americans with a dilemma that had not been fully anticipated. The letter, as Johnson's first reply noted, raised "grave questions regarding the whole relationship between the responsibilities and benefits of the alliance," but Johnson held off from being more specific.[20]

In preparing a full response to de Gaulle's letter, Bator was guilty of considerable understatement when he suggested to the president that "your advisors may disagree." Was there a distinction between the treaty and the organization? Bator put forth a strong case for not yet pressing the issue. He appealed to Johnson's common sense: "It is a fact of geography that a U.S. threat to deprive France of our protection is at best barely credible and at worst, just plain silly. It is like threatening to abandon Kentucky in the face of a land attack by Canada. It is hard to do unless one is prepared to throw in Ohio. If we are going to defend the Germans against the Russians, we cannot help but defend France too."[21] Bator stressed that the Germans would "look to us for guidance," in any response to de Gaulle, and urged Johnson to approach the issue cautiously. The real problem, as his White House staff stressed to LBJ, was "as always, . . . not France but Germany—and the more we agitate the alliance the more we may bring this potentially divisive issue to the fore."[22]

On the other side of this issue, powerful emotions were at work. After de Gaulle told him that every American soldier must leave France, Rusk replied, "Does that include the dead Americans in military cemeteries as well?"[23] The State Department's reaction reflected this indignation, urging what one critic called a "clarion call to propaganda battle."[24] It wanted to push an accelerated program of integration in NATO, in effect arguing that the best way to stop de Gaulle "is to beef up the alliance—make it more integrated rather than less."[25] On this point, Rusk and Ball received support from their formerly reluctant ambassador in France, Charles Bohlen. Bohlen had been an advocate of restraint in dealing with de Gaulle, but he now felt the general had gone one step too far. He told LBJ that the French withdrawal had radically changed the situation, amounting to a "complete destruction . . . of the entire NATO organization and cooperative defense efforts." To accept de Gaulle's move with equanimity would, in Bohlen's words, "have a chilling effect upon the opposition in France," and lead to a "panic in French public opinion."[26] Although State took the lead in proposing a tougher policy, it could count on support from the departments of Defense and the Treasury, as well as the senior "Wise Men" like Dean Acheson and John McCloy, whom Johnson brought in for advice on the issue.

Johnson resisted their advice, and he was determined to retain control of his administration's response to de Gaulle. Historians have generally not given Johnson credit for resisting the temptation to exploit the French action for his own short-term political gains.[27] Polls at the time demonstrated that an overwhelming majority of Americans disapproved of de Gaulle's action, and Johnson, in the midst of the Vietnam conflict, could have chosen to exploit this issue as a diversion.[28] Johnson chose not to arouse passions, and he stressed instead the last sentence of his response to de Gaulle's letter that "as our old friend and ally her place will await France whenever she decides to resume her leading role."[29] Johnson insisted that he saw "no benefit to ourselves or to our allies in debating the position of the French government," and that "our task is to rebuild NATO outside of France as promptly, economically, and effectively as possible."[30] George Ball noted that Johnson "incessantly restrained me from making critical comments," about de Gaulle.[31] And in one of his most famous remarks, the president told McNamara, "When a man asks you to leave his house, you don't argue; you get your hat and go."[32]

Although Johnson asserted a line of restraint in response to de Gaulle, this approach was still subject to implementation by members of his government who did not share his preference. This became clear as the various issues were addressed, including questions of allied overflights of French territory, the continued transportation of oil across France, and reentry rights for NATO forces into France in the event of war. One of the most important of these was the issue of French troops stationed in Germany. Consisting of air and army units comprising approximately 76,000 personnel, these forces posed less of a military question than a political one.[33] The French government made it clear that although these forces would no longer come under NATO command, they would remain in Germany if the German government wanted them. The German government faced a dilemma: If it insisted that French troops could remain only if they remained committed to NATO, it would precipitate a French withdrawal and cause a major setback in Franco-German relations, with important domestic political consequences. The Gaullists in the Christian Democratic Party, led by such figures as Franz Josef Strauss and having the support of the former chancellor Konrad Adenauer, would vigorously protest such a move, and they would have significant public support.

With notable understatement, the American ambassador in Bonn, George McGhee, reported that "If the present confrontation results in a withdrawal of French forces, . . . German public opinion will not react with exhilaration." Indeed, McGhee suggested that such a clear failure in the attempt to "build Europe" would lead the Germans to a renewed focus on "the other elusive goal of German foreign policy-reunification," a game in which, McGhee commented, the "key cards are held by the other side."[34] Conversely, if Germany agreed to seek a new arrangement with the French, that would seem to reward de Gaulle's nationalism, and it raised questions about a special status for France that would be particularly irritating to Washington. In effect, de Gaulle's policy was forcing the Germans to choose between Paris and Washington, a choice no German political leader wanted to make.

On this issue, most of Johnson's advisers wanted to take a very firm stand. At a meeting on April 4, 1966, with Rusk, McNamara, Ball, and

Acheson present, they decided that the United States "should fully support" the Germans if they took a hard line toward the French and their troops in Germany, "and do nothing to dissuade them." If the Germans decided to try to negotiate an agreement with de Gaulle about the troops, the "U.S. should urge them to incorporate in these new arrangements effective safeguards assuring their use in accordance with NATO requirements and an adequate quid pro quo giving to other allies in Germany facilities in France such as transit and overflight rights."[35] These conditions were designed to be unacceptable to the French and call their bluff. They were the basis for the instructions given to John J. McCloy, the president's special envoy, as he prepared for talks with Chancellor Erhard a week later.

Johnson was at his ranch when the State Department finished drafting the instructions for McCloy. George Ball sent them to the president, with the note that this "will constitute Mr. McCloy's instructions."[36] When Bator saw Ball's message, he objected to what he perceived as pressure on the Germans to take a hard line. He believed that such pressure would both complicate Erhard's position in German politics and go against Johnson's own clear preference for a muted response to de Gaulle's challenge. He feared that "if under U.S. pressure, German-French negotiations fail, and French Divisions withdraw, Germans will join other Europeans in blaming us for resulting grave damage to German-French relations." The desire to avoid choosing between Paris and Washington, Bator warned, is "still at the center of German politics." Bator immediately cabled LBJ at his ranch, asking him to change McCloy's instructions. Bator urged a less conditional American approach, offering the Germans support for whatever they decided to do about the French troops.[37] Johnson, who was on vacation and "wanted to focus on his cows," did not look at Bator's message until later in the week, after McCloy had already met with Gerhard Schröder, the German foreign minister, and delivered the tougher message. However, when Johnson read Bator's message, he immediately told Rusk that he agreed with Bator, and that the secretary should change McCloy's instructions. Johnson wanted the Germans to know, as McCloy subsequently told Chancellor Erhard, that the "United States should support any position taken by the FRG [Federal Republic of Germany] that recognized the seriousness of the situation and provided an adequate response to the French. The FRG must itself decide the position it wishes to occupy in Europe. We are not thinking of forcing the FRG toward any policy or decision."[38]

The Germans ultimately decided that the political importance of the French troops outweighed any other considerations. Faced with a major electoral defeat in a key provincial election in July 1966, Erhard "must have given de Gaulle the impression the Germans would never invite the French troops to leave no matter what."[39] Although the arrangements governing French troops in Germany were not finalized until Erhard was replaced by the Grand Coalition of the Christian Democratic Union / Christian Social Union and the Social Democratic Party (SPD), which was formed in December 1966, they were clear once the United States decided not to make it a decisive issue. France was allowed to keep its troops in Germany on its own terms, free, as Lawrence Kaplan noted, "from alliance obligations and free, for that matter to leave whether or not the Germans or Americans wished them to go."[40]

Johnson's "soft" treatment of de Gaulle aroused the fury of his advisers, notably Dean Acheson, who told Bator at a Washington dinner party that "you made the greatest imperial power the world has ever seen kiss de Gaulle's arse."[41] Acheson's fury was not confined to Bator, and he exploded directly at LBJ during a White House meeting in May 1966. The president continued to insist that everyone in the administration remain "scrupulously polite in references to the General," and on this point his advisers found him unyielding.[42] Almost a year later, Acheson was still complaining, this time to former British prime minister Anthony Eden. "I have been sadly wondering what LBJ might have done if he had persevered in the plans which McCloy and I had started to get the French troops out of Germany," Acheson told his British friend. The American was convinced that "this would have been clear notice to France and the French Army that de Gaulle's attack on NATO has failed. But irresolution and feeble councils prevailed."[43]

This portrait of conflict between Johnson and his advisers over the French issue is only part of the picture. The other part is the recognition by Johnson and his aides that the French move constituted an opportunity to solve many alliance-related issues, from Flexible Response, to nuclear sharing, and even the financial burdens of the U.S. presence. Acheson himself, despite his occasional outbursts, played a vital role in this process, abandoning his earlier stance in favor of the MLF and embracing a careful détente as an objective of the alliance. So much more was now possible with France out of the picture, at least for the immediate future. As Harlan Cleveland, the U.S. permanent representative to NATO, would put it: "In recent years France has been a drag on NATO.... We are increasingly able to take advantage of the new surge of life which this vessel, even with all its barnacles, begins to feel now that it is no longer trying to drag a bucket."[44]

The Acheson committee's recommendations focused on "emphasizing, clarifying and implementing NATO's political function" and in particular its political function in organizing the West's approach toward a détente with Eastern Europe. The committee acknowledged the danger of "leaving the field of East-West relations" to General de Gaulle, and it proposed a more positive policy toward improving the "Central European environment." It urged that "at every stage in policymaking and execution scrupulous attention must be paid to German interests and sensitivities," a concern that clearly met with the president's approval.[45]

Although Johnson wanted to keep U.S. relations with Germany at the center of his concerns, events and other priorities worked against his intention. In the summer of 1966, it became increasingly clear that Germany would not be able to pay its offset costs, that is, those contributions, in the form of purchases of American weapons, that were designed to "offset" the expense of stationing U.S. troops in Germany. The German economy was experiencing a minor slowdown, and Erhard's party had suffered a serious political defeat in a *Land* election in North Rhine Westphalia. At the same time, the British were also experiencing difficulties in affording their expenditures for the British Army on the Rhine (BAOR), and they were demanding increased German payments or threatening to withdraw their troops. In response to both de Gaulle's withdrawal and the offset issues, Senator Mike Mansfield (D-Mont.) was pushing for an American withdrawal of up to half of U.S. forces in Europe. In the midst of these disintegrating forces, it became clear that Johnson might be able to reach a deal to move ahead with the Soviet Union on the NPT, if the United States would agree to language that largely eliminated any possibility of an MLF or Atlantic Nuclear Force. There were even indications that the Soviets might consider some type of mutual troop withdrawal from Central Europe.[46]

The Trilateral Negotiations and Johnson's European Speech

In late August 1966, the administration in Washington suggested a form of "Trilateral Negotiations" between the United States, the United Kingdom, and Germany to resolve the offset problem. Earlier in the summer, Bator had suggested to Johnson the creation of some type of "mixed commission" of the United States, the United Kingdom, and Germany that might "protect our balance of payments" and hammer out a consensus "on an allied defense posture in Europe which will provide deterrence and the insurance of a reasonable conventional option."[47] Now, through Bator and other channels, the Americans sought to convince the Germans that, although they would insist on the current offset being met, changes in the manner of future payments were negotiable.

However, Erhard refused to agree to the arrangement, stubbornly insisting on seeing Johnson personally before he agreed to the talks. With Erhard's political position in Germany now precarious, Bator told LBJ that "for us it is important—even more than Erhard's survival—that we not appear the culprit if he falls."[48] Press reports made it clear that Erhard "badly needs a success at the White House,"[49] but Johnson, backed strongly by McNamara and the Treasury Department, would not allow a "stretching out" of the current offset payments.[50] Both Cabinet secretaries were thinking of the possible congressional reaction to an American retreat. But Johnson also seems to have made the judgment that Erhard could no longer deliver politically, that any deal he might make with the weakened chancellor was unlikely to stick. In a long and painful meeting, Erhard pleaded that a potential successor might "not show the same loyalty and determination to cultivate close ties to the United States."[51] However, in the end Erhard remained true to form and put up little resistance.[52] When he returned to Germany without a success given by his American friends, his government collapsed. The new government consisted of a "Grand Coalition" between the Christian Democrats and the Social Democratic Party. Kurt Kiesinger from the Gaullist faction of the Christian Democratic Union became chancellor, with SPD leader Willy Brandt taking over as foreign minister.

The collapse of Erhard's government was a blessing in disguise for Johnson's European policy. Erhard had been the most loyal of allies, and Johnson felt a genuine warmth toward him. However, Erhard was increasingly ineffective as a political leader, and his weakness had shown at the polls in *Länder* elections.[53] In the weeks preceding the trip, his top aide had resigned and his defense minister only barely survived a vote of confidence. One recent analysis notes that "in Germany the prevailing opinion was that Erhard's fate was sealed anyway and the visit to Washington was just the last straw."[54] With his resignation and the coming of the Grand Coalition, Johnson now had a stronger, if more independent minded, German government to deal with, one more capable of taking risks and far more interested in moving forward on détente.[55] Most important, however, Johnson and his advisers recovered rapidly, using the crisis to push for a solution that dealt with both the security and economic issues underlying NATO.

In the midst of the political crisis in Germany, Johnson decided to deliver his most significant speech on Europe, a speech designed, as one news report put it, to signal "a bold new initiative on the part of the United States to achieve East-West reconciliation."⁵⁶ Preparation of the speech had been in the works since the Acheson committee had delivered its report in early June. That report had suggested that by September, "when most of the decisions had been taken to respond to the disruptive actions of France, the president should make a major address expressing the continuing U.S. interest and participation in NATO."⁵⁷ Johnson's advisers were also sensitive to the timing of the speech, recognizing that a summer speech would have far less impact in Europe than something in the autumn.⁵⁸ In the speech of October 7, 1966, Johnson told a New York conference of editorial writers that "we want the Soviet Union and the nations of Eastern Europe to know that we and our allies shall go step by step with them as far as they are willing to advance." Johnson listed a number of steps he would take to hasten "peaceful engagement" with the East with the hope of shaping "an entire new political environment." The president argued that this would have important consequence in the long run for Germany: "We must improve the East-West environment in order to achieve the unification of Germany in the context of a larger, peaceful, and prosperous Europe."⁵⁹

The speech was an important signal, and it expressed "a doctrine congenial in Europe, different from de Gaulle's, without quarrelling."⁶⁰ Johnson also affirmed that the United States respected "the integrity of a nation's boundary lines" and encouraged the removal of territorial and border disputes, a none-too-subtle reference to Germany's refusal to recognize the Oder-Neisse line and the loss of its eastern territories. The Bonn embassy had sought a last-minute change that would have softened the reference, but the State Department insisted it remain, to provide "gentle support to those people in Germany who want slowly to back away from a self-defeating position."⁶¹ In effect, the Johnson administration was lending its support to moderate SPD politicians in Germany like Willy Brandt, who as foreign minister in the Grand Coalition had initiated his policy of *Ostpolitik.*⁶²

These U.S. steps—the refusal to make concessions to Erhard, the advocacy of an NPT, the talk of troop withdrawals—amounted to a form of shock therapy to Germany, and one measure of that shock is the precipitous drop in support and sympathy for the United States. The rhetoric was extraordinarily heated; the new Chancellor Kiesinger referred ominously to the "atomic complicity" between the two superpowers, while Franz Josef Strauss, in the Grand Coalition as finance minister, referred to an NPT as a "new Versailles."⁶³ To try to mend relations, and to handle the trilateral negotiations, Johnson appointed John J. McCloy, the former American high commissioner in Germany.[64] McCloy strongly opposed significant troop reductions, and he argued against the idea that the level of forces should depend on the offset payments. Opposing him was McNamara, who advocated a reduction of two divisions and personally favored an even more drastic cutback. In presenting the options to the president, Bator stressed that this "decision will cast a very long shadow on our relations with Germany and Europe, with consequences for domestic politics."[65]

Johnson now took command. Through a series of meetings with the congressional leadership and his negotiators, he laid down the path he wanted to follow. With the members of Congress, he "managed" a breakfast, taking a hard line "more arbitrary than I like, which made it difficult for them to disagree with the president of the United States." With McCloy, Johnson insisted that the former high commissioner pressure his German friends "that they have to be realistic." Noting that the Fredericksburg, Texas, Germans with whom he grew up were "great people; but by God they are as stingy as Hell," Johnson told McCloy that "they have got to put in some money." They would have to help the British as well, because a BAOR withdrawal would encourage demands for a similar American action. Johnson feared that without a German offer, he would have to cut two divisions. When McCloy warned that "you are on the verge of the collapse of the alliance," Johnson replied, "Jack, I know that; I'll try to hold this alliance together longer than anybody else will, longer than the British will, and longer than the Germans. But they have got to put something in the family pot."[66]

The Germans did. They agreed to purchase and hold some $500 million in U.S. government medium-term securities, and even more important, agreed to make public their intention to refrain from buying gold.[67] The so-called Blessing Brief was a significant German concession, one that would be extremely helpful in managing the balance of payments deficit.[68] In effect, as Bator told the president, the United States had also scored a victory against the French, "negotiating the world onto a dollar standard," and to "recognition of the fact that, for the time being, the U.S. must necessarily play banker of the world and that the continuing threat to convert gold is simply unacceptable."[69] Bator expected that America's concessions to the Germans in the trilateral talks would contribute to gaining German support in the ongoing negotiations dealing with both the Kennedy Round of trade talks and the question of international money.[70] The United States withdrew one division and ninety-six aircraft, although for appearance's sake, these forces remained committed to NATO.[71]

The Trilateral Agreements also witnessed the finalization of a U.S.-German-British compromise over the issue of Flexible Response, although this question remained largely in the background during the talks. Through the working groups dedicated to an overall strategic review, as well as the efforts of McNamara's Nuclear Planning Group, the United States and Germany moved closer together over the issue of the use of tactical nuclear weapons, with the Americans accepting a greater role than had originally been foreseen in the Flexible Response strategy, while the Germans agreed that NATO had to take greater measures for a non-nuclear forward defense. This paved the way for NATO's final adoption of Flexible Response as its strategy in its meetings in May and December 1967.[72]

Though something of a stopgap measure, the agreements secured the alliance's financial basis—and protected the dollar—giving Johnson the weapon he needed to fend off congressional challenges. More important, they were one of the first examples of genuine burden sharing within the alliance. Helga Haftendorn noted the "greatest success of the trilateral talks" was that the offset question, rather than becoming an "explosive issue" within the alliance, "paved the way for its consolidation."[73] And Bator proved correct in recognizing that German assistance could prove helpful in securing a trade agreement in the Kennedy Round in May 1967, and agreement on Special Drawing Rights or international money in August. The NPT would prove more complicated, but despite German objections, it was signed in July 1968. Indeed, Johnson might well have capped his presidency with a journey to Moscow to sign a Strategic Arms Limitation Talks agreement had it not been for Moscow's decision to crush the Prague Spring.

Conclusion

The French-NATO crisis offers one reason to revise past historical estimates of the Johnson administration and foreign policy. Johnson was able to assert enough control over the institutions and Cabinet departments of his government to construct a set of priorities for the United States in Europe, priorities that shifted the American focus from confrontation to détente, and provided an appealing countervision to that of French president de Gaulle. This investigation of American policymaking also reveals the degree to which even during the worst moments of the "French" crisis, the American focus remained on Germany, and the need to keep its "special relationship" with the Bonn Republic intact. Johnson shared this sentiment, even though he was willing to bargain hard and push German domestic politics in directions that would further the alliance's—and American—objectives. To this extent, from the American perspective, the strategic triangle was never an equilateral one, and the choices made reflected those priorities and objectives.

Finally, the NATO crisis highlights the degree to which questions of strategy, transnational relationships, economic restraints, and domestic politics were intertwined in the resolution of this alliance crisis. Perhaps the very vitality of the NATO alliance, and even its ability to outlive the Cold War, owes much to the degree to which Western leaders have been able to bring all these questions to the table and to negotiate issues with the common assumption that all politicians must answer to their electorates. Lyndon Johnson understood that, and although he never surmounted his own credibility gap on Vietnam, he did respond effectively to the alliance's "crisis of credibility."[74]

Notes

1. Lewis L. Gould, "The Revised LBJ," *Wilson Quarterly* 24 (Spring 2000): 80.
2. Most notably, H. W. Brands, ed., *The Foreign Policies of Lyndon Johnson: Beyond Vietnam* (College Station: Texas A&M University Press, 1999).
3. Eric F. Goldman, *The Tragedy of Lyndon Johnson* (New York: Alfred A. Knopf, 1968), 378.
4. Alonzo L. Hamby, *Liberalism and Its Challengers: From F.D.R. to Bush,* 2nd ed. (New York: Oxford University Press, 1992), 232.
5. Alain Peyrefitte, *C'était de Gaulle,* vol. 2, *La France reprend sa place dans le monde* (Paris: Fayard, 1997), 48.
6. Henry Brandon, *Special Relationships: A Foreign Correspondent's Memoirs from Roosevelt to Reagan* (New York: Athenaeum, 1988), 200.
7. Robert Dallek, "Lyndon Johnson as a World Leader," in *Foreign Policies of Lyndon Johnson,* ed. Brands, 8–9.
8. Robert Dallek, *Flawed Giant: Lyndon Johnson and His Times, 1961–1973* (New York: Oxford University Press, 1998), 90.
9. H. W. Brands, *The Wages of Globalism: Lyndon Johnson and the Limits of American Power* (New York: Oxford University Press, 1995), 94.
10. *Time,* June 12, 1964, 42.
11. Richard J. Barnet, *The Alliance: America, Europe, Japan—Makers of the Postwar World* (New York: Simon & Schuster, 1983), 240.
12. U.S. Department of State, *Foreign Relations of the United States (FRUS), 1961–1963* (Washington, D.C.: U.S. Government Printing Office, 1988), vol. 8, 544.
13. Thomas A. Schwartz, "Lyndon Johnson and Europe: Alliance Politics, Political Economy, and 'Growing Out of the Cold War,'" in *Foreign Policies of Lyndon Johnson,* ed. Brands, 44–48.

14. Francis Bator, interview with the author, Cambridge, Mass., December 16, 1995.
15. U.S. Department of State, *Foreign Relations of the United States (FRUS) 1964–1968* (Washington, D.C.: U.S. Government Printing Office, 1992), vol. 13 (hereafter *FRUS 1964–68), 258.
16. *FRUS 1964–68,* 309.
17. Ibid., 254, 304.
18. Ibid., 254–57.
19. Ibid., 325.
20. Ibid., 326.
21. Ibid., 327.
22. Ibid., 337.
23. Thomas J. Schoenbaum, *Waging Peace and War: Dean Rusk in the Truman, Kennedy, and Johnson Years* (New York: Simon & Schuster, 1988), 421.
24. *FRUS 1964–68,* 337.
25. Ibid., 336.
26. Bohlen to Rusk, March 7, 1966, Central Files, DEF 4 NATO, Box 2186, National Archives.
27. As respected a historian as Warren Cohen wrote, "Perhaps as a result of advice from men like Bundy and Bohlen, his ambassador to France, Johnson was uncharacteristically tactful in all of his dealings with the French president." Warren I. Cohen, *Dean Rusk* (Totowa, N.J.: Cooper Square Publishers, 1980), 262. However, Bundy had left the government by this point, and Bohlen's response to de Gaulle's step broke from his earlier advocacy of restraint.
28. The Gallup Poll found that well over half of all Americans did not believe France was "a dependable ally of the United States," and these figures were almost two-thirds for college-educated Americans. George H. Gallup, *The Gallup Poll; Public Opinion, 1935–1971* (New York: Random House, 1972), 2017.
29. *FRUS 1964–68,* 349. Frank Costigliola argues that this sentence contains a "gender-coded" formulation that indicates the continuing American desire to dominate both France and the Alliance. Frank Costigliola, *France and the United States: The Cold Alliance Since World War II* (New York: Twayne Publishers, 1992), 145–146.
30. *FRUS 1964–68,* 376.
31. George W. Ball, *The Past Has Another Pattern: Memoirs* (New York: W. W. Norton, 1982), 336.
32. Lyndon Johnson, *The Vantage Point: Perspectives of the Presidency, 1963* (New York: Holt, Rinehart & Winston, 1971), 305.
33. *FRUS 1964–68,* 357.
34. Ibid., 376.
35. Ibid., 354.
36. George Ball, Memorandum for the President, "Guidance for John J. McCloy," April 10, 1966, National Security Files (NSF), Agency File, NATO, vol. 3, Lyndon B. Johnson Library (LBJL).
37. Bator to LBJ, telegram, April 11, 1966, Bator Papers, Chronological File, Box 3, LBJL.
38. *FRUS 1964–68,* 367.
39. Ibid., 441.
40. Lawrence S. Kaplan, *NATO and the United States: The Enduring Alliance* (Boston: Twayne Publishers, 1988), 121.

41. Bator, interview with the author, Cambridge, Mass., December 16, 1995.
42. *FRUS 1964–68,* 391–92. For Acheson's own account of this meeting, and his subsequent rapprochement with LBJ, see his letter to Anthony Eden, June 29, 1966, in *Among Friends: Personal Letters of Dean Acheson,* ed. David S. McLellan and David C. Acheson (New York: Dodd, Mead, 1980), 279.
43. Acheson to Eden, March 15, 1967, folder 118, box 9, Papers of Dean Acheson, Yale University.
44. Cleveland to Leddy, November 5, 1966, Central Files, DEF 4 NATO, Box 1567, National Archives.
45. *FRUS 1964–68,* 407–8.
46. Ibid., 632.
47. Ibid., 455.
48. Bator to LBJ, September 25, 1966, NSF, National Security Council (NSC) History, Trilateral Negotiations and NATO, 1966–67 (TNN), box 50, LBJL.
49. *Time,* September 30, 1966, 29.
50. To meet an estimated yearly gap of $500 million between what the Germans would pay and what the costs were, McNamara advocated reducing American spending in Europe by $200 million, and considering the withdrawal of a significant number of American combat personnel, which he acknowledged would have a "traumatic" effect on NATO. McNamara to LBJ, September 19, 1966, NSF, NSC History, TNN, box 50, LBJL.
51. *FRUS 1964–68,* 473.
52. George McGhee, *At the Creation of a New Germany: From Adenauer to Brandt —An Ambassador's Account* (New Haven, Conn.: Yale University Press, 1989), 192–93.
53. Dennis L. Bark and David R. Gress, *A History of West Germany, Vol. 2: Democracy and Its Discontents 1963–1988* (Oxford: Blackwell, 1989), 57. Although Bark and Gress repeat the argument that American obstinacy caused Erhard's downfall, the evidence they present suggests otherwise.
54. Hubert Zimmermann, "Dollars, Pounds, and Transatlantic Security: Conventional Troops and Monetary Policy in Germany's Relations to the United States and the United Kingdom, 1955–1967" (Ph.D. diss., European University, Florence, 1997), 241.
55. Rusk was particularly impressed with Brandt's appearance at NATO, noting that he demonstrated that the new German government "will not be bound by the rigid theology of the Adenauer period." *FRUS 1964–68,* 517.
56. *Newsweek,* October 17, 1966, 42.
57. *FRUS 1964–68,* 409.
58. Bator to LBJ, August 16, 1966, Chronological File, box 3, Francis Bator Papers, LBJL.
59. Speech to Editorial Writers, October 7, 1966, NSF Speech File, box 5, LBJL.
60. Rostow to LBJ, October 6, 1966, NSF Speech File, box 5, LBJL.
61. Bator to LBJ, October 13, 1966, NSF Speech File, box 5, LBJL.
62. I am not arguing that the United States deserves the credit for *Ostpolitik,* only that at this time it was ahead of the Germans on the issue and capable of lending considerable political support to those in Germany who wanted to move in that direction. For the signs of interest in Germany for such a policy, see Roger Morgan, *The United States and West Germany, 1945–1973; A Study in Alliance Politics* (London: Oxford University Press, 1974), 155–58.
63. Ibid., 160–62.

64. Kai Bird, *The Chairman: John J. McCloy, The Making of the American Establishment* (New York: Simon & Schuster, 1992), esp. 590–93.

65. *FRUS 1964–68,* 535.

66. LBJ to McCloy, March 1, 1967, and Memorandum for the Record, "President's Conversation with John J. McCloy," March 2, 1967, NSF, NSC History, TNN, box 50, LBJL.

67. McCloy to LBJ, May 17, 1967, NSF, NSC History, TNN, box 50, LBJL.

68. Memorandum for the President, March 8, 1967, Bator Papers, Chronological File, box 4, LBJL.

69. Memo to the President, February 23, 1967, Bator Papers, box 4, LBJL.

70. Memorandum for the President, April 21, 1967, Bator Papers, Chronological File, box 4, LBJL.

71. McCloy to LBJ, March 22, 1967, NSF, NSC History, TNN, box 50, LBJL.

72. On this point, I am reliant on Helga Haftendorn, *NATO and the Nuclear Revolution: A Crisis of Credibility, 1966–1967* (Oxford: Clarendon Press, 1996), 388–89.

73. Haftendorn, *NATO and the Nuclear Revolution,* 397. Kaplan ends his study by noting that John Leddy's 1968 conclusion that "NATO is in a better state of health than the pessimists predicted a few years ago," may have understated Johnson's achievement. See Lawrence Kaplan, "The US and NATO in the Johnson Years," in *The Johnson Years, Vol. III: LBJ at Home and Abroad,* ed. Robert A. Divine (Lawrence: University Press of Kansas, 1994), 143.

74. Haftendorn, *NATO and the Nuclear Revolution,* 4.

Part III

Dealing with the Collapse of Bretton Woods

Chapter 6

The Search for a New Monetary System: Germany's Balancing Act
Michael Kreile

The search for a new international monetary system was forced upon the major industrial countries when the Bretton Woods system of fixed exchange rates was undermined by an escalating crisis of confidence in the dollar. Efforts to stabilize the system gave rise to a complex game of monetary diplomacy. It took place in the context of an eroding American hegemony and reflected a new correlation of forces between the United States, Western Europe, and Japan.

For Germany, the crisis and the breakdown of the Bretton Woods system created new challenges and opportunities. As a successful trading state, West Germany had thrived under the Pax Americana and the old international economic order. American hegemony was not objectionable as a matter of principle, but it collided with German interests when it became a source of inflation. The transition to flexible exchange rates therefore eliminated a major constraint on German domestic monetary policy. At the same time, the process of international monetary crisis management and International Monetary Fund (IMF) reform put Germany in a situation where it had to achieve a difficult balancing act not only between domestic and international stabilization requirements but also between economic policy priorities and alliance solidarity, with the United States and France making competing claims on solidarity. This explains the variable combination of unilateralism, mediation, and concerted action that characterized German monetary diplomacy during the 1970s.

Turmoil in the World Economy and the Elusive Quest for Institutional Reform

On August 15, 1971, U.S. president Richard Nixon announced his decision to close the "gold window," that is, to suspend the convertibility of dollars held by foreign central banks into gold. He also imposed a 10 percent surcharge on goods imported into the United States and called upon America's trading partners to cooperate in "the necessary reforms to set up an urgently needed new monetary system."[1] The Nixon decision unilaterally terminated the gold dollar standard which had been one of the pillars of the Bretton Woods system of fixed exchange rates. It opened the way to a general realignment of currencies including a devaluation of the dollar, "that ultimate and unmentionable calamity whose consequences are the more dreaded for never being described," as James Tobin wrote in 1964.[2] However, the stabilization of the fixed exchange rate regime achieved with the Smithsonian Agreement of December 1971 was rather short-lived. The spring tides of currency speculation forced the major Western industrial countries to float their currencies against the dollar. This decision made by fourteen industrial countries in March 1973 marked a watershed in the history of international monetary relations.[3]

The collapse of the Bretton Woods system "was one of the most accurately and generally predicted of major economic events."[4] It can be explained as the outcome of three interrelated structural problems, which were exacerbated by discordant government policies in the context of liberalized capital movements: the problem of international liquidity, the problem of confidence in the key reserve currency, and the problem of balance of payments adjustment.[5] With the expansion of international trade and payments and the official price of gold fixed at $35 an ounce, international gold production was not sufficient to cover the rapidly growing liquidity needs of a dynamic world economy. That is why international liquidity was primarily created by the United States running current account deficits, providing foreign central banks with dollar reserves. During the period of postwar reconstruction, when the Western European countries and Japan suffered from a "dollar gap," central banks were eager to accumulate dollar reserves. The dollar was all the more attractive as a reserve currency because the U.S. Treasury guaranteed the convertibility of dollar reserves into gold.

However, when the "dollar gap" turned into a "dollar glut" (due to generous American foreign aid and military expenditure abroad), confidence in the dollar was bound to erode. "As outstanding dollar liabilities held by the rest of the world monetary authorities increased relative to the U.S. monetary gold stock, the likelihood of a run on the 'bank' increased. The probability of all dollar holders being able to convert their dollars into gold at the fixed price declined."[6] This problem became known as the "Triffin dilemma."[7] Under the system of fixed but adjustable parities, an asymmetry of adjustment obligations between deficit and surplus countries developed. Countries running persistent balance of payments deficits were forced to change economic policies or to devalue when they had exhausted their reserves and credit facilities in exchange market interventions. Surplus countries could just accumulate currency reserves without being forced to revalue to correct a fundamental disequilibrium in the balance of payments.

Moreover, devaluation was resisted by deficit countries as it came to be considered a political defeat. A specific asymmetry in adjustment obligations consisted in the "exorbitant privilege" of the United States, as de Gaulle called it, to run deficits without having to take corrective economic policy measures. Unlike other countries, the United States was thus able to finance deficits by printing more of its own currency. This aggravated the confidence problem when the costs of the Vietnam War and President Lyndon Johnson's "Great Society" programs resulted in an expansionary fiscal and monetary policy with negative effects on the balance of payments.

Yet, confidence in the gold dollar standard had already begun to weaken soon after the Bretton Woods system had started to function normally with the introduction of convertibility by the countries of Western Europe at the end of 1958. In fact, American external monetary policy in the 1960s can be read as a series of attempts to prevent a "run on the bank" and the devaluation of the dollar.[8] Economic dollar reserves were increasingly replaced by "political dollar reserves," because the willingness of key central banks to keep or increase their stock of dollar reserves became a function of their countries' political and security dependence on the United States. Under the presidency of Charles de Gaulle, France adopted a policy of systematically exchanging dollar holdings into gold.[9] This policy was aimed at undermining American hegemony in general and at promoting a reform of the international monetary system, reflecting French preferences for a more symmetrical mechanism of adjustment.

The opposite approach was taken by Germany. Starting in 1961, the Federal Republic concluded offset agreements with the United States providing for German arms purchases in the United States, which compensated for the foreign exchange costs of American troops stationed in Germany. Moreover, the Bundesbank, with the famous "Blessing letter" of March 1967, committed itself to supporting the dollar "by refraining from dollar conversions into gold from the United States Treasury."[10] The French reserve policy was a calculated risk and did not jeopardize the whole international monetary system as long as countries like Germany continued to support the dollar.[11] In a way, French policy toward NATO followed a similar pattern.

Given the precarious and politically contentious nature of the gold dollar standard, the ten leading industrial countries (the Group of Ten, or G-10) in 1963 started discussions on a new reserve system, which was supposed to meet the growing liquidity needs of the world economy. The ensuing negotiations, which led to the creation of the Special Drawing Rights (SDRs) in 1968, were characterized by the antagonism between France and the United States. The Federal Republic of Germany tried to act as a mediator. The United States emphasized the risk of insufficient liquidity, whereas France challenged the privilege of the dollar and advocated the creation of a reserve unit linked to gold and "composed in fixed proportions of the currencies of the G-10 countries."[12] Germany favored a strengthening of multilateral surveillance of economic and monetary policies according to agreed-on rules. The six European Community (EC) member countries managed to secure a veto on SDR allocation with the introduction of a qualified majority requirement of 85 percent of IMF voting power.

Although the SDRs were clearly a major conceptual and technical innovation, they failed to stabilize the international monetary system. After the SDRs had been activated in 1969, monetary expansion in the United States "resulted in an explosion of dollar liquidity," which made "the primary task of the SDR in supplying adequate global liquidity . . . very evidently redundant."[13] The French offensive against the dollar via gold purchases had been defeated by the students and workers of France in May 1968. Speculation against the franc led to a G-10 ministerial meeting in Bonn in November 1968, which was marked by a quarrel over who had to change the par value of its currency. De Gaulle refused to devalue as a matter of national pride. The Kiesinger government ruled out deutsche mark (DM) revaluation, a decision hailed by the tabloid *Bild* as a sign that the Germans had become number one in Europe.[14] After de Gaulle had resigned from office, the franc was devalued by 11 percent in August 1969. Following the Bundestag election of September 1969, the new Social Democratic Party–Free Democratic Party coalition government decided to revalue the DM by 9.3 percent.

In 1970–71, a crisis of confidence in the dollar caused massive capital outflows from the United States, which in large part went into Germany. To curb imported inflation, the German government turned to the only available remedy after the proposal of a common float against the dollar had been rejected by the EC and decided to float the DM unilaterally.[15]

The currency crises of the late 1960s and early 1970s did not only originate in the structural defects of the Bretton Woods system; they were also driven and magnified by the large volumes of short-term international capital movements. The expanding international mobility of capital (epitomized in the development of the Euromarkets) made it increasingly difficult for governments and central banks to operate pegged but adjustable exchange rates. "In a world of high capital mobility, defending a parity required unprecedented levels of foreign-exchange-market intervention and international support. Support of this magnitude was something countries hesitated to extend when they doubted the willingness and ability of a government to eliminate the source of the payment imbalances."[16] For large countries like the United States and Japan, it was therefore rational to opt for flexible exchange rates. For the European countries, the alternative to the Bretton Woods exchange rate regime was its reproduction on a regional scale.

International Monetary Fund Reform

The search for a new international monetary system started a few months after the Smithsonian Agreement had brought about a realignment of parities and the widening of permitted margins for exchange rate fluctuations (2.25 percent instead of 1 percent each side of the central rate). Because the gold convertibility of the dollar was not restored, de facto a dollar standard applied. The task of institutional reform was entrusted to the "Committee of Twenty" established by the Board of Governors of the IMF. It first met in September 1972 and delivered its final report together with an Outline of

Reform in June 1974.[17] The committee debates, as summarized by Harold James,

> revolved around the conflict between an American position and a widely held alternative viewpoint that came to be most articulately and forcefully presented by France and its representatives. The United States insisted on the establishment of some automatic mechanism for forcing surplus countries to reduce their surplus positions. The Europeans responded by arguing that the principle of equality in the international system required a provision for the convertibility of dollar reserves into gold or foreign exchange. As epitomized in the phrases "adjustment" (United States) and "asset settlement" (Europe), these positions resulted in a complete deadlock.[18]

By the time the committee published its Outline of Reform without having reached agreement on major issues,[19] international economic conditions had changed radically. The final breakdown of the Bretton Woods system had occurred, and the world was struggling with the consequences of the oil price shock. With oil prices set in dollars, the oil-exporting countries had become increasingly restive about the relative decline of their export revenues due to worldwide inflation and dollar devaluation. The Yom Kippur War and the Arab oil embargo provided the Organization of the Petroleum Exporting Countries (OPEC) with a strategic opportunity. The posted price for Arab light crude was raised from $2.90 in mid-1973 to $11.65 in December 1973.[20] The surge in oil prices shattered one of the pillars of the postwar international economy, the availability of cheap energy. The current account of the major oil-importing countries deteriorated dramatically while OPEC countries reaped record surpluses. The oil price increase fueled worldwide inflation and triggered the recession of 1974–75.

No wonder then that the problem perceptions of policymakers changed as the crises unfolded. Consequently, the international agenda was very much determined by the priorities of crisis management. The problem of the dollar overhang in the composition of international reserves vanished as oil-importing countries had to cope with a dramatic increase in their oil bills. Dollar reserves now served as valuable cushions in the process of adjustment to higher oil prices,[21] and the dollar standard was greatly legitimized by the OPEC action. At the same time, a comprehensive reform of the international monetary system was doomed to failure. The economic repercussions of the oil price shock frustrated the European efforts to move toward Economic and Monetary Union. They also rekindled the forces of protectionism and complicated the Tokyo Round of trade negotiations under the auspices of the General Agreement on Tariffs and Trade (GATT).

At the end of the 1970s, it became evident that the search for a new international monetary system had only yielded piecemeal reforms and limited adjustments to new economic and political realities. Institutional reforms according to ambitious blueprints were not attainable, given the divergent interests of the major actors and the state of turbulence that plagued the world economy. In the end, it was highly personalized summit diplomacy combined with technocratic pragmatism that led to the Jamaica Agreement of January 1976.[22]

The agreement was formalized in the Second Amendment of the IMF Articles of Agreement, which came into force in April 1978. It legalized the practice of floating exchange rates. The proponents of a return to fixed exchange rates obtained the face-saving provision according to which members of the IMF assumed the obligation "to assure orderly exchange arrangements and to promote a stable system of exchange rates." However, the reintroduction of "a widespread system of exchange arrangements based on stable but adjustable par values" was subject to the requirement of an 85 percent majority, which now applied to all important decisions.[23] The United States thus kept its veto power although its share of quotas was reduced to less than 20 percent.

As a compromise between the EC countries and the United States, the official price of gold was abolished and central banks were authorized to trade gold freely at market rates. The Jamaica Agreement ratified the transition to a nonsystem, under which governments and central banks relinquished some of their management functions to financial markets. It was only in the regional framework of the EC that a system of fixed but adjustable exchange rates could be restored.

Germany's Approach to Monetary Crisis Management and IMF Reform

A successful strategy of export expansion was one of the hallmarks of West Germany's economic and social development in the postwar period. Rising trade surpluses and a strong currency symbolized economic success. The Pax Americana provided a congenial international environment for German export expansion, as world trade flourished under the rules set by a liberal hegemonic power. With the gradual decline of American hegemony, the Federal Republic's external monetary policy became increasingly a function of Germany's dependence on the United States for its security. German reliance on American nuclear and conventional protection produced, as Susan Strange put it, "a docility and compliance with American wishes which was the more remarkable as German economic strength continued to grow and to be acknowledged."[24] Various devices designed to shore up the U.S. balance of payments position were dependent on German cooperation. Because the Bundesbank refrained from converting dollars into gold, a commitment laid down in the Blessing letter of 1967, Germany prolonged the viability of the Bretton Woods system. German readiness to cooperate with the United States was, however, limited by the need to establish a delicate balance between loyalty to the United States and EC solidarity. EC solidarity and cohesion in turn rested on Franco-German entente.

At the same time, monetary policy had to meet the requirements of price stability and export competitiveness. Monetary policy played a crucial role in securing export competitiveness, as it kept German inflation rates below those of its trading partners. Yet, the overriding importance attributed to price stability essentially derived from domestic concerns. The memories of two great inflations, voters' expectations, the conviction of policymakers that a functioning market economy requires a stable currency, and the aversion of Bundesbank officials to the spendthrift habits of modern "mass democracy"[25] worked together to establish price stability as a super-goal to which full employment had to be sacrificed, if necessary. However, during the 1950s and 1960s, exchange rate policy was committed to parity maintenance, thus causing a chronic undervaluation of the DM and rising export surpluses. Under the system of fixed exchange rates and free capital movements, parity maintenance was bound to conflict with domestic stabilization. Anti-inflation policy proved to be self-defeating when it induced capital inflows, which aggravated the balance of payments surplus and countered efforts to bring liquidity under control.

Parity changes, however, were bound to hurt the interests of the powerful export sector. According to German policymakers, there was only one remedy to fundamental balance of payments disequilibria: The burden of adjustment had to be shouldered by deficit countries, which had deviated from the path of monetary discipline. Germany, for its part, assumed the task of exporting stability to its partners.[26] This position was advocated with dogmatic zeal and managed to bring about recurrent clashes with Germany's transatlantic and European allies. Parity changes were only resorted to as an ultima ratio—as in 1961 and 1969—when imported inflation gravely imperiled price stability.[27] It can therefore be argued that West Germany's economic policies were mainly shaped by domestic priorities, which allowed for the pursuit of a neomercantilist strategy.

This was dramatically illustrated by the G-10 meeting in Bonn in November 1968 mentioned above. The German government was subject to strong international pressure to revalue the DM, and the Bundesbank strongly recommended such a move. The United States preferred a German revaluation to a French devaluation because the latter might have weakened the British pound. The British government even "threatened the withdrawal of British troops from Germany if there was no action on the exchange rate."[28] De Gaulle ruled out franc devaluation as an absurdity and strongly pushed for DM revaluation.[29] Nevertheless, the Grand Coalition government headed by Chancellor Kurt Kiesinger remained inflexible because DM revaluation was considered to be detrimental to German exports and economic recovery.

In this case, the main cleavage of interests was that between deficit and surplus countries. The notion of a strategic triangle composed of Bonn, Washington, and Paris must therefore be taken with a pinch of salt when applied to international monetary diplomacy. Of course, for Germany the strategic triangle constituted the framework within which foreign policy had to be formulated and conflicting interests reconciled. However, in the field of international monetary diplomacy, Germany acquired considerable leeway in the conduct of its policy and managed to a significant extent to resist the imposition of American or French policy preferences. As the currency crises of 1971 and 1973 demonstrated, Bonn's political stature did not match West Germany's economic weight, but the economic weight offered opportunities for German action that redefined the context in which collective crisis management had to operate. Moreover, the dynamics of the currency crises very much determined the choice of policy instruments.

In the wake of the Nixon decision of August 1971, while the foreign exchange markets were closed, the German government tried to convince the other EC member states to form a floating bloc vis-à-vis the dollar, a proposal that Economics and Finance Minister Karl Schiller had already made in the May 1971 crisis after having floated the DM unilaterally as an emergency measure.[30] This would have warded off the inflow of dollars and the resultant inflationary impulse while, at the same time, leaving the parities as well as the terms of competition within the EC intact. The French government, represented by the secretary general of the presidency, Michel

Jobert, proposed the creation of a common two-tier foreign exchange market. Financial transactions (including those between EC countries) would take place under a floating rate regime, whereas commercial transactions would be governed by the fixed exchange rates that had applied before August 15. This measure would have ruled in speculation and would have preserved the terms of competition between EC economies worldwide. In this context, the floating of the DM vis-à-vis the dollar was criticized by President Georges Pompidou as German support for the U.S. position. The German government rejected the Jobert proposal on the grounds that it would entail enormous bureaucratic controls. The two-tier market would also have led to a DM appreciation against the French franc in the financial sector, which would have predetermined the DM/franc rate in the prospective realignment of currencies.

The Franco-German disagreement obviously precluded a common EC course of action. That is why the European foreign exchange markets reopened on August 23 with three different exchange rate regimes: France with its two-tier market, Germany and Italy with unilateral floating, and the Benelux countries with a common bloc floating at unchanged parities among their currencies. Britain, Switzerland, and the Scandinavian countries had also opted to float. The central banks of the float countries intervened occasionally in the foreign exchange market to limit the appreciation of their currency, a practice for which the term "dirty float" was coined. U.S. Treasury secretary John Connally made a blatant attempt to exploit the rift between France and Germany by offering to lift the import surcharge for Germany in exchange for a clean German float. This obliged Chancellor Willy Brandt to call for a prompt return to fixed exchange rates.[31]

The negotiations leading to the Smithsonian Agreement largely centered on the percentage points by which parities were to be changed in a general realignment among the G-10 countries ("Germany is reluctant to move more than 5 percent above France; Japan wants to move no more than 5 percent above Germany; and Italy, Britain, and some smaller Europeans will not move at all unless France moves.")[32] In this neomercantilist bazaar, France enjoyed a clear tactical advantage as the two-tier foreign exchange market had allowed for a continuous de facto devaluation of the "franc commercial" vis-à-vis the floating currencies. At a meeting between Brandt and Pompidou (upon German request) in early December, the French president accepted a change in the DM/franc cross-rate in line with the German position. In return, he obtained an unofficial mandate to represent the European Community at the Franco-American summit in mid-December. In addition to this symbolic satisfaction, Pompidou extracted from Nixon the concession that the gold parity of the franc would be maintained. The main French concession was that France no longer insisted on the reopening of the "gold window" as a condition for its participation in the realignment. As Rolf Kaiser has argued, a multilateral solution to the 1971 crisis crucially depended on an agreement with the one actor in the G-10 who was prepared to exert maximal obstruction and able to afford doing so.[33]

Domestic Stabilization and the Exchange Rate Regime

The fifteen months following the Smithsonian Agreement were a period of trial for the German monetary authorities. American benign neglect toward the balance of payments, a more general lack of commitment to the new central rates,[34] and the weakness of the British pound triggered new waves of speculation and massive capital inflows into the DM. Disagreement among policymakers over the appropriate reaction to the pound crisis of June 1972 led to Karl Schiller's resignation as minister of economics and finance. The Bundesbank had proposed to require official approval for the sale of fixed-interest securities, a measure that Schiller rejected as an interventionist sin. However, his alternative, namely, a common floating of the EC currencies against the dollar, was unlikely to be adopted without lengthy negotiations. The government followed the Bundesbank's advice, and Schiller's offer to resign was accepted.

His successor, Helmut Schmidt, came close to a clash with the central bank in February 1973, when the Bundesbank Directorate asked the government to be relieved of its obligation to defend the DM/dollar parity. Schmidt opposed floating the DM on the grounds that this would be contrary to German obligations under international law (i.e., the Smithsonian Agreement) and involve conflict with France and the Benelux countries. A collision was avoided due to the blitz mission undertaken by Paul Volcker, the undersecretary for monetary affairs at the U.S. Treasury, who managed to put together—within barely a week—an exchange rate realignment.[35] The success of the Volcker mission crucially depended on both Japanese and European cooperation. According to Volcker's account, the "Europeans all accepted that our approach was more promising than any alternative they had considered. Conceptually, a joint float of European currencies against the dollar was an option, but it would in effect constitute a declaration of monetary independence from the

United States. I felt they doubted they had either the political cohesion or the technical ability to manage it successfully."[36]

Yet, only three weeks later, another wave of speculation against the dollar precipitated the decision that neither the German government nor the other EC countries had wanted to make in February. On March 2, 1973, the German government closed the foreign exchange market and left no doubt that the DM would be floated unilaterally unless the EC countries agreed to a joint float. Six out of nine EC members decided to participate in the joint float, while Britain, Ireland, and Italy stayed outside. Although France had been very keen on British participation, this was ruled out when the chancellor of the exchequer, Anthony Barber, laid down "certain essential conditions for a British participation in the coming float, including unconditional mutual financial support without limits of amount, without guarantees, without specific obligations to repay."[37] For the German monetary authorities, the transition to a regime of generalized floating was a momentous event.[38] It finally enabled the Bundesbank to conduct, once again, an effective stabilization policy. The sealing of the "open external flank" represented a turning point in monetary policy, for it permitted a decoupling of the Federal Republic from the international inflation trend.[39] It should be pointed out that this was the result neither of a political strategy nor of a paradigm change in monetary thinking but rather, as Otmar Emminger put it, was an act of self-defense.[40]

The negotiations on IMF reform in the Committee of Twenty were, at least initially, based on the assumption that the transition to floating was only temporary and that a return to a par value system was both desirable and feasible. According to Emminger's account, by the late autumn of 1973, it became clear that the work of the committee was leading to an impasse. The centerpiece of the reform project, the restoration of stable but adjustable parities, had become a rather remote scenario. Other elements—like the consolidation of the dollar overhang in a substitution account with the IMF, the U.S. proposal for a symmetrical adjustment mechanism, or the French demand for a system of multicurrency intervention—"were from the outset too ambitious and unrealistic."[41] As for the future exchange rate regime, the German position largely coincided with the American one. French insistence on a return to fixed exchange rates was referred to by German officials as a "Maginot doctrine" and attributed to an ideological fixation.[42] Given the polar positions taken by the United States and France, a Franco-American compromise was required to reach agreement on IMF reform. As in 1971, Germany accepted France acting as representative of

European interests. The good personal relationship between the former finance ministers Schmidt and Valéry Giscard d'Estaing clearly facilitated a Franco-German understanding. And the pragmatism of the technocrats in charge of Franco-American negotiations, Jacques de Larosiére and Edwin Yeo, smoothed the way to the Jamaica Agreement.[43]

The Jamaica Agreement was very much the result of a crisis-driven process of adjustment to new economic realities rather than the outcome of a competition between grand designs. In the triangular game of monetary diplomacy between Germany, France, and the United States, a pattern of convergent and conflicting interests put Germany in a position where a clear-cut choice between the two allies had to be and could be avoided. This holds true even if one leaves aside the political requirements stemming from German security dependence on the United States and EC solidarity with France. In contrast to France, Germany in the 1960s supported the de facto dollar standard and thereby maintained the Bretton Woods system. Yet, at the same time, the strength of the DM contributed to undermining it. Both France and Germany wanted to impose some discipline on American fiscal and monetary policy. The United States and France (together with Britain) had a common interest in getting the surplus countries to adjust. When it came to managing currency crises, in 1971 unilateralism carried the day in Washington, Bonn, and Paris. For Germany, however, floating the DM unilaterally was only a second-best solution as long as a concerted EC float was not forthcoming. In 1973, this finally came true. Negotiations on currency realignments were marked by straightforward neomercantilist bargaining as every country tried to protect or improve its export competitiveness. On key issues of international monetary reform, such as the exchange rate regime and the role of gold, Germany was closer to the United States than to France, and in 1975 graciously Germany acceded to the Franco-American compromise. The preference of German policymakers for flexible exchange rates at the global level was essentially determined by the fact that this regime met the requirements of domestic stabilization policy.

Alternatives to Systemic Reform: European Monetary Integration and Trilateral Policy Coordination

The story of Germany's monetary crisis management would be incomplete without taking into account the regional component. In a recent article, Randall Henning has argued "that disturbances in the international system provided strong incentives for European governments to cooperate on exchange rates and monetary matters at numerous critical junctures over the last four decades."[44] The European reactions to American "benign neglect" in the late 1960s, the Nixon shocks, and the economic policies of the Jimmy Carter administration provide substantial evidence in support of this thesis. For Germany, the regional framework of the European Community was of crucial importance, given the regional concentration of West German foreign trade and the pattern of asymmetrical interdependence that characterizes the Federal Republic's economic relations with its European partners. Within the triangle of international monetary diplomacy, the bilateral Franco-German relationship was both privileged and sensitive. It was privileged because the two countries constituted the core of the European Community. It was also highly sensitive and involved considerable friction because Bonn and Paris not only held different views on international monetary reform but also represented opposing camps in the debate on European monetary integration. The debate between "economists" and "monetarists" on the appropriate strategy for reaching Economic and Monetary Union (EMU) reflected the cleavage between surplus and deficit countries and the related views on adjustment obligations.

EMU was put on the community agenda by the Hague summit at the end of 1969, and it was elaborated in the Werner Report of 1970. France and Belgium, the "monetarists" in the Werner group, gave priority to monetary integration and advocated narrower fluctuation margins for exchange rates as well as the pooling of currency reserves. This would then lead to the coordination of national economic policies. The "economists"—that is, Germany, Italy, and the Netherlands—argued that only a gradual harmonization of national economic policies would prepare the ground for monetary integration. France was primarily interested in a common system of credit facilities. Germany, however, anticipated the risk of having either to provide generous currency loans without adequate conditionality or to accept higher inflation. The Werner Report reconciled the two positions by proposing the parallel and gradual pursuit of both economic policy coordination and unification of monetary policy. According to the report, by 1980, EMU was to be completed with a European system of central banks taking over responsibility for monetary policy.[45] However, in March 1971, the Council of Ministers only managed to reach agreement on some measures to be implemented in the first stage of a projected three-stage process, such as the narrowing of intra-European fluctuation margins and better consultations on economic policy.

The Search for a New Monetary System 163

International economic conditions were not propitious for European monetary unification. The first stage of EMU fell victim to the dollar crisis of the spring of 1971. The joint float proposed by Germany was not accepted by the EC Council. As we have seen above, in August 1971 the EC countries were divided over how to react to the Nixon decisions. It was only after the Smithsonian Agreement that they tried to achieve some damage control. Under the agreement, the exchange rate fluctuation margins against the dollar had been widened from ±1 to ±2.25 percent, which allowed for intra-EC fluctuations of up to ±4.5 percent. This was considered an excessive range, and the EC countries agreed to narrow the margins of their bilateral rates to ±2.25 percent. This arrangement, the "snake in the tunnel," came into force in April 1972 and included the six EC member countries, plus Britain, Denmark, and Ireland as future members.[46] The central banks of the snake members were bound by rules for joint intervention and granted each other very-short-term credit facilities for that purpose.

The snake soon became an exercise in variable membership. Britain left it in June 1972, Italy decided to float the lira in February 1973, and the floating bloc formed in March 1973 by six European currencies against the dollar lost France in January 1974. The franc returned to the snake in July 1975 but withdrew again in March 1976.[47] With Norway and Sweden as associate members and Austria pegging the schilling informally to the DM, the snake survived as a DM zone. "It was rather ironical . . . that the core countries of the 'economist' group had chosen to remain in the regional exchange rate system, while France, the leader of the 'monetarists,' had been forced to leave."[48] For weak-currency countries, membership in the snake was simply too burdensome in terms of reserves to be spent in the defense of parities and too much of a constraint on domestic economic policies. The differential impact of the oil crisis on the European economies and the different responses by national governments excluded the convergence of economic policies that progress toward EMU required. Flexible exchange rates promised more autonomy in fiscal and monetary policy, but in cases like Britain and Italy also contributed to accelerating inflation.

The Franco-German proposal to create a European Monetary System (EMS) submitted to the European Council in Bremen in July 1978 therefore "surprised the world (and the Bundesbank)."[49] In fact, Schmidt and Giscard d'Estaing had never ceased to believe in the virtue of exchange rate stability. By 1978, they felt that the time was ripe for a new European initiative. Without going into a discussion of Schmidt's motives,[50] it can be stated with a reasonable degree of certainty that he was convinced of the need to isolate

Europe from the disorder in foreign exchange markets. He clearly perceived the unchecked decline of the dollar as a manifestation of political irresponsibility on the part of the Carter administration. And he was eager "to dampen DM appreciation by helping weak-currency countries impose macroeconomic discipline rather than either devalue or impose trade restrictions."[51] The establishment of a zone of exchange rate stability, which included Germany's most important trade partners, was thus expected to protect German export markets. French participation in the EMS initiative was made possible by the defeat of the French left in the parliamentary elections of March 1978. A victory of the Socialist-Communist alliance would hardly have favored Franco-German leadership in European monetary integration. Remarkably enough, in spite of a good deal of skepticism in the U.S. Treasury, the Carter administration early on took up a supportive stance on the EMS project and thereby distanced itself from British opposition.[52] The reproduction of the Bretton Woods system on a regional scale with some significant alterations[53] turned out to be the most durable and successful institutional reform that emerged from the turbulence of the 1970s.

In the absence of systemic reform, trilateral policy coordination was invented as a strategy for facilitating balance of payments adjustment between the major industrial countries. The theoretical case for policy coordination looks convincing: Under conditions of economic interdependence, coordinated fiscal and monetary policies were likely to produce better results than autonomous action by national governments and central banks. However, the first attempt at trilateral policy coordination, the "locomotive" experience of 1978, left a bitter taste in Germany as it became associated with the subsequent steep rise in public debt and the traumatic current account deficits of 1979–81.

In spite of the first oil price shock and a significant appreciation of the DM, up to 1978, the German balance of payments showed consistent trade and current account surpluses. Soon after the Carter administration had entered office, it began to press the German and Japanese governments for more expansionary fiscal policies. Faced with rising trade deficits and an inflation differential that weakened the dollar against the DM and the yen, the U.S. government called upon its allies to assume their international economic responsibilities and to act as locomotives for the world economy. German resistance to reflationary measures was overcome at the Bonn summit of the Group of Seven in July 1978, where the U.S. position was supported by EC countries, the Organization for Economic Cooperation and

Development, and the IMF. Foreign pressure succeeded as it shifted the domestic balance of forces in Germany in favor of the Social Democratic Party's labor wing, which advocated demand expansion by the state to counter rising unemployment. Even the Bundesbank was prepared to accept a higher public deficit.[54] The government package providing for tax relief and social policy measures amounted to a fiscal stimulus of about 1 percent of gross national product. The Japanese government also committed itself to a reflationary program. The Carter administration pledged to reduce U.S. energy imports. The summit also paved the way for a successful conclusion of the Tokyo Round of the GATT.

However, the United States refused to commit itself to exchange market interventions in support of the dollar.[55] There is no doubt that "the Bonn accords represent a rare and perhaps even unique example of international coordination of economic policies."[56] But in Germany—and in Japan—they acquired a negative image as they were overshadowed by the effects of the second oil price explosion. By the mid-1980s, the large-scale balance of payments disequilibria resulting from Reaganomics and supply-side economics German-style triggered yet another dispute over adjustment responsibilities and the purpose of international policy coordination.

Conclusion

The "locomotive" experiment in trilateral policy coordination was enacted by three key players—the United States, Germany, and Japan—which owed their roles to the size of their economies and to the distribution of deficit and surplus positions. In the episodes of monetary diplomacy discussed in this chapter, the constellation of actors was different. From Germany's point of view, both the United States and France were indispensable partners across the dimensions of security, trade, and money. Japan mattered as a competitor, but it was clearly of secondary importance. So was Britain, because of its reluctance to play the European card. The role of France in monetary diplomacy is particularly intriguing, to the extent that France did not act from a position of economic strength but derived its stature from acting as America's chief antagonist on international monetary reform. Germany, conversely, was philosophically less inclined to challenge American hegemony, but in fact it did so as a result of its virtuous domestic economic policy.

Looking back at Germany's international monetary policy during the years 1968–79, one finds a wide range of behavior: confrontation with partners calling for DM revaluation, unilateral floating of the DM, acquiescence in Franco-American bilateralism, joint floating of EC currencies, and Franco-German leadership in European monetary integration. Policy choices were often short-term reactions to crises and hardly inspired by a consistent strategy. Yet, at the risk of reductionism, it can be argued that there was one rationale guiding German policymakers, namely, the primacy of price stability coupled with a neomercantilist export strategy. They had no ambition to reshape the international monetary system according to some well-designed blueprint and were satisfied to live with the post-Jamaica system combining flexible exchange rates with a dollar standard. At the regional level, Franco-German cooperation created an architecture for monetary integration, in which the DM assumed the key currency role, and in which the Bundesbank imposed both the constraints and benefits of monetary stability on partner countries.

Notes

1. Text of President Nixon's television address, quoted from Rolf Kaiser, "Die Interdependenz politischer und ökonomischer Interessen in der Weltwährungskrise 1971" (Ph.D. diss., University of Tübingen, 1976), 260–66; the quotation here is on 264.

2. Ibid., 88.

3. Barry Eichengreen, *Globalizing Capital: A History of the International Monetary System* (Princeton, N.J.: Princeton University Press, 1996), 136.

4. Peter M. Garber, "The Collapse of the Bretton Woods Fixed Exchange Rate System," in *A Retrospective on the Bretton Woods System: Lessons for International Monetary Reform,* ed. Michael D. Bordo and Barry Eichengreen (Chicago: University of Chicago Press, 1993), 461.

5. See Michael D. Bordo, "The Bretton Woods International Monetary System: A Historical Overview," in *Retrospective on the Bretton Woods System,* ed. Bordo and Eichengreen, n. 4, 50–73.

6. Ibid., 51.

7. Robert Triffin, *Gold and the Dollar Crisis: Yesterday and Tomorrow,* Essays in International Finance 132 (Princeton, N.J.: Department of Economics, Princeton University, 1978); Eichengreen, *Globalizing Capital,* 116.

8. See, e.g., Uwe Andersen, *Das internationale Währungssystem zwischen nationaler Souveränität und supranationaler Integration* (Berlin: Duncker & Humblot, 1977), 272–96; and Harold James, *International Monetary Cooperation since Bretton Woods* (Oxford: Oxford University Press, 1996), 159–65.

9. See Garber, "Collapse," 465.

10. The Bundesbank pledge was part of a trilateral package deal between the United States, Britain, and the Federal Republic regarding the financing of the foreign exchange costs incurred by the United States and the United Kingdom by stationing troops in Germany. On March 30, 1967, the president of the Bundesbank, Karl Blessing, wrote to Federal Reserve chairman Martin a letter stating, "You are, of course, well aware of the fact that the Bundesbank over the past few years has not converted any of the dollars accruing out of German foreign exchange surpluses into gold from the United States Treasury. . . . By refraining from dollar conversions into gold from the United States Treasury, the Bundesbank has intended to contribute to international monetary cooperation and to avoid any disturbing effects on the foreign exchange and gold markets. You may be assured that the Bundesbank intends to continue this policy and to play its full part in contributing to international monetary cooperation." I am indebted to Helga Haftendorn for making a copy of this letter and other relevant materials available to me. Blessing to Martin, March 30, 1967, National Security Files, Trilateral Negotiations, box 50, Lyndon Baines Johnson Library. In a memorandum of March 8, 1967, Francis M. Bator, deputy special assistant to the president for national security affairs, characterized the "Bundesbank agreement to a public pledge not to convert dollars into gold" as "a major breakthrough." "In effect it will put the Germans on a dollar standard." Ibid. See also Elke Thiel, *Dollar-Dominanz, Lastenteilung und Amerikanische Truppenpräsenz in Europa* (Baden-Baden: Nomos, 1979), 72–78.

11. Andersen, *Das internationale Währungssystem zwischen nationaler Souveränität*, 274–75. See also Jonathan Kirshner, *Currency and Coercion: The Political Economy of International Monetary Power* (Princeton, N.J.: Princeton University Press, 1995), 192–203.

12. James, *International Monetary Cooperation,* 170; see also Michael D. Bordo, Dominique Simard, and Eugene White, *France and the Bretton Woods International Monetary System: 1960 to 1968,* NBER Working Paper 4642 (Cambridge, Mass.: National Bureau of Economic Research, 1994).

13. James, *International Monetary Cooperation,* 173.

14. Otmar Emminger, *D-Mark, Dollar, Währungskrisen* (Stuttgart: Deutsche Verlags-Anstalt, 1986), 148.

15. James, *International Monetary Cooperation,* 214–16.

16. Eichengreen, *Globalizing Capital,* 137.

17. Committee on Reform of the International Monetary System and Related Issues (Committee of Twenty), *International Monetary Reform:. Documents of the Committee of Twenty* (Washington, D.C.: International Monetary Fund, 1974).

18. James, *International Monetary Cooperation,* 246–47.

19. See Brian Tew, *The Evolution of the International Monetary System 1945–88,* 4th ed. (London: Hutchinson, 1988), 170–71.

20. See Daniel Yergin, *Der Preis: Die Jagd nach Öl, Geld und Macht* (Frankfurt: Fischer, 1993), 763.

21. Tew, *Evolution of the International Monetary System,* 176.

22. James, *International Monetary Cooperation,* 265–77.

23. Ibid., 271–72.

24. Susan Strange, *International Monetary Relations,* vol. 2 of *International Economic Relations of the Western World 1959–1971,* ed. Andrew Shonfield (London: Oxford University Press, 1976), 46–47. See also Michael Kreile, "West Germany: The Dy-

namics of Expansion," in *Between Power and Plenty: Foreign Economic Policies of Advanced Industrial States,* ed. Peter J. Katzenstein (Madison: University of Wisconsin Press, 1978), 195–97.

25. Emminger, *D-Mark,* 25; Manfred G. Schmidt, "West Germany: the Policy of the Middle Way," *Journal of Public Policy* 7 (1987): 148–54.

26. William P. Wadbrook, *West German Balance-of-Payments Policy* (New York: Praeger, 1972), 251.

27. Kreile, "West Germany," 213–16.

28. James, *International Monetary Cooperation,* 195.

29. See Wolfram F. Hanrieder, *Germany, America, Europe: Forty Years of German Foreign Policy* (New Haven, Conn.: Yale University Press, 1989), 269.

30. The discussion of the 1971 crises is mainly based on Kaiser, "Die Interdependenz politischer," n. 1.

31. Ibid., 171–72.

32. C. Fred Bergsten, "The New Economics and U.S. Foreign Policy," *Foreign Affairs* 50 (1971–72): 199–222, quoted in Kaiser, "Die Interdependenz politischer," 183.

33. Kaiser, "Die Interdependenz politischer," 199.

34. Paul A. Volcker and Toyoo Gyohten, *Changing Fortunes: The World's Money and the Threat to American Leadership* (New York: Times Books, 1992), 103.

35. See Emminger, *D-Mark,* 217–24, 232–39; Volcker and Gyohten, *Changing Fortunes,* 106–11.

36. Volcker and Gyohten, *Changing Fortunes,* 110.

37. Emminger, *D-Mark,* 247.

38. Karl Otto Pöhl, "International Monetary Policy: A Personal View," in *Russian Reform/International Money,* ed. Yegor Gaidar and Karl Otto Pöhl (Cambridge, Mass.: MIT Press, 1995), 69.

39. Otmar Emminger, "Deutsche Geld- und Währungspolitik im Spannungsfeld zwischen innerem und äußerem Gleichgewicht (1948–1975)," in *Wirtschaft und Währung in Deutschland 1876–1975,* ed. Deutsche Bundesbank (Frankfurt: Fritz Knapp Verlag, 1976), 487.

40. Emminger, *D-Mark,* 251.

41. Ibid., 294 (my translation).

42. Ibid., 296, 301.

43. Ibid., 296–301; James, *International Monetary Cooperation,* 267–70.

44. C. Randall Henning, "Systemic Conflict and Regional Monetary Integration: The Case of Europe," *International Organization* 52 (1998): 538.

45. Michael Kreile, "Das Europäische Währungssystem: Inflationsgemeinschaft oder DM-Imperialismus?" in *Eurosozialismus,* ed. Gerhard Kiersch and Reimund Seidelmann (Cologne: Europäische Verlagsanstalt, 1979), 51–53.

46. The three countries joined the snake on May 1.

47. See the chronology of the snake in Eichengreen, *Globalizing Capital,* 156.

48. Loukas Tsoukalis, *The New European Economy: The Politics and Economics of Integration,* 2nd rev. ed. (Oxford: Oxford University Press, 1993), 181.

49. Pöhl, "International Monetary Policy," 84. See also Peter Ludlow, *The Making of the European Monetary System* (London: Butterworth Scientific, 1982), 95.

50. See Andrew Moravcsik, *The Choice for Europe: Social Purpose and State Power From Messina to Maastricht* (Ithaca, N.Y.: Cornell University Press, 1998), 238–59.

51. Ibid., 253; Emminger, *D-Mark,* 364.

52. Ludlow, *Making of the European Monetary System,* 117–22.
53. See Emminger, *D-Mark,* 369; Eichengreen, *Globalizing Capital,* 160–63.
54. Robert D. Putnam and Nicholas Bayne, *Hanging Together: Cooperation and Conflict in the Seven-Power Summits,* rev. and enlarged ed. (Cambridge, Mass.: Harvard University Press, 1987), 73–92.
55. See Helga Haftendorn, *Sicherheit und Stabilität, Außenbeziehungen der Bundesrepublik Deutschland zwischen Ölkrise und NATO-Doppelbeschluß* (Munich: Deutscher Taschenbuch Verlag, 1986), 72–78.
56. Putnam and Bayne, *Hanging Together,* 89.

Chapter 7

France, European Monetary Cooperation, and the International Monetary System Crisis, 1968–1973

Eric Bussière

The restoration of an international monetary order is certainly one of the fields in which the notion of the "strategic triangle" is particularly valuable to explain French attitudes and decisions at the end of the 1960s and the beginning of the 1970s. During these years, the international monetary system moved from the Bretton Woods model, characterized by the central position of the dollar, to a bipolarized or tripolarized model with the emergence of new reserve currencies. At that time, the pound sterling no longer played its previous international role and was, furthermore, not taken into account by the French authorities as a crucial element of the debate. Up to 1967, British monetary policy was considered by the French government to be closely connected to American preferences. After the devaluation of sterling in October 1967, as one of the "weak" currencies of the international monetary system, sterling and the British monetary authorities were not able to influence the system and its dynamic anymore.

The emergence of the deutsche mark (DM) as a major international currency was consolidated, from the French point of view, by the monetary crisis that affected the franc as a consequence of the crisis of May 1968. From fall 1968 onward, the DM benefited from the weakness of the dollar; in consequence, the rise of the DM created strong pressure on the other European currencies. At the same time, the ability of the French government to exert political pressure on the German government and German monetary authorities was less important than at the beginning of the 1960s; the age of de Gaulle was over even before Georges Pompidou was elected as the French president in June 1969. This new ability of the Germans to "just say no" was revealed in November 1968, when the German government resisted strong French and American pressure to revalue the DM.

What were the challenges for French international monetary policy between 1968 and 1973? One can identify three main objectives during this period. The main one was certainly to establish and maintain a system that preserved monetary stability, especially the stability of exchange rates that provided for a deep economic integration in the European and international economies. A consequence of this aim was the preference for a neutral monetary system that avoided the domination of one single national currency for economic and political reasons, which were strongly linked. Thus, French monetary authorities focused on the dollar during the 1960s, and on the dollar and the DM after 1968.

The second objective was European monetary cooperation. This cooperation was essentially seen during this period as a way to preserve stability, but from differing points of view. During the 1960s, European cooperation was essentially considered by the French government as a way to counterbalance American leadership in the international monetary system, and to promote a reform of the system according to French interests. After the monetary crisis in 1968, a second aim for European cooperation was considered: to set up a specific European monetary fund to support European countries facing serious monetary difficulties. After 1971, European monetary cooperation became a way to create a space of regional monetary stability to counterbalance the negative effects of floating exchange rates. But from this time onward, the debate began to change substantially, because monetary integration, in lieu of cooperation, became a feasible option.

The third objective was to promote national aims. During the 1960s, those were mainly modernization of the French economy and attempts to create a political equilibrium between France, Europe, and the United States. The years after 1968 were shaped by an accelerated economic modernization (by a strong rate of national investment), but also by the fear of new social challenges, which implied a sufficient autonomy of national economic and social policy. But this autonomy had consequences in the monetary field.

The prevalent element in the international context between 1968 and 1973 was the debate about flexibility and the advent of floating rates. Analyzing this debate is useful for elucidating the French government's policy toward Europe and the United States during these years in general, and especially between 1971 and 1973. At that time, the choice for France was less between fixed or floating exchange rates than between a peg to the dollar or to the DM. The French preference for European solidarity was evident, but it had to be balanced with the loss of economic autonomy that this choice entailed. In January 1974, the French defection from the "European currency snake" (see below for a discussion of the "snake") showed that the French authorities were ready for European monetary cooperation but not yet for monetary integration. However, both options were discussed, and momentous decisions in this matter were made after 1982.

Who shaped monetary policy in France during this period? One of the distinctive national features in this field was the strong dependence of the French central bank, the Banque de France, on the government. One consequence of this dependence was the polarization of decisionmaking among the French Finance Ministry and the Elysée Palace, as was shown by many recent publications.[1] President Pompidou and his finance minister, Valéry Giscard d'Estaing, paid strong attention to international monetary policy both for its economic implications and its political consequences. The president and the finance minister were guided and advised by high-ranking civil servants, such as the director of the Treasury and by the governor or vice governor in charge of international monetary policy of the Banque de France, who represented France in the European Monetary Committee and in the committee of governors of central banks of the European Community (EC).

France and European Monetary Solidarity after May 1968: European Consolidation and the National Interest

The Hague European summit meeting in December 1969 is generally described as a new start for European monetary cooperation on the initiative of President Pompidou, followed by the establishment (in March of 1970) of an ad hoc group under the chairmanship of Pierre Werner to elaborate a plan for an economic and monetary union. At that time, the devaluation of the French franc in August and the revaluation of the DM in October had put an end to the immediate consequences of the French crisis of May 1968. In fact, the first attempt of French authorities to establish a new basis for European monetary cooperation took place at the very beginning of September 1968, just between the speculative crisis against the franc in May and June and the second wave of massive speculative outflows of capital in November. What were the aims and the results of this attempt?

The French initiative was introduced at the Monetary Committee session on September 4, 1968, by René Larre, director of the Treasury, the most important civil servant of the Finance Ministry. Larre's proposal was to bolster monetary solidarity between members of the EC in the field of exchange reserves; he justified his proposal by the strong interdependence between the EC economies.[2] These ideas were clearly connected with proposals from the vice president of the EC Commission, Raymond Barre, in his two memoranda of February 1968 and February 1969. In this second memorandum, Barre clearly linked the need for better monetary cooperation with the consolidation and preservation of the common market, and he repeated this argument at the EC finance ministers' conference of April 1969, declaring that, if the members rejected the French monetary proposal, they should not have launched the customs union of the six on July 1, 1968.[3] The second justification of Larre's proposal was the growing size of the speculative flows with which the EC countries were confronted, and the inadequacy of the usual instruments of credit used by central banks as swaps or drawings from the International Monetary Fund; here again, the convergence with the Barre memorandum of February was very strong.[4]

Larre's arguments were developed further after the crisis of November by Daniel Deguen, Larre's successor, through strong criticism of Europe's feeble cooperation toward France's difficulties in October and November.[5] At the end of 1968, the French position on European monetary solidarity was clear: France wanted the creation of new instruments of monetary solidarity among the Europeans; these instruments had to be sufficient to prevent speculative attacks; and, because they were the consequence of economic integration, France did not propose any counterpart to their creation, especially in the field of economic coordination. This strategy was also the position of the Bank of France. In June 1969, when the creation of a short-term facility—that is, drawing rights—between European central banks was under discussion, Governor Olivier Wormser supported the unconditional character of this facility, as had been the case during recent years with the American and the British central banks.[6]

The reception of the French proposals was not very enthusiastic among EC countries, especially by Germany and the Netherlands. In the Monetary Committee discussions about the crisis of November 1968, they argued that this crisis was more due to the divergence between national economic policies—especially to the French policy of expansion following the political crisis of May—than to external causes. As a result, they proposed better coordination of economic policies as a more effective measure to prevent speculative attacks than any short- or medium-term facilities. If the creation of such facilities were decided, they could only contribute to assuaging the effects of cyclical lags between European economies, not to counterbalancing the effects of major crises such as the one of May 1968. For Wormser's colleagues, efficient procedures of economic coordination had to precede the establishment of short- or medium-term facilities, and the number of these facilities had to be moderate; this point of view was opposed to the French position.[7]

The isolation of the French government concerning these points was only progressively reduced. Debates in the Monetary Committee were unfavorable for the French delegation until the spring of 1969, and the report presented by the president of the Monetary Committee, Émile van Lennep, to the ministers of finance in April 1969 was still very restrictive; the short-term facility was dependent on the decision of the governors who were skeptical about it, and the medium-term facility hinged on the vote of national parliaments. The advice that the Committee of Governors transmitted to the president of the EC Commission in July 1969 was also quite restrictive with regard to the short-term facility. Such a facility implied a strong coordination of national policies and their overall amount.[8]

The crises of November 1968 and May 1969 contributed to the end of the deadlock. Though French policy was criticized in November, the Germans faced strong opposition from all their partners in May 1969 because of their refusal to revalue the mark. At the session of the Monetary Committee in May, the president of the Bundesbank, Otmar Emminger, had to deplore this attitude himself. All the members of the Monetary Committee were asking for better cooperation in the spring of 1969.[9] This context was an opportunity for the Commission to promote its project of monetary integration; in February 1969, the second Barre plan was supported by Luxembourg and Belgium, and it was a compromise between the French and the German points of view.

In the summer of 1969, the political change in Paris and the election of Pompidou as president contributed to a better climate for cooperation. In July, just before the French devaluation, the finance ministers decided on a parallel process: Both aspects would be implemented. Monetary cooperation, through the creation of short- and medium-term facilities, and the coordination of economic policies advanced together. The devaluation of the franc in August and the revaluation of the DM in October contributed to creating conditions that permitted the decisions of the Hague summit in the monetary field in December 1969.[10]

What were the core tenets of the French evaluation of monetary cooperation at the beginning of 1970, that is to say, just a few weeks before the Werner committee was created? The analyses of the Finance Ministry's experts and of President Pompidou were very similar. As for the former, two notes from the director of the Treasury to the finance minister, of October 1969 and of January 1970, address the issue. On January 23, 1970, Larre recognized that the Hague conference had positive consequences for the work of the experts, especially the governors. But the result of their work was still under the requirements of a real European monetary area that needed much bigger means, especially if one wanted to narrow margins as in the Barre project. This objective also included some constraints in the field of economic coordination that Larre was not yet ready to accept. In his note of October 1969, he wrote: "Considering the weight of the Federal Republic in the EEC, France should be obliged to follow the evolution of German prices and wages—in nominal value—or be submitted to the domination of German products taken to their extreme consequences, including the elimination of enterprises that could not succeed in containing their costs within the German limits."[11]

If this solution was necessary to contain the inflationist tendencies of trade unions and of employers, Larre questioned the willingness of his fellow citizens to accept the stability of prices and wages, and he shunned the risks of social and political destabilization that such a policy implied. He also refused the risk of a relative decline of French industry. His point of view was very close to that of President Pompidou, who said before the Hague conference that "we have to be ready to accept and propose only that which can be achieved rapidly, that is, no commitment in the long term but a medium-term cooperation with prudent objectives."[12]

France, European Monetary Cooperation, and the Problem of Flexibility, 1970–1971

During 1970, the Werner group, in charge of the development of a plan for a European economic and monetary union, was the more visible place of the debate among Europeans about monetary affairs. In addition, one needs to take into consideration the debates among the members of the Monetary Committee and of the Committee of Governors. These three forums were closely connected through personal links; Bernard Clappier, president of the Monetary Committee, and Baron Hubert Ansiaux, president of the Committee of Governors were members of the Werner group. But there were also very narrow connections between the object of their debates. The Werner group was in charge of the design of a long-term project, while the two committees had to assess the two major problems that were going to determine the environment of the first step of monetary union, the problem of flexibility and the financial cost of cooperation.

The debate about flexibility became one of the crucial points of discussion concerning the reform of the international monetary system from 1970. This point was strongly linked with the question of margins reduction between European currencies, which was considered an intermediate step toward fixing exchange rates and, eventually, toward monetary union. Such a margins reduction could be absolute if the rules inside the international monetary system were not changed; or if the system decided to widen margins generally, the Europeans could choose not to move. Confronted with the American pressure for flexibility, the Europeans emerged divided. In fact, the real question was the possibility of a common European attitude in case the United States ended convertibility of the dollar into gold.

The French position was firmly epitomized by Governor Wormser: absolute opposition to flexibility in the international monetary system. In his opinion, it was clear that a partial flexibility was only a step toward floating exchange rates, which he repudiated. On May 11, 1970, he informed the Committee of Governors that his position had become that of the French government. He was all the firmer in his attitude because he knew that some of his European partners were less determined. If the Belgians and the Dutch were close to the French position, the Italians were favorable to monetary flexibility and the German position, which adapted Emminger's views, favoring a more flexible international monetary system as a way toward European monetary individualization.[13]

The conflict became more serious at the end of the summer of 1970. The Monetary Committee had a discussion on the subject on September 3 to prepare the conference of finance ministers that was to be held in Luxembourg on September 9 and 10. Once more, the Italians, represented by Rinaldo Ossola, supported flexibility. Emminger advocated flexibility as a way for the Europeans to protect themselves from the negative effects of American monetary policy, and as a way for a European *Individualisierung*. Cécil de Strycker of the National Bank of Belgium contested this point of view very strongly, feeling that European monetary integration, as presented by Emminger and Ossola, was only a pretext to promote flexibility. On behalf of France, Larre stuck with his basic opposition to flexibility. He could accept wider margins between European currencies and others only if real cooperation among the six could be established. Clappier, president of the Monetary Committee, ended the debate without a clear conclusion to gain time and delay the debate about flexibility at the international level to permit the organization of cooperation among the six. But Clappier's point of view was overly optimistic, as was Emminger's, who expected a delay of about two years before the achievement of the reform of the international monetary institutions. They obviously overestimated the time at their disposal.[14]

A few days after this session, Larre drew the main conclusion from the debate on flexibility for the finance minister. His advice was to link a positive French attitude on flexibility at the international level with the achievement of cooperation within Europe.[15]

For the French authorities, the discussions about the medium-term facility were a test concerning the willingness of the six to institute real monetary solidarity in the EC. The main debate among the Europeans focused on the amount to mobilize. The French Ministry of Finance wanted about $2.5 billion to $3 billion, whereas the German government proposed only $1 billion or $2 billion. There were also diverging opinions with regard to the rate of these facilities; the French representatives proposed a low rate, lower than the international monetary system facilities to make the use of European facilities attractive. This position was clearly upheld by the director of the Treasury in February 1970, when he contended that a stronger monetary cooperation would be an effective measure for the Europeans to show their solidarity and to reinforce their means of defense in a context of growing uncertainty about the international monetary system.

The debate between ministers at the Paris conference of February 23 and 24, 1970, showed the strong opposition between Karl Schiller and Valéry Giscard d'Estaing. The German minister regarded a medium-term facility as a secondary step of his plan for European monetary cooperation; the first step should be the liberalization of monetary and financial markets in Europe and the harmonization of economic policies. During the second "probationary" step, the convergence of national economic performances had to be achieved, so that the establishment of the medium-term facility would be the consequence of the convergence. For the French delegation, the monetary solidarity was a necessary condition to economic coordination, and Giscard d'Estaing told his colleagues that the monetary approach would be "the Ariadne's clew of economic integration."[16] The French delegation received the support of Raymond Barre, the vice president of the Commission in charge of economic and monetary affairs. For the Commission, the medium-term facility was to be established as a first step with the beginning of liberalization of money markets; the convergence of economic policies had to take place during a second step. At the Paris conference, Barre's point of view was strongly opposed by Schiller and Johannes Witteveen, of the Dutch delegation.

The debate about the means of solidarity continued during the following months within the Monetary Committee. The French delegation, supported by the Belgians and the Commission's representatives, advocated relatively unrestrictive conditions for the medium-term facility; they based their arguments on the failure of the short-term facility due to the restrictive conditions imposed by the governors.[17]

The attitude of President Pompidou toward the Werner plan in the fall of 1970 was in line with his position during the preparation of the Hague conference, but also in the same vein as the debates of 1970 about cooperation and flexibility. In Luxembourg, in June 1970, the European Council accepted the general purpose of a first step toward monetary union as being the reduction of margins between the six and the medium-term facility. In October, the final report was more precise regarding the institutions of the proposed economic and monetary union, especially concerning the second step in creating the union: the emergence of specific responsibilities for the union in the field of economic policies and for the Committee of Governors in the field of monetary policies.

Pompidou strongly opposed this evolution, so that the decisions made by the six in February and March 1971 fell short of the hopes of the supporters of monetary union.[18] In fact, the French opposition to the institutional aspects of the Werner plan during the winter of 1970–71 had not only a political origin but was also the result of a balancing of interests between the advantages of monetary cooperation and the constraints represented by a progressive loss of autonomy in economic policies. In the fall of 1970, as one year earlier, it was clear that the most important partners of France in the EC, especially Germany and Holland, were not ready to accept a strong and costly monetary cooperation. The consequences of this attitude were amplified in the context of uncertainty caused by the debates about flexibility. President Pompidou had to take into account the risk of a reform of the international monetary system with the introduction of partial flexibility and possibly the advent of floating exchange rates. In that case, the need for strong European cooperation would be greater than the risk of a loss of autonomy of national economic policies.

President Pompidou expressed his doubts concerning the attitudes of France's partners to Michel Jobert, general secretary of the presidential staff, in December 1970 contending that he would accept European monetary integration "the day when European countries will be able to ask the United States to take back their dollars and return gold in exchange."[19] Thus, for Pompidou, the decision to reduce the margins made on March 21, 1971, was a test of the willingness of France's partners to cooperate, and it also meant to create a viable link between them in order to resist American pressure toward flexibility. In case of success, further steps toward European monetary union would have been possible, but only under this condition.

Monetary Cooperation and the European Snake

The crisis of the international monetary system initiated by the floating of the DM in May 1971 and the Nixon shock in August confirmed the French position with regard to the ways to establish European monetary cooperation. For the French authorities, the establishment of the snake would be a way to preserve stability inside the EC and a way to force the United States to accept a reform of the international monetary system that excluded large flexibility or even floating currencies. President Pompidou could play a major role as a mediator between the Europeans and the Americans at the Azores conference in December because of the relative isolation of the Germans in Europe on the issue of flexibility.

The German decision of May 1971, and the proposal by Schiller for a collective floating of European currencies vis-à-vis the dollar, were rejected firmly by the French authorities. Pompidou as well as Giscard d'Estaing and Wormser completely agreed on this point. The Germans were also strongly criticized inside the Monetary Committee by Claude Pierre-Brossollette with the support of the other non-German members, even if their remarks were more moderate. All of them advocated stronger controls against hot money in Germany.[20] The French resistance against floating proved to be effective. When Pompidou and German chancellor Willy Brandt met in Germany on July 5, Pompidou stipulated a widening of the margins in the international monetary system and the return to fixed rates.[21] A few days later, on July 11, Governor Karl Klasen admitted at the meeting of governors that larger margins could help the return of the DM to fixed rates. The same day he announced new steps in Germany to resist capital inflows. Discussions at the Monetary Committee session on July 20 consolidated the evolution toward a compromise consisting of limited and controlled flexibility inside the international monetary system and return of the DM to fixed rates.[22]

The American decisions of mid-August 1971—including temporary wage and price controls, an import surcharge of 10 percent, and a suspension of the convertibility of the dollar into gold—did not really change the nature of the debate among the Europeans. If the proposition of a concerted floating of European currencies vis-à-vis the dollar was disputed among European finance ministers on August 19, the French position still was to give priority to a global solution at the international monetary system level and to define new parities between the dollar and European currencies. In fact, when Pompidou flew to the Azores in mid-December 1971, the scheme he was going to promote drew upon the general compromise established inside the Monetary Committee in July and was further refined between Pompidou and Brandt at their Paris meeting on December 3 and 4. The day when Pompidou engaged the debate with President Richard Nixon on December 13, the European central banks, in the Committee of Governors, also resumed their studies about margin reductions in the EC.[23]

The creation of the European snake in April 1972 was a way for the French authorities to link the European governments and central banks in a common attitude toward the United States. The snake was a commitment by the six EC members to keep their exchange rates within 2.25 percent of each other by using periodic exchanges of assets linked to gold and to foreign exchange. This range of fluctuation was half the 4.5 percent that had been stipulated in the Smithsonian Agreement of December 1971, and this action reduced the range of flexibility among EC currencies as well as between EC currencies and the dollar. But again, one of the major problems was the organization of solidarity among European central banks. Because the Americans did very little to defend the new parities, most of the efforts had to stem from the Europeans and especially the Germans to resist speculation. The burden for the Bundesbank was the obligation to support not only the dollar but also European currencies unable to resist asymmetric pressures inside the snake.

The discussions about the European monetary cooperation fund (EMCF) were the stumbling block for the tentative solidarity among the members of the snake. The Commission wanted a prompt organization of the EMCF, with a pooling of reserves and the coordination of exchange rate policies. This position was supported by the French representatives in the Monetary Committee and in the Committee of Governors. In June 1972, Clappier, president of the Monetary Committee, advocated a progressive increase of the means of the fund by way of a partial pooling of reserves so that the EMCF would progressively assume the missions of a European federal reserve system. But the Germans, especially Klasen, were more prudent and wanted a simple instrument of coordination without any financial means and real responsibility or autonomy. In June 1972, the French position was reinforced by the Italians, who were exposed to strong speculative pressures and who also advocated a larger solidarity; but the Germans and the Dutch maintained their prudent attitude because of the risk of imported inflation involved by interventions in the market.[24] As a consequence of these discussions, and as decided at the Paris European summit in October 1972, the EMCF was created in March 1973 with limited resources and responsibilities.[25]

As a counterpart to financial solidarity, the German authorities emphasized (especially in the second half of 1972) the coordination of economic and monetary policies where risks of inflation were concerned. In this respect, the Commission supported the German position. On October 16, Emminger expressed to his colleagues in the Monetary Committee that the Bundesbank wanted to promote in the EC a progressive reduction of the increase of the money supply, and the Bank of France's representative also supported this attitude. A few days later, during the session of the Committee of Governors, Emminger mentioned the coordination between the Bundesbank and the Bank of France concerning the rates of interest.[26]

At the end of 1972, in the context of the European summit of Paris, all the information at our disposal shows that the French authorities were determined to gear their strategy in the monetary field toward European solidarity. As a result, they accepted the German positions about inflation, but they adopted this priority without receiving guarantees about strong solidarity.

The debate about flexibility, relaunched by the discussions about the reform of the international monetary system from the summer of 1972, revealed once again the divergence between French and German conceptions. The Paris agreements of October 1972 did not solve anything, as the debates inside the Monetary Committee in January 1973 revealed. Emminger supported the flexibility of exchange rates and free movement of capital as a way to preserve European economies from imported inflation, even if one had to accept the rise of exchange rates for European currencies. The French representatives merely accepted a limited flexibility with control of capital movement; for them, stability of exchange rates between European currencies was also an objective, but it should not be traded for inflation caused by excessive costs of solidarity. For the French, the main objective was stability of exchange rates at both the world and European levels.

Thus the new crisis of the international monetary system in February and March 1973 did not have the same meaning for the Germans as it did for the French. For the French authorities, it implied a very difficult choice about whether to maintain the franc in the snake, which implied paying a higher price. For the Germans, it seems that the choice had already been made, as was revealed by the unilateral features of their monetary policy during the following months.

During the crisis of February and March 1973, the French made a final attempt to preserve fixed exchange rates, and they succeeded in February—probably because of the isolation of the Germans at that stage of the crisis. The debates inside the Monetary Committee on February 6 and 7 focused on the issue of proposed controls over capital movements, defended by the Commission and the French, but refused by the German representatives. Most of the members, including the Dutch, opposed floating.[27] However, the devaluation of the dollar was considered as a last attempt to preserve the world from floating exchange rates. Debates at the supervisory board of the Bank of France revealed the absence of illusions about this last attempt to preserve fixed exchange rates.[28] The crisis of March corroborated this opinion. By that time, the positions were reversed between the Germans and the French, who were isolated at the Monetary Committee session of March 3, as if everyone were convinced that the floating of currencies was inevitable.

Despite the strong disagreement between the finance minister's main adviser, Claude Pierre-Brossolette, and the state secretary, Karl-Otto Poehl, on March 3 the French agreed to maintain the snake out of the tunnel.[29] This decision was confirmed by the finance ministers on March 11. But once again, the guarantees were very weak concerning the return of the lira and the pound sterling to the snake and for the eventuality of more control over capital flows in Germany.

The decision made by the French authorities to remain a member of the snake represented a risk, as the experts understood. Raymond Barre, who had just left his position as vice president of the Commission, declared at the supervisory board of the Bank of France on February 15, that following the rate of the DM implied guarantees from Germany, such as controls and bigger facilities, and the return of the lira and the pound to the snake. But Barre was skeptical about the possibility of these currencies returning to the snake. As for Pierre-Brossolette, his advice to track the dollar was also based on the risks implied by an overvalued franc, pushed upward by the DM.[30]

Why was this risky decision made? Pompidou probably played a role in this difficult choice. In February 1972, he supported the point of view of Giscard d'Estaing to put the priority on European monetary cooperation, convinced of the weakness of the Smithsonian agreements. The following July, after Karl Schiller was dismissed from the Finance Ministry in Germany, the president maintained this option for stronger cooperation among Europeans so that the decision of March 1973 was consistent with this evolution. As for Giscard d'Estaing, the fact that the ballot of March 1973 in France gave an advantage to the Independents and the view of Giscard's party as more "European" than the Gaullist party of Pompidou can help explain the decision to follow Germany. In any case, the president as well as his finance minister were informed of the risk they took. They realized that the decision of March 1973 was an experiment and a test of the willingness of the partners of France, especially Germany, to play the card of European solidarity. For its part, the French government was ready to pay the price.

From the French point of view, the success of the experiment begun in March depended on the possibility of reinserting the lira and sterling into the snake. In the spring of 1973, hopes of succeeding rose as shown by a note from the director of the Treasury to the minister of finance. It seems also that Brandt wanted to help the British rejoin the snake.[31] But this hope was short-lived, and the chancellor had to abandon his project due to the opposition of the monetary authorities. On June 22, 1973, Pompidou and Brandt had to admit failure and the necessity to delay the second step of building economic and monetary union. This position was reiterated later on in November.[32]

The Bank of France came to view the experiment of keeping the franc in the snake as a costly failure of cooperation among central banks. The speculative crisis of June 1973 was interpreted by the bank as the result of the selfish attitude of German monetary authorities, especially regarding the interest rates that induced a unilateral revaluation of the DM on June 29. In

Basel, on July 7, 1973, Governor Wormser advocated a more symmetric sharing of efforts between central banks, but Klasen emphasized the costs of heavy interventions in the market of European currencies, alluding to the internal objectives of stability in Germany.[33] In July, August, and, September of the same year, Wormser decided to raise the interest rates in France, especially to support the franc vis-à-vis the DM. He justified these decisions at the Bank of France Supervisory Council on September 20.[34] On the one hand, Wormser admitted the lack of cooperation and information sharing among central bankers in Europe and acknowledged that this was not a favorable setting for pursuing massive and costly efforts to support the franc. On the other hand, Wormser recognized that the policy pursued by Germany, which consisted of high interest rates and revaluation of the DM, had proved to be efficient from an economic point of view because it had had no negative consequences for German exports. At this meeting, both Raymond Barre and Jacques Delors supported a policy of high interest rates to fight inflation.

The reasons behind the French government's decision to leave the snake in January 1974 are still not fully known. Probably, officials concluded that the price to be paid to maintain the franc in a monetary zone dominated by the DM when the coordination of monetary policies was weak was too high. Another complicating factor was the oil crisis of October 1973, which diminished hope for quick reform of the international monetary system and confronted France with the necessity of increased exports. The beginning of a new speculative crisis in January provided an opportunity to leave the snake.

Conclusion

Very early in the process of the collapse of the Bretton Woods system, European financial experts linked the problems of European monetary cooperation on the one hand, and the stabilization of a monetary order in the world on the other hand. This conceptual approach is one of the most important elements in explaining European efforts toward monetary integration during the 1980s and 1990s, as well as the first serious attempt in that direction between 1969 and 1973.

In this context, the French position revealed a profound change between these two dates that can be summarized as follows:

- France was an early advocate of European monetary cooperation and sponsored a first initiative in that direction just after the monetary crisis of the summer of 1968. At that time, specialists could design a strategy

to preserve a reformed international monetary system, but the French authorities were not ready to pay the price for the necessary European cooperation in terms of national economic constraints.
- In 1971–72, France moved beyond this initial position and tried a form of transatlantic compromise between Europe and the United States. The European snake became an element of global monetary stabilization, and the French government anticipated that there would be a sharing of the economic burdens of this stabilization between the United States and Europe.
- In 1973, the failure of the tunnel—as designed in the Smithsonian Agreement—was also the failure of the French system, but France decided to maintain the franc within the snake and to accept more economic burdens as the price for European monetary stability. Although this attempt was interrupted in January 1974, it started an evolution toward a policy that was definitively adopted ten years later.

The evolution of French policy is connected with the relative economic positions of France and its two partners. In this perspective, France was certainly the minor partner in the strategic triangle, especially after 1968. Up to that date, the strong position of the franc allowed President de Gaulle to compete with the United States in international monetary debates, to denounce "dollar imperialism," and to advocate a common position of the EC countries toward the United States.

After 1968, economic and social conditions prohibited adhering to these Gaullist positions. Confronted with social and political instability and in accordance with President Pompidou's goal of a thorough and rapid modernization of the economy, France had to adopt a more flexible attitude and to preserve more autonomy in its monetary policy. Though it was able to pretend to exercise a form of leadership in Europe in the monetary field between 1963 and 1967, Paris had to give up this role in 1968 and was obliged to comply with the monetary policy of Germany. For Bonn, the support of monetary flexibility was a comfortable way to pursue its national interest and to further its economic leadership in the EC.

Notes

1. See Association Georges Pompidou, *Georges Pompidou et l'Europe: Colloque, 25 et 26 novembre 1993* (hereafter *Georges Pompidou et l'Europe*) (Brussels: Éditions Complexe, 1995), especially the contributions of Franck, Fabra, de Boissieu, Bossuat, and Paye.

2. Monetary Committee (MC) Session, September 4, 1968, file DDPE 43 1397/15, Bank of France Archives (BF).

3. "Memorandum de la Commission au conseil sur la coordination des politiques économiques et la coopération monétaire au sein de la Communauté, II," Mons Conference, April 20–21, 1969, B 50 479, Finance Ministry Archives (F 30), 5–7.

4. Ibid., 15.

5. MC Session, December 18, 1968, DDPE 43-1397/16, BF.

6. Olivier Wormser to President of Committee of Governors, June 23, 1969, DDPE 43-1397/18, BF.

7. Directeur des etudes, note, December 2–3, 1968, DDPE 43-1397/16, BF; M. Dickhaus, "La Bundesbank et l'Europe," *Histoire, économie et société* 18 (1999): 775–95; J. Barebdregt, "Les Pays-Bas et l'Europe monétaire après la deuxième guerre mondiale," *Histoire, économie et société* 18 (1999): 815–22.

8. Mons Conference, April 20–21, 1969, B 50 479, F 30; text in DDPE 43-1397/18.

9. MC Session, May 9 and 19, 1969, DDPE 43-1397/17, BF.

10. Service des affaires internationals, note, September 18, 1969, B 50 484, F 30.

11. Notes for Finance Minister, October 20, 1969, and January 23, 1970, B 12 544, F 30.

12. G. Bossuat, "Le président Pompidou et les tentatives d'union économique et monétaire," in *Georges Pompidou et l'Europe,* 408.

13. Committee of Governors (CG), April 13, 1970, and May 11, 1970, BF.

14. MC Session, September 3, 1970, DDPE 43-1397/21, BF.

15. R. Larre, note, September 8, 1970, B 12 544, F 30.

16. Conference of Finance Ministries, February 23–24, 1970, B 50 479, F 30.

17. MC Session, March 10, 1970, DDPE 43-1397/19, BF.

18. Bossuat, "Le président Pompidou," 411–19.

19. President Pompidou, note, December 9, 1970, M. Jobert Archives; quotation by Bossuat, "Le président Pompidou," 414.

20. MC Session, June 23, 1971, DDPE 43-1397/23, BF.

21. Georges-Henri Soutou, "L'attitude de G. Pompidou face à l'Allemagne," in *Georges Pompidou et l'Europe,* 291–92.

22. MC Session, July 20, 1971, DDPE 43-1397/23, BF; CG, July 11, 1971, BF.

23. CG, September 8, 1971, and December 13, 1971, BF; Boussuat, 424.

24. CG, June 10, 1972, and July 10, 1972, BF.

25. Bossuat, "Le président Pompidou," 430.

26. MC Session, October 16, 1972, DDPE 43-1397/28, BF.

27. MC Session, February 6–7, 1973, DDPE 43-1397/29, BF.

28. Conseil general, February 15, 1973, BF.

29. MC Session, March 3, 1973, DDPE 43-1397/29, BF. This meant France would maintain the 2.25 percent range with EC currencies, but would go outside the Smithsonian tunnel of 4.5 percent if necessary for other exchange rates.

30. Director of the Treasury to Finance Minister, note, March 3, 1973, B 12 536, F 30; Director of Treasury to Finance Minister, note, March 11, 1973, B 54 757, F 30.

31. Bossuat, "Le président Pompidou," 432; note for the Finance Minister, May 14, 1973, B 50 484, F 30.

32. Note for the Minister, September 20, 1973, B 50 484, F 30; Bossuat, "Le président Pompidou," 434, 447 nn. 125, 128.

33. CG, July 8, 1973, BF.

34. Conseil general, September 20, 1973, BF.

Chapter 8

The United States and the Search for a New Economic and Monetary System in the 1970s
William H. Becker

In the summer of 1971, the Bretton Woods fixed exchange rate system faced what turned out to be its last "dollar crisis." For more than a decade, the growing outflow of dollars from the United States had threatened the convertibility of the dollar for gold at the official rate of $35 per ounce. By the late 1960s, foreign confidence had waned in the fixed-rate gold-backed dollar as the anchor of the international economy's monetary system. As early as 1958, the total value of dollars abroad held in reserves exceeded the value of official American gold stocks. As these stocks declined in the 1960s while dollar flows overseas increased, the international monetary system became less secure. Dollar crises occurred when foreign central banks had to intervene in private currency markets to defend the fixed value of the dollar.

This predicament posed a major challenge to the United States and its Western European allies. Diminishing confidence in the dollar meant that traders and monetary officials in Europe and Japan doubted that the fixed gold-backed exchange rate could be sustained. In effect, they feared that the United States would have to devalue its currency. If that occurred, foreign governments, businesses, and individuals holding dollars would suffer losses. But, of more importance, abandoning convertibility and fixed exchange rates was a leap into the unknown. Few were confident enough to predict with authority what might be the consequences.

How, then, were the United States and its allies either to manage the troubled fixed exchange rate system or come up with something less prone to crisis? During the late 1950s and 1960s, Presidents Dwight Eisenhower, John Kennedy, and Lyndon Johnson adopted stopgap measures to cope with the problem. These included programs to counter the outward flow of dollars from the United States by stimulating American exports or increasing foreign investment in the United States. There were also efforts—for the most part halfhearted—to slow American expenditures for overseas military and economic assistance. Kennedy supported tying American aid to purchases of American goods. Johnson imposed controls on American foreign investment. When runs on the dollar occurred, crisis management usually entailed American officials rallying Western European (often West German) and Japanese central bankers to purchase dollars at the fixed exchange rate in money markets and to refrain from cashing in their dollars held as reserves.[1]

Despite the weaknesses in the Bretton Woods system, informed American opinion believed that the fixed exchange rate and dollar/gold convertibility had contributed to the post–World War II recovery and prosperity of Western Europe and Japan.[2] Central bankers in West Germany, Britain, and Japan also accepted that fixed exchange rates were on balance beneficial. But during the 1960s, there were growing concerns about the inflationary costs large influxes of dollars imposed on Western European economies. Clearly, the system needed to be adjusted, and there were a series of stopgap maneuvers to cope with the weaknesses of the Bretton Woods arrangements during the 1960s. For its part, France after 1965 tried to discipline the U.S. dollar outflow by routinely demanding gold for its dollar reserves. The other Western European countries preferred a less confrontational approach to the United States and a more gradual adjustment of the postwar international monetary system. American officials were certainly inclined to go slow, because the Bretton Woods system seemed advantageous to U.S. interests.[3]

Nevertheless, what to do about Bretton Woods was settled in a drastic fashion on August 15, 1971. President Richard Nixon unceremoniously abandoned American adherence to its precepts in a nationwide television address. He shocked the United States' German, French, British, and Japanese allies. Nixon seemed unconcerned with what many feared would be grave consequences to the international economy. Nor was he solicitous of the standing and prestige of the leaders of the United States' allies who were not consulted, nor even warned in advance of the impending change.

Why did President Nixon act as he did? Why did he suddenly abandon one of the key elements of the postwar order in such a precipitous manner? Whatever one's assessment of Nixon's role in domestic American politics, he seemed comparatively surefooted when it came to the international scene. Yet Nixon ended the Bretton Woods system without displaying any of the finesse he employed in dealing with other international issues.

Revisiting why Bretton Woods ended as it did provides useful insights for understanding the intricacies of the American foreign economic policy process. To be sure, the international economic issues of the new twenty-first century differ significantly from those of the 1970s. But the forces at work in policymaking still remain to influence the way in which the United States deals with the international economy. These considerations will be taken up again at the end of this chapter after examining the reasons Nixon behaved as he did in confronting probably the most important foreign economic policy issue the West faced at the time,[4] as well as the short-term and long-term consequences for both the international economic system and the United States' allies in West Germany and France.

Nixon, Grand Strategy, and the Problems of the Dollar

Richard M. Nixon took office as president in January 1969. Before his election, a speculative run on the dollar had occurred in 1967–68. Though the Johnson administration contained that crisis, the systemic weaknesses of the international monetary system remained. Nevertheless, these problems were of little concern to the United States' new chief executive. Initially, Nixon believed that international monetary problems were a technical matter, best left to lower-level offices in either the departments of State or Treasury.[5]

Instead, two big ideas preoccupied Nixon's presidency. One involved fundamentally reshaping the terms of the Cold War rivalry between the United States and the Soviet Union; the other focused on the long-term role of the Republican Party in American politics. These two overriding concerns provide a compass by which to track how Nixon approached many issues, including eventually and grudgingly the increasing problems of fixed exchange rates and dollar convertibility.

Grand idea number one encompassed the place of the United States in international relations. Nixon believed that the United States had an opportunity to change the dynamics of the Cold War. Increasing tensions between the Soviet Union and the People's Republic of China in the 1960s, Nixon thought, provided the United States with an opening to gain greater leverage with the Soviets. Helping to shape and deepen the new president's ideas was his national security adviser, Henry Kissinger, one-time Harvard University professor and later secretary of state. In any event, Nixon had concluded that America's isolating China handed the Soviet Union an advantage in its dealings with the United States. In the 1950s and 1960s, despite tensions with Moscow, China had no place to turn for substantial support other than the Soviet Union. In fact, Nixon's rapprochement with China in 1972—formal relations were established in 1979—did add leverage to the United States' relationship with the Soviet Union. Nixon was able to make progress on détente, arms control, and trade with the Soviets. Of most significance, the two countries signed the first Strategic Arms Limitation Talks treaty (SALT I) in May 1972, which was ratified by the U.S. Senate in October 1972.[6]

Thus, Japan and Western Europe were secondary to Nixon's concerns about the possibilities of a triangular relationship with the Soviet Union and China. Western Europe was important to the United States, to be sure, but its interests were subordinate to Nixon's overriding concern with Cold War grand strategy. There was, in his opinion, no way to reverse the growing independence of the reviving European states. This was a reality to be managed, not reversed. What the United States would have to determine, however, was how to cope with a new European assertiveness on trade and monetary issues, among others. Kissinger hoped that the Atlantic alliance would conduct its relations through frequent consultations. Indeed, within a month of taking office, Nixon made a European trip to visit with heads of state. This allowed the leaders of the Atlantic alliance to take the measure of the new American president, and he of them.[7]

But U.S.-European relations, and much else, were also subordinated to the second of Nixon's grand ideas. He hoped to do no less than bring about a political realignment in the United States. His goal was to make the Republicans the majority party in order to dominate American politics for decades to come. He would create his new majority by permanently capturing Democratic Party constituencies disaffected by their party's policies in the 1960s, especially on civil rights. Winning reelection in 1972 became for Nixon essential to achieving the long-term objective.

Nixon's 1968 election owed much to the bitter divisions in public opinion brought about by American involvement in the Vietnam War. He got the votes of those critical of Lyndon Johnson's management of the war. Equally important, though, were voters (Democrats included) angry at the vocal and growing antiwar movement.

But Nixon's election also reflected a growing more general discontent with Democratic Party policies, especially with regard to social issues and race relations. Initially, when civil rights for African Americans became a national political issue in the United States in the late 1950s, many outside the highly segregated South were supportive. Substantial numbers approved ending racial segregation and guaranteeing the voting rights of African Americans. Later efforts to further extend civil rights, however, encountered more resistance and engendered much discontent. Causing the most opposition were programs of "affirmative action," that is, federal government policies designed to help minorities make up for past discrimination in, for example, hiring, job promotion, and university admissions. Critics saw such programs as providing racial preferences or encouraging "reverse discrimination." A particularly volatile issue was busing students from one neighborhood to another to create racially integrated schools.[8]

Nixon saw an important political opportunity in these developments. Many of those opposing affirmative action and busing, along with the antiwar movement, were Democrats. A number of these usually Democratic voters were also union members. Nixon hoped to wean these voters away from the Democratic Party, capturing constituencies for the Republicans, creating what he referred to as a "New Majority." The key to changing the balance in American politics was to keep these former Democratic voters loyal to the Republican Party. In particular, he had to be more attentive to the interests of organized labor than was usually the case for a Republican. More generally, his task was to depict the Democrats as unable or unwilling to maintain law and order, and as favoring preferential treatment for racial minorities. Nixon also endeavored to portray the Democratic Party as untrustworthy in protecting the United States' foreign interests, in particular its apparent failure to understand the need to end the Vietnam War with "honor." These were divisive and controversial issues, but ones Nixon was willing to exploit to get reelected in 1972.[9]

Governing

Bold as Nixon's strategic thinking was about foreign policy and electoral politics, he found that once in office governing demanded attention to less grand issues. None was more mundane to the new president than the issue of the performance of the domestic economy and the problems of the international monetary system. He was not a close student of economics and, consequently, relied heavily on advisers. As one of them observed, "Mr. Nixon may have . . . had a psychological block about economics," for he attacked the subject much "like a little boy doing required lessons."[10] Many of the advisers were professional economists who often exasperated the president by their conflicting interpretations of current economic conditions and what to do about them. During his years in office, Nixon usually singled out one adviser on whom to rely so as to avoid having to make choices about complex, often technical economic issues he did not fully understand or care very much about. For most of the Nixon years, this key adviser was either George Shultz or John Connally.

Nixon came to office without much interest in economic issues per se. Indeed, in his entire inaugural address, he only mentioned the economy in one line of the speech, and what he offered were platitudes about continuing prosperity. What he was keenly aware of, however, was the potential political impact of economic conditions in the United States. Invariably, he viewed domestic and international economic issues in terms of their political importance. He had learned the importance of the politics of economics from a recession in 1958–60 that he believed cost him the close presidential election of 1960.[11]

During the 1960s, the United States enjoyed a booming economy, helped along by large spending for the Vietnam War toward the end of the decade. There was no recession between 1960 and 1968. During the Kennedy and the early Johnson administrations, inflation and unemployment attained relatively low levels—the best numbers were 2.7 percent inflation and 4 percent unemployment. These critical indicators became the benchmark by which Nixon and the public judged the economy's performance in his years as president. But once in office, Nixon soon confronted a reversal in the positive economic conditions. After 1965, his predecessor, Lyndon B. Johnson, funded an ambitious and expensive social program—"The Great Society" —and the Vietnam War at the same time. Because of the war's unpopularity, Johnson dared not raise taxes significantly and so financed it by deficit spending. When Nixon took office, the government was running a budget deficit of $25 billion and facing a 5 percent rate of inflation. The vast spending for the war stimulated demand for both domestic and imported goods. Inflationary prices also reduced American exports, which in turn lessened the country's trade surplus and increased its balance of payments deficit.[12]

In addition, Nixon was the first president to confront the structural economic issues that economists would later refer to as "stagflation." Rising inflation in the 1970s was accompanied by a surprising development—higher levels of unemployment. Thus, Nixon was bedeviled by the unusual twin economic phenomena of increasing prices in a time of recession, that is, in a period with increasing levels of unemployment.[13]

In his first two years in office, Nixon focused his economic policy on reducing inflation. This was the course championed by Paul McCracken, chairman of the Council of Economic Advisers, and George Shultz, head of the Office of Management and Budget, the president's initial economic policy guru. Both were academic economists. Shultz, with a Ph.D. in economics from the University of Chicago, was a disciple of Milton Friedman. To cut inflation, the administration presented a budget with no deficit and convinced the Federal Reserve Board to limit the growth of the money supply. The Federal Reserve pushed up interest rates in April 1969, which produced a recession by the end of the year. But inflation also kept creeping upward. It continued to increase in the next year—it was 6 percent for 1970—with unemployment over 5 percent. The congressional elections of November 1970 demonstrated the political failure of this economic policy. Nixon's hopes for significant Republican gains were disappointed, at best postponing the electoral realignment the president so ardently wanted.

Consequently, early in 1971, Nixon reversed his economic policy. He proposed a budget with an $11.6 billion deficit as a stimulus to the economy. The newly appointed chairman of the Federal Reserve Board (Arthur Burns) complied with his request to increase the growth of the money supply and lower interest rates. Nixon unabashedly championed an expansion to secure his primary political objective of reelection in 1972. He calculated that high levels of unemployment would doom his electoral chances with union members. He clearly preferred to risk further inflation to ensure a robust economy by election time.[14]

Nevertheless, by July 1971, Nixon encountered growing criticism because of the growing rates of inflation (6 percent) and unemployment (6.2 percent). He was constantly under attack by Congress, the press, and Wall Street. Voters were also unhappy. One public opinion poll in July found that 73 percent of respondents lacked confidence in Nixon's handling of the economy; another poll reported that 50 percent favored a freeze on prices and wages.[15]

In the latter part of July 1971, Nixon decided that something drastic had to be done. Bolstering his conviction was an unlikely ally. In December 1970, the president had appointed John Connally secretary of the Treasury. In 1971, Connally supplanted Shultz to become Nixon's closest economic adviser. Connally was a three-term former governor of Texas, and a Democrat. He had come to national attention when President Kennedy was assassinated in 1963. Then-governor Connally and his wife were riding in the car with the Kennedys in Dallas when the president was shot. Even though Connally was a protégé of Lyndon Johnson, the Texas governor became increasingly disenchanted with the Democratic Party during the 1960s.

Connally came to Nixon's attention when he served on a White House commission to study government reorganization early in 1970. Connally's work on the commission impressed Nixon enormously, and they grew closer. Connally was an imposing political figure. Subordinates found him highly intelligent and a fast learner. He was also ruggedly handsome, supremely self-assured, and an effective, articulate speaker. He could be warm and charming, but also quite ruthless when necessary. Nixon came to believe that Connally might be the right man to succeed him as president, a man who could appeal to the same electoral constituencies that Nixon hoped to forge into his new majority.[16]

In any event, Nixon and Connally worked together in July 1971 to cope with the political problems brought about by the performance of the American economy. By early August, they agreed that drastic measures were needed to cope with rising inflation. Nixon was to take the extraordinary step of imposing temporary price and wage controls in peacetime to hold down inflation. At the same time, there would be more conventional steps— a cut in taxes—to stimulate the economy and increase employment. Initially, they planned to announce these changes in September when Congress returned from a recess.[17]

Nixon, Connally, and the End of Bretton Woods

But in late July and early August 1971, another dollar crisis forced Nixon and Connally to move more quickly. Ultimately, to signal that the administration was boldly dealing with the country's domestic and international economic problems, they combined announcing price and wage controls with the jettisoning of the Bretton Woods system, of closing the gold window and abandoning fixed exchange rates. Nixon announced both new policies in a nationwide television broadcast on the evening of August 15, 1971.

As with the decision on price and wage controls, Connally was essential in Nixon's decision to abandon Bretton Woods. Connally knew little about international economic issues when he took office. Initially, he focused on trade issues instead of the international monetary system. What he learned about the United States' trade policy influenced how he, and ultimately Nixon, coped with the final crisis in the Bretton Woods system in July and August 1971.

Connally's tutor on trade issues was Peter Peterson, himself a novice in the area of foreign economic policy. Even though the Treasury Department had some of the most able staff members in Washington, Connally distanced himself from them.[18] He believed that they had their own agendas and were too influenced by economic theory. Connally showed his disdain for economic theorizing in comments about comparative advantage to the Senate Finance Committee: "The reason I do not understand [the theory of comparative advantage] is that I am not an economist. But if I were an economist, I would not want to understand it because I do not believe it is going to work."[19]

In any event, Connally turned to Peterson as his guide on trade policy. Peterson came to the administration at around the same time as Connally. Nixon appointed him in late 1970 to serve as chairman of a new Council for International Economic Policy. This body was made up of representatives from government agencies with some responsibility in that policy area. Peterson had been something of a managerial wunderkind as the president of the Bell and Howell Company in the 1960s. He expanded and diversified the camera company's operations, markedly increasing its profitability. A business news publication called the relatively young Peterson the "most brilliant" executive of the time.[20]

Peterson's first assignment from Nixon was to prepare a study of how the world economy was changing. This was an unfamiliar area for Peterson—Bell and Howell did not have major overseas markets—but he threw himself into the task. In April 1971, he presented a confidential report to the president that greatly impressed Nixon and Connally.[21]

What Peterson produced was a decidedly mercantilist interpretation of where the United States stood in the international economy of the early 1970s. His report was an early expression of fears about America's declining competitiveness, an issue that was destined to shape U.S. policy discussions for much of the later 1970s and 1980s. The United States, the report emphasized, placed last among industrial countries in rates of gross investment, and it only bested Britain in comparative rates of economic growth. Peterson also focused on the declining place of American manufactures in world output and of its exports in the share of world exports. Since 1964, American exports had increased 110 percent, compared with 200 percent for Germany and 400 percent for Japan. The United States ran its first trade deficit with Japan in 1965. By 1971, this deficit had grown to $3 billion, which almost equaled the country's trade deficit with the rest of the world. The study provided data on the growing place of imports in key American markets—in 1970, 49 percent of sewing machines, 52 percent of black and white television sets, 70 percent of radios, and all 35-millimeter cameras came from overseas.[22]

These data of course were not unknown to government statisticians and professional economists.[23] But what made Peterson's effort so important was his forceful interpretation of the material he had assembled. He argued powerfully that devaluing the dollar would not be enough to reverse the trends in investment and trade he found so ominous. He maintained that the United States had to combat the unfair practices of its competitors and consider policies—an industrial policy—to revitalize American business.[24]

In the months following the submission of his report, Peterson elaborated on his findings. Though he was positively alarmist about Japan's threat to the United States, he made the case for concern about Europe as well. In testimony to the Senate Committee on Finance, he laid out in stronger than usual language a case that had of course been made before. Western Europe restricted American agricultural imports; had discriminatory bilateral trade arrangements with Mediterranean and African countries harmful to U.S. trade; and kept Japanese imports to 7 percent while the United States took 30 percent of Japanese exports. He rehearsed the arguments about the longstanding concern that Europeans only paid $800 million of the $1.7 billion annual cost of keeping American troops there for the defense of Europe. Peterson concluded that even though the United States had a trade surplus with Europe, America needed to counter the protectionist tendencies of the European Economic Community.[25]

Peterson's report left economists on Nixon's staff aghast. It contained every fallacy about foreign trade that economic theory had worked so hard to debunk. Trade, according to standard economic theory, was about mutual benefits. It was not a zero-sum game where for some to gain others had to lose. Economists in the White House also pointed out that the United States maintained its share of restrictive measures that barred foreign goods from the country.[26]

Nevertheless, Connally enthusiastically bought into Peterson's ideas. In the spring of 1971, he went about convincing Nixon that it was time to end America's "benevolent" approach to the world. Connally stated publicly that our allies "have grown accustomed to our being relaxed, fairly generous, always forgiving, always easy in our dealings with them. Consequently, they have built up tariff arrangements, they have built up trade restrictions against U.S. goods. . . . And they expect us to like it." Or, as Connally put it rather crudely to his Treasury colleagues, "My basic approach is that foreigners are out to screw us. . . . Our job is to screw them first." Connally and Peterson were not arguing for protectionist policies in the United States. But what they favored was a much more forceful approach to trade issues in order to get foreign governments to play by the rules.[27]

Nixon wholeheartedly accepted Connally's analysis and prescription. Connally succeeded with the president because he connected trade issues to Nixon's overriding concerns for the United States' place in the world and about reordering American electoral politics. The president accepted, as he said at a meeting with business leaders in June 1971, that "it's terribly important that we be #1 economically because otherwise we can't be #1 diplomatically or militarily."[28]

What most caught Nixon's attention in Connally's and Peterson's call for economic nationalism were the domestic political implications. Peterson's study came as Nixon faced increasing criticism of his economic policies, especially his apparent inability to halt rising unemployment, an issue of particular concern to organized labor. So Nixon became intrigued with Peterson's argument that growing exports increased jobs. Peterson estimated that every $1 billion increase in exports translated into 60,000 to 80,000 jobs. Connally and Nixon knew that a crusade to increase American exports might not work in time for the next election. But they both concluded that taking a strong stance against foreign restrictions would have a political payoff, especially with union leaders. These leaders in the 1960s had been among the first to become concerned about the growing competition from imports. As Nixon's key aide H. R. Haldeman put it in his diaries, all that the administration needed to do was show labor "an interest in protecting their jobs. We don't have to solve the problem, just work towards it, showing visible understanding and articulation."[29]

A truculent attitude toward the country's major trading partners ripened just as there was another dollar crisis. On July 28, the public release of data about the growing size of the U.S. trade deficit ($597 million by the end of June 1971) precipitated a run on the dollar. In 1970, the United States had a trade surplus of $2.7 billion. If such deficits continued to mount, 1971 would be the first year since 1893 that the United States would face an overall trade deficit. The official publication of these data set off the frenzied selling of dollars in overseas markets, as there was open talk in Western Europe of the need for devaluation.[30]

Problems with the dollar had been building throughout the first months of 1971. One could make the case that the major cause was Nixon's altered economic policy. To stimulate the economy, the Federal Reserve lowered interest rates in early 1971. As a result, there was a large exodus of dollar-denominated short-term capital from the United States looking for better rates overseas. In 1970, European central banks had absorbed $10 billion to prop up the dollar. Accelerating dollar outflows in 1971 made it look like the total for that year would be $30 billion.[31]

By May, the situation had gone too far for West Germany. On May 4, traders dumped $1.2 billion for deutsche marks, which they anticipated might be revalued upward. In the first forty minutes of trading the next day, $1 billion were turned in, at which point the German currency markets were closed. Though Western European finance ministers were unanimous in their anger at the United States, they could come to no common policy. Consequently, official German policy moved on its own and took the drastic step of stopping the purchase of dollars. In the resulting float of currencies, the deutsche mark increased about 4 percent against the dollar. This pacified markets for the moment, along with lower interest rates in Europe that moved closer to American rates.[32]

However, the trade figures announced late in July ended the calm. In the face of the crisis, the Treasury's undersecretary for monetary affairs, Paul A. Volcker, advocated that the United States close the gold window and begin negotiations to revalue the grossly overvalued dollar. Connally rejected these ideas out of hand. The United States was not going to be a supplicant. He preferred the image of himself as "the bully boy on the manicured playing fields of international finance." He called devaluation "monetary magic" that would not work. Instead, he wanted to force open Western European markets to American goods and proposed a temporary 10 percent border tax on imports coming into the United States. The United States would remove the border tax in exchange for concessions on trade restrictions on American goods.[33] As the crisis continued, Connally reversed his initial opposition to ending dollar/gold convertibility. He apparently bought into the idea of a Treasury consultant who argued that a 10 to 15 percent devaluation would stimulate enough exports to create 500,000 jobs.

On August 2, Connally presented Nixon with a package of recommendations on how to meet both his domestic economic problems and the international monetary crisis. Thus, Nixon and Connally decided on wage and price controls, tax cuts (to stimulate the economy), closing the gold window, and the border tax. Overall, the package promised political benefits. It would quiet the critics of his domestic economic policies and appeal to a labor constituency perhaps more worried about imports than any other group in the United States at the time.[34] Initially, Nixon and Connally planned the announcement for early September when Congress returned from recess. But a further crisis in money markets accelerated the timetable. The markets, already nervous following the publication of data on the U.S. trade deficit, became more volatile when on August 6 Congress's influential Joint Economic Committee released a report favoring devaluation. Heavy selling of the dollar followed in Western European markets. Treasury officials warned Connally that a full-scale market panic was in the offing. And so, on Sunday evening, August 15, Nixon made his nationally televised address announcing his "New Economic Policy," which featured wage and price controls and, in effect, the end of the Bretton Woods system.[35]

Aftermath

Nixon's speech shocked Western European officials. In terms of the usual diplomatic niceties, the U.S. administration had treated the leaders of its European and Japanese allies very badly. Kissinger spent the following months trying to maximize what might be obtained from the United States' stunned allies without provoking serious retaliation.[36]

There were also significant short-term economic consequences overseas from the United States' unilateral suspension of gold convertibility. Allied governments had two unpleasant choices in the aftermath of Nixon's New Economic Policy. They could either hold onto nonconvertible dollar reserves or sell them on the currency markets, which in effect forced a revaluation of their own currencies. The American devaluation was thus done without the consultation so much at the heart of the Bretton Woods system. Because the dollar had been overvalued for so long, there was no place for it to go but down in relation to other currencies. A devalued dollar helped American exports, and the balance of payments problems would also be eased by the temporary 10 percent border tax, which proved an enormous irritant to Western European officials.[37]

In mid-December 1971, the United States, the Western Europeans, and the Japanese came to an understanding. In the so-called Smithsonian Agreement—following meetings in Washington—the United States dropped the 10 percent border tax in return for an official revaluation of currencies. On average, the dollar was devalued about 10 percent against European currencies and 17 percent against the Japanese yen. To salvage some semblance of fixed exchange rates in a more difficult environment, the participants agreed to widen the band in which currencies could fluctuate—the range went to 2.5 percent from the 1 percent allowed during Bretton Woods.[38]

The effort to maintain fixed exchange rates in the established dollar band did not last. By March 1973, the major currencies were allowed to float. Fixed rates did not survive, because there remained large numbers of dollars ($90–100 billion) still circulating freely—the so-called eurodollars. Essentially, eurodollars were dollars held in banks outside the United States, including American banks located overseas. Deposits of eurodollars earned interest, and the banks holding them made loans in dollars.[39]

The dollar also remained important because of the Organization of the Petroleum Exporting Countries (OPEC). When the United States devaluated the dollar, the major oil companies increased the per-barrel price of petroleum. In the fall of 1973, OPEC quadrupled the per-barrel oil price and—despite the hostility of its member countries to the United States—retained the long-standing practice in the industry of accepting payment only in dollars. Thus, as countries scrambled to pay the higher prices for petroleum, the dollar—which by the mid-1970s had depreciated almost 30 percent against the deutsche mark—regained its significance in international monetary transactions. But the economic disruptions to various countries brought about by OPEC price increases proved so destabilizing that they ended attempts for most of the 1970s to peg rates. What resulted in Western Europe were floating rates anchored to the deutsche mark.[40]

Once currencies began to float, the dollar fell against the Western European currencies at different rates. It depreciated most against the deutsche mark, least against the lira. This led to greater volatility among the Western European exchange rates, which prompted uncertainty in business and intergovernmental transactions. By the end of the 1970s, the leaders of the European Community's (EC's) governments (the European Council) instituted the European Monetary System (EMS), which formally began its work in March 1979. The EMS was a coordinating agency that served to establish and adjust as necessary exchange rates among the EC currencies. Its highly flexible exchange rate mechanism allowed the central banks of the EC to adjust rates with relative ease. Consequently, the system responded well to OPEC's doubling of petroleum prices in 1979, and the resulting decline in growth rates, increasing unemployment, and political changes in member countries. The success of EMS in coordinating exchange rates raised confidence—in the minds of some at least—in centralizing control over the supply of money in the EC. The December 1991 Maastricht Accord for European Monetary Union, and the adoption of a common European currency, are both results of the EMS.[41]

The United States' Foreign Economic Policy Process

America's abandoning of Bretton Woods provides another example of the axiom that there is often little "foreign" in foreign policy, in this instance foreign economic policy. That the short-run political interests of leaders played a role in decisions about foreign economic policy, even such momentous decisions as those associated with Bretton Woods, should not come as a surprise. What is perhaps unusual in this instance is the relentlessness of Nixon's pursuit of domestic political advantage to the exclusion of almost all other considerations with regard to the international monetary system.

Even so, one can find other constants in the American policymaking process in examining how the Nixon administration dealt with Bretton Woods. Nixon and Connally were deeply suspicious of the Department of the Treasury. Those who have followed the public career of Henry Kissinger know of his skepticism about the Department of State. This is a persistent theme in American administrations, where presidents often were suspicious of the "permanent government," which was there before they arrived in the White House and which would outlast their tenure. What was also remarkable about Nixon was his willingness to accept the voice of amateurs (Connally and Peterson) over that of the professionals and experts in the executive branch departments and the White House itself. Academics will surely bristle at the short shrift their colleagues received at the hands of Nixon and his closest advisers. Yet there was nothing particularly new about this. Suspicion of experts certainly varies from administration to administration. However, the constant is suspicion of highly theoretical explanations for problems of policy that politicians see, at least in part, as being political but that academics and other experts often see only in technical terms.

Notes

1. Diane B. Kunz, "Cold War Diplomacy: The Other Side of Containment," in *The Diplomacy of the Crucial Decade: American Foreign Relations during the 1960s,* ed. Diane B. Kunz (New York: Columbia University Press, 1994), 80–107.

2. Some recent scholarship questions the causal relationship between Bretton Woods and prosperity. Indeed, the argument is the longevity of the system was a result of prosperity. See Barry Eichengreen, *Globalizing Capital: A History of the International Monetary System* (Princeton, N.J.: Princeton University Press, 1996), 93.

3. A standard treatment of the subject is David P. Calleo, *The Imperious Economy* (Cambridge, Mass.: Harvard University Press, 1982).

4. Recently, the U.S. National Archives has opened papers from the Nixon administration. Included are the notes Nixon arranged to be taken at every meeting he attended as president. These sources provide unique insights into Nixon's thinking about issues and policy.

5. Allen J. Matusow, *Nixon's Economy: Booms, Busts, Dollars, and Votes* (Lawrence: University Press of Kansas, 1998), 118–19.

6. Robert Schulzinger, *Henry Kissinger: Doctor of Diplomacy* (New York: Columbia University Press, 1989) provides a balanced review. On these events, there are also books by Nixon and Kissinger. See Richard M. Nixon, *In the Arena: A Memoir of Victory, Defeat, and Renewal* (New York: Simon & Schuster, 1990); Nixon, *RN: The Memoirs of Richard Nixon* (New York: Grosset & Dunlap, 1975); and Henry Kissinger, *White House Years* (Boston: Little, Brown, 1979).

7. Kissinger, *White House Years,* 73–111; Matusow, *Nixon's Economy,* 119–21.

8. Terry H. Anderson, *The Movement and the Sixties: Protest in America from Greensboro to Wounded Knee* (New York: Oxford University Press, 1995); and William J. Berman, *America's Right Turn: From Nixon to Bush* (Baltimore: Johns Hopkins University Press, 1994).

9. Herbert Parmet, *Richard Nixon and His America* (Boston: Little, Brown, 1990). For a contemporary analysis of the electoral dynamics of the time, see Kevin Phillips, *The Emerging Republican Majority* (New York: Anchor Books, 1970).

10. The quotation is from Paul McCracken, Nixon's first chairman, Council of Economic Advisers, in Matusow, *Nixon's Economy,* 16.

11. Matusow, *Nixon's Economy,* 18–19; Richard M. Nixon, *Six Crises* (Garden City, N.Y.: Doubleday, 1962), 310.

12. Diane B. Kunz, *Butter and Guns: America's Cold War Economic Diplomacy* (New York: Free Press, 1997), 103–11; Matusow, *Nixon's Economy,* 116, 125–26.

13. See Michael A. Bernstein, ed., *Understanding America's Economic Decline* (New York: Cambridge University Press, 1994).

14. Matusow, *Nixon's Economy,* 87–98. In fact, the inflation and unemployment figures were not so serious by European standards, nor indeed by the considerably worse record of the American economy later in the 1970s. But Nixon judged the economy's performance—as did most of the American public—on the remembrance of the low-inflation, rapidly expanding economy of the 1960s.

15. Ibid., 108–15.

16. Ibid., 84–87; Kissinger, *White House Years,* 951.

17. Matusow, *Nixon's Economy,* 111–14.

18. Indeed, had Connally been interested in a study of international monetary prob-

lems, there was a report close at hand. In the first year of the administration, Paul Volcker, Treasury undersecretary for monetary affairs, later chairman of the Federal Reserve, had prepared a lengthy report on the options the United States faced in dealing with Bretton Woods. Matusow, *Nixon's Economy,* 126–31. A close study of the events leading to the end of Bretton Woods is Thomas Forbord, "The Abandonment of Bretton Woods: The Political Economy of U.S. International Monetary Policy" (Ph.D. diss., Harvard University, 1980), 74–111. Also see Henrik S. Houtakker, "The Breakdown of Bretton Woods," in *Economic Advice and Executive Policy: Recommendations from Past Members of the Council of Economic Advisers,* ed. Werner Sichel (New York: Praeger, 1978), 45–64.

19. Quoted in Matusow, *Nixon's Economy,* 139.
20. Ibid., 131–37; Kissinger, *White House Years,* 951–53, 957.
21. Matusow, *Nixon's Economy,* 131–33. Nixon's speechwriter observed later that for a period because of his report Peterson became "number one intellectual concubine" in the White House; see William Safire, *Before the Fall: An Inside View of the Pre-Watergate White House* (Garden City, N.Y.: Doubleday, 1975), 498.
22. Matusow, *Nixon's Economy,* 133–34; Peter G. Peterson, *The United States in a Changing World Economy,* 2 vols. (Washington, D.C.: U.S. Government Printing Office, 1971).
23. See, e.g., U.S. Department of Commerce, *Business Statistics, 1973* (Washington, D.C.: U.S. Government Printing Office, 1974), 110, 115.
24. Matusow, *Nixon's Economy,* 133–34.
25. Ibid., 134.
26. Ibid., 138–39; for a discussion of the problems of professional economic advisers, see Herbert Stein, *Presidential Economics: The Making of Economic Policy from Roosevelt to Clinton,* 3rd ed. (Washington, D.C.: American Enterprise Institute for Public Policy Research, 1994).
27. The Connally quotation is in *U.S. News & World Report,* April 12, 1971, 55; the second Connally quotation is found in John S. Odell, *U.S. International Monetary Policy: Markets, Power, and Ideas as Sources of Change* (Princeton, N.J.: Princeton University Press, 1982), 263; Matusow, *Nixon's Economy,* 135.
28. Quoted in Matusow, *Nixon's Economy,* 136.
29. Ibid., 136–37; quoted from *Haldeman Diaries,* June 27, 1971.
30. Brian Tew, *The Evolution of the International Monetary System, 1945–77* (New York: John Wiley & Sons, 1977), 145–50; Kunz, *Butter and Guns,* 199–204.
31. Matusow, *Nixon's Economy,* 143–44; Leland B. Yeager, *International Monetary Relations: Theory, History, and Policy,* 2nd ed. (New York: Harper & Row, 1976), 435, 516–17.
32. Tew, *Evolution of the International Monetary System,* 145–50; Susan Strange, "The Dollar Crises of 1971," *International Affairs* 48 (April 1972): 191–215; Matusow, *Nixon's Economy,* 144–45.
33. Quotes from Matusow, *Nixon's Economy,* 144–45, 147.
34. Ibid., 147; Forbord, "Abandonment of Bretton Woods," 244–60.
35. Matusow, *Nixon's Economy,* 147–55; Joanne S. Gowa, *Closing the Gold Window: Domestic Politics and Bretton Woods* (Ithaca, N.Y.: Cornell University Press, 1983), 44, 88–97, 100.
36. Kissinger, *White House Years,* 957–67.
37. Eichengreen, *Globalizing Capital,* 133–36.

38. Ibid., 133–37, 140, 145, 155–57; Tew, *Evolution of the International Monetary System,* 72–74.

39. The eurodollar market began early in the 1950s when the Soviet Union refused to deposit the dollars it acquired in American banks. Instead it opened a branch of its own bank, Moscow Narodny Bank, located in the City of London to deposit dollars. For much of the 1950s, dollars acquired in Europe were quickly used for transactions. But as dollar supplies increased beyond what was needed for immediate transactions in the late 1950s, separate accounts of what became known as eurodollars appeared. Banks holding this currency began to lend it out; indeed, beginning in 1957, eurodollars were used to buy large bond issues. In the 1960s, the eurodollar market burgeoned as banks holding dollars put them to use by lending them. They found a ready market for such loans among large American multinational corporations trying to cope with the restrictions the U.S. government had put on foreign investment, restrictions designed to stop the outflow of dollars from the United States. Thus, a growing supply of dollars in banks outside the United States met a growing demand. See Howard M. Wachtel, *The Money Mandarins: The Making of a Supranational Economic Order,* rev. ed. (Armonk, N.Y.: M. E. Sharpe, 1990), 94–100; Susan Strange, *Sterling and British Policy: A Political Study of an International Currency in Decline* (New York: Oxford University Press, 1971), 203–7; and Tew, *Evolution of the International Monetary System,* 139–47.

40. Eichengreen, *Globalizing Capital,* 136–44; Wachtel, *Money Mandarins,* 85–87.

41. Larry Neal and Daniel Barbezat, *The Economics of the European Union and the Economies of Europe* (New York: Oxford University Press, 1998), 141–67; Eichengreen, *Globalizing Capital,* 157–72.

Part IV

Ostpolitik and Détente

Chapter 9

German *Ostpolitik* in a Multilateral Setting

Helga Haftendorn

German *Ostpolitik* is a typical example of German preunification policy. Its subject matter is the relationship with the Soviet Union and the Eastern European countries within the context of Germany's division. At its core is the crucial question of the country's future, whether in division or unity. In this chapter, *Ostpolitik* refers to efforts taken by the Willy Brandt–Walter Scheel government to normalize relations with Moscow, Warsaw, and—last but not least—East Berlin. The strategies they used took their cues from the international environment—more than from the domestic setting—and the tactics they employed mixed adaptation to allies' priorities with independent approaches to further Germany's interests. *Ostpolitik* had many precursors; to be successful, it required a convergence of positive international and special domestic factors.

This chapter details the origins, motives, and setting of German *Ostpolitik*, focusing on the Brandt-Scheel government (1969–72) and the negotiations on the Moscow and Warsaw treaties that were a political precondition for a rapprochement between Bonn and East Berlin.[1] Looking at the strategies and tactics employed by the government of the Federal Republic, and at the international environment that affected *Ostpolitik*, the quadripartite negotiations on Berlin are treated here as an enabling as well as a controlling factor, along with the Conference on Security and Cooperation in Europe project that provided a multilateral arena for what basically had been a bilateral *Ostpolitik*. The chapter concludes by asking whether the strategic triangle had any impact on the outcome of *Ostpolitik*, and what this impact was.

The Federal Republic clearly had an *Ostpolitik* right from its origins in 1949. At its core was the German question, and all initiatives toward Moscow or reactions to Soviet policy moves were shaped by considerations on how to overcome the division of the country without risking its bonding to the Western alliance. Because Moscow intended either to separate Germany from the West or keep the country divided, Bonn's *Ostpolitik* in the 1950s and 1960s was mostly defensive and negative. With no room for maneuvering, German governments stuck to a policy of relying on the responsibility of the Four Powers for reunification—as specified in the 1945 Potsdam Accord and confirmed in the 1952–54 Bonn and Paris agreements—while at the same time remaining concerned that no legal positions were relinquished by recognizing the German Democratic Republic (GDR) or improving its international standing. A central aspect of this policy was known as the "Hallstein doctrine," which considered diplomatic recognition of the GDR by any state other than the Soviet Union and its allies as an unfriendly act that was to be punished by Bonn's breaking off diplomatic relations with the offending country.[2]

In the mid-1960s, after the Berlin and the Cuban crises had died down, the Soviet Union as well as Germany's partners sought to overcome the Cold War by a new policy of détente. Most significant, although disturbing in Bonn's eyes, were President Lyndon B. Johnson's "bridge building speech" of October 7, 1966, and President Charles de Gaulle's overtures toward Moscow and Warsaw.[3] To prevent it from being isolated from its partners and continuously ostracized by Moscow, the German government on March 25, 1966, sent a diplomatic note to all countries with which it maintained diplomatic relations. This note detailed the principles of German *Ostpolitik* and underlined Bonn's commitment to détente. The Federal Republic suggested a number of arms control and confidence-building measures. Specifically, it proposed an exchange of declarations on the mutual renunciation of force.[4] Although the note, especially its tone, signified a departure from Bonn's previously rather inflexible stand, it was rightly criticized for not showing any flexibility in substance on the most controversial issues of the status quo, such as Poland's western frontier at the Oder-Neisse, the invalidity of the 1938 Munich agreement, and the diplomatic recognition of the GDR.

Reactions from both West and East proved disappointing to officials in Bonn. Though Germany's partners applauded the note's style and tone but asked for bolder steps, the Soviet Union and the Eastern European countries criticized Bonn for continuing to stick to its policy of nonrecognition of the GDR. The Foreign Office state secretary, Karl Carstens, was quite concerned that Bonn would risk international isolation if it did not modify its course on *Ostpolitik* and the German question. In a secret memorandum to Chancellor Ludwig Ehrhard and the Cabinet, he suggested a modification of the Hallstein doctrine and urged for a more forceful public presentation of German political goals.[5]

Because of the change of government in Bonn, the administration did not follow up on Carsten's memorandum. However, the Grand Coalition of the Christian Democratic Union / Christian Social Union (CDU/CSU) and the Social Democratic Party (SPD), which had been formed in December 1966, showed a bit more flexibility on recognizing the status quo. In his Bundestag address when taking office, Chancellor Kurt-Georg Kiesinger (of the CDU) took note of the "existence" of the GDR and suggested that it should be included in the détente process.[6] His foreign minister, Willy Brandt (of the SPD), wanted to go even further. His vision of a European order of peace was to replace the military confrontation and heal the political division of the continent, including Germany's. He was very disappointed when the Soviet Union not only broke off the renunciation of force talks,[7] but he also intervened in Czechoslovakia in August 1968, crushing the "Prague Spring."

The military intervention in Czechoslovakia put détente back into the doldrums for a time. But by the summer of 1969, there were increasing indications that the two world powers wanted to revive the détente process. Washington sought an exit strategy from the Vietnam War, for which it needed at least tacit Soviet support; and Moscow was troubled by increasing tensions with China, which peaked in armed exchanges in the Far East on the Ussuri and Amur rivers. When visiting Germany in February 1969, President Richard Nixon in an offhand remark speculated about the possibility of new East-West talks, above all on improving the situation in and around Berlin.[8] The West was challenged to react when the Warsaw Pact countries in their Budapest Declaration of March 1969 called for the convening of a European security conference.[9] Though constrained by imminent Bundestag elections, the Bonn government followed suit and resumed its talks with Moscow on a renunciation of force. Not only had this issue received added importance after the Warsaw Pact intervention in Czechoslovakia, but renunciation of force declarations could also be used as a means of confidence building. Bonn also agreed to participate in a European security conference if the United States and Canada participated on an equal standing and if a modus vivendi was achieved on the German question. Détente was back on track, although a breakthrough was not yet in sight.

A New Start by the Brandt-Scheel Government

For the new Socialist-Liberal coalition, *Ostpolitik* was of crucial importance. Brandt knew that there was no alternative to a vigorous policy of détente if the Federal Republic did not want to risk isolating itself from international developments. Moreover, a normalization of relations with the Soviet Union and West Germany's Eastern European neighbors was also in Bonn's best interest. A modus vivendi on the disputed question of frontiers and status was a precondition for a rapprochement with the GDR that Brandt and his colleagues sought. Their objective was not reunification, at least not in the near future, but improving the situation for the people in both German states and keeping alive the feeling of national identity among them. Economic considerations were an added objective.

When the Brandt-Scheel government took office on October 21, 1969, the blueprint for a new *Ostpolitik* was already at hand. While head of the policy planning staff in the Foreign Office during Brandt's tenure as foreign minister, Egon Bahr had developed a strategy on how to proceed.[10] His central goal was inner-German rapprochement, but he fully realized that this could only be achieved after a normalization of relations with Moscow. This made the Soviet Union Bonn's primary interlocutor in the ensuing negotiations on the so-called Eastern treaties. But the German government was also aware that it could only negotiate successfully with the Soviet leadership if it had the full backing of its Western partners. Bonn therefore had to dispel the many apprehensions held even by those politicians who had previously advised it to display more flexibility in relations with the East. Now many in Washington, Paris, and other Western capitals were concerned that the Socialist-Liberal coalition's *Ostpolitik* might unlock a dynamic of its own that could tempt Germany to follow a new "Rapallo type" policy of changing alliance orientations to achieve German reunification.[11]

Even before the coalition had formally taken office, Brandt sent Bahr to Washington to inform the U.S. administration about his intentions and to dispel doubts that his government could waver in the Western orientation of its policy.[12] For Henry Kissinger, national security adviser to President Nixon, a central consideration was to harness the process of East-West détente and German *Ostpolitik* to make it conform to U.S. interests and strategies.[13] To assure that Bonn was involved in a dense net of consultations, a back channel was instituted between the White House and the chancellor's office in Bonn that enabled secret communications between Kissinger and Bahr.[14] As the German documents show, Bahr used this channel to regularly inform Kissinger about his negotiations in Moscow.[15]

Another reassuring message was sent to Paris. To overcome French apprehensions, Brandt in a personal letter to President Georges Pompidou promised German concessions on European affairs, including "financial sacrifices" on funding the European Community's Common Agricultural Policy.[16] The French president distrusted Brandt and Bahr, for he assumed that their ultimate goal was the reunification of Germany. He was concerned that for this objective they were prepared to accommodate Soviet requests.[17] When France later supported German *Ostpolitik*—though with apprehensions[18]—it did so for two reasons. The Moscow and Warsaw treaties were not only an element of European détente; they also solidified the status quo, including the frontiers in Europe and the partition of Germany. The most positive reaction to *Ostpolitik* came from London. The Labour government welcomed Bonn's new approach, and it hoped that progress could be reached in East-West arms control and détente. But, like Paris and Washington, London insisted that the rights and responsibilities of the Four Powers not be weakened.

Though aware of the need to cooperate closely with its partners, the Brandt government did not feel it needed prior approval for its *Ostpolitik*. Rather, its partners would be informed, and if necessary consulted, but their advice would not be solicited. Though annoyed at first, Kissinger came to prefer this procedure. "The last thing we wanted was to be held responsible for German negotiating positions that were turning into a bitter domestic issue in Germany."[19] But the U.S. administration provided the support that was indispensable for Bonn's *Ostpolitik* to succeed, just as German *Ostpolitik* would not have been possible without an American policy of détente. The CDU/CSU thus misinterpreted the skeptical noises emanating from Washington, especially from old European hands at the State Department, for the official U.S. position. On Berlin, the situation was different. There the allies held the rights and responsibilities while "Brandt . . . had to ask the Western Allies for permission to do what he wanted to do. The consultations which resulted from this 'request' turned out to be one of the great strong points in the ensuing period of *Ostpolitik.*"[20]

Negotiations with Moscow, Warsaw, and East Berlin

As expected, the negotiations with Moscow were arduous. Thanks to his stubbornness, single-mindedness, and ingenuity, the German chief negotiator, Bahr, won an agreement only eight months after the German-Soviet talks began in December 1969. During the first phase, both sides tried to gauge the other's room for maneuvering. The German ambassador, Helmut Allardt, presented new drafts for renunciation of force declarations, and the Soviet foreign minister, Andrej Gromyko, suggested a treaty on the formal recognition of the status quo in Europe, including a recognition of the GDR under international law and a confirmation of existing frontiers. This was not a very promising start, but the German side correctly interpreted Gromyko's participation in the talks as an indication of Soviet interest.[21]

After additional positive signals, at the end of January 1970 the German government resolved to continue and felt secure enough to entrust Bahr with the negotiations. This architect of *Ostpolitik* remained Brandt's closest foreign policy adviser, now serving him as a junior minister in the Chancellor's Office (*"Staatssekretär"*). Among the most difficult problems Bahr encountered in his talks with Gromyko were the diplomatic recognition of the GDR, the issue of European frontiers, the observance of allied rights and responsibilities in Germany as a whole and in Berlin, and the future of ties between Berlin and the Federal Republic. Bahr argued that a full diplomatic recognition of the GDR was not possible because it would infringe on Four Power rights, thus also on Soviet rights. "The diplomatic recognition of the GDR by us which the Soviet Union demanded was by no means acceptable. This was the nucleus of the matter. . . . If we had not been able to insist on this crucial point, or if the Soviet Union had not compromised, I would have had to leave Moscow without any success, and I had left."[22]

The issue of frontiers was of equal delicacy. Finally, both sides agreed on the formula that all frontiers were inviolable—not immutable, as Moscow had originally demanded. Both the Federal Republic and the Soviet Union confirmed that they had no territorial claims against anyone, nor would they assert such claims in the future. This formula was compatible with the 1945 Potsdam Accord, according to which a final settlement of the German frontiers was deferred to an eventual peace treaty. Further, all specific clauses were subordinated to the principle of renunciation of force in accordance with article 2 of the UN Charter. Therefore, articles 53 and 107 of the Charter, the so-called enemy clauses that Moscow wished to retain, lost in importance, as did the treaty's character of a border treaty. Although the agreement made no direct reference to Berlin, the German side felt assured because the treaty recognized that a normalization in Europe and the evolution of peaceful relations among all European states had to proceed from the actual situation existing in this region. In addition, Bahr and Gromyko agreed on a number of declarations of intent. The Federal Republic indicated that it intended to conclude similar treaties with Poland, Czechoslovakia, and the GDR. The Federal Republic also agreed that it would develop relations with the GDR on the basis of sovereign equality, nondiscrimination, and nonintervention in domestic affairs. This was different from the full diplomatic recognition that Moscow had initially demanded, though it went as far as Bonn could go without infringing on the stipulations of the Federal Republic's constitution. On balance, Bonn was not able to exchange "pure" renunciation of force declarations, but it had succeeded in upholding its view on the "European realities" and kept its essentials intact.

Bahr and Valentin Falin, Gromyko's aide, recorded these terms in a secret minute that they submitted for final approval to their governments on May 22, 1970.[23] When opponents of a German-Soviet rapprochement leaked this paper to the press, it caused a tempest of protest. Members of the CDU/CSU opposition, representatives of the refugee organizations, and large segments of the conservative press challenged the government on political and constitutional grounds. They argued that the agreements had been negotiated too quickly, not professionally and carefully enough (e.g., not by career diplomats or experienced politicians). Of more weight was the charge that the Socialist-Liberal coalition, in clear violation of the Federal Republic's Basic Law, was about to recognize the GDR and thus give up its claim to national reunification. The Bavarian state government even put this charge to the Constitutional Court, which upheld the constitutionality of the Eastern treaties in its ruling of July 31, 1973. But in a politically charged climate, the government had to watch its step, especially because its slim parliamentary majority was dwindling when a number of SPD and Free Democratic Party members critical of *Ostpolitik* crossed party lines. Thus, on May 17, 1972, the Moscow and Warsaw treaties were only ratified after an agreement on Berlin had been achieved and after a complicated domestic tug of war.

For domestic consumption, on the one hand, and for intragovernment bargaining, on the other, the Cabinet entrusted the foreign minister, Walter Scheel—and not Bahr—with the concluding negotiations in Moscow. The documents reveal that this was a mock performance because Scheel was either badly briefed by his staff or not enough interested in the treaty. As soon as the meeting in Moscow had opened on July 27, 1970, he asked Bahr to take the lead. The result of this third round of German-Soviet negotiations did not differ substantially from the earlier Bahr-Falin accord. A new element was a letter on Germany's claim to national unity,[24] which the Soviet side accepted without formally noting. It had been designed to dwarf the opposition's challenge that the government neglected the constitutional mandate regarding national unity. On August 12, 1970, the Moscow Treaty was signed in a splendid ceremony by Chancellor Brandt, Minister President Alexei Kosygin, and foreign ministers Scheel and Gromyko. To inform Germany's partners and to dispel doubts about the intentions of the Moscow Treaty, Scheel briefed the three Western ambassadors in Moscow about the agreement. He further instructed the German ambassadors in the Western capitals to fully inform their host governments.[25] Brandt, to mark the historic event and to calm domestic apprehensions, addressed the German people with a televised message while still in Moscow. He assured his viewers that the treaty gave nothing away that had not been gambled away long ago, and that it in no way infringed on the close mooring of the Federal Republic to the West. Instead, he declared that the treaty was to safeguard peace in Europe and to enable peaceful relations among its people.[26]

Negotiations with Poland began in February 1970, but their pace was much slower than that of the Moscow talks. Because the major breakthroughs had to be achieved in Moscow, the Warsaw negotiations were relegated to a secondary role. The German delegation was led by State Secretary Ferdinand Duckwitz, an experienced career diplomat with an impeccable wartime record (as a diplomat in occupied Denmark, he had warned the country's Jews of their imminent deportation and thus enabled most of them to escape) and a strong leaning toward Socialist-Liberal policies, and by deputy Polish foreign minister Jósef Winiewcz. Not unexpectedly, the most difficult agenda item was the recognition of Poland's western frontier at the Oder and Neisse line. Initially, the German side had sought to solve this problem by offering Warsaw renunciation of force declarations and stating its willingness to observe this frontier until a final ruling in a peace treaty was achieved.[27] During the negotiations, however, the German negotiators learned that an agreement with Poland could only be had if Bonn recognized the Polish desire to live in secure frontiers. Besides declaring their respect for the inviolability of their frontiers, both sides stated that the borders demarcated in Potsdam constituted Poland's western frontiers. Another difficult issue that was successfully solved was the permission for a certain number of Polish citizens of German origin to join their families in the Federal Republic. Bonn repudiated the Polish claim for reparations for wartime damages, although a few years later it offered financial subsidies to Poland if it further facilitated the emigration of German descendants. Before the Warsaw Treaty could be signed on December 7, 1970, more details and emotional problems had to be overcome.[28] To improve the climate of the talks, Brandt wrote a personal letter to Party Secretary Władysław Gomułka and promised to attend the signing ceremony. He wanted to be as forthcoming as possible toward the Polish government, although he could not disguise the fact that the crucial agreements had to be effected in Moscow, not in Warsaw.

The Prague Treaty was the last to be concluded with Germany's eastern neighbors,[29] apart from that with the GDR. The reason was not that particularly controversial problems had to be tackled. On the contrary, both sides were in full agreement that the 1938 Munich Accord was nil, although they disagreed on the exact date it became invalid. The Czech side argued that it never had any validity because it had been forced on the Czechs, while the Germans preferred to leave the exact date open because they wanted to legally protect their citizens who had acted in the belief of the accord's validity. The late conclusion of the Prague Treaty on December 11, 1973, was rather due to the tremendous workload that the German administration, above all Bahr, had to cope with while negotiating with the GDR on the inner-German arrangements. Further, there was no diplomatic pressure from any of Germany's Western partners. Their primary attention had been directed at détente with the Soviet Union and, to a lesser degree, with Poland, although this country had been the first victim of World War II. Though the German government was apprehensive about domestic opposition, especially from the Sudeten Germans who had been forced to leave Czechoslovakia in 1945, neither Washington nor Paris showed much interest in an agreement. They had little regard for the strictly pro-Moscow regime of Gustav Husak, and there were no large communities of Czech émigrés in the West who could exert pressure on their host governments.

The Basic Treaty was indeed the apex of *Ostpolitik's* architecture. For a

German patriot like Bahr, the other treaties were but necessary preconditions for an agreement with the GDR that could hold the promise of easing the fate of the people in divided Germany and eventually bring about "change through rapprochement."[30] In his first message to the Bundestag, Brandt had recognized the existence of two states in Germany that could not be foreign to each other. He proposed the initiation of bilateral talks resulting in an agreed-on cooperation below the level of diplomatic recognition.[31] The GDR's head of state, Walter Ulbricht, had responded with the proposition that both states conclude a formal treaty in which they agree on the establishment of diplomatic relations based on their full equality.[32] Not only did Bonn's and East Berlin's starting positions thus vary, but also their general approach toward détente and a relaxation of intra-German tensions differed widely. This was most visible when Brandt and Willi Stoph (then the GDR head of government) met at Erfurt and Kassel.[33]

After the Bahr-Falin memorandum became known, the East Berlin leadership feared that Moscow would block the GDR's goal of full diplomatic recognition. It thus tried to achieve in direct talks with Bonn what Moscow no longer seemed willing to deliver. But the Federal Republic was no more forthcoming than the Soviet Union had been. The way out of the impasse were talks on traffic questions between Bahr and Michael Kohl (nicknamed "red cabbage"[34]). The need for improvements on inner-German traffic was obvious. Further, it was assumed that the Four Powers would agree on general arrangements concerning the traffic to and from Berlin, but leave details to be arranged between the two German states. When Kissinger was informed about these talks, he was concerned that a German-German dynamic might undercut a Four Power arrangement on Berlin.[35] Neither Bonn nor East Berlin, in fact, were quite immune against reaching a joint accord: Bonn wished to use the inner-German talks to speed up the quadripartite negotiations; East Berlin insisted that regulations on intra-German traffic and the exchange of visitors fell within the sovereign authority of the GDR. When the Four Powers had concluded their quadripartite negotiations on Berlin and instructed the two German governments to negotiate on implementing the Berlin Four-Power Agreement, both already had a negotiation forum at hand. They could resume their negotiations without prior exploratory talks. After three months, the agreements were in hand.

The next logical step was a German-German Traffic Treaty, which was initialed in May 1972. It was the first international agreement between the two German states and thus signified an important step toward an international recognition of the GDR. A few months later, negotiations on a treaty between the German states began. The most difficult question was what form of recognition of the GDR the Federal Republic was to concede, and, above all, whether the GDR would accept anything less than full diplomatic recognition. What could the Federal Republic offer in exchange? Disagreements also existed on other questions of status, such as the exchange of permanent representatives and the nature of the inner-German frontier, as well as on a multitude of humanitarian issues. Bonn knew that it could not block the GDR's international recognition much longer, because many of its friends wanted to normalize relations with East Berlin. Its only card was admission to the United Nations, because any of the three Western powers could veto the GDR's request for membership. Time thus was running out, the more so as Bonn wanted to settle the intra-German issues before a European security conference convened. Finally, a few days before Christmas, a Basic Treaty between the two German states, together with a number of additional protocols and letters, was signed. Ratification was no problem, for the Socialist-Liberal coalition had won a large majority in the 1972 general elections, which were mainly fought on the issue of *Ostpolitik*. Now, for the first time since 1949, the two German states had normal relations with each other—at least nominally. Bahr's comment was prophetic: "Until then we had no relations with each other, now we will have bad relations."

The Four Powers carefully observed the inner-German negotiations, and behind the scenes they were directly involved in them. The 1945 Potsdam Accord as well the 1952–54 agreements between the three Western powers and the Federal Republic, and the 1954–55 treaty between the Soviet Union and the GDR, had given the Four Powers overall authority on questions relating to Germany as a whole and especially to Berlin. Their rights and responsibilities gave them a means of control, which they intended to retain. In their participation in these negotiations, while in the background, they carefully watched that the two German states did not overstep their boundaries and infringe on allied rights. In identical notes to the three Western powers and to the Soviet Union, the Federal Republic and the GDR later confirmed that the Basic Treaty did not touch on any relevant quadripartite agreements, decisions, and practices.[36]

The International Setting of *Ostpolitik:*
The Berlin Agreement and the Conference
on Security and Cooperation in Europe

German *Ostpolitik* was embedded in a web of mutual linkages and multilateral arrangements. Because the security of Berlin was not adequately dealt with in the Moscow Treaty, the Federal Republic made its ratification contingent on the successful conclusion of an arrangement on Berlin. The Soviet Union, in return, announced that the quadripartite agreement on Berlin would not enter into force unless the Moscow and Warsaw treaties had been ratified by the German Bundestag. A third, although somewhat weaker, linkage made the convening of a European security conference contingent on a previous inner-German accord. The Eastern Treaties, the Quadripartite Agreement on Berlin, and the Conference on Security and Co-operation in Europe were thus inextricably linked.

The uncertainty about the future of Berlin, the drain on its people, its insecure access, and the frequent harassment of Berliners and West Germans alike made an agreement on Berlin urgent. Moreover, the Soviet Union could use the situation in and around the city at will to put pressure on the West. This was an untenable predicament. When President Nixon, on his first visit to Germany, referred to the possibility of East-West talks on Berlin, the German government was quick to support a pertinent initiative. In the past, the Western partners of the Federal Republic had been quite reluctant to propose negotiations on Berlin. Being the demandeurs, they were skeptical whether such talks would yield positive results. When in 1969 both the Soviet Union and the United States, although for different reasons, were interested in gestures of détente, the prospects for positive results looked somewhat brighter.

After a slow beginning in March 1970, the quadripartite negotiations between the representatives from France, Britain, the Soviet Union, and the United States gained in speed, while Bonn and Moscow were finalizing their arrangements on a modus vivendi on the status quo in Europe. Washington now wished to use the Berlin negotiations to control the dynamic of *Ostpolitik*. Because the Federal Republic, because of the allied rights and responsibilities, could not negotiate on Berlin, it needed the Four Powers to effect what the Federal Republic was not entitled to do. However, it was deeply involved in devising a joint Western negotiating strategy. The most important forum for this was the "quad," a group of governments and embassy officials of the three Western powers and of the Federal Republic, as well as its formal and informal subgroups.[37] Another bilateral German-American link was provided by the back channel between Bahr and Kissinger. Though the quad was most effective in the preparatory stages of the quadripartite negotiations and during their apex, the back channel was used to reassure a concerned partner, or to overcome deadlocks. If the Western allies participated on the sidelines in the negotiations on a Basic Treaty with the GDR, so did the Federal Republic at the Berlin talks.

The Berlin Agreement had three parts. The first, most important part had been negotiated by the Four Powers and contained regulations on the integrity and the accessibility of West Berlin, as well as on its ties with the Federal Republic. Though Moscow guaranteed the survivability of the city, the West recognized that it was not governed from Bonn. The second part of the agreement was negotiated by the two German states. It contained the operative clauses on traffic to and from West Berlin, its borders, and the status of enclaves on the state's territory. After this agreement had been reached, the Four Powers reconvened to take note of the inner-German arrangement and set the whole Quadripartite Agreement into force. More than anything else, this procedure symbolized the interdependence of Western détente and German *Ostpolitik*.

The project of a European security conference (ESC) was an old Soviet idea from the 1950s, but it was regularly retabled in consecutive years—although with changing purposes. It was geared toward the recognition of the postwar status quo in Europe and putting a break on any kind of German revisionism. It was further advertised as an instrument of détente. With it, Moscow sought to establish itself as the prime guarantor of peace and security in Europe, decoupling the West from U.S. military protection. For these reasons, the Western powers were reluctant to swallow this bait. In 1968, NATO instead proposed to hold negotiations on Mutual and Balanced Force Reductions (MBFR). When in 1969 Finland offered its good services to bring about a European security conference, the European countries agreed on preparatory talks, although in veiled language. They made their consent contingent on the full participation of the United States and Canada, the inclusion of military and arms control issues in the agenda, and the improvement of the situation in Berlin.

Brandt's view on a European security conference had undergone significant changes since the 1960s. When he was foreign minister, he saw a solution of the German question in the framework of—as he liked to call it—a "European order of peace." In Brandt's view, a European order of peace was more than a European security system that concentrated on the security and military elements of the confrontation, which should be diminished and ultimately overcome. But a European order of peace also implied that political tensions would be reduced and cooperation and rapprochement between nations deepened.[38] This concept had initially been developed by Bahr, who foresaw it as a bridge between the two opposing alliances, NATO and the Warsaw Pact—and eventually as a replacement for them. In this concept, the ESC was an instrument to bring about a rapprochement between the two German states. When, after 1969, direct negotiations with

Moscow and the other Eastern European neighbors on renunciation of force treaties proved successful, the ESC was relegated to a secondary role. Instead of being used as an enabling device, it was now to safeguard multilaterally what had been achieved bilaterally. Therefore, the conference should only take place after the German issues had been settled.

The German position on the ESC—now called the Conference on Security and Cooperation in Europe—was only haltingly supported by the U.S. administration. Washington was not very enthusiastic about an all-European conference, even with American and Canadian participation. Kissinger once remarked that he did not think it was appropriate if now the Portuguese and the Poles were negotiating on European security. When the conference project took shape in the course of 1972, the participation of the United States and Canada was assured, and other conditions were met, the United States reluctantly joined its Western partners in agreeing to hold this conference. However, Washington, Paris, and Bonn differed substantially on political preferences. For the United States, MBFR was a top priority and the CSCE was something that could not be avoided. France, for its part, supported the CSCE because it resented the bloc-to-bloc approach of MBFR. The Federal Republic wanted both CSCE and MBFR, and it preferred a close linkage between the two.

After difficult intra-alliance negotiations in May 1972, President Nixon and Soviet Party Secretary Leonid Brezhnev agreed in a direct bilateral exchange that CSCE and MBFR talks should take place but be conducted as separate and parallel activities. The specific conference strategy and tactic for the CSCE was left to the Europeans to work out. Most active were the members of the European Community, especially the Federal Republic and France, as well as a number of neutral and nonaligned countries such as Finland and Switzerland. Due to heavy domestic opposition,[39] the United States displayed an attitude of benign neglect. It only intervened in the final stages of the conference, to break deadlocks and to assure that provisions on freedom of speech and on the liberties of journalists were agreed on. When Kissinger in his memoirs claims a dominant American role at the CSCE, he certainly overstates his government's input.[40]

German *Ostpolitik* in a Strategic Triangle: Findings

In chapter 10 of this volume, Georges-Henri Soutou contends that—as seen from Paris—there was no French-German-American triangle on *Ostpolitik* and détente. Instead, he sees two other major triangles at work: "one between Paris, Moscow, and Bonn, mostly about the European aspects of détente; and one between Paris, Washington, and Moscow, mostly about the international aspects." The view from Bonn was slightly different. Of the two triangles Soutou describes, the first was considered to be very weak and overshadowed by the second. Any French-Soviet rapprochement, as indicated by Pompidou's visit to Moscow in October 1970, raised suspicions in Bonn that Paris wanted to claim a dominant role in European affairs, as a spokesman for Europe toward Moscow, laying out the blueprint for a European order of peace. If French interests combined with those of the United States and the Soviet Union, fears of a new Potsdam were raised in West Germany.

Regarding German *Ostpolitik,* the triangle had constraining as well as enabling effects. The three Western powers in the 1952-54 Paris and Bonn treaties had reconfirmed their rights and responsibilities regarding Germany as a whole and Berlin. Their special rights were in the well-understood self interest of the Federal Republic because they carried the commitment to support German reunification and to safeguard Berlin. In return, they called for a close cooperation with Paris and Washington (as well as with London) on all issues where the German question was involved, such as *Ostpolitik.* Before the Socialist-Liberal coalition could embark on its détente policy, it had to attain the support of the three powers. It turned out that the British Labour government was quite sympathetic to *Ostpolitik* and détente, whereas French and American support had to be won with a policy of confidence building and with special reassurances. Their concern that German *Ostpolitik* could acquire a dynamic of its own, and therefore needed harnessing, limited Bonn's room for maneuvering.

At the same time, the triangle was used by Bonn to support *Ostpolitik* and détente, as was done during the German negotiations with Moscow and Warsaw. The quadripartite negotiations on Berlin, however, showed that Western interests were not completely identical. France was very concerned that détente might be endangered if too many concessions were extracted by the Soviet Union, or France's quadripartite rights might be abrogated.[41] However, France also felt that a more forthcoming attitude to Bonn's concerns would strengthen its transatlantic coupling. In this situation, the triangular mechanism was used by Bonn to have Washington convince Paris of the merits of its position. The triangle thus served as an enabling structure for Germany.

This opportunity was lost when, during and after the 1973 Arab-Israeli war, French-American relations were marked by a recurrent pattern of controversies. During the oil crisis, the conflict was about interest and power in Southwest Asia—or the "Proche Orient," as the French called it. During the debate on Kissinger's ill-fated proposal for a "Year of Europe," the conflict was about the American role in Europe. In both areas, it was a struggle about a hegemonic role, for which there was no solution. The triangle thus became a liability for the Federal Republic. The French-American controversies deprived the Socialist-Liberal coalition of any support it might need with regard to Moscow. Fortunately, *Ostpolitik* was mostly completed, although the implementation of the Quadripartite Agreement on Berlin, and the interpretation of its ambivalent language, were hampered by these disagreements. Problems arose about the ties between West Berlin and the Federal Republic, which Paris and Moscow interpreted in a very restrictive sense, while Washington tended to support Bonn's more extensive position —as long as its rights and responsibilities were not infringed.

In general, there was a basic congruence of interests and positions among the Western powers concerning Germany. This was especially true on German *Ostpolitik*. Under these conditions, the strategic triangle constituted a strong enabling factor.

Notes

1. German *Ostpolitik,* however, has to be seen in the context of overall German foreign policy. See my *Coming of Age: German Foreign Policy since 1945* (Lanham, Md.: Rowman & Littlefield, 2006); chap. 5, 157–95, deals with *Ostpolitik* and détente.

2. See "Government Declaration, 28 June 1956: The Hallstein Doctrine," in *Politics and Government in the Federal Republic of Germany: Basic Documents,* ed. Carl-Christoph Schweitzer et al. (Lexington, Mass.: Berg Publishers, 1984), 298–99.

3. See "The Atlantic Alliance and European Policy: Address by President Johnson to the National Editorial Writers Conference, New York, October 7, 1966," in *Documents on American Foreign Relations 1966,* ed. Richard P. Stebbins (New York: Harper & Row, 1967), 73–80; see also Centre d'Études de Politique Étrangère, "Modèles de sécurité européenne," *Politique Étrangère* 32 (1967): 519–41.

4. See "Note From the Federal Republic of Germany to the United States and Other Powers on West German Efforts to Improve Relations with the Soviet Union and Eastern European Countries, March 25, 1966" [extract], in *Documents on Germany 1944–1985,* ed. U.S. Department of State (Washington, D.C.: U.S. Department of State, 1985), 914–18.

5. See "Aufzeichnung des Staatssekretärs Carstens," October 17, 1966, doc. 333, in *Akten zur Auswärtigen Politik Deutschlands* [hereafter AAPD] 1966, ed. Institut für Zeitgeschichte (Munich: Oldenbourg, 1997), 1374–83; and Karl Carstens, *Erinnerun-*

gen und Erfahrungen, ed. Kai von Jena and Reinhard Schmoeckel (Boppard am Rhein: Boldt, 1993), 761–62.

6. See "Address by Chancellor Kiesinger Before the Bundestag on the Foreign Policy Goals of the New Coalition Government on the Federal Republic of Germany, December 13, 1966" [extracts], in *Documents on Germany,* ed. U.S. Department of State, 935–41.

7. See Presse- und Informationsamt der Bundesregierung, ed., *Die Politik des Gewaltverzichts* (Bonn: Presse- und Informationsamt der Bundesregierung, 1968); and Auswärtiges Amt, ed., *Dokumentation zum Gewaltverzicht* (mimeo), July 12, 1968.

8. See "Remarks by President Nixon at the Siemens Factory, West Berlin, February 27, 1969" [extracts], in *Documents on Germany,* ed. U.S. Department of State, 1032–34.

9. See "Communiqué Issued by the Political Consultative Committee of the Warsaw Pact Appealing for a Conference on European Security" [extracts], Budapest, March 17, 1969, in *Documents on Germany,* ed. U.S. Department of State, 1035–37; and "Address by Foreign Minister Gromyko Before the Supreme Soviet of the U.S.S.R. Regarding Germany and European Security" [extracts], July 10, 1969, in *Documents on Germany,* ed. U.S. Department of State, 1046.

10. See "Aufzeichnung des Ministerialdirektors Bahr," September 18, 1969, doc. 295, *AAPD 1969,* 1030–47. Various Foreign Office papers built on these ideas later on; see "Aufzeichnung des Ministeraldirektors Ruete," October 29, 1969, doc. 333, *AAPD 1969,* 1173–84; and "Aufzeichnung des Ministeraldirektors Ruete," December 30, 1969 (including draft treaty with the GDR), doc. 415, *AAPD 1969,* 1471–76.

11. For French apprehensions, see chapter 10 in the present volume by Georges-Henri Soutou; and Henry Kissinger, *White House Years* (Boston: Little, Brown, 1979), 529. Willy Brandt was very much aware of these sentiments; see his *Begegnungen und Einsichten: Die Jahre 1960–1975* (Hamburg: Hoffmann & Campe, 1976), 385–86.

12. See "Aufzeichnung des Ministerialdirektors Bahr," October 14, 1969, doc. 314, *AAPD 1969,* 1114–18, for a German report on this visit; and Henry Kissinger, *White House Years* (Boston: Little, Brown, 1979), 409, for the U.S. reaction. In his memoirs, Kissinger details his skepticism about German *Ostpolitik.* It took him a while before he realized that the United States had few alternatives to a pragmatic support.

13. See former state secretary Paul Frank, who recalls in his memoirs that Kissinger once had told him: "I will tell you something: If a policy of détente with the Soviet Union is contemplated, then it will be us doing it." *Entschlüsselte Botschaft: Ein Diplomat macht Inventur* (Stuttgart: Deutsche Verlags-Anstalt, 1981), 287.

14. See Kissinger, *White House Years,* 409.

15. See the numerous memos from Egon Bahr to Henry Kissinger, in *Egon Bahr, Aufzeichnungen, Berichte, Gespräche: Aus den Akten zur Auswärtigen Politik der Bundesrepublik Deutschland 1970,* ed. Institut für Zeitgeschichte (Munich: Oldenbourg, 2000).

16. See letter from Chancellor Brandt to President Pompidou, "Bundeskanzler Brandt an Staatspräsident Pompidou," November 27, 1969, doc. 380, *AAPD 1969,* 1346–47.

17. See chapter 10 in this volume.

18. For the French attitude, see the report from the German minister and ambassador in Paris, "Gesandter Blomeyer-Bartenstein, Paris, an das Auswärtige Amt," June 10,

1970, doc. 258, *AADP 1970*, 942–44; "Botschafter Ruete, Paris, an das Auswärtige Amt," July 23 , 1970, doc. 331, *AADP 1970*, 1230–31.

19. See Kissinger, *White House Years*, 530.

20. "From U.S. Mission Berlin to Department of State," Department of State Airgram, August 12, 1980, confidential (in the author's possession).

21. See Helmut Allardt, *Politik vor und hinter den Kulissen: Erfahrungen eines Diplomaten zwischen Ost und West* (Düsseldorf: Econ, 1979).

22. See interview by Staatssekretär Egon Bahr with Günter Gaus, June 4, 1972, in a TV program "Zur Person," in *Entscheidung in Bonn: Die Entstehung der Ost- und Deutschlandpolitik 1969/1970,* ed. Günther Schmid (Cologne: Wissenschaft und Politik, 1979), 48; see also Bahr's conversation with Gromyko, "Gespräch des Staatssekretärs Bahr, Bundeskanzleramt, mit dem sowjetischen Außenminister Gromyko in Moskau," January 30, 1970, doc. 28, *AAPD 1970,* 105–28.

23. See "Leitsätze für einen Vertrag mit der UdSSR," May 20, 1970, Doc. 221, *AAPD 1970,* 822–24; For an English version of the "Bahr-Paper" and the "Treaty Between the Federal Republic of Germany and the Soviet Union, Signed at Moscow, August 12, 1970," see *Documents on Germany,* ed. U.S. Department of State, 1101–5.

24. See "Letter From the Federal Republic of Germany to the Soviet Union Regarding German Reunification, August 12, 1970," in *Documents on Germany,* ed. U.S. Department of State, 1105.

25. See "Bundesminister Scheel, z. Z. Moskau, an Staatssekretär Freiherr von Braun," August 4, 1970, doc. 359, *AAPD 1970,* 1366–68; "Staatssekretär Frank, z. Z. Moskau, an Staatssekretär Freiherr von Braun, 4 August 1970," doc. 363, *AAPD 1970,* 1378–81; also "Bundesminister Scheel, z. Z. Moskau, an die Botschafter von Hase (London), Pauls (Washington) und Ruete (Paris)," August 5, 1970, doc. 370, *AAPD 1970,* 1399–1402; "Gespräch des Bundesministers Scheel mit den Vertretern der Drei Mächte in Moskau," August 6, 1970, doc. 372, *AAPD 1970,* 1405–6.

26. See TV Address by Chancellor Brandt at Moscow, August 12, 1970 in Presse- und Informationsamt der Bundesregierung, ed., *Der Vertrag vom 12 August 1970 zwischen der Bundesrepublik Deutschland und der Union der Sozialistischen Sowjetrepubliken* (Bonn: Bundesdruckerei 1970), 26–28; the citation here is on 28.

27. See "Abkommen zwischen der Bundesrepublik und Polen," Working Paper (Entwurf, April 22, 1970, doc. 174, *AAPD 1970, 644–45*; For guidelines from the Bundesregierung for the negotiations with Poland, see "Aufzeichnung des Ministerialdirektors Ruete," November 13, 1969, doc. 316, *AAPD 1969,* 1275–81.

28. See "Treaty Between the Federal Republic of Germany and Poland Concerning the Basis for Normalizing Their Mutual Relations, Signed at Warsaw, December 7, 1970," *Documents on Germany,* 1125–27; see also Presse- und Informationsamt der Bundesregierung, ed., "Information der polnischen Regierung," *Der Vertrag zwischen der Bundesrepublik Deutschland und der Volksrepublik Polen* (Bonn: Bundesdruckerei 1970), 13–15.

29. See "Treaty of Mutual Relations Between the Federal Republic of Germany and the Czechoslovak Socialist Republic, Signed in Prague, December 11, 1973," *Documents on Germany,* 1256–58.

30. "Wandel durch Annäherung" (change through rapprochement) was the catchword of a talk which Egon Bahr, director of the Berlin Press and Information Office, had given in 1963. See "Vortrag des Leiters des Presse- und Informationsamtes des Landes Berlin, Bahr, in der Evangelischen Akademie Tutzing," July 15, 1963, Bundesminis-

terium für Innerdeutsche Beziehungen IV, ed., *Dokumente zur Deutschlandpolitik* (cited as DzD) Series, Vol. 9/1963 (Frankfurt am Main: Alfred Metzner, 1978), 572–75.

31. See "Statement by Chancellor Brandt Before the Bundestag on the Goals of the New West German Government Respecting Germany and European Security, October 28, 1969" [extracts], in *Documents on Germany*, 1049–50.

32. See "DDR-Staatsratsvorsitzender Ulbricht: Schreiben an Bundespräsident Heinemann und Entwurf eines Vertrages," in *Texte zur Deutschlandpolitik* (cited as *TzD*), vol. 4, ed. Bundesministerium für Innerdeutsche Beziehungen (Bonn–Bad Godesberg: Vorwärtsdruck 1969), 143–47.

33. For Stoph's and Brandt's statements at Erfurt, see "DDR-Ministerratsvorsitzender Stoph: Grundsätzliche Ausführungen anlässlich des Erfurter Treffens" and "Bundeskanzler Brandt: Grundsätzliche Ausführungen anlässlich des Erfurter Treffens," March 19, 1970, *TzD*, vol. 4, 327–65; for their statements at Kassel, May 21 1970, see *TzD*, vol. 5, 96–170. For a good summary of this meeting, which uses recently released East German archival material, see M. E. Sarotte, *Dealing with the Devil: East Germany, Détente and Ostpolitik, 1969–1973* (Chapel Hill: University of North Carolina Press, 2001), chap. 2.

34. The German word "Kohl" means "cabbage." This nickname further distinguished East German Michael Kohl from the CDU politician and later chancellor Helmut Kohl.

35. See Kissinger, *White House Years,* 531–32.

36. See "Treaty on the Basis of Relations Between the Federal Republic of Germany and the German Democratic Republic and Supplementary Documents, Signed at Berlin, December 21, 1972," in *Documents on Germany,* ed. U.S. Department of State, 1215–30; the citation here is on 1221.

37. See Helga Haftendorn and Henning Riecke, ". . . *die volle Macht eines souveränen Staates . . . ," Die Alliierten Vorbehaltsrechte als Rahmenbedingung westdeutscher Aussenpolitik 1949–1990* (Baden-Baden: Nomos 1999), 37–80 (61 ff). For an English-language account on the quad, see Helga Haftendorn, "The 'Quad': Dynamics of Institutional Change," in *Imperfect Unions: Security Institutions over Time and Space,* ed. Helga Haftendorn, Robert O. Keohane, and Celeste A. Wallander (Oxford: Oxford University Press, 1999), 162–94.

38. See Willy Brandt's radio interview with *Deutschlandfunk,* July 2, 1967, reprinted in *Bulletin der Bundesregierung,* July 8, 1967, 604–7; and his interview with Sonntagsblatt, February 14, 1968, reprinted in *Bulletin der Bundesregierung,* February 16, 1968, 165–67. See also his address to the Consultative Assembly of the Council of Europe in Strasbourg, January 24, 1967, *Bulletin der Bundesregierung,* January 26, 1967, 59–61. For a somewhat heavy-handed American criticism on Bahr's and Brandt's ideas, see Walter F. Hahn, *Between Westpolitik and Ostpolitik: Changing German Security Views* (Beverly Hills, Calif.: Sage, 1975).

39. See Henry Kissinger, *Years of Renewal* (New York: Simon & Schuster, 1999), 653.

40. See *Verwaltete Aussenpolitik: Sicherheits- und entspannungspolitische Entscheidungsprozesse in Bonn,* ed. Helga Haftendorn, Wolf-Dieter Karl, Joachim Krause, and Lothar Wilker (Cologne: Wissenschaft und Politik, 1978); Kissinger, *White House Years,* 412–16, 534, 948, 1128.

41. See "Gespräch des Bundeskanzlers Brandt mit Staatspräsident Pompidou in Paris," January 30, 1970, doc. 29, *AAPD 1970,* 119–26; the citation here is on 125.

Chapter 10

President Pompidou, *Ostpolitik,* and the Strategy of Détente

Georges-Henri Soutou

Georges Pompidou, president of the French Republic from 1969 until his death in 1974, was fully aware of the revolution in international affairs that took place during those years: the "Nixon shock," détente, and *Ostpolitik.* He basically favored détente because it could enhance stability in Europe. He believed détente was the best framework within which to try to settle the German problem, which preoccupied him because he feared the basic instability of Germany and the temptation of a deal with Moscow that came from the partition of the country.[1] For him détente, provided it was prudently managed without provoking the Soviet Union, was the only possible way to give more leeway to Eastern Europe in its relations with Moscow. It was also the best framework to help the forces slowly transforming the Soviet Union into a modern industrialized society less hostile to the West.

At the same time, Pompidou adamantly wanted to preserve the basic independence of French foreign policy, true to the essence of Gaullism. But he did not simply copy Charles de Gaulle's actual policy. As we shall see, he had his own, partly different agenda, largely because he felt that de Gaulle had often been not pragmatic enough and had uselessly isolated France. His strategy toward détente was complex, partly because the situation as such was complex, and partly because he could not afford to antagonize the most Gaullist part of his constituency. He was also a master tactician. He was not always perfectly candid, and his words should not be taken at face value, particularly his exchanges with the Russians and to a much lesser degree with the Germans. He was probably at his sincerest (outside the Elysée Palace and outside the French government) with his American partners.[2]

In my view, there was no real French-German-American triangle about détente. Apart from the fact that Washington and Paris agreed generally on a very prudent and not overly enthusiastic view of *Ostpolitik,* there were no systematic consultations between the three capitals about it, with the exception, as we shall see, of the Berlin settlement of 1971 (which also included the United Kingdom). It is for European affairs and the development of the European Community that such a triangle was very much in evidence—the Americans trying to control the European Economic Community (EEC) through an extension of the scope of the Atlantic alliance, the French resisting that trend, and the Germans trying to mediate between Paris and Washington or aligning themselves with one or the other capital.[3] It has frequently been asserted that there existed in European affairs a triangle between Paris, Bonn, and London, Pompidou supposedly accepting in 1970 the British entry into the European Community in order to balance Germany. This is an overly simplistic view; Pompidou was more sophisticated than that, and from the beginning he had been more concerned with the fact that Britain could block from the outside any progress of the EEC if it were kept out.[4] To balance Germany, Pompidou counted on Moscow and Washington, not on London.

With regard to détente proper, there were two major triangles: one between Paris, Moscow, and Bonn, mostly about the European aspects of détente; and one between Paris, Washington, and Moscow, mostly about the international aspects, such as the Strategic Arms Limitation Talks (SALT), China, or the Middle East. The whole point for Paris was to try to remain at the apex of each of those three triangles, enhancing its world role through its European position as leader of the European Community and conversely using its world role to legitimate its leadership of Europe.

Pompidou's Views of the Soviet Union, Germany, and the United States

Pompidou already had a clear vision of international relations before becoming president of the French Republic in 1969. His views were basically Gaullist: He was adamant about French independence; he was very much on guard against a perceived American policy to use NATO to control Europe; he was very ambivalent toward Germany, feeling that it should be closely controlled in a French-led Europe; and he was in favor of détente with the Soviet Union and of a special French role in Moscow to enhance France's influence in the world.[5] At the same time, he was quite ready to have better relations with Washington, believing that the military and economic coherence of the West was an absolute necessity.[6] As for Russia, he distrusted Soviet geopolitical aims toward Europe and the Middle East and deeply feared the totalitarian expansive force of communist ideology. But at the same time, he believed Marxism was ultimately doomed, if only because of the failure of Soviet economy;[7] he did not share de Gaulle's vision of a "Europe from the Atlantic to the Urals," and instead he believed that through economic, social, and political evolution, the Soviet Union would ultimately become part of the Western, industrialized world. Conversely, he feared from the beginning a possible Soviet-American condominium over Europe.[8]

Those views differed from those of de Gaulle; or, more accurately, Pompidou was more pragmatic, wishing to follow a rationalized form of Gaullist foreign policy, without the sudden impulses of his predecessor, feeling that in the long term one could accomplish more by being more prudent.[9] At the same time, his political constituency as president included centrist and bourgeois rightist parties that wanted better relations with Washington and had been deeply suspicious of de Gaulle's Soviet policy. Politically, of course, Pompidou could not afford to depart too openly from de Gaulle and did not wish to do so; but at the same time he was convinced that a change was necessary, particularly a change from the last period of de Gaulle's foreign policy, starting in 1963–65 with the deep transatlantic quarrel and culminating in 1966 with the departure from the integrated command of NATO and the trip to Moscow. For instance, it is not widely known that de Gaulle, when he went to Moscow in June 1966, endorsed the principle of a European security conference without American participation.[10] This amounted to the formation of a new European security system relying on a Franco-Soviet entente without the United States.

As for Germany, de Gaulle stated as early as 1964–65 that the perennial German problem could only be solved through a set of European negotiations, including the eastern and western neighbors of Germany; the country would be reunified, but within the framework of a European security system established among Europeans, and would have to renounce the Oder-Neisse territories and nuclear weapons.[11] Actually, de Gaulle certainly did not mean quick and full reunification (he told Leonid Brezhnev in 1966 that he was "neither adamant nor in any hurry" to see Germany reunited),[12] but some kind of German confederation, heavily dependent on the new pan-European security system.[13] In practical terms, this would have amounted to joint Franco-Soviet control over Germany, with America being pushed to the periphery. This was the real meaning of de Gaulle's two famous formulas: "Détente, entente et cooperation," and "Europe from the Atlantic to the Urals."

Pompidou and Détente

Pompidou had quite different views, even if, once again, he was no Atlanticist and absolutely determined to uphold French independence. For him Western solidarity in the face of the still-present Soviet menace was very important, the United States should remain fully committed in Europe, and for the time being the best solution for Germany was partition. The present balance between East and West was preferable to dangerous innovations along the line of a grand pan-European security concept, which could only lead to either an American-Soviet or a German-Soviet condominium, both detrimental to French interests. Détente was useful because it kept war away, brought stability, and could in the long run help Eastern Europe to get more freedom from Moscow. But it could not be used as a shortcut to advance French ambitions in Europe. France's role in the world would rely on its leadership of Western Europe, not on tacit cooperation with the Soviet Union.

Pompidou understood quite well that there was a fine line between détente as a useful way to increase stability between East and West and détente as a series of unilateral Western concessions playing into the hands of the Soviets.[14] He feared particularly the tendency toward disengagement, which was evident in American public opinion and in the U.S. Congress (e.g., the campaign of Senator Mike Mansfield [D-Mont.], for a reduction of American troops in Europe), and which he suspected was present even inside the

Richard Nixon administration. That is the reason why, for him, détente had to be indivisible and had to concern not only Europe but also the rest of the world, specially the Middle East and Asia. He feared that if détente was to be limited to Europe, it might lead to a form of American-Soviet condominium over the continent.[15] He particularly feared that Moscow and Washington could strike an implicit deal at the expense of the Europeans in order to concentrate their energy on their converging feud with China.

The Period 1969–1970: Initial Contacts with Moscow

President Pompidou was immediately, and was to be constantly, tested by the Soviets and challenged to follow in the steps of de Gaulle's foreign policy.[16] He of course repeatedly assured them that such was the case.[17] Politically, he could not afford to abandon de Gaulle's legacy in that respect (we shall see that some Gaullist quarters exerted strong pressure on him on that point), and at the same time he did not want to. The relationship with Moscow nurtured since 1964 was now a card in the French game and, as he told Soviet foreign minister Andrej Gromyko in June 1970, in his first important talk with a Soviet leader, the two countries did have common interests: peace, Europe's independence from America, and the future of Germany. Both countries had more or less parallel views on the two crisis areas of the time, the Middle East and Vietnam. Pompidou was willing to develop bilateral relations with Moscow in all fields—trade, culture, and political consultations—to achieve common views and positions about serious European and world problems. He was also ready to accept the old Soviet proposal of a European security conference at a time when no other Western leader had yet endorsed it.[18]

Apparently, it was all well in line with de Gaulle's very French-centered détente policy. But all that should not be taken at face value. Trade was probably the field where Pompidou sincerely wished to develop Franco-Soviet relations and expected the most from détente.[19] But, for instance about the Middle East and Vietnam, Pompidou was less than candid with Gromyko; actually, between 1969 and 1973 the French gave Washington important diplomatic support to try to end the war in Indochina, particularly in the last crucial phase in 1972, and were much more cooperative than in the previous period and abstained from provocative public statements, which was a considerable change from de Gaulle and his well-known 1966 speech in Pnom Penh.[20] Another important departure from de Gaulle was that Pompidou ceased to insist on Four Powers concertation on the Middle East and to seek a special role for France in that region through a privileged Franco-Soviet relationship but agreed with Washington that the only practical way out of the crisis was for the United States and the Soviet Union to explore possible solutions bilaterally.[21]

As for the European security conference, Pompidou's views were complex. On one side he favored it, against the initial opposition of the Quai d'Orsay, which well realized that the Soviet aims were to achieve recognition of the 1945 settlement and to divide Western Europe from America. For Pompidou, it was a way to escape from the "two blocks," a very Gaullist concern that he constantly supported. Anyway, he felt sure the other Western countries would end up embracing the Soviet proposal and that the urge for détente was simply too powerful. He did not see why France could not take advantage of being the first, and this was the only concession he could bring to Moscow for his first visit, scheduled for October 1970. But at the same time, he saw in the European conference a way to achieve a modicum of freedom from Moscow for the Eastern Europeans, particularly for countries like Poland, Romania, and Yugoslavia, and to alleviate the consequences of the "Brezhnev doctrine."[22] And, in a major difference with de Gaulle, he felt that the United States should "naturally" participate in such a conference, and he did not hesitate to state explicitly that they were not "foreign to European problems."[23]

In anticipation of Pompidou's visit, the Soviets suggested that it should be the occasion for a more formalized Franco-Soviet political relationship and the conclusion of a "treaty of friendship and cooperation." Although this proposal was supported by the French ambassador in Moscow, Roger Seydoux, who felt that France should stay ahead of Germany in developing relations with the Soviet Union,[24] the French president refused to bow to Soviet pressure and be stampeded into accepting a proposal that appeared to him quite dangerous.[25] The most that Pompidou was willing to accept was a "protocol" signed at the end of his trip, which for the first time stated the necessity of true "political cooperation" between the two countries and stipulated "periodical" meetings between both foreign ministers, who would meet in principle twice a year.[26] This became the model for other such documents signed by the Soviets, for instance with Italy, but it was not the treaty Moscow had wanted and would try again to achieve.

Apart from this protocol, three main topics were discussed during Pompidou's visit to Moscow. First, he assured his Soviet counterparts that France would not return to the integrated NATO command structure, and it is evident from the archives now accessible that he had absolutely no intention of doing so. Second, the participants discussed the United States. Referring evidently to de Gaulle's visit in 1966, Brezhnev asked if Pompidou, like his predecessor, also agreed with the view that "American influence in Europe should be progressively eliminated." The French president stressed that he remained true to the basic principles of Gaullism, but in a significant intellectual twist, went on to explain that if the United States were influential in Europe it was largely because it was militarily supporting European countries against "the immense weight" of the Soviet Union. He was all in favor of an evolution allowing "Europe to be fully Europe," but there could be no question of exchanging "what you fear to be American tutelage" for a Soviet one: "We want to be friends, but we intend to be free."[27] He also clearly stated on the first day of his visit that "France was a Western country and fully intended to remain such."

The third topic to be discussed at length was Germany. Pompidou repeatedly assured his partners that France would never accept Germany gaining access to nuclear weapons, and he expressed his satisfaction with the Soviet-German treaty signed in August, because it helped détente and confirmed the existing borders and the partition of Germany. But he asked searching questions about the future of the German problem, stressing that Germany was always an uncertain factor that had repeatedly become dangerous. He noted that both Germanys were not free to "get more acquainted" and asked how far this would be allowed to go and where the Soviets stood regarding reunification. It is interesting to note that Brezhnev escaped into platitudes about the need for the Federal Republic of Germany to respect the independence of the German Democratic Republic without committing himself clearly against reunification, as Pompidou would have wished.[28]

In these talks, Pompidou was evidently promoting his own agenda. He was both following in de Gaulle's steps, when he reaffirmed French independence and refusal to come back into NATO, and following a very different line, when he stressed the need for an American military presence in Europe and made no mention at all of his predecessor's grand security concept for Europe relying on a Franco-Soviet entente. He was much more prudent toward Moscow. As for Germany, his views were much more complex then what he told the Soviets. He did want Germany to remain divided, but not so much because he feared Germany as such but because he believed that reunification could be a lever allowing the Soviets to control Germany and thus Europe. At the same time, if he stressed the German menace, it was because he felt that the Soviets were obsessed by it and that he could use this obsession to France's advantage, to enhance its importance in Soviet eyes. France, in particular, could help prevent Germany from getting access to nuclear weapons. Thus France could retain an important international role, despite the fact that in the beginning move toward détente the Soviets were bound to negotiate first with Germany and the United States.

Pompidou and the First Period of *Ostpolitik*

Pompidou was not opposed to the first period of *Ostpolitik,* that leading to the treaties between Germany and the East in 1970–72. After all, it had been constant French policy since de Gaulle's press conference of February 5, 1964, that the German problem could be solved only after the reconciliation of Eastern and Western Europe, and that Bonn should renounce the Oder-Neisse territories. Pompidou himself publicly observed that *Ostpolitik* was an application of this Gaullist legacy on August 11, 1970, when Willy Brandt was in Moscow to sign the Soviet-German treaty the next day.[29]

Apart from Pompidou's wish in a general way for détente in Europe, there was a very specific reason for his support of *Ostpolitik's* treaties: They consolidated the partition of Germany. French internal documents from Pompidou's cabinet office allude indirectly to that consideration. And from 1972 onward, Pompidou insisted that the German Democratic Republic should be treated by the French as a fully independent country. The president was unequivocal when he visited Brezhnev in October 1970: He told him that France looked favorably towards the international recognition of the German Democratic Republic, and that it "believed that one should not deprive Germany of the hope of reunification, but that (Paris) was in no hurry."[30]

But from the beginning, Pompidou distrusted Brandt's and Moscow's ulterior motives. The heart of the matter was that, if Pompidou was clearly willing to support the first stage of *Ostpolitik* (the recognition of realities and especially of the division of Germany), he was much less enthusiastic over the possible further evolution of Bonn's policy toward the East for the use that Moscow could make of it and for Brandt's suspected ulterior motives. Pompidou and his advisers (for Germany, especially, the diplomat Jean-Bernard Raimond, diplomatic counselor at the Elysée) were convinced, as early as December 1969, that Bonn wished through *Ostpolitik* ultimately to weaken the East German regime and to absorb East Germany.

But this policy could misfire; the growing contacts between both Germanys could well play into the hands of the Soviets and lead instead to a "destabilization of the East," to a destabilization of the West, and to increased Soviet influence.[31] More generally, Pompidou was convinced that Brandt's first foreign policy objective was reunification and that it influenced the rest of Bonn's policies. Particularly, Pompidou was convinced that Bonn no longer wanted the construction of a strong Western Europe, which could hamper its search for a broad settlement with Moscow. He saw a risk of a divided Western Europe negotiating piecemeal with Moscow from a dangerous position of inferiority (he told Brandt as much on January 25, 1971).

Evidently, Pompidou did not realize that *Ostpolitik* was a very-long-term perspective, putting reunification in the very far future at best. It should be noted that Pompidou had no first-hand knowledge of Germany, and that the Elysée staff provided him with a traditional geopolitical diplomatic view, not with an explanation of the psychological and political aspects of *Ostpolitik* in terms of German internal politics. This probably led to some distortion, to some exaggeration in the president's view of German foreign policy at the time. What were at times tendencies or working hypotheses in Bonn were taken in Paris for definite policies. Pompidou was also probably informed by the French secret service that Brandt and some of his aides and political allies had been quite close to the Komintern in the 1930s and perhaps were the object of Soviet penetration.[32]

The third fear of Pompidou about *Ostpolitik* (the first being the prospect of German reunification, the second being the possibility of a "Finlandization" of the Federal Republic) was that it would lead, through the lever that Moscow possessed over Bonn through the partition of Germany, to a vast Soviet-German agreement and to a kind of Soviet-German condominium over Europe, under the paramount influence of Moscow. It should be noted here that some proponents of *Ostpolitik*, certainly Egon Bahr and probably Brandt himself, were actually contemplating the formation of a European security system based upon a broad Soviet-German agreement as a means of promoting a solution of the German problem, even if they were not sure about the possible timetable for such an evolution.[33]

In private talks with French journalists, Pompidou stated as early as September 1970 that he feared both the new German assertiveness toward the Western allies and the fact that the Soviet Union had now strong leverage over Bonn. He feared an eventual withdrawal of American troops from Europe (this was to be his constant obsession), which might lead to a Soviet-German agreement. Germany might then become reunified, neutralized, and armed with nuclear weapons—three nightmares for the French! The only defense was to anchor Germany to a strong Western Europe in such a way that it could no longer detach itself.[34] Pompidou was convinced that there was a strong link between the European problem and the German question, and that the prudent nurturing of real practical solidarities among Europeans was the best way to funnel the evolution of the German question in a way that would prevent both a German escape from the European framework and the risk of a Soviet-German condominium. Thus Pompidou rejected the Gaullist scheme of a German confederation controlled in a European security framework dominated by Russia and France and returned to the much simpler policy of "double security," which had been followed by most French leaders since the 1950s: France's security toward (or at least superiority over) Germany would be provided by its partition, and France's security against the Soviet Union would be achieved through a strong Western Europe and the Atlantic alliance, both incorporating and controlling the Federal Republic.

Franco-American Relations and Détente, 1969–1971

Pompidou's first contacts with the Americans were largely positive. He did not hesitate to state that Europe and France needed the Atlantic alliance.[35] The Nixon administration noted with satisfaction the immediate change of atmosphere between the two countries.[36] Of course there were differences; for example, about the international monetary system, but also about the military aspects of détente. Paris feared that the SALT negotiations (which started in earnest in 1969) could reduce the American nuclear guarantee to Europe and drive Washington and Moscow to look on third nuclear powers as destabilizing and in need of being controlled in time of crisis. Paris was also against the proposal made in late 1969 by the Atlantic alliance, with strong American support, for a conference about mutual and balanced force reductions in Europe (MBFR). Apart from the well-established French opposition to any negotiation "between the blocks," Pompidou feared that it could further worsen the existing imbalance in conventional forces and lead to a kind of neutralization of Central Europe. On the other side, Paris supported the European security conference, which Washington still opposed. But the French were quite willing to have serious exchanges with Washington about all those questions. There was to be a non-stop Franco-American dialogue on all questions pertaining to détente, which amounted to a renewed intimacy after the frosty years since 1963.[37]

Despite incidents with Jewish groups, Pompidou's visit to the United States in February 1970 was a success. The French president's talks with President Nixon on February 24 and 26 showed there was a broad area of agreement about the evolution of the international system toward a multipolar system (with the poles being the United States, Soviet Union, Western Europe, China, and Japan), about the need for a prudent attitude toward the Soviet Union, about the importance of not isolating China, and about the need to ask the Germans to keep their Western partners fully informed about the development of *Ostpolitik*[38] Nixon accepted the French independent foreign and military policy and did not try to bring France back into NATO. Both presidents decided to restart Franco-American strategic talks and military cooperation, which had basically been stopped since 1962. This led to very important developments under Pompidou and his successor, Valéry Giscard d'Estaing.[39] The Franco-American rift since 1963–66 was about to be bridged. There was agreement to follow quite closely Brandt's *Ostpolitik,* not out of fear of any German danger as such, which both French and Americans believed outdated, but over the risk of excessive German concessions to the Soviets.[40]

However, this Franco-American understanding began to sour in 1972–73, partly because of the ultimate failure of the Azores summit of December 1971 on the crucial problem of the international monetary system,[41] but largely because of growing differences about détente, particularly about SALT and MBFR. As early as 1971, Paris realized that a Soviet-American SALT agreement was likely to be completed. It might have negative consequences for France, reducing the political and military value of its own deterrent.[42] As for MBFR, France feared the negotiations could lead to a withdrawal of American troops from Europe and to a neutralization of Central Europe, allowing Moscow to exert constant and considerable pressure on Europe.[43]

At the Azores summit in December 1971, Pompidou stressed that France belonged to the West and remained true to the Atlantic alliance. His aim was to be recognized by Nixon as the spokesman of the European Community and to put France in a strategic privileged position of intermediary between America and Europe. But Nixon did not deliver on the monetary compromise reached at the Azores. The failure of the summit meant the failure of Pompidou's concept of a Western Europe led by France and collaborating with the United States on an equal footing. This led to a realignment of Pompidou's policy toward the United States after 1972: His aim was henceforth less to be the privileged intermediary between Europe and the United States and much more to gather the Europeans to balance American influence, which was in a way a return to Gaullism. The American Embassy in Paris sensed this already in September 1972.[44]

The Year 1971: Prudent Relations with Moscow

Despite growing tensions with Washington, however, Pompidou still considered America France's only real partner when trying to steer détente in the right direction and to avoid its pitfalls. He knew he had to be very cautious with the Soviets, who were in his view trying to use détente to further their permanent aims in Europe[45] and who were pressuring the French to go beyond the Protocol of 1970 and to put Franco-Soviet relations on a treaty basis comparable to the Franco-German Elysée Treaty of January 1963.

The French reacted to this pressure by dividing themselves. Pompidou and the Elysée staff realized that Moscow wanted to play the Western countries against each other and to compromise France; Roger Seydoux in Moscow and Foreign Minister Maurice Schumann wanted instead to go along with the Soviet proposal, true to the Moscow-centered orientation of late Gaullism and feeling that France should stay ahead of the pack in the rush for détente. They even prepared a treaty draft without instruction from the Elysée. This divergence led to a short-lived but amazingly strong tension between the Quai d'Orsay and the Elysée, which in fact reflected a deep-seated distrust in some Gaullist circles about the orientations of President Pompidou and the continuing wish in some quarters for a privileged Franco-Soviet relationship.[46]

The Soviets stepped up the pressure until the eve of Brezhnev's trip to Paris in October 1971, trying to achieve, if not a treaty, at least a "declaration on the principles of political cooperation" between both countries amounting to a political alliance and also endorsing the Soviet concept of a permanent organism for European security that could be decided by the future security conference.[47] The French managed to leave out the word "political" in the title of the "Declaration on Principles of Cooperation between France and the USSR," but Gromyko insisted in keeping the expression "political cooperation" in the preamble of the text. In the end, Pompidou and his aides were satisfied that the Soviet proposal had been watered down and added actually nothing of importance to the "protocol" signed the previous year.[48]

Brezhnev's visit in Paris at the end of October 1971 revolved around three main topics: Germany, the European security conference, and MBFR. About Germany, both leaders agreed that Brandt should be helped, despite his slender majority, to get the Bundestag to ratify the *Ostpolitik* treaties.[49] Pompidou did deliver on his promise. In his meeting with the leader of the Christian Democratic Union (CDU), Rainer Barzel, on March 22, 1972, he insisted forcefully that the CDU should not impede the ratification of those treaties.[50] Barzel then decided ultimately that the CDU should abstain at the time of the crucial vote, instead of voting against them, as had been his first intention. It is thus possible to state that Pompidou played an important part in the ratification of the Eastern Treaties.

About MBFR, Pompidou stated once again his resolute opposition, explaining in a very candid way that he feared those negotiations could lead to a withdrawal of foreign troops from both Germanys and ultimately to the emergence of a reunited and uncontrolled Germany.[51] Another reason why the French opposed MBFR (but of course Pompidou did not say as much to Brezhnev) was that they felt the West was already inferior in conventional armaments and that further reductions could imperil its defense. Thus the Western allies would jeopardize their security for a mere appearance of détente. Paris staunchly refused to have anything to do with the preparations inside the alliance for MBFR.[52]

On the European security conference, President Pompidou was adamant that it should not be delayed any longer, and he exerted strong pressure on the Western allies to that effect.[53] At the same time the French, to ensure the success of the conference, were ready to tone down the anti-Soviet tendency of the objective they originally followed (to give more freedom from Moscow to the Eastern European countries) and to content themselves "with a slow and progressive development of exchanges" between both Europes. But they fully realized that the Soviet concept of a permanent security body for Europe would allow Moscow to exert considerable pressure on Western Europe, and they opposed the establishment of such a body.[54] They were actually walking a tightrope between a conference they wanted for the sake of stability in Europe and to keep some common ground with Moscow and a special role for France between East and West, and the fear that the aftermath of such a conference could lead to a kind of "Finlandization" of Western Europe (the expression appeared in informed circles at the time).

Reservations about the Berlin Settlement

Nothing better epitomizes Pompidou's prudence toward the Soviets than his attitude about the negotiations for a settlement in Berlin. The French played an important part in the negotiation of the quadripartite agreement on Berlin of September 1971. But it was the French Foreign Office that supported the negotiation, while the president was very skeptical from the beginning and urged utmost caution. He refused the idea of a different treatment for West and East Berlin; he refused the idea that West Berlin could become a full-fledged West German *Land;* he refused to make an agreement on Berlin the condition of a broad East-West détente; he would have preferred to limit the negotiation to practical matters concerning the life of West Berliners. As he stated as early as October 1969: "One must not alter the status of Berlin."

Of course France could not remain isolated and had to go along with the negotiation. But it would seem from the record that Pompidou played an important role at the end: In August 1971, the negotiation was stalled by the problem of Soviet responsibility for the access to West Berlin. Moscow wanted to mention in the agreement the German Democratic Republic as co-responsible with the Soviet Union for the access: Pompidou urged the French negotiators to resist adamantly this demand, and they won, which meant that the September 3 agreement remained in the framework of the quadripartite status of Berlin.

Why was the defense of this strictly quadripartite status so important for Pompidou? Because he was convinced that Berlin was the fulcrum of the East-West balance. In a long handwritten note of March 26, 1970, the president wrote "that quadripartism was capital because it implicated the USSR." Any other solution would enable the East to blackmail the Federal Republic through Berlin, and the city, as the president told Brandt on July 3, 1970, and again told Barzel on June 3, 1971, was "the crucial and determining factor of the balance between eastern and western Europe." For him, the whole East-West balance and the evolution of the German question hinged on Berlin; if the status of Berlin was altered, Moscow could pressure the Federal Republic, and the West (and above all France) would lose their best instrument to control the evolution of the German problem: their rights in Berlin. This relates evidently to Pompidou's fears of a quick German reunification and of a big German-Soviet deal.[55]

The Period 1972–1973: The Rising Fear of a "Soviet-American Condominium"

In 1972–73, the fear of a German-Soviet deal was compounded by the fear of an American-Soviet one. Paris was concerned by the SALT agreements of May 1972 and their possible implications for France. On the strategic side, they reduced the value of the American military guarantee to Europe.[56] On the political side, the French president asked himself in front of Gromyko on June 13 if these agreements "did not amount more or less to a sort of will to establish a condominium on the rest of the world." This theme would now be heard frequently.[57] And Nixon did not hide the fact that the Soviets had already tried and would try again to take French nuclear forces into account in the disarmament negotiations. Pompidou was absolutely opposed to that.[58]

Paris was concerned by the whole revolution in the international system that took place between the spring of 1972 and the spring of 1973. French officials took satisfaction in Nixon's trip to China and the beginning of the Conference on Security and Cooperation in Europe (CSCE) in November 1972, which would lead to the foreign ministers' conference in Helsinki in July 1973. But they had deep misgivings about two new developments: the negotiation of an agreement "to prevent nuclear war" that Brezhnev was to sign during his visit to California in June 1973; and the "Year of Europe" announced by Henry Kissinger on April 23, 1973, which was supposed to see the transatlantic relationship defined anew in an "Atlantic Charter."

Pompidou and his very Gaullist foreign minister, Michel Jobert, looked upon those developments with anxiety. Were not the Americans going to strike a deal with the Soviets at the expense of Europe? On April 23, Kissinger had spoken of Europe as a regional gathering with limited interests. Did not Washington want to achieve the role of leader of a vast transatlantic grouping?[59] All those fears were at the time subsumed under the frequently used expression of "American-Soviet condominium."

There was now a big rift emerging between Paris and Washington about the very strategy of détente. Pompidou and Kissinger had a very important and candid talk about that strategy on May 18, 1973, shortly before the Nixon-Pompidou Reykjavik summit.[60] In this meeting, Pompidou raised two points that went to the core of Washington's détente policy: About the agreement to prevent a nuclear war, the problem was not so much the risk of an outright Soviet aggression but rather of more Soviet expansionism under the threshold of war, as with Czechoslovakia in 1968 or perhaps with Yugoslavia or China at the death of Tito or Mao; Pompidou asked, "Was there an American tactic to stop an undercover Soviet advance, taking place without the use of force but as a progressive torrent?" He also warned Kissinger not to be tempted to support the Soviet Union against China.

Kissinger explained America's real strategy: There was no intent to establish an American-Soviet condominium or to choose the Soviets against China, but the idea was to support Beijing against Moscow to prevent it from crushing China, allowing it afterward to Finlandize Europe and isolate the United States. But to prevent the Chinese-American connection from serving as a pretext for a Soviet attack against China, Washington had at the same time to continue the détente policy with Moscow in order "to win time, to paralyze the USSR, ... to entangle her." We should note that Kissinger gave exactly the same explanation to the Chinese at the time and that these were the administration's views, not just his own.[61] To convince his partner, Kissinger added that a strong Europe, with France playing a pivotal role, belonged fully in this overall concept.

In the French view, this positive attitude was contradicted by the semifailure of the Reykjavik meeting between Nixon and Pompidou in late May 1973. The two leaders surveyed the international situation at length, but rather inconclusively. They did not agree either on the reform of the international monetary system or about the Atlantic Charter. The most successful part of the summit revolved around military and strategic matters: Pompidou publicly told the press at the end of the summit that he was in favor of the American military presence in Europe, which was indeed a new departure for leaders of the Fifth Republic. And they agreed that the very secret Franco-American military talks already in progress should be extended to cover the technology of nuclear weapons. The Nixon administration was ready to go this far because it dearly wanted to win acceptance for its various great schemes in Paris, for both the Atlantic Charter and the strategy of détente. France, it was implied, could choose to enjoy the same privileged position in Washington as Britain if it supported those concepts.[62]

But the new round of military and nuclear talks stopped at the end of 1973 (they were to resume only under Pompidou's successor, Valéry Giscard d'Estaing), because the Americans balked at helping the French to perfect their new, quite advanced generation of missiles and "MIRVed"

(MIRV means multiple independently targetable reentry vehicle) warheads. The French concluded that Washington did not want their nuclear force to become too effective and wanted to retain a certain degree of control over its modernization. Washington especially did not want to make the next round of SALT more difficult. Pompidou reacted by stopping the exchange and by deciding in February 1974 on a new defense directive for the armed forces that marked a renewed insistence on the independence of the French nuclear deterrent. This was again a certain return to Gaullist orthodoxy. The growing difference about détente had led Pompidou to revert to a more independent stance toward Washington.

Growing Contradictions in France's Soviet Policy, 1973–1974

America was not France's only problem, however. Already in 1972 the French had realized that Moscow took scant notice of their wishes and interests. Generally speaking, the Soviets were transacting their business with the United States without properly informing Paris and only according to their own interests. But instead of drawing the evident conclusion that France's policy toward Russia since 1966 had failed and left it isolated, Pompidou's aides tried to salvage it and preserve French "originality" in dealing with Moscow by making concessions on the CSCE. France decided to reduce its emphasis on expanding freedom for the Eastern European countries, because it displeased the Soviets.[63] And Pompidou, at the end of 1972, was contemplating French support for the Soviet concept of a permanent security organization in Europe, following the CSCE.[64] Meeting Brezhnev at Zaslavl (near Minsk) in January 1973, the French president told him that Paris had no intention of insisting at the CSCE on an extension of cultural exchanges and freedom of information between the two parts of Europe in a way that might hurt the interests of the Soviets. One would, rather, have to reach "a balanced and satisfactory settlement" for those questions. And he gave his agreement in principle to the permanent security organism for Europe that the Soviets wanted.[65]

Pompidou was true to his word. The French delegation in Helsinki, where the diplomatic chiefs of mission were preparing the CSCE, was instructed to support the Soviet wish for a permanent organism and to suggest a very general and unbinding arrangement for the exchange of people and ideas between the two Europes, despite strong suspicions in the other

Western delegations that the French had gone too far in appeasing the Soviets at Zaslavl.[66]

However, despite France's accommodating stance, the Soviets were putting more pressure on Paris, constantly accusing the French of drifting toward the West.[67] And Moscow had not yet renounced the idea of a "new step" with France, resulting in a political treaty.[68] The French realized that their relations with Moscow were actually deteriorating. Bilateral consultations remained limited in scope and openness and never reached a real harmonization. Sometimes the positions were opposed, as was the case for MBFR and its relationship to the German problem. The French also realized that since Nixon's trip to Moscow, the Americans were more interested in MBFR and SALT and in favor of a quickly concluded CSCE. Paris feared a quick conference could achieve only what the Soviets actually had in mind, a mere legalization of the status quo in Europe without any real provision for more freedom for Eastern Europe, a goal the French still cherished even if they were ready to water it down enough to placate the Soviets.[69]

The French sought to counteract those tendencies. They toned down the communiqué that was to be issued after Zaslavl to avoid any impression of excessive intimacy between Paris and Moscow.[70] The French understood full well that the Soviets, who through the SALT agreements had achieved a nuclear balance between the United States and the Soviet Union and thus tended to reduce the extended American deterrent, now wanted to reduce the conventional options of the Atlantic alliance through MBFR and also to establish a special military status for the territory of the Federal Republic. They particularly feared this last development because of its possible consequences for the evolution of the German question and because it would preclude in the future the possibility of a European defense system (a new consideration that appeared in 1973). They also feared it because it might give the Americans the occasion they were seeking anyway, as Paris saw it, to reduce or withdraw altogether their troops from Europe. Generally speaking, they saw in the SALT and the MBFR the outline of a great Soviet-American deal leading to a kind of condominium over Europe, both countries giving priority to their relationship to each other, particularly the Soviets because of their problem with China.[71]

During the autumn of 1973 and the following winter—a period of a worsening international situation linked with the Yom Kippur War and its consequences for Europe (the energy crisis)—the Soviets stepped up their pressure on Paris. Moscow insisted once again that France should participate in the MBFR, which had started in Vienna in January,[72] and criticized vehemently several allusions made in November by Foreign Minister Michel Jobert to a possible European defense system.[73] Pompidou's aides understood very well that the Soviets were seeking, through the CSCE and the MBFR, to divide Europe from the United States and to neutralize it in a new security system while preventing the emergence of a European foreign policy and defense identity. They noticed that for Moscow's ideologues, the energy crisis heralded a deep crisis of the capitalist system and the opening of vast opportunities for radical revolutionary transformations. They noticed the growing criticism in the Soviet press about French internal and defense policy and the renewed cooperation between the Soviets and the French Communist Party intended to step up pressure on the French government. At the same time, the Soviets were still extolling the "exemplary character" of Franco-Soviet relations and they wished, even if Washington was now their first partner, to retain some possibility for maneuvering with the most independent partner of the Atlantic alliance. One had to admit that relations between the two countries were, at best, "ambiguous."[74]

Despite this pessimistic assessment, Pompidou, during the last weeks of his life, tried to salvage the Franco-Soviet relationship.[75] Already very ill, he went to Pitsunda in March and told Brezhnev that he wished that there would remain a special relationship between Paris and Moscow, despite the fact that other Western countries had also through the process of détente developed important links with the Soviet Union. He hinted at the fact that France did not intend to support China against Russia (an indirect critique of Kissinger's policy). He was rather accommodating on the problem of human rights at the CSCE. He told Brezhnev he had no intention of letting the United States establish control over Western Europe through the guise of a common energy policy. At the same time, he repeated that France had no intention of participating in SALT or MBFR. He pressed Brezhnev to accept at the CSCE a formula about the inviolability of borders in Europe that the West Germans could accept, "in the long-term interest of peace in Europe" and to help Chancellor Brandt, who was now in a difficult political situation.[76]

It would seem that French policy toward Russia was now stuck in a deep contradiction. On one side, Soviet policy was hardening. If anything, the Soviet Union remained dangerous, and France did not enjoy much influence over Soviet policy. On the other side, France wished to retain a special role in Moscow and was ready to be accommodating with the Russians to enhance French influence in the world while trying to balance both the Federal Republic and the United States, or more exactly to prevent an American-Soviet condominium or a German-Soviet one. To try to bridge that contradiction, Paris was once again reaffirming with energy the Gaullist dogmas about national independence. It is most likely that this convoluted policy toward Moscow was largely explained by the problems and disillusionment encountered in the last months with both Bonn and Washington relating to the strategy of détente.

The Period 1973–1974: Rising Qualms about *Ostpolitik*

The importance of Brezhnev's visit to Bonn in May 1973 and the scope of the economic agreements concluded on that occasion made a significant impression on French officials. There were also growing differences with West Germany about the strategy of détente. Paris feared the consequences of MBFR for Western defense in Europe; Bonn was in favor of them because it hoped it would be possible, through disarmament, to some day achieve a new security order in Europe that would make reunification possible.

As for the CSCE, Paris favored it as a means to make Soviet interventions in Eastern Europe more difficult, and as a good instrument of détente. But Bonn was very reticent because it understood that Moscow's first aim was to achieve international recognition of the new borders in Europe and of Germany's division. At the end of 1972 and the beginning of 1973, the divergence between Paris and Bonn was growing. Bonn was more and more in favor of MBFR, and Pompidou, after his trip to Zaslavl in January 1973, was more and more in favor of CSCE.[77]

Ostpolitik seemed to the French to evolve more and more in the direction of those ulterior motives that Paris had feared from the beginning. On November 23, 1973, Jean-Bernard Raimond wrote for the president that Bonn wanted to promote MBFR as a means to achieve a European security system "relying on the withdrawal of foreign troops [hence the departure of American troops in Europe] and with the guarantee of the superpowers," that is, along the lines that had been suggested by the Soviets for twenty years.[78] Pompidou's unease was increased by what Brandt had told him on June 21, 1973. The German chancellor alluded to the possibility of a European defense organization "doubling or replacing NATO," expressing the view that the Franco-German strategic dialogue should now become "more practical." He made it clear that in such an organization, Germany could not content itself with a second-rate role, even if it was not now seeking to acquire nuclear weapons. Without fully closing the door to a European defense, Pompidou remained very noncommittal. On November 9, German foreign minister Scheel took up the subject once again with his French counterpart, Michel Jobert. He was more precise than Brandt, telling Jobert that the European Community would have eventually to "free itself from its dependence" on NATO and acquire a nuclear defense capability. Coming from the foreign minister of a country purporting to be the staunchest supporter of NATO on the European continent, this was a rather startling statement.

What Jobert answered on November 9 is not known. But his reaction can be inferred from his speech before the assembly of the Western European Union (WEU) on November 21[79] and from an article in *Le Monde* on November 27, which was visibly inspired by him. On those two occasions, Jobert stressed the necessity of the Atlantic alliance, of the permanence of American troops in Europe, and of the American nuclear guarantee. To the Europeans, he suggested only "an effort of dialogue and reflection" in the framework of the WEU. A European defense "was a long-term affair, about which one could only say that it was not for tomorrow." This was a very low-key answer to Scheel's suggestions indeed.

Evidently Paris reacted quite negatively to the German overture. When Brandt broached the subject once again with Pompidou on November 26 (five days after Jobert's speech), Pompidou did not answer. Pompidou's prudent attitude was certainly also explained by his refusal to renounce the dogma of French nuclear independence in some kind of European sharing with Germany. But it was also explained by the very ambiguous nature of the German overtures, compounded apparently by what Egon Bahr told Jobert on November 20.[80] This could very well lead to the establishment of a European military defense without the Americans, who could be connected in a neutral way to this European security system based on a German-Soviet agreement that some were contemplating in Bonn and that the French feared. Apparently Pompidou's last answer to what he perceived as a drift of *Ostpolitik* toward neutrality was, in the autumn of 1973, to restart the process of European political collaboration through the regular meeting of European chiefs of state and chiefs of governments, which was to lead ultimately to the creation of the European Council.

Worsening Relations with Washington from Mid-1973

The differences between Paris and Washington about the strategy of détente grew rapidly from the summer of 1973 onward. The turning point was the "agreement to prevent a nuclear war" signed by Brezhnev in California on June 22. For Paris, the most disquieting feature of this agreement was the clause concerning mutual consultation in case of a conflict between two other powers. Pompidou sensed the danger "of a kind of tutelage over Europe," as he wrote to Nixon on July 13.[81] The suspicions about a Soviet-American condominium were growing fast—the more so because Paris believed there was a convergence between the June 22 agreement, SALT, and MBFR.[82]

Those suspicions were compounded by the draft of a "Common Declaration of Principles for the Atlantic Alliance," which was prepared in Washington during the summer. Jean-Bernard Raimond explained to the president on July 4 that the draft would give the United States a leading role for all kinds of problems in a vast transatlantic grouping, that it implied a de facto return of France to NATO, and that it would prevent the European Community from developing progressively "its autonomy and its political personality respective to the United States." He was convinced that Kissinger sought through the declaration to maintain American leadership despite the revolution taking place in international affairs.[83]

The Yom Kippur War of October 1973 and its consequences (the oil shock) complicated Franco-American relations even further. Apart from a fundamental disagreement about the situation in the Middle East, the French interpreted Nixon's invitation on January 9, 1974, to hold a conference in Washington about energy as a means of relaunching Kissinger's Atlantic Declaration and to form under American direction a vast grouping between the United States, Europe, and Japan.

A serious crisis had developed between Paris and Washington, with the more Gaullist political and media circles in Paris, and particularly Foreign Minister Michel Jobert, pleading for a full return to late Gaullism and for an uncompromising stance toward Washington. But the Elysée staff was in favor of a much more prudent attitude, and the president supported them. On February 6, Michel Jobert was instructed to attend the Washington conference. He was not to make any concession to American views about a cartel of oil-consuming countries to resist the Organization of the Petroleum Exporting Countries, and he was not to agree to any kind of permanent organization between industrialized countries, but he was to avoid a major break.[84]

In the same way, under the more prudent advice from the Elysée staff, a break about the Atlantic Declaration was avoided. Instead of an outright rejection, Jobert drafted on October 3, 1973, a French version for the declaration on instructions from Pompidou.[85] This text epitomized all French current worries about détente. It reaffirmed the necessity for transatlantic solidarity and for the continuing presence of American forces in Europe, but it also stressed the need for nuclear deterrence in light of the suspicion that the Americans were drifting toward a non-nuclear stance and against any possible negative consequence of SALT. The French version stressed that the United States would not let Europe be submitted "to an external pressure, political or military, which might affect its freedom." This was of course intended to block the possible consequences of the June 22 Soviet-American agreement. The French text underscored the "specificity" of Europe's defense and the value of the contribution to the Atlantic alliance of European conventional forces and also of the nuclear deterrents of Britain and France. This was a way to get the alliance to recognize the usefulness of the French Force de Frappe and also to pave the way for a future European defense identity, which Michel Jobert was going to suggest in his well-known speech at the Assembly of the WEU on November 21.

The French draft was a major success. Kissinger wisely preferred to withdraw his own draft, and thus the French one found its way into the Ottawa Declaration decided by the Atlantic Council on June 19, 1974, after Pompidou's death. Thus the French had managed to bring the alliance to endorse some of their more important views about nuclear deterrence, about détente, and against the "condominium." At the same time, they had reaffirmed Atlantic solidarity at a time when the Germans (at least Brandt and Scheel) were exploring the possibility of a new European security system and of a European defense outside NATO. We have here the quintessential rationalized Gaullism of Georges Pompidou—steadfast defense of French independence but basic solidarity with the United States in the face of the Soviet danger and the risk of Germany drifting towards neutralism.

Conclusion

For Pompidou, détente meant a relaxation of tensions on the basis of the status quo and some improvement for the Eastern Europeans, giving time for a withering of communist ideology and for structural change in both the Soviet Union and in East-West relations. But he was from the beginning and, even more after 1972–73, very pessimistic about détente, at least as it was managed by Moscow, Washington, and Bonn. He feared the establishment of an American-Soviet condominium over Europe and particularly the possible excesses of *Ostpolitik*. That pessimism, bordering after 1973 on an outright gloomy view of the world, is very important to understand Pompidou's reactions (and sometimes overreactions).

Pompidou's attitude toward *Ostpolitik* was at the heart of his détente policy, and very revealing about his fears and objectives. He did not want *Ostpolitik* to drift toward an alteration of the East-West balance, and to give Moscow new means to influence Germany and Western Europe. Pompidou was very much on guard against the ulterior motives of *Ostpolitik*. First the Soviet motives, which he saw as the wish to "Finlandize" Germany and hence Western Europe. Germany seemed to him on the verge of compromising the western front against Russia, an even more sobering perspective in the context of the quick removal of American troops that most Europeans feared at the time.

But Pompidou also distrusted German ulterior motives and policy. He reacted along geopolitical lines and did not grasp the psychological and even moral aspects of the debate in Germany. This led him to overreact to some aspects of *Ostpolitik,* while underestimating the depth of the German people's commitment to the West. He sensed in Bonn the wish to construct a new European security order, with a much smaller role for America, and based on a broad agreement between the Soviet Union and a Germany that was hinting also at a new European defense system without NATO and equipped with nuclear weapons. Once again, those fears were probably overstated. But they were not purely theoretical, as the talks between President Pompidou and his German partner, as well as the debates in Bonn at the end of the Brandt administration, would seem to confirm.

Pompidou's first reaction was to revert to a classical (since 1945) French policy of "double security," security both toward Germany and the Soviet Union by a system of interlocking balances: balancing the Soviet Union with Europe and the United States, balancing Germany with the Soviet Union. This was Gaullism, but with three important differences: France was no longer a lone player; for him, the United States belonged at the heart of this European balance system, not at its fringe (as for de Gaulle); and he never contemplated making Moscow the major partner of France in this system, as de Gaulle did in 1966–68.

In the short term, however, Pompidou's reaction was rather contradictory, probably because he could not and did not want to abandon all aspects of de Gaulle's foreign policy. On one side, despite all differences, he ultimately retained the basic Cold War solidarity with Washington. Although he realized with anxiety that Soviet influence and power were growing, that

Franco-Soviet relations were deteriorating, and that now Moscow's real partners in the West were the Federal Republic and the United States, he remained, because of his distrust of the Germans and the Americans, fixed in his language with the Soviets upon formulas of French independence from both "blocs." This position was very Gaullist but at the same time showed that Paris had reached an impasse.[86]

In the long term, Pompidou certainly believed that a deepening of European solidarity, possibly extending to foreign policy and defense, was the only way to steer détente into safe waters, to contain the Soviets, to keep Germany firmly in the West, and to force Washington to take better account of European interests.[87] In his press conference of September 27, 1973, he suggested that the European chiefs of state and heads of governments should meet regularly to discuss political cooperation. This was to lead to the Summit of the Nine in Copenhagen in December 1973 and, ultimately, to the present European Council and later to the Common Foreign and Security Policy endorsed by the Maastricht Treaty in 1992.

Notes

1. He expressed those fears frequently, for instance to British prime minister Edward Heath on May 21, 1973; quoted by Eric Roussel, *Georges Pompidou* (Paris: J. C. Lattès, 1994), 653.
2. For Pompidou's foreign policy, see Roussel, *Georges Pompidou;* see also Association Georges Pompidou, ed., *Georges Pompidou et l'Europe* (Brussels: Complexe, 1995). See also the memoirs of Henry Kissinger, *White House Years* (Boston: Little, Brown, 1979); and *Years of Upheaval* (Boston: Little, Brown, 1982). Also see the memoirs of Michel Jobert, *Mémoires d'avenir* (Paris: Grasset, 1974); and *L'autre regard* (Paris: Grasset, 1976).
3. In the context of this chapter, I cannot expand here; see my "L'attitude de Georges Pompidou face à l'Allemagne," in *Georges Pompidou et l'Europe*, ed. Association Georges Pompidou.
4. Meeting between Pompidou and Quai d'Orsay officials on June 1, 1962, shortly after his nomination as prime minister and less than one year after the first British application to the EEC (private papers).
5. For Pompidou's views before 1969, see Alain Peyrefitte, *C'était de Gaulle*, vol. 1, *La France redevient la France* (Paris: Fayard, 1994); and Cyrus Sulzberger, *An Age of Mediocrity* (New York: Macmillan, 1973).
6. Sulzberger, *Age of Mediocrity*, 216–17.
7. Georges Pompidou, *Le Noeud Gordien* (Paris: Flamarion, 1974).
8. See Alain Peyrefitte, *C'était de Gaulle*, vol. 2, *La France reprend sa place dans le monde* (Paris: Fayard, 1997), 25; and Sulzberger, *Age of Mediocrity*, 4, 406.
9. For this very important point see Peyrefitte, *C'était de Gaulle*, vol. 1, 499.

10. Georges-Henri Soutou, *L'Alliance incertaine: Les rapports politico-stratégiques franco-allemands de 1954 à 1996* (Paris: Fayard, 1996); and private papers.
11. See Soutou, *L'Alliance incertaine;* and Alain Peyrefitte, *C'était de Gaulle*, vol. 3, *Tout le monde à besoin d'un France qui marche* (Paris: Fayard, 2000), 195–207.
12. Private papers.
13. An official document of the Centre d'Etudes de Politique étrangère to that effect was published in 1967 (in the 1967, no. 6, issue of *Politique étrangère*), "Modèles de sécurité européenne." This unsigned text (a telltale sign of its official significance) raised many eyebrows in Bonn and Washington.
14. See an annotation by him on a telegram from the French embassy in Moscow on January 2, 1971, Paris, Archives Nationales (hereafter AN), 5AG2 1017.
15. He quite bluntly told as much to Brezhnev on October 29, 1971, AN 5AG2 1018.
16. Note from Gaucher, at the time diplomatic counselor at the Elysée Palace, October 1, 1969, quoting a letter from the ambassador in Moscow Roger Seydoux, AN 5AG2 1017.
17. See his talk with Soviet ambassador Zorin on September 9, 1969, and with Foreign Minister Andrej Gromyko on June 2, 1970 (his first talk with an important Soviet leader), AN 5AG2 1018.
18. See Pompidou's talk with Gromyko on June 2, 1970, quoted above.
19. Very numerous notes from him to that effect, particularly for oil and raw materials, can be found in AN 5AG2 1017.
20. Henri Froment-Meurice (director for Asia at the Foreign Ministry), *Vu du Quai: Memoires 1945–1983* (Paris: Fayard, 1998); talk between Kissinger and Maurice Schumann on September 22, 1972; note from Kissinger to Nixon about a conversation between General Walters and Pompidou on October 30, 1972, Washington, National Archives, Nixon Presidential Materials, National Security Council (NSC) 679 / France, vol. 10.
21. Conversation with Sargent Shriver, the American ambassador in Paris, on July 23, 1969; AN 5AG2 1022.
22. See several documents in AN 5AG2 1041, particularly a note by Raimond on August 7, 1969, and a conversation between Pompidou and Jean de Lipkowski, secretary of state (i.e., undersecretary) at the Quai d'Orsay, on January 6, 1970. See also a note from the Quai d'Orsay with passages underlined by Pompidou, from October 2, 1970, AN 5AG 1018.
23. Conversation of Pompidou and Rogers from December 8, 1969, AN 5AG2 1022, and National Archives, RG59 / 67-69 / box 2103; notes from Jean-Bernard Raimond, diplomatic counselor at the Elysée, for the President, on November 18, 1969, and January 21, 1970, AN 5AG2 1041. Letter from Pompidou to Nixon on July 1, 1972, AN 5AG2 1021.
24. Letter from Roger Seydoux to the General Secretary of the Quai d'Orsay, Hervé Alphand, March 23, 1970, and note from Raimond to Pompidou on September 17, 1970, AN 5AG2 1018.
25. Note from Raimond to the President on May 26, 1970, AN 5AG2 1018.
26. Marie-Pierre Rey, "Georges Pompidou, l'Union soviétique et l'Europe," in *Georges Pompidou et l'Europe*, ed. Association Georges Pompidou, 155–57.
27. Talk with Brezhnev and Pompidou on October 13, 1970, AN 5AG2 1018.
28. Talk between Pompidou and the Soviet leaders on October 7, AN 5AG2 1018.
29. Roussel, *Georges Pompidou*, 391–92.

30. Roussel, *Georges Pompidou*, 395 ff.

31. This point of view was expressed by Raimond in two notes from November 6 and December 8, 1969, see my quoted paper.

32. See Pierre de Villemarest, *Polyarnik: Histoire d'un chef d'État espion* (Paris: Godefroy de Bouillon, 1999), and Villemarest, *Le coup d'Etat de Markus Wolf: La guerre secrete entre les deux Allemagnes 1945–1991* (Paris: Stock, 1991). See Reinhard Müller, *Die Akte Wehner: Moskau 1937 bis 1941* (Berlin: Rowohlt Berlin, 1993).

33. See Werner Link's account in *Republik im Wandel 1969–1974: Die Ära Brandt*, vol. 5/I of the *Geschichte der Bundesrepublik Deutschland*, ed. W. Jäger and W. Link (Stuttgart: Deutsche Verlags-Anstalt, 1986), 169 ff.

34. Roussel, *Georges Pompidou*, 393–94.

35. As with Shriver, on July 23, 1969.

36. E.g., see the conversation between Secretary of State William Rogers and André Fontaine, journalist from *Le Monde*, on December 15, 1969, National Archives, Nixon Presidential Materials, NSC CF/676/France, vol. 4.

37. Conversation between Pompidou and Rogers on December 8, 1969, AN 5AG2 1022 and National Archives, RG59 / 67-69 / box 2103; notes from Jean-Bernard Raimond for the President on November 18, 1969, and January 21, 1970, AN 5AG2 1041.

38. In his private conversations after the meeting Nixon expressed himself quite satisfied; see Sulzberger, *Age of Mediocrity*, 614–15.

39. See my "Le Président Pompidou et les relations entre les Etats-Unis et l'Europe," *Journal of European Integration History* 6, no. 2 (2000): 111–28.

40. As Henry Kissinger told the French ambassador, Charles Lucet, on April 13, 1970, letter from Lucet to Maurice Schumann on April 14, 1970, AN 5AG2 1021.

41. See Soutou, "Le Président Pompidou et les relations entre les Etats-Unis et l'Europe."

42. Annotation from Georges Pompidou on May 13, 1971, AN 5AG2 1041.

43. Note from Jean-Bernard Raimond for Pompidou on October 8, 1971, AN 5AG2 1018.

44. Telegram from Paris on September 20, 1972, National Archives, RG 59 / Num 70-73 / box 2278.

45. E.g., see an annotation from July 2, 1971, on a telegram from the embassy in Moscow about the so-called Soviet peace offensive, AN 5AG2 1017.

46. Note by Jean-Bernard Raimond from August 2, 1971, with annotations by Pompidou, criticizing the draft prepared by Seydoux and Schumann and devastating handwritten note by Edouard Balladur, deputy general secretary of the Elysée, of the same day, AN 5AG2 1017.

47. Note from Raimond for Pompidou from October 18, 1971, AN 5AG2 1017.

48. Note by Raimond on October 23, AN 5AG2 1017. See also two notes from Schumann to Raimond and to Pompidou on October 20, a note from Raimond to Michel Jobert, general secretary of the Elysée, on the same day. See also a long note for the historical record of the negotiation (and also for his own defense) by Seydoux on November 20.

49. Second meeting between Brezhnev and Pompidou on October 26, 1971, AN 5AG 1018.

50. AN 5AG2 1011.

51. Fourth talk on October 29, confidential part, AN 5AG2 1018.

52. Note by Jean-Louis Lucet, from the diplomatic staff at the Elysée, for Pompi-

dou on January 12, 1972, and annotations by Pompidou on May 11, 1970, and June 11, 1971, AN 5AG2 1041.

53. Note from Raimond to Jobert on December 9, 1971, relating the trivial objections of the allies and answer from Jobert with Pompidou's instructions to Maurice Schumann at the Atlantic Council: "Aucun compromise . . . Il faut être intraitable!" AN 5AG2 1041.

54. See a note from Raimond to Pompidou on October 8, 1971, AN 5AG2 1018.

55. For a more detailed account, see my "L'attitude de Georges Pompidou face à l'Allemagne."

56. Note by Raimond for Pompidou on June 12, 1972, commenting upon a document of the Foreign Office, AN 5AG2 1018.

57. AN 5AG2 1018.

58. Letter from Nixon to Pompidou on June 13, 1972, commenting upon a document of the Foreign Office, AN 5AG2 1018.

59. Note from Raimond on May 3, 1973, for Pompidou, AN 5AG2 1021.

60. AN 5AG2 1022.

61. William Burr, ed., *The Kissinger Transcripts: The Top Secret Talks with Beijing and Moscow*, National Security Archive Document Reader (New York: New Press, 1998). Note from Kissinger to President Nixon before Reykjavik, Nixon Presidential Materials, NSC CF / 949 / Pompidou-Nixon Meeting.

62. For a more detailed account see Soutou, "Le Président Pompidou et les relations entre les Etats-Unis et l'Europe."

63. Note from Raimond to Pompidou on June 8, 1972, AN 5AG2 1018.

64. Pompidou's annotations on telegrams from the French embassy in Moscow from September 23, 1973, and November 3, AN 5AG2 1041.

65. Meeting of January 12, 1973, AN 5AG2 1019.

66. Annotation by Pompidou on February 15, 1973, and note from Raimond on February 20, AN 5AG2 1041.

67. The infamous "journalist" Victor Louis played his part in this campaign (see a letter from Seydoux on December 29, 1972, AN 5AG2 1017) as did Defense Minister Marshall Grechko during his visit to France at the end of 1972 (see his talk with his French counterpart Michel Debré on November 27, AN 5AG2 1018).

68. Note from Raimond on June 23, 1973, after a conversation with Vimont, the ambassador to the Soviet Union, AN 5AG2 1017.

69. Note by Raimond on January 10, 1973, AN 5AG2 1041.

70. Note from Raimond to Jobert on December 18, 1972, AN 5AG2 1019.

71. Three notes from the Quai d'Orsay from June 19 and 20, 1973, AN 5AG2 1019.

72. Telegram from Moscow recounting Defense Minister Robert Galley's talks with the Soviet leaders, December 7, 1973, AN 5AG2 1017.

73. Telegram from Moscow, November 28, 1973, AN 5AG2 1017.

74. Notes from Gabriel Robin, successor of Jean-Bernard Raimond, to Pompidou on February 13, 1974, and March 6, AN 5AG2 1019.

75. Upon instructions, Robin established on the eve of the trip to Pitsunda a list of points by which the French could accommodate Soviet views; Pompidou actually followed rather closely this advice in Pitsunda; note from Robin to Balladur (the general secretary of the Elysée) on March 11, AN 5AG2 1019.

76. Talks with Brezhnev on March 12 and 13, 1974, AN 5AG2 1019.

77. For a more detailed account, see my "L'attitude de Georges Pompidou face à l'Allemagne."

78. See Link's account, in *Republik im Wandel,* vol. 5/I, *Geschichte der Bundesrepublik Deutschland,* ed. Bracher, Jäger, and Link, 231, about the contradictions in Brandt's cabinet at a time of renewed difficulties in Moscow in the autumn of 1973. See also Link, in the next volume of the *Geschichte der Bundesrepublik Deutschland,* 5/II, 291 ff, about the debate in Bonn at the time of Brandt's fall.

79. See *Le Monde,* November 23.

80. Jobert, *L'autre regard,* 348.

81. AN 5AG2 1021.

82. Note from the Quai d'Orsay on June 20, 1973, AN 5AG2 1019.

83. AN 5AG2 1021.

84. AN 5AG2 1021, note from Gabriel Robin, successor of Jean-Bernard Raimond, on January 10 for Balladur, with annotation from Balladur, and attached documents.

85. AN 5AG2 1021.

86. The memorandum of his conversations with Brezhnev at Pitsunda on March 12 and 13, 1974, is quite revealing on this point, AN 5AG2 1019.

87. Soutou, "L'attitude de Georges Pompidou face à l'Allemagne."

Part V

Testing Détente and Relaunching Europe

Chapter 11

The United States Tests Détente
Gale A. Mattox

For the United States, détente addressed and resolved a number of practical problems confronting U.S. policymakers in the 1970s. It provided an avenue to divert attention from the domestic agony and international embarrassment over the emerging debacle in Vietnam. Détente also gave President Richard Nixon an opportunity to showcase the statesman image he sought. The arms control negotiations with the Soviet Union, the centerpiece of détente for the United States, were designed to cap the quickly growing Soviet nuclear arsenal and lower the tensions and thus potential for conflict in Europe. But the Helsinki Conference in 1975, acclaimed as a glowing manifestation of the benefits of détente and as the first step to peace in Europe, in fact actually initiated a gradual disillusionment with détente in the United States, fueled in large part by partisan politics of the mid-1970s and underpinned by a substantial ideological divide in American politics.

The views expressed in this chapter are those of the author and do not represent the views of the U.S. government or the institutions with which the author is affiliated.

For Europeans, détente signified a very fundamental change in approach to relations with the Soviet Union, with implications for the daily life of Europeans (to include Russians) on both sides of the East-West divide, while for the United States, in contrast, détente was a shift in policy that lost its following when the Soviets fell short of expectations. Perhaps also, by nature, Americans were more anxious for immediate and visible success, whereas the European concept of détente carried a longer-range perspective. For the Soviet Union, détente served very specific political and economic purposes by lowering tensions with the West and slowing the arms race, but not at the price of a breakup of either its own system of governance or its goal of spreading its ideology abroad. When East-West relations experienced hills and valleys, the Europeans, who had witnessed a greater impact on their lives and had a more pragmatic approach to détente, much more easily adapted than did the United States. The Europeans were willing to compromise to an extent in view of the longer-term advantages of lowered tensions and stability, for example in Berlin. The Americans were far less willing to abide by what they saw as a retreat from the "détente deal" struck with Moscow and withdrew their enthusiasm and support for détente.

Finally, the differences in expectations for détente were also influenced by the striking divergence in outlook between the European regional and American global perspectives. Although this difference had been less pronounced just after World War II, it grew as France and Britain shed their colonies and began to build a European community. Germany maintained its low profile and turned to the European Economic Community (EEC) and NATO to provide avenues by which to expand its interests, albeit within fairly strict parameters. With its efforts to block the spread of communism and encourage democracies, the United States' responsibilities became increasingly more global.

Defining Détente

Both the Europeans and the Americans viewed potential gains to be achieved in the pursuit of détente when they adopted the concept in relations with the Soviet Union. For the Europeans, détente meant lowered tensions and more opportunities for their publics—in trade, in travel, and in reduced frictions on a broad spectrum of issues. For the Germans, in particular, détente meant abandonment of the Hallstein doctrine, normalization of relations with the Soviet Bloc, and the benefits of greater contacts with the East—including long-term political and economic cooperation. A series of agreements and treaties affecting in particular East Germany, Poland, and the Soviet Union were designed to improve the conditions of Eastern Europeans and, specifically, East German citizens. For the Americans, first and foremost, détente permitted at least a respite from the ongoing Berlin crises and the German division, but also "détente successfully linked the whole range of issues between East and West all around the world; . . . [and] if the Soviets were to reap the benefits of the relaxation of tensions, they, too, were obliged to contribute to détente."[1]

In his book *Diplomacy,* Henry Kissinger, former national security adviser and secretary of state to Presidents Nixon and Ford, explicitly addresses the wide range of issues on which the United States felt it would be able to engage the Soviet Union through détente—from the most prominent, the German question, to the Middle East to other parts of the world.[2] Kissinger argues that just the fact that Chancellor Willy Brandt could pursue an *Ostpolitik* with Moscow and other Eastern Bloc states that recognized the borders after World War II gave the Soviets "a big incentive for restrained conduct, at least while they (the treaties) were being negotiated and ratified." Among other implications, it meant that "Moscow's response was muted" when President Nixon "decided to mine North Vietnamese harbors and to resume the bombing of Hanoi."[3] This muted response was argument enough for many adherents to a policy of détente.

Kissinger has also detailed the decision of the Nixon and then Ford administrations to pursue a policy of détente in various books since his time in office. He offered his own analysis of why détente served U.S. national interests in a speech in March 1976 during the Ford administration:

> Soviet strength is uneven; the weaknesses and frustrations of the Soviet system are glaring and have been clearly documented. Despite the inevitable increase in its power, the Soviet Union remains far behind us and our allies in any overall assessment of military, economic, and technological strength; it would be reckless in the extreme for the Soviet Union to challenge the industrial democracies. And Soviet society is no longer insulated from the influences and attractions of the outside world or impervious to the need for external contacts.[4]

Not only would détente bring about a necessary reduction in tensions to permit pursuit of a range of issues by the United States and Europe, it also made possible a series of important arms control agreements and treaties (Strategic Arms Limitation Talks, or SALT; and the Anti–Ballistic Missile; as well as Incidents at Sea and others) that were beneficial to the Soviet Union.

Former president Nixon later offered his advice on dealing with the Soviets, based on his experiences during the early days of détente:

> How we structure and approach talks with Moscow will largely determine our success in them. Gorbachev will take us to the cleaners in negotiations unless we use the tactic of linkage. The two sides do not have the same degree of interest in progress on all issues. . . . If we fail to link the two sets of issues—he will dominate the negotiating agenda.[5]

Several factors led to the "testing of détente" and its eventual demise. Those factors fell into two general categories: the impact of Soviet international behavior; and American domestic considerations as the country dealt with Watergate and then moved politically to the right by the end of the decade. In terms of Soviet behavior in its international dealings, this involved the retreat, in the eyes of the United States, by the Soviet Union from the "détente deal" as demonstrated by (1) Soviet involvement through Cuban surrogates in Angola and Vietnamese in Kampuchea/Cambodia, as well as support for rebels in Nicaragua and elsewhere,[6] (2) the introduction of the SS-20 nuclear missile into Europe and, finally, (3) the intervention by the Soviets in Afghanistan.

These international events obviously affected as well U.S. domestic political considerations, but it is also clear that the political arena had a dynamic of its own, including (1) the increasing weakness of President Nixon during and after Watergate; (2) the subsequent absence of a strong advocate and an inability to protect the policy from domestic critics to the right and left and; finally, (3) a challenge from the right during the 1976 election, but, more seriously, during the 1980 election. When the Soviets failed in a number of respects to "reform" their activities, or even adhere to their agreements, support for détente deteriorated among the informed public in the United States. Though many have dated the demise of détente to the invasion of Afghanistan, the "testing of détente" was already well-established before 1979.

At the basis of this national debate—or national elite debate, to be more precise—was the fact that Nixon (read Kissinger also) "saw détente as a tactic in a long-term geopolitical struggle: his liberal critics treated it as an end in itself while conservatives and neoconservatives rejected the geopolitical as so much historical pessimism, preferring a policy of unremitting ideological confrontation."[7] Certainly, in retrospect, it is clear that détente served a very useful purpose in walking the line between these groups; but, in so doing, détente was oversold to the public. It was this divisive difference in the expectations of the policy of détente that even before the 1975 Helsinki Conference on Security and Cooperation in Europe had begun to undermine its foundation and eventually result in its demise.

Soviet Involvement Outside Europe

In the evaluation and testing of détente, not only were there differences of opinion in the area of arms control, there were also clear divergences at points over the impact of Soviet involvement in activities outside Europe. These differences in the evaluation of the impact on détente of Soviet activism ranged from stark disagreements with the French, who expressed less concern about activities that did not pose a direct threat to the Germans. Germany—whose forces, unlike those of the French, were constitutionally restricted to the North Atlantic area—were not inclined to divert resources outside the continent. The Germans had the additional priority of retaining U.S. support and presence in the Atlantic alliance. For the United States, the Soviet actions abroad abrogated what it viewed a basic tenet of détente: to avoid tensions and the potential for conflict.

Soviet activism outside the Soviet Union's borders ranged from what the United States regarded as Cuban surrogate action in Angola—U.S. estimates were that Cuba received $8 million a day from the Soviets—to later support of Vietnam in Cambodia and of the Sandinistas in Nicaragua, the latter long considered the U.S. backyard. President Jimmy Carter derisively reports that Soviet general secretary Leonid Brezhnev insisted to him that

> you continue to complain about Cuban troops and the Cuban leaders themselves. However, we do know that the troops are sent only in response to specific requests for assistance by the recognized governments in Angola and Ethiopia. The American leaders should remember that many foreign troops fought with George Washington during your own revolution.[8]

For the United States, these activities were viewed with alarm. At his 1979 summit with Secretary Brezhnev, President Carter minced no words about U.S. dissatisfaction in these areas as well as in the Middle East (especially Iran and Syria) and elsewhere in Africa. During the 1979 Vienna summit for the signing of the SALT II agreements, President Carter used the occasion to admonish the Soviet Union on its activities abroad and noted that the United States expected the Soviets to remain out of the internal affairs of other states.[9] For the United States, it was becoming clear that Soviet actions outside arms control belied the "true" Russian intentions in pursuing détente, and the policy had become a liability in a number of ways. President Carter's admonishment to Secretary Brezhnev preceded the Russian march into Afghanistan by six months!

A Nuclear Imbalance?

For the United States, the January 1979 meeting at Guadeloupe was a turning point in recognizing a perceived force imbalance that had arisen in Europe as a result of two factors: (1) the equal ceilings negotiated in the SALT I Treaty and reinforced in the follow-up Vladivostok Agreement; and (2) the introduction of the SS-20s into the nuclear arsenal of the Soviet Union capable of reaching Western Europe, a category of nuclear weapons not included in the SALT negotiations. These two factors appeared for the Americans to pose a potentially unsettling and dangerous challenge to peace on the European continent.[10] The situation clearly needed to be addressed, and the meeting on the island for the first time included German chancellor Helmut Schmidt. Germany was perhaps the most unsettled participant because of its vulnerable position, but it also recognized the need to resolve this new and threatening situation more than any of the others.

In fact, the most vocal concerns over the direction of SALT II, a centerpiece of détente, and the lack of European input into the negotiations—when the outcome could potentially have substantial consequences for the NATO alliance—emanated from the Germans. Their discontent had been building from the early days of the Carter presidency to the summit. For one, in the spring of 1978, a controversy over the enhanced radiation weapon (known familiarly as the "neutron bomb") had made Chancellor Schmidt skeptical of the direction of U.S. policy. In this case, Schmidt was left after a trip to Washington with the impression that the introduction of the neutron bomb was certain. He proceeded to convince his Cabinet of its necessity only to have the rug—figuratively speaking—pulled out from under him when the United States decided to defer production of the neutron bomb.

The neutron bomb was to be a "high yield weapon . . . effective for stopping Russian tanks, but . . . also (able to) kill or severely injure many NATO soldiers and German civilians and . . . devastate much West German territory."[11] Though many proponents of the neutron bomb argued for its deterrent value "against Soviet aggression in Europe and to make the Alliance more secure from Soviet political and military pressure," the political fallout for such a potential deployment was substantial.[12] As the experts acknowledged, "the effects of induced and residual radiation could make the occupation and recovery of the affected territory a lethal prospect for some time."[13] It had not been an easy sell, and the retreat from the decision was embarrassing for Schmidt.[14]

From the perspective of President Jimmy Carter, it was the Europeans, especially the British and Germans (in that order), who made it impossible to decide to produce or deploy the neutron warhead. He wrote in his diary on March 20, "I became more and more convinced that we ought not to deploy the neutron bomb. We've not gotten any firm commitments from a European nation to permit its deployment on their soil, which is the only place it would be deployed."[15] Despite an April Bundestag conditional acceptance and a reassuring call from Chancellor Schmidt, Carter further comments with irritation in his memoirs that "the fact is that to this day no European government has been willing to agree to their (ERW [enhanced radiation weapons]) deployment"[16]—despite the fact that Schmidt "subsequently complained to many listeners that the United States had unilaterally aborted plans to produce and deploy neutron weapons."[17] Given the European indecision on the issue, President Carter was obviously livid with Schmidt over his complaints. But it is interesting that despite the tension caused in the relationship, both leaders appeared to agree on using the issue to "induce additional restraints among the Soviets in other arms control negotiations."[18]

This neutron bomb "crisis" had followed the failure of the Comprehensive Proposal presented in Moscow for SALT II by the new Carter administration in the spring of 1977, a proposal that had not been vetted or even discussed in any detail by the U.S. administration in Europe. Not only did Chancellor Schmidt want closer consultation on SALT II, he was also convinced that SALT III could potentially deal with European-dedicated nuclear weapons and he wanted to be sure that there was European input. Helmut Schmidt, the more pragmatic successor to the architect of *Ostpolitik* Willy Brandt, expressed his concerns in a very public forum in the fall of 1977 at the International Institute for Strategic Studies in London.[19] In his Alastair

Buchan Memorial Address, he lamented the imbalance that had been created by SALT and the need to address the European theater in the future.

For the Americans, the options to resolve this conundrum were limited. From their perspective, the overwhelming qualitative superiority of the American nuclear arsenal was sufficiently reassuring to counter the negotiated equal ceilings in SALT. The perception of overall imbalance on the part of the Europeans was unsettling—while the United States was willing to station large numbers of forces in Europe to symbolize its commitment to European defense should there be a challenge from the Soviets across the border, there was no way either the American public or the newly created American volunteer force could match the Soviet conventional forces. The American public was weary from the Vietnam War and only beginning to heal internally.

The election of Jimmy Carter over Gerald Ford had been driven in part by the desire of Americans to put behind them both the agony of a demoralizing loss to a small nation in Southeast Asia that few Americans before 1968 could find on a map and the wrenching demise of a previously popular President Nixon whose actions in the Watergate scandal had threatened the political fabric of the nation. A national political will to engage in a more substantial way in Europe was clearly absent and not likely to be aroused by the makers of U.S. foreign policy, who themselves were not sure that the situation created by SALT was as dire as the Europeans portrayed.

But even these considerations of political will aside, the American volunteer force was in crisis, and the possibility of stationing larger numbers of troops in Europe was clearly not an option. The military forces, and particularly the army, were confronted with a serious shortage of labor power. The willingness of young men and women to volunteer for the armed services had substantially dropped after Vietnam and the elimination of the draft in 1973. Though the military was still attracting recruits, it was not attracting the type of recruit that it needed for the demands of an emerging technological revolution. The numbers of recruits with a high school education was at a low point.[20] Training and readiness were affected, as was the overall morale and standing within society generally. In short, the bottom line of deterrence against attack from the East had to remain American nuclear capabilities.

After the Guadeloupe summit, the United States pondered how it should address the European concern that the nuclear balance now struck in the strategic arms control regimes, coupled with the clear Soviet conventional superiority, had created a serious credibility gap in the ability of the United

States to deter Soviet attack across the vulnerable German plain. There were a range of alarmist voices in the debate who cited new data on the estimated time it would take for the Soviet army to roll through the Fulda Gap and reach the Rhine River—figures that estimated a decrease in time from two weeks to a matter of days. The NATO doctrine of Flexible Response adopted ten years earlier had posited the potential to respond to an attack either with conventional or with intercontinental nuclear weapons, or anything in between. Though the Soviets had long had SS-4s and SS-5s in their force, the SS-20 represented a considerable qualitative advantage.[21] The problem was that the allies only had battlefield nuclear weapons in that span between conventional and strategic response. What if those battlefield weapons (numbering more than 7,000 atomic artillery shells, mines, short range missiles, etc.) were insufficient for the task?

The agreed-on response at the December 1979 NATO summit was the "dual-track" decision, which proposed to resolve the dilemma through two tracks. The first would continue to pursue an active arms control negotiation with the Soviets to remove the SS-20 threat; and failing such a resolution, the second track would counter the SS-20 with the introduction of modernized Pershing IIs in Germany and the new ground-launched cruise missile (GLCM) in the five NATO countries, Germany, Britain, the Netherlands, Belgium and Italy.[22] The one interesting factor was that the second part of the equation—the Pershing IIs and GLCMs—would not be operational in any case for a year or two at best. A date of 1983 was established as the point at which either there would have been success at the negotiating table or the new modernized arsenal of intermediate-range nuclear forces (INF) would be introduced. It was a unique and innovative approach.[23] For the United States, it demonstrated commitment to arms control while testing a new intermediate-range weapon that would provide one more escalatory option in a spiraling crisis short of strategic nuclear force use.[24] The double-track nature of the decision would put pressure on the Soviets to negotiate without immediately introducing a new weapon to expand an even more frenetic arms race.[25]

SALT II: A Crowning Achievement Challenged

On June 19, 1979, President Jimmy Carter and General Secretary Leonid Brezhnev met in Vienna to put their signatures to the SALT II Treaty. The event was superbly choreographed to showcase a young vigorous U.S. president jogging through Vienna's stately Hapsburg Hofgarten while the Russian interlocutor had to be supported by aides on either side. It was a triumphant president who returned to the United States on Air Force One following the summit eager to trumpet his success in convincing the Soviets to reduce for the first time, albeit not in large numbers, their strategic nuclear arsenal.

Almost from the point of landing, however, Carter began to experience problems with ratification. A measure of both partisan politics and skepticism over the intentions of the Soviets colored the debate. Soviet actions—mostly through surrogates—in Central America and in Angola had prompted questions about the true motivations of the Soviet Union in agreeing to SALT II. The rapid buildup of SS-20s clearly aimed at NATO countries had also begun to have an impact.[26] In terms of partisan politics, the mood in the American public was swinging to the right, and that swing was being influenced heavily by former California governor Ronald Reagan. Not taken seriously in the 1976 race and passed over for the incumbent President Gerald Ford, Reagan had spent three years assuring that he would not be passed over again for the Republican nomination. His message was one that this time resonated with Republicans and began to make inroads into the swing voters who were tiring of "Preacher" Jimmy Carter. By mid-1979, the fight among Republicans was already moving the party to the right, and President Carter was realizing the impact of this shift on his party as well. Over the next year, the voters more generally edged rightward as the 1980 election got into gear.

Skepticism toward the Soviets, combined with the looming 1980 U.S. presidential campaign, had an interesting effect on SALT II ratification. The initial response to the treaty was positive after the June 1979 signing and by July, when former secretary of state Kissinger voiced cautious support, it appeared that treaty ratification was in sight. One issue, however, continued to dog the treaty: verification, which embodied both the above factors—to wit, the right (led by Reagan) had been consistently opposed to past arms control treaties signed with the Soviets on the grounds that Russian leaders could not be trusted. How could a governmental system rooted in an ideology committed to burying the West and stamping out capitalism and democratic regimes be trusted to adhere to treaties, especially treaties with such implications for the American way of life? Given the high visibility of the SALT II agreement and its close identification with Jimmy Carter, it was also convenient as an issue on which the opposition (Republicans but also

Democrats who were beginning to perceive Carter as vulnerable within the party for the nomination) could challenge the incumbent.

During the August summer break, the chairman of the Senate Foreign Relations Committee, Frank Church, who was presumably feeling the heat from the right, raised a red flag over the introduction of "new" units of Soviet troops in Cuba. Where the truth lies remains unclear—assertions ranged from a new threat to the U.S. mainland to the contention that these were no more than fresh units replacing Soviets rotating home. But the Senate that returned after the August break appeared increasingly skeptical of the SALT II treaty; and when the hearings reconvened, ratification had been thrown into question. After numerous experts testified, there seemed to be a general agreement from moderate Republican members to Democrats who seemed to want to support the president that the main stumbling block was whether treaty compliance could be reliably verified.

The treaty called for more stringent verification measures than previous agreements and specifically allowed "National Technical Means" (NTM) of verification. But could NTM catch Soviet violations? There were those who felt that no treaty could ever catch the necessary sum total of the cheating incidents and should never be accepted, but most senators appeared to accept the administration's standard for a treaty able to capture violations that would threaten the United States or its allies; that is, less substantial, potential violations were disturbing but would not outweigh the advantages of the treaty. But there remained the question of how verifiable the treaty really was. In large part, there was a general turning to Senator John Glenn (D-Ohio) for this expert determination, but he was slow in making a public statement about where his threshold for tolerance was and if SALT II met that tolerance.[27]

Before Glenn announced his final verdict on the ability of SALT II to be verified, an unrelated incident occurred with a resulting impact on the treaty. In November 1979, radical students overran the U.S. Embassy in Tehran and took fifty-four hostages. U.S. installations were seized throughout the country, and the incident confronted the administration with a situation that would deny the sitting president any chance of reelection and would set back U.S.-Iranian relations at least twenty years. Moreover, the Iranian seizures proved to have included "listening posts" on the Iranian northern borders that were critical to U.S. verification of its arms control treaties. It was a devastating situation that put the SALT II ratification into serious question by raising substantial doubts about the verifiability of the treaty.

The Soviet Invasion of Afghanistan

But if the Iranian seizures represented a nearly fatal blow to SALT II, the Soviet invasion of Afghanistan in late December 1979 put the final nail in the treaty's coffin. For Americans, the Afghanistan invasion represented an end to détente.[28] There is little question that the atmosphere over the year 1979 had slowly become less supportive of the U.S.-Soviet relationship in a number of respects. The Soviet use of surrogates in various regions, the introduction of the SS-20 in a threatening position to Europe, and the poor performance of the Eastern Bloc on the Conference on Security and Cooperation in Europe (CSCE) / Helsinki agreements had all sparked a more cautious attitude toward the Soviet Union. Equally important was the shift to the right in U.S. domestic politics, which made all aspects of détente into an intensely partisan issue.

Following the Afghanistan invasion, President Carter announced his "disappointment" with the Soviet Union. Among steps announced in reaction to the invasion, he canceled the planning for an exchange of consulates (Kiev/ New York), reduced the presence of the Russian government airline Aeroflot, canceled U.S. participation in the 1980 Moscow Olympics, and canceled the shipments of grain to the Soviet Union that had been planned and were an element of the broader U.S.-Soviet détente relationship. Finally, Carter withdrew the SALT II treaty from consideration by the U.S. Senate.

The Reagan Attack on Détente

As the 1980 campaign heated up, the Republican nominee Reagan continued his attack on the naiveté of the incumbent President Carter in his dealings with the East. The American public appeared to agree, particularly after the hostage taking, but also with respect to relations with the Soviet Union. Less recognized perhaps is the fact that the U.S. administration was also moving rightward in response to the attacks, as well as in recognition of the public mood and Carter's own disillusionment. A review of increased defense spending during this period confirms this direction by the administration. But the arguments of Reagan caught the attention of Americans, and in November 1980, the voters refused Carter a second term and elected Reagan the next president of the United States.

Given his later comments in support of disarmament and a zero solution, President Reagan's real thoughts about arms control and nuclear weapons are interesting topics. Immediately on assuming office, he announced a review of arms control that effectively blocked all negotiations for more than a year. It also gave rise to a nuclear freeze movement in the United States in reaction.[29] For the INF negotiations, the arms control track of the dual-track decision, the delay was a significant factor in the European public demonstrations that began in 1980 and crested in 1982 with the largest total number of protestors seen on the streets since World War II. Those protests against INF deployments were particularly large in Germany, Britain, Belgium, the Netherlands, and to a lesser extent Italy, all countries slated to receive the new INF weapons. By contrast, French protests were proportionately and considerably smaller.

President Reagan's rejection of the arms control negotiations inherited from his predecessor were part of his general disdain for the U.S.-Soviet détente policy more generally. He took little time in making his views of the 1970s U.S.-Soviet relationship known. In his first press conference nine days after taking office, he "labeled the Soviet Union an outlaw empire" prepared "to commit any crime, to lie, to cheat" to achieve its goals.[30] This proved the precursor to the later much-quoted "evil empire" label he accorded the Soviet Union in 1983.

The Soviet Pipeline: European Pragmatism Meets U.S. Opposition

The controversy over the Soviet Yamal pipeline provides a good example of the differences in approach to détente between the United States and the Europeans. The Western Europeans developed a plan with the Soviet Union for a natural gas pipeline running from the Yamal gas deposits in Siberia through Germany and into a number of European states. The pipeline was to be financed by loans from the Europeans to be repaid by the Russians through the sale of the gas that would then flow. The United States was aghast over this proposal and argued that it would permit the Russians leverage over the Europeans and their energy supplies. This type of leverage could in turn have substantial implications for the East-West balance in Europe itself and even the strategic balance between the superpowers. Furthermore, there would be a transfer of hard currency to the Soviet Union from the West for the development and construction of the pipeline as well as later when the gas began to flow. The impact of such a flow of hard currency could be negative, and the idea of subsidizing the Soviets did not fall on happy U.S. ears![31]

For the Europeans, the planned gas pipeline made eminent sense after the 1973 Middle East energy shortages. It was uncertain when the next crisis might affect the energy supply, and this pipeline from western Siberia would diversify energy sources for the Europeans. At least eight European countries would be helped in their gas needs, and the Soviet Union would be tied to the West.[32] Whereas the Europeans found this mutual dependence to be potentially stabilizing, the United States worried about undue influence and pressure from the Russians on other issues once the gas began to flow. As one critic commented, "It is not a problem for France to be dependent on Holland; it could be a problem, a very serious one, when France is dependent on the Soviet Union."[33]

The end result was a compromise solution whereby the pipeline was developed but within an energy grid that would particularly avoid an overreliance by Germany, the most militarily vulnerable to potential attack from the East. The plan also included facilities to regulate the flow on the part of the West and provide other safeguards. The debate was fierce, and the arguments reflected some of the fundamental differences in approach to the Soviet Union—the United States was demonstrating the skeptical stance it had adopted toward Moscow since Afghanistan, while the Europeans took a much more pragmatic approach based on their own economic needs and perceived overdependence on the potentially volatile Persian Gulf energy resources.[34] For the Europeans, in contrast to the United States, the pipeline potentially had direct and positive consequences for the daily lives and standard of living of its citizens.

The CSCE Review Conference: A U.S.-European Clash over Concepts of Détente

With Reagan at the helm, détente as it had been conceived and pursued in the 1970s was effectively over. In an interesting final gasp, the CSCE process—once thought the embodiment of détente—was in the midst of a scheduled review that had begun in November 1980 in Madrid but had come under attack after the declaration of martial law in Poland during the new Reagan administration. The Yamal pipeline disagreement had centered on issues related to economics and military security, while the issues confronted in the CSCE discussions were directly related to the evaluation of the Russian performance in terms of human rights as well as the array of confidence-building measures adopted in Helsinki.[35] Human rights had

The United States Tests Détente 275

been an ongoing irritant between Washington and Moscow. Even at the last plenum of the June 1979 SALT II summit, with General Secretary Brezhnev impatiently looking at his watch as the meeting went into overtime, President Carter had commented that

> the subject of human rights is very important to us in shaping our attitude toward your country. You voluntarily signed the Helsinki accords, which made this issue a proper item for state-to-state discussions. We have been gratified at the more liberal emigration policies you have established in recent months.[36]

At Madrid, not only was the Eastern Bloc's lack of adherence to Basket Three human rights widely criticized, the Soviet Union itself was charged as well with abrogating a number of the agreed-on terms from all the negotiated CSCE three baskets. In addition, the Soviet Union had moved ships into the waters off Poland in a show of force during the Solidarity demonstrations and subsequent announcement of martial law. This was clearly in violation of the CSCE agreement for signatories to inform other signers of maneuvers of a proscribed size.[37] Ambassador Joerg Kastl of Germany described the change in atmosphere as follows:

> When the delegates began on 9 September 1980 to prepare the proceedings for the main meeting in Madrid, it was immediately clear that the world political atmosphere had deteriorated considerably. In Helsinki (1975), hopes of a progressive détente had overshadowed concern about the Soviet Union's incipient intervention in the Third World. In Belgrade (1977–1978), disappointment over the disregard of human rights by the Warsaw Pact countries was already predominant. By 1980, détente had become questionable for many participating states.[38]

But despite the shared subdued reaction generally to the Helsinki process, the United States and Europe reacted differently with respect to the Polish situation. The U.S. reaction was to move to cancel the CSCE Review Conference scheduled to resume in Madrid. For the United States, the Soviets had also lost their right to be treated equally after the Afghanistan invasion. In contrast, the Europeans argued that the West should not isolate the Soviet Union and should hold the talks to continue engaging Moscow. Ambassador Kastl describes the European position:

Foreign Minister Genscher strove hard to keep the meeting going, trying to gain some success in Madrid for the people of Europe, despite all the disappointments. He introduced the theme that it was not the West that must yield ground in the humanitarian field or in the matter of military security, but the East; not the West that must be seen to be on the defensive, but the East. If there were to be a lengthy adjournment, the East would blame it on the West for not having been willing to negotiate and thus . . . extricate itself from the unwanted criticism of implementation. . . . Had (the CSCE process) not proved to be a platform from which attention could be focused on such issues as the renunciation of the threat or use of force, on non-intervention, human rights and the creation of greater military openness in Europe?[39]

This clash of concepts over the appropriate approach to the Soviet relationship vividly underscores the differences between the European and the U.S. perceptions of détente. For the Europeans, the prospect of completely severing relations with the Soviets would return the relationship to the standoff of the 1960s. This was not a desirable outcome. In their calculation, the cost such a radical retreat would incur politically, economically, and otherwise was simply not worth the unlikely benefits. Détente was logical and natural to most Europeans by that point—did it not make sense to be on a speaking basis with neighbors? Was it not better to have established avenues of communication with a potential foe through which misunderstandings could be addressed and not escalate to dangerous proportions?

In contrast, just as the United States had canceled participation in the Olympics after Afghanistan, the U.S. response to the imposition of martial law in Poland followed by the buildup of Soviet forces without notification as required under the terms of the Helsinki CSCE agreement was naturally to take steps against the Soviet Union to show its displeasure. The American public was much less informed than the Europeans on the U.S.-Soviet relationship and certainly did not feel an ownership or particular value in the pursuit of détente. Unlike the Europeans, the majority of Americans experienced no direct benefit from détente, such as travel, family contact, and others as a result of the détente relationship with the Soviet Union. To the contrary, the burgeoning war in Nicaragua, the constant threat of Cuba ninety miles away, the violations of human rights against groups within the Soviet Union, and a history of tension over "hot spots" such as Germany had left few warm feelings in the U.S. public toward the Russian "Bear."

The issue of Soviet trustworthiness also played a large role. Central to the American sense of security since 1945 had been the U.S. nuclear capability and superiority in the field. As the Soviet arsenal increased, so did acceptance of the concept of Soviet-American cooperation on arms control to prevent any further potentially uncontrolled growth of Russian nuclear forces. This acceptance was eroded, if not before, then after the 1980 campaign built on the charges by the Republicans of a "window of vulnerability."[40] Détente, and with it arms control, was only acceptable with a high level of trust; when the Soviets abrogated that trust, as they had in Afghanistan and now in Poland and elsewhere, any remaining willingness to be understanding evaporated.[41]

The Europeans were adamant in their insistence that the CSCE Review Conference continue, and a compromise was finally struck; the United States would agree to attend if the conference was used to drive home Western dissatisfaction with an array of Soviet misdeeds against the spirit of Helsinki, if not the letter of the obligations made in 1975. According to a member of the U.S. negotiating team, the Washington delegation's mood was extremely skeptical when traveling to Madrid in February 1982. But the general U.S. delegation assessment at the conclusion was that, contrary to expectations, the conference proved a tremendous platform for the West to drive home the Soviet failures in meeting their agreements made in Helsinki.[42] The German ambassador gave considerable credit to the U.S. ambassador, Max Kampelman: "An eloquent advocate of human rights, he knew how to demonstrate to his government the benefits of achieving success in Madrid."[43] The conference rules for statements enabled the Western allies to showcase especially the Soviet repression of a range of human rights. One after another, the Western ambassadors rose to charge the Soviets and others in the Eastern Bloc not only on the issue of Poland but also on the suppression of the media, religious groups, and other human rights abuses in the communist states.

Détente Fails the Test

The United States embarked on détente for a number of reasons quite different from those of Europe. The impetus for the new policy of détente was twofold. First, the quantitative parity reached in strategic nuclear forces in 1967 and the disinclination of a U.S. government embroiled in a war to address the emerging parity with additional weapons prompted Washington to seek redress through arms control. Second, the ability to finally resolve the

German question and a range of outstanding border issues, at least sufficiently to reduce the tensions in Central Europe, was attractive. Furthermore, a détente relationship could provide an avenue whereby other issues (in the Middle East, Latin America, and elsewhere) could be discussed and possibly resolved if dialogue could be opened between the East and West.

Once embarked upon this relationship, whose crowning achievement was the Helsinki Agreement, the Americans found that the CSCE Agreement was an efficient mechanism by which to pressure the Eastern governments on their human rights records and pursue various confidence-building measures. The Helsinki process, in fact, found even more resonance in the Eastern Bloc than was at that time recognized. Groups such as Czech Charter 77 and others in the Eastern European communist states drew strength and followers from the news of the Helsinki and later agreements between the United States, Soviet Union, and Western and Eastern Europeans. The West's condemnation at the Madrid CSCE Conference of the Polish suppression of Solidarity and the massing of Soviet troops raised the hopes of dissidents throughout the Eastern Bloc and, many assert, was important in the eventual demise of the Soviet Union. Former playwright and activist Václav Havel, who left jail after the Velvet Revolution to assume the Czech presidency, seldom misses an opportunity to trumpet the impact of the CSCE agreements in encouraging Soviet and Eastern European publics in their efforts to change their repressive political and economic systems.[44]

The expectations for détente were high in the West. The failure of détente was correspondingly monumental. For the United States, détente had promised a "reformed" Soviet Union both internally in its behavior toward individuals and groups previously suppressed and externally in its dealings with the developing world. For the Soviet Union, détente meant the advantages of closer relations with the United States and Europe for arms control and lowered tensions, but it did not require a break with the fundamental ideological basis of the regime. It did not mean disruptive individual rights over group rights, nor did it mean that a severing of ties to comrades abroad or even the struggle side-by-side in the revolutions that were inevitable in communist ideology. This latter point distinguished the United States from Europe—European states saw détente from a regional perspective. Though Russian actions in Angola and Afghanistan were disturbing, the European disillusionment with détente came considerably later when Poland was affected. This regional versus global perspective was important to understanding the very different reactions of American and European elites to détente, not to mention the even larger divide between American and European publics.

In announcing the steps to be taken against the Soviet Union after Afghanistan, President Jimmy Carter announced his "disappointment" in the Soviet Union. The guffaws from his critics were audible and underscored how far away from policy the American public had moved. The nomination and election of Ronald Reagan to the presidency completed the demise in American minds of this approach to the superpower bilateral relationship. The subsequent actions of the Soviets in Poland, Nicaragua, and elsewhere merely confirmed the conviction of détente's opponents that their opposition had been well grounded.[45] The announcement by the new President Reagan in 1981 of a review of all arms control agreements and the cessation of all negotiations until an exhaustive review was completed later reinforced the intentions of the new administration.

After the Atlantic alliance crisis of INF public demonstrations in the West over the proposed nuclear force modernizations and the slow pace of arms control, NATO chose to proceed with INF deployment in November 1983 in light of the unwillingness of the Soviet Union to conclude an arms control treaty. As one scholar observed in December 1983, there was now a battle being waged over the public, but it was no longer an East-West battle for public opinion. Rather, "East and West are battling over the basic principles to govern their relationship in the eighties and beyond, while Western political elites are battling each other over the guidelines for Western policy towards the East."[46]

The U.S.-Soviet détente relationship developed during the Nixon administration was tested by a number of foreign policy challenges in the late 1970s and early 1980s, but also by a determined and increasing domestic opposition. This confluence of factors resulted in the testing and finally collapse of détente.

Limited Success for the Strategic Triangle

In the approach to détente, France, Germany, and the United States held divergent assumptions about the impact of a shift in the relationship with the Soviet Union. Different perceptions of the desired results of a détente policy led to divergent expectations. As the previous chapter argued, the United States perceived détente as a means to lower tensions with the Soviet Union and thereby enhance stability in a number of conflict areas, particularly in Europe, but also in Southeast Asia, the Middle East, and elsewhere. Such reduced tensions were expected to slow the escalating nuclear arms race and permit negotiations to cap or even reduce the threatening numbers of nuclear weapons. Though there was general public support initially, the public did not expect a direct advantage, as did many Europeans, especially the Germans. Because the Iranian hostage crisis left the public feeling uncomfortably vulnerable and a general disillusionment with President Carter set in, the domestic challenge from the right by Ronald Reagan became increasingly attractive. Why, many voters questioned, should we reach out to the Soviet Union given its ideology and history of repression? What basis was there to trust the Soviets to fulfill agreements or treaties? What assurances were there that the Soviet Union really would alter is behavior? When the Soviets marched into Afghanistan in December 1979, support for détente plummeted in the United States. Reagan rode the shift in public mood easily into office. The mobilization of Soviet troops in the Baltic region shortly after Reagan's assumption of office reinforced the skepticism over Soviet intentions, and the era of the "evil empire" began.

For Germany, détente represented a fundamental and strategic shift in policy. The underlying assumption for German policy embodied in its Basic Law was the eventual unification of the two German states, East and West. A 1950s decision that this goal might be achieved through tying its security, economy, and essentially identity to the West—particularly the United States—had been manifested in the Hallstein Doctrine, an explicit policy against relations with the communist East. This policy proved only minimally successful and certainly not a solution to the objective of unification. Détente offered another avenue to unification, and Germany eagerly followed the U.S. lead in concluding agreements with the East to lay out the outlines of the new relationship.

While Europe as well as the United States had the goal of stability on the continent by ensuring that any future change would not occur through conflict but through peaceful means, the German objective of unification manifested itself in additional benefits of détente not shared by the Americans. For Germany, détente and the agreements that came to be associated with policy such as the Helsinki Agreement of 1975 and agreements with East Germany offered German families sometimes the first personal contact with the Eastern half of their families. It lightened the burdens on the "West" Berliners and greatly assisted travel and trade with the East. It was not unification, but the road to that end appeared more discernible and, more important, even now possible. An additional element convincing for both German policymakers and publics was the tremendous economic miracle of the 1950s and 1960s, which had brought prosperity and a greatly improved standard of living to the West. Once the East experienced this prosperity and became itself more open, unification would surely follow in time.

For all these reasons, the Germans initially embarked hesitantly on the new détente policy, but they embraced it wholeheartedly as the benefits and potential became clear. When the Americans began to question the policy of détente and abandoned it with the Soviet march into Afghanistan, the Germans kept open the door to the relationship with the East, to a large extent informally and largely through the person-to-person programs. This split in the official policy of taking a hard line against the Soviets, for instance in the response to the Soviet introduction of SS-20s aimed at the West, and the reluctance of at least a portion of the public to respond was evidence of the high hopes détente had engendered on a very human level in the German population. Though the Germans accepted the Atlantic alliance's decision to introduce a counter to the Soviet SS-20s if negotiations failed to remove them, the Germans never severed the relationship to the East in the 1980s, even under the Christian Democratic government, to the extent the United States did.

For the French, détente posed still other issues, some of which were shared with the United States and some with Germany, while others were uniquely French. The change to a policy of détente in the 1970s permitted France to forge a relationship with Moscow within the parameters of the broader evolving East-West relationship. On European issues, France pursued a dialogue with the Russians that gave it a more prominent status within Europe. This role matched more closely French global aspirations, which had diminished with the end of the colonial era. The prospect of again exercising influence in the international community by virtue of a new role as interlocutor with the Russians was attractive. Furthermore, it fulfilled the long-term vision of the French of a broader secure Europe beyond the western World War II borders.

The French-Russian relationship was also insurance against an overly eager German role. Though officially favoring German unification in the long term, France has always only thinly veiled its nervousness with respect to unification, which would thrust Germany into a dominant position in population as well as territory in the middle of Europe. The Soviet Union shared the French nervousness with respect to Germany and certainly saw the French as a natural balance to any wayward German behavior. In addition, the French viewed détente policy as an opportunity to not only counter the Germans but also counterbalance the U.S. dominance in Europe.

The strategic triangle worked smoothly when the United States pursued détente. Germany and France each also saw advantages in détente, and the trio could cooperate even if for somewhat divergent reasons. But when the United States moved away from détente because of aggressive Soviet behavior outside Europe, Bonn and Paris were disappointed by Washington's new hard-line policies and tried to salvage as much of détente as they could.

Notes

1. Henry Kissinger, *Diplomacy* (New York: Simon & Schuster, 1994), 737.
2. Ibid.
3. Ibid.
4. Ibid., 747; from a speech titled "America's Permanent Interests," before the Boston World Affairs Council, March 1, 1976.
5. Richard Nixon, *In the Arena: A Memoir of Victory, Defeat, and Renewal* (New York: Simon & Schuster, 1990), 325.
6. The Soviet Union clearly entered into détente with a set of very different objectives beyond the scope of this chapter, which did not include heightened expectations from its own public or the willingness to abandon its goal of spreading the communist ideology. For an interesting compilation of Soviet views, see Georgi A. Arbatov and Willem Oltmans, *The Soviet Viewpoint* (New York: Dodd, Mead, 1983).
7. Kissinger, *Diplomacy,* 745. He goes on to comment that "Nixon's nightmare was geopolitical vulnerability to creeping Soviet expansionism (while) conservatives' fear was moral disarmament or an apocalyptic nuclear showdown . . . by Soviet technological breakthrough (and) liberals' concern was American overemphasis on military security." This latter became a focus on human rights in the Carter administration (author's note).
8. Jimmy Carter, *Keeping Faith: Memoirs of a President* (Toronto: Bantam Books, 1982), 256.
9. Carter, *Keeping Faith,* 254.
10. Lynn E. Davis, who later (1993–98) became the undersecretary of state for international security policy, argued late in 1975 that both the United States and Europeans feel that the enemy needs to feel that it will receive unacceptable damage if he attacks, but "Americans emphasize the need to design rational strategies for the use of particular weapons systems in the event that deterrence fails. . . . In contrast, Europeans emphasize the uncertainty which must exist in the mind of the enemy about how particular weapons will be used . . . focus on what they call the 'political' dimension underlying deterrence." In part, this difference played a role as well in the debate over what was necessary to address the 'new' circumstances after SALT I/II. Lynn Etheridge Davis, *Limited Nuclear Options: Deterrence and the New American Doctrine,* Adelphi Paper 121 (London: International Institute for Strategic Studies, 1975), 13.
11. Fred M. Kaplan, "Enhanced-Radiation Weapons," in *Progress in Arms Control?*

Readings in Scientific American, ed. Bruce M. Russett and Bruce G. Blair (New York: W. H. Freeman, 1979), 159.

12. Kent F. Wisner, "Military Aspects of Enhanced Radiation Weapons," *Survival* (November–December 1981): 246–51; the citation here is on 247.

13. Kaplan, "Enhanced-Radiation Weapons," 159. Both Wisner, "Military Aspects," and the Kaplan article discuss the details of the effects and planned deployments of the enhanced radiation weapons (ERW) as a Lance modernization. See the Wisner piece for a chart of the radiation to personnel protected by armor and the blast to urban structures. While the ERW Lance (1–5 kilotons, or KT) would have the "same radii of prompt radiation effects against armored forces as a fission weapon of tenfold greater yield (a fission warhead of 1–50 KT)," military planners argued that the "major difference between the two Lance warheads, therefore, is that the ERW would offer significantly less collateral damage for the same military effectiveness." Wisner, "Military Aspects," 249.

14. See brief discussion in Jonathan Carr, *Helmut Schmidt* (Munich: Knauer, 1987), 158.

15. Carter, *Keeping Faith,* 227.

16. Ibid., 229.

17. Ibid., 228–29.

18. Ibid., 228.

19. Chancellor Schmidt had expressed his concerns in March 1977 in Washington privately, but he clearly decided that this was insufficient. (Note: this was the trip on which he was given assurances about the U.S. intention to deploy a neutron bomb, and then the United States changed its mind). For Schmidt's International Institute for Strategic Studies remarks, see "1977 Alastair Buchan Memorial Lecture," *Survival* (January–February 1978): 2–10.

20. This problem of finding qualified recruits, i.e., with a high school diploma, plagued the military until later in the 1980s and required an intensive focus.

21. In contrast to the SS-4s and SS-5s, the SS-20 was a qualitative improvement in three basic respects: (1) Its greater range based forward could reach as far as Northern Africa; (2) it carried three rather than one warhead; and (3) its circular error probable was a considerable improvement in accuracy.

22. See NATO, "Special Meeting of Foreign and Defense Ministers, December 12, 1979," *NATO Final Communiqués 1975–80* (Brussels: NATO Information Service, 1980), vol. 2, 121–23.

23. This was by no means a universally shared assessment of the dual-track decision, particularly when the negotiations became stalemated. See, e.g., William G. Hyland, "Soviet Theater Forces and Arms Control Policy, *Survival* (September–October 1981): 194–99. Hyland is critical of the Eastern demand that NATO do away with its programs and in return the USSR would freeze its deployments; as well as the Western insistence on a link between deployments and negotiations. He suggested either beginning with a discussion of broad principles or offering a specific "take it or leave it" proposal (198). In the end, a 1987 agreement was able to achieve a total withdrawal.

24. A good discussion of the arms control efforts during this period may be found in Theodore H. Winkler, *Arms Control and the Politics of European Security,* Adelphi Paper 177 (London: International Institute for Strategic Studies, 1982).

25. The December 12, 1979, communiqué of the Special Meeting of Foreign and Defense Ministers, Brussels, paragraph 8, states: "Ministers attach great importance to the role of arms control in contributing to a more stable military relationship between

East and West and in advancing the process of détente. This is reflected in a broad set of initiatives being examined within the alliance to further the course of arms control and détente in the 1980s" (p. 122). This sentiment is reinforced a day later in the December 13–14 communiqué of the North Atlantic Council, Brussels, in paragraph 3, which includes "Reviewing developments in East-West relations since they last met, Ministers . . . recalled their commitment to détente and stressed the defensive nature of the alliance" (p. 124). NATO, *NATO Final Communiqués 1975–1980.*

26. The introduction of the SS-20 to replace the SS-4s and SS-5s was reported to have begun as early as 1976.

27. As a result of his astronaut experience and training, Senator John Glenn was highly regarded on both sides of the aisle for his technical expertise and honesty. He had acquired a reputation in the Senate for his thoughtful deliberations on such matters and many of the senators deferred to him on technical issues.

28. It is less clear that the Afghan invasion had as significant implications for the Europeans.

29. See, e.g., Ground Zero, *Nuclear War: What's In It for You?* (New York: Pocket Books, 1982); Helen Caldicott, *Missile Envy: the Arms Race and Nuclear War* (New York: Bantam Books, 1984); or *Hawks, Doves and Owls,* ed. Graham T. Allison, Albert Carnesale, and Joseph S. Nye, Jr. (New York: W. W. Norton, 1985), which attempts to portray the wide chasms in the thinking on this topic at the time. For a thorough analysis of the topic, see Paul Lettow, *Ronald Reagan and His Quest to Abolish Nuclear Weapons* (New York: Random House, 2005).

30. Kissinger, *Diplomacy,* 767, from Reagan's first presidential press conference January 29, 1981.

31. For an in-depth study of the economic and other implications of the Yamal pipeline, see Thomas Blau and Joseph Kirchheimer, "European Dependence and Soviet Leverage: The Yamal Pipeline," *Survival* (September–October 1981): 209–14.

32. The pipeline was scheduled to bring 40 billion cubic meters (BCM) to Germany, 12 BCM to France, and the rest (8 BCM) to Italy, Sweden, Belgium, the Netherlands, Austria, and Spain; Blau and Kirchheimer, "European Dependence," 209.

33. Blau and Kirchheimer, "European Dependence," 214. He also cites "USSR Offers Italy Energy It Lacks," *L'Unita* (Milan), June 24, 1980, 2.

34. Many critics maintained that the Europeans had ample alternatives to the Yamal Pipeline; see Blau and Kirchheimer, "European Dependence," for a discussion of some of them.

35. The skepticism of the United States about CSCE is clear in the memoirs of former president Ford when he comments on the Soviet idea for a thirty-five-nation conference on security: "Initially the United States had been cool to the idea because we didn't see any advantages to be gained." He goes on to mention the concessions then offered by the Soviets, including conventional force reduction and an East-West agreement on Berlin. He underscores the "victory for our foreign policy" that national borders could only be changed by peaceful means. But the impact the agreement would have in the 1980s on the governments of Central Europe and eventually the Soviet Union through democratic revolutions was beyond any expectations at the time of the Helsinki 1975 summit signing. Gerald R. Ford, *A Time to Heal: The Autobiography of Gerald R. Ford* (New York: Harper & Row, 1979), 298–99.

36. Carter, *Keeping Faith,* 260.

37. The limits set by Helsinki and adjusted downward thereafter were at that time

for two levels of performance—one, it was mandatory for members to notify other signatories of all maneuvers over 25,000 within twenty-one days or more of the movement whereas, two, it was deemed permissive, i.e., voluntary, for other smaller maneuvers or additional information to be conveyed. It is interesting that the Soviet Union had never offered additional information, but that it had adhered to the required notification provisions since the Helsinki Act had entered into force. See John D. Toogood, "Military Aspects of the Belgrade Review Meeting," *Survival* (July/August 1978): 155–58.

38. Joerg Kastl, "The CSCE Review Meeting in Madrid," *NATO Review* 31, no.5 (1983): 13.

39. Kastl, "CSCE Review," 15.

40. The use of such labels has not been limited to the Republicans—Democrat John F. Kennedy used similar warnings in 1960 of a "missile gap" to win the presidential election. In both instances—1960 and 1980—whether the United States faced a real threat (gap or vulnerability) has been challenged later.

41. This probably reflects a uniquely American element in its character—witness the widely related (and probably only folklore) tale of George Washington admitting to chopping down the cherry tree—as long as he told the truth, all was forgiven. In contrast, many during the Clinton impeachment maintained that his indiscretions may have been forgiven, if he had not lied to the American public!

42. Related by a staff member of the U.S. delegation, 1982.

43. Kastl, "CSCE Review," 19.

44. Czech president Václav Havel often comments on the importance of 'Helsinki' to Charter 77, the underground group which monitored Czech compliance (or lack of compliance) as well as many other underground groups throughout the Warsaw Pact states. See speech given in New York City at the annual awards dinner by the East-West Institute, 1997.

45. Neil Macfarlane discusses Afghanistan and Angola, as well as Chad, Ethiopia, and Somalia, and the Horn of Africa in *Intervention and Regional Security,* Adelphi Paper 196 (London: International Institute for Strategic Studies, 1985).

46. Gregory Flynn, "Public Opinion and Atlantic Defense," *NATO Review* 31, no. 5 (1983): 11.

Chapter 12

From Euromissiles to Maastricht: The Policies of Reagan-Bush and Mitterrand

Samuel F. Wells Jr.

The 1980s saw significant changes in both Europe and the United States. A notable Franco-German rapprochement led by François Mitterrand and Helmut Kohl stimulated European politics and laid the foundation for a major advance in European integration through the creation of the single market. In Washington, Ronald Reagan brought about new departures in economic policy as well as a more assertive foreign policy. In European-American relations, the major issue was the deployment of new intermediate-range missiles to counter the Soviet introduction of SS-20 missiles and, ultimately, the revival of arms control and détente with Moscow.

For leaders in France and Germany, the strategic triangle formed by their nations and the United States was an important factor in shaping international policy. Neither Bonn nor Paris wanted to be isolated from both its main European partner and Washington at the same time. If Germany, for example, was to be at odds with Washington over critical issues in policy toward the Soviet Union, officials in Bonn would work especially hard to coordinate policy with Paris.

In Washington, the officials of the Reagan administration sought cooperation with France and Germany, but the fundamental structure of U.S. policy for Europe involved a rectangular relationship that gave a significant role to Britain. This was especially true because Margaret Thatcher, the British prime minister, was President Reagan's closest friend among foreign leaders. As a superpower and the acknowledged head of the Western alliance, the United States had its most important relations in a different strategic triangle with the Soviet Union and China. These additional elements meant that the French-German-U.S. triangle was less determining in Washington's decisionmaking than it was in Bonn and Paris.

In this international system, Reagan posed a major problem for European leaders. His main objectives were to create a vigorous government in Washington and reassert U.S. leadership in the world, but his top priorities were in domestic affairs. He wanted to reduce the size of government, cut federal regulations, and unleash the American economy to achieve a new level of growth and prosperity. A devoted anticommunist, Reagan sought to rebuild U.S. military power and use it to resist the Soviet Union in all its adventures around the world. He brought to Washington a political program built on a few broad principles, and his operating style established in eight years as governor of California was to leave the design and implementation of policy to trusted aides.[1]

Responding to the Soviet Threat

The Reagan administration's foreign policy officials identified their principal mission as reacting vigorously to a range of challenges initiated by Moscow. They believed that Soviet leaders were exploiting the United States' weakness and lack of political will in the aftermath of Vietnam, the oil shocks, and the Iranian hostage crisis. On the basis of a massive expansion of conventional and nuclear arms, the Soviet Union had increased the stakes in the Cold War with its invasion of Afghanistan in December 1979. It threatened Western interests and international stability with its military support of terrorism and hostile regimes in the Middle East and the Horn of Africa. With the backing of Fidel Castro's Cuba, Moscow gave vital support to the Socialist government of Nicaragua in its effort to overthrow elected governments in El Salvador and Honduras. In Europe, the Soviets were threatening the security balance by their deployment of intermediate-range SS-20 missiles and the support of antinuclear movements among America's European allies.[2]

To demonstrate that it had adopted a significantly different policy, the new administration launched a broad defense buildup and a new counteroffensive strategy. In his second month in office, Defense Secretary Caspar Weinberger submitted formal revisions to the budgets before Congress, requesting an additional $7 billion for fiscal year (FY) 1981 and $26 billion for FY 1982. Taken together, these revisions in the budgets proposed by President Jimmy Carter projected a 10.1 percent real annual growth in obligational authority for FYs 1981–86, bringing defense spending to an average of 7 percent of gross national product. This new funding would expand procurement on the most advanced conventional and nuclear weapons, increase high-technology research and development, and move toward the goal of the 600-ship navy. In his annual report for 1982, Weinberger described his new strategy by saying the United States, if attacked, would respond with force "at places where we can affect the outcome of the war," striking at both political and military targets of sufficient importance to "offset" the original attack. This policy of horizontal escalation would require more military forces, especially for the navy.[3]

In its first two years, defense policy drove the Reagan administration's international agenda more than diplomacy. The administration provided aid to the government of El Salvador and covert support to the opponents of the Sandinista regime in Nicaragua. Massive assistance also went to the mujahedeen in Afghanistan. Washington gave strong military and diplomatic support to Israel and launched an active campaign against terrorism around the world. Led by Defense Department officials, the administration placed additional limits on the transfer of military or dual-use technology and tried to restrict trade and credit for the Soviet bloc. U.S. officials encouraged the NATO allies to implement the deployment of U.S. intermediate-range nuclear force (INF) missiles in response to the Soviet SS-20s. Initially the administration moved slowly on arms control in the hope that the U.S. military buildup would show Moscow that it would have to make a clear choice between negotiating arms reductions or facing an arms race with the United States.[4]

Sizing Up the Allies

Focused on passing a major tax cut bill and expanding defense programs, the Reagan administration took few significant international actions but did assess its main European partners. The president had a prior relationship with Margaret Thatcher from the time when both were out of leadership positions, and more important they shared a conservative philosophy of minimal government and a strong foreign policy based on national interests in a European environment dominated by Socialist governments with a firm commitment to détente. Thatcher would be Reagan's first state visitor in February 1981, and she was received in Washington with great respect and high ceremony.

Administration officials were skeptical about Helmut Schmidt in Germany, because his party seemed to have deserted him on INF deployment and his government appeared threatened in the forthcoming elections. In France, the new Socialist government of François Mitterrand was viewed with even more unease due to its left-wing economic program and the inclusion of four Communist ministers. As the months passed, U.S. officials came to take a much more positive view of Mitterrand when they understood how much he agreed with U.S. policy toward the Soviet Union and on the need to fight European neutralism by deploying the INF missiles.[5]

Allied leaders showed concern and dismay at U.S. officials' early statements on the use of nuclear weapons and the need to defer strategic arms control negotiations. It was bad enough to have senior officials who had campaigned against the second Strategic Arms Limitation Talks treaty and European pacifism, but now these same individuals were discussing nuclear demonstration shots in congressional testimony and the president himself talked about a limited nuclear exchange in Europe with a group of newspaper editors. Such remarks helped fuel the antinuclear demonstrations in October and November 1981 in Bonn, London, and Florence. Officials in each country where these demonstrations took place expressed their distress to Washington and asked for help in winning public support for the INF missiles scheduled for deployment on their territory.

In deciding how to go to the negotiating table on INF, officials in the Reagan administration underwent the first of what would be a long series of battles on arms control and security issues between the Pentagon and the Department of State. Leading the fight for each side was Richard Perle for the Pentagon and Richard Burt for State. They ultimately came to seize on a version of zero deployments in exchange for zero missiles left deployed by the Soviets as their solution, but there were many variations between their approaches. Ultimately, President Reagan chose the Pentagon's version because of its clear simplicity and the ease with which it could be explained. This was to be zero pure and simple, which Richard Perle, as all of those around him knew, hoped would prove unnegotiable.[6] Working hard on the speech himself, President Reagan made a dramatic proposal for the elimination of all INF missiles in Europe with his "zero-option" proposal at the National Press Club on November 18, 1981. Many in Europe breathed easier when INF negotiations between U.S. and Soviet delegations opened in Geneva on November 30. These talks would drag on for more than six years before the decisive intervention of the new Soviet leader Mikhail Gorbachev would lead to the signing of an INF treaty in December 1987.[7]

The Polish government's imposition of martial law in December 1981 gave Reagan administration hard-liners an opportunity to send a strong message to the allies about economic relations with the Soviet adversary. Arguing that the Soviet Union had forced the Polish government to suppress Solidarity with martial law, which we now know was wrong, the Reagan administration announced on December 29 a series of sanctions that were primarily aimed at restricting U.S. exports to build a natural gas pipeline from Siberia to Germany. The purpose of the sanctions was twofold: to delay the construction of the pipeline, and, more important, to instruct the Western Europeans on how dangerous it was to become dependent on Soviet energy supplies.

The European governments and press were shocked at the U.S. sanctions and argued against them, using the logic of détente and the need to create mutual interests in trade and arms control. The pipeline debate became part of the agenda at the June 1982 Versailles economic summit, where a heated debate between Reagan and Mitterrand produced an ambiguous deal whereby the United States would not push sanctions any further while the Europeans would restrict credits to the Soviet Union. At a NATO summit in Bonn a few days later, this deal was neither clarified nor recorded, so that after the meeting Reagan and Mitterrand each gave a different version of what had been agreed to. In a recent interview, Burt (at the time director of the Bureau of Politico-Military Affairs at the Department of State) said that the gas pipeline decision "was a total fiasco."[8]

On his return from Europe, Reagan received strong criticism from conservatives for not winning the support of the allies for pipeline sanctions. The president's top White House staff decided to take a strong stand on the pipeline issue as a way of striking back at Secretary of State Alexander Haig, whom they blamed for not getting a better result in Europe. Judge William P. Clark, the national security adviser, called a meeting of the National Security Council (NSC) for June 18, when Haig had to be at the United Nations in New York. At this session, the staff pushed through a set of expanded sanctions to include subsidiaries of U.S. firms operating abroad and European firms using technology under American licenses. This claim of "extraterritorial sanctions" brought a howl of protests from European capitals, including a strong lecture from Thatcher, who was in Washington for a visit shortly after the decision.

The NSC action did produce the resignation of Alexander Haig, who was replaced by George Shultz. And, as Burt says, "We had a full-blown crisis within the alliance where even Reagan's natural allies like Margaret Thatcher were very distressed, very unhappy." Shultz suddenly found himself inheriting this mess, and "he handled it in a great way. He got a dialogue started and listened to people and finally reached agreement with the French in which we were at least able, in lifting our sanctions, to get people to focus on the problem and began a dialogue on what the security consequences were of this kind of trade with the Soviets. But it was a difficult, prolonged process." As an official in the Elysée Palace put it, in order to maintain a generally cordial relationship with Washington, "a lot of water was put in the wine." But the memory remained of how little the Reagan administration seemed to know or care about European views on alliance unity or the value of détente as part of a balanced approach to the Soviet Union. The evolution of the gas pipeline crisis reflects two basic trends within the administration: that policy choices could be shaped by battles among the president's senior staff and that policy for Europe was essentially a derivative of strategy toward the Soviets.[9]

Some new information has recently come out concerning Central Intelligence Agency (CIA) estimates of Soviet strength and Soviet behavior and how these were used during the Reagan administration. These were published in a volume by the CIA under the title *CIA's Analysis of the Soviet Union, 1947–1991,* edited by Gerald K. Haines and Robert E. Leggett. A conference at Princeton University in March 2001 discussed the validity and the use made of these assessments. One example, on the natural gas pipeline discussed above, was made in August 1982 and evaluated the prospects for the Siberia–to–Western Europe pipeline. After reviewing the elements of technology involved and the likelihood that the Soviets would be able to get from other sources many of the things which the sanctions would deny them, the analysis concluded that the new export pipeline could probably begin functioning in late 1985 and reach nearly full volume in 1987, a delay of roughly one year as a result of the sanctions. On the negative side, it pointed out that the Western Europeans needed the relatively low-priced Soviet gas and viewed the pipeline as creating employment for their citizens and creating a form of economic interdependence that would "lead to more responsible Soviet behavior." The analysis pointed out that the Western Europeans are "deeply angry about the U.S. decision, especially the extraterritorial and retroactive features of the measures, which they regard as a serious infringement of their sovereignty."

This estimate was quite accurate and essentially confirmed information that was available from unclassified economic analysis, but in many other ways the conference pointed out that during the Reagan and George H. W. Bush years, the CIA was a key part of the process of overemphasizing most dimensions of the Soviet threat. At the conference, Raymond Garthoff, a long-time CIA military analyst, admitted that "there were consistent overestimates of the threat every year from 1978 to 1985." Douglas MacEachin, a thirty-two-year CIA veteran and former deputy director, "identified the biggest single trap for intelligence estimates was Soviet intentions." He went on to say that the agency completely missed the extent to which the Soviet military industrial complex drove its own institutional growth and was motivated in part by their perceptions of American military strength. He said that the CIA overestimated the accuracy of Soviet missiles and the quality of their equipment.

Other analysts pointed out that the CIA's economic estimates had significantly exaggerated the Soviet Union's economic well-being and had been very slow to catch on to the fact that the Soviet Union had been encountering serious economic problems starting in the early 1970s. A former chairman of the National Intelligence Council, Fritz Ermarth, said that the agency's first paper indicating that the heavy level of military production was creating domestic stress on the system was produced only in the fall of 1985, a date that was "embarrassingly late."[10]

In the pipeline crisis and with other issues, the Reagan administration paid no attention to the operation of a Bonn-Paris-Washington triangle. U.S. officials took little notice of signs of German dissatisfaction with administration policies or of a series of French initiatives to strengthen security cooperation with Germany. Disturbed by the rise of neutralism in Germany and the weak response to the imposition of martial law in Poland, the French government had given strong support for the deployment of INF missiles in Germany, culminating in Mitterrand's dramatic speech before the Bundestag on January 20, 1983. France proposed a new security dialogue, which was endorsed by Helmut Schmidt in February 1982 and reaffirmed by Helmut Kohl when he came to Paris on his first day as chancellor, October 4, 1982. The French government also revived the Western European Union (WEU) as an instrument of enhanced security cooperation with a group of allies that included Germany. And France created a new rapid intervention force, the Force d'Action Rapide, to signal its commitment on the Central Front in times of crisis. None of these steps received much attention in the upper levels of the Reagan administration. In fact, at a Woodrow Wilson International Center for Scholars meeting in October 1984, a senior Defense Department official was openly dismissive of the military capabilities and significance of the Force d'Action Rapide.[11]

For most of 1983, U.S. and allied diplomacy focused on deploying INF missiles and strengthening conventional defenses. Washington's actions concentrated on providing support for nations pledged to deploy the INF missiles, especially West Germany. In a critical vote after a two-day debate, the Bundestag voted to deploy the assigned cruise and Pershing II missiles on November 22, 1983. The Soviet Union walked out of the INF negotiations in Geneva in protest the next day. By the end of December, German defense officials announced that the first group of Pershing II INF missiles were operational at their German bases.[12]

As INF missiles were deployed, Washington officials pressed for strengthened conventional defenses, including a new operational doctrine of Deep Strike into enemy territory and increased European contribution to defense costs. Coming at a time of stagnant European economies, the demand for increased burden sharing was not received. To make matters worse, many in Europe questioned the need for improved conventional defenses. One widely read analyst, Josef Joffe, opposed high-technology conventional defense and preferred to rely on the strategy of Flexible Response. He argued that "the system has worked too well to be lightly abandoned in favor of reform-minded conventionalism. Nuclear deterrence in Europe has a track record, conventional defense has not, and four decades of ultrastability are an impressive argument for the status quo."[13]

A respected German policy analyst, Walter Schütze, seriously questioned whether Germany could continue to function as the centerpiece of the alliance. The battle over the deployment of INF missiles, he believed, had broken the consensus on security policy and defense that had lasted for more than twenty years. Contending that pressure on the Europeans to spend more such as the Nunn amendment of 1984 might well be counterproductive, he concluded that "by and large Germans are convinced that they do their fair share within the overall Western defense effort. . . . And that, after all, better security cannot be bought by more armaments but by arms-control agreements with the other side. As Chancellor Kohl said in a recent Bundestag debate: 'We want peace with less weapons!'"[14]

The Wild Card: The Strategic Defense Initiative

As Reagan's ideas about nuclear weapons became known, civilian and military specialists who had endorsed the strategy of nuclear deterrence felt under attack. On March 23, 1983, the president addressed the American people on national security and defense issues. After a lengthy review of the Soviet military buildup of the past twenty years and what his administration was doing to redress the inadequacies of U.S. defenses, Reagan offered to share "a vision of the future which offers hope." He raised the possibility of defending against missile attack and called on the American scientific community "to give us the means of rendering these nuclear weapons impotent and obsolete." He announced a comprehensive program of research and development to build defenses against missiles that would eventually allow their elimination through arms control. And he concluded with the pledge: "We seek neither military superiority nor political advantage. Our only purpose—one all people share—is to search for ways to reduce the danger of nuclear war."[15]

Only a few defense experts took the president's call for missile defense seriously, but this was a mistake. The need to eliminate the threat of nuclear weapons was one of Reagan's most strongly held beliefs. Combined with his unlimited faith in American technological ingenuity, this belief created the dream of a world freed from the terror of nuclear weapons. Many officials in the administration, such as Deputy National Security Adviser Robert McFarlane, advanced the idea of missile defense, hoping to trade it in negotiations with the Soviets for large cuts in numbers of weapons. But McFarlane and other supporters for tactical reasons would be disappointed. Reagan would not give up his dream of a nuclear free world. As the arms control expert Strobe Talbott told the Reagan biographer Lou Cannon, Reagan "was a romantic, a radical, a nuclear abolitionist." The president's chief Strategic Arms Reduction Treaty (START) negotiator, Lieutenant General Edward L. Rowny, declared privately in 1985: "People are in for a surprise. Reagan really wants to abolish nuclear weapons, and he is confident the people will support him against the arms control establishment."[16]

Reagan's Strategic Defense Initiative (SDI) speech came as a total surprise to Richard Burt, who was completely absorbed in the INF negotiations. Burt recalled: "My initial reaction was of a kind of unpleasant distraction because it appeared with so little consultation and so little preparation that it did disturb the alliance." He pointed out that the Germans were upset with the potential decoupling of the alliance and by the reduction of any sense of risk sharing that would be involved. But he went on to emphasize that "the people who reacted first and foremost and the strongest were the British. Mrs. Thatcher was upset and she probably did more than anyone to put a fence around SDI." This was really brought to completion when she got President Reagan to sign onto her list of agreed points during a meeting at Camp David.[17]

Allied reaction was mild and limited to complaints that the U.S. president's speech had undermined alliance strategic doctrine and public confidence in deterrence. Meanwhile, the Pentagon reorganized the missile defense efforts of the various services into the SDI and by the end of 1990 would have spent $17 billion on the program. Defense Secretary Caspar Weinberger propelled European political leaders into action when he wrote them on March 26, 1985, asking for their participation in SDI research and giving sixty days for a reply. In explaining the delayed reaction to SDI, a senior French diplomat declared, "we felt it was just another Reagan Sunday speech like those about the evil empire or school prayer. But when we realized that American generals were touring Europe with their checkbooks open ready to sign up our best technology firms, we knew we had to respond in a substantive way."

The European governments gave a mixed reaction to the proposed research cooperation on SDI. France, Germany, and Britain firmly let it be known that they had reservations about strategic innovations that undercut nuclear deterrence, but they all wanted to benefit from the new high-technology research. The French government insisted that it would not endorse research participation, but it quietly allowed French companies to sign contracts for SDI-sponsored research.[18]

Responding to initiatives from Paris, the allies generated several responses to SDI. In April 1985, the Mitterrand government announced the creation of Eurêka as a cooperative program of civilian technology research and development ranging from microelectronics and computers to advanced industrial turbines. This program would involve eighteen European nations in cooperative projects and would generate significant partnerships among firms in France, Germany, the Netherlands, and the United Kingdom. Meeting in June 1985, the European Council endorsed proposals to revive activity in the Western European Union. Franco-German defense cooperation also picked up, with joint maneuvers involving 150,000 troops in 1986 and, on the suggestion of Chancellor Kohl, the creation of a Franco-German brigade the following year.[19]

Franco-German defense cooperation won Washington's polite approval, provided it did not divert resources from NATO. Assistant Secretary of State Burt conveyed the message about protecting the uniqueness of NATO in unusually direct fashion in February 1985. The State Department let it be known that it saw no particular need to revitalize the WEU and it felt that cooperation in armaments could be done through the Eurogroup. Basically, the U.S. government wanted the Europeans to improve their conventional defenses, pay more of the costs of NATO, and follow policies made in Washington for high-technology research, the completion of the INF deployments, and the reduction of battlefield nuclear weapons as had been agreed. Privately, defense officials in the United States discounted Eurêka and the Franco-German brigade as largely exercises in symbolism.[20]

The Search for Arms Control

After 1985, senior officials of the Reagan administration devoted a large part of their time to conventional and strategic arms control negotiations, and these issues remained vital to the George H. W. Bush administration up until the start of the Persian Gulf War in January 1991. This unanticipated result stemmed from the conjunction of three very different sets of events. Ronald Reagan shifted his policy toward Moscow with a speech on January 16, 1984, in which he began to focus on the threat of war. "Reducing the risk of war—and especially nuclear war—is priority number one," he asserted. From this point on, the president was more conciliatory toward the Soviet Union and consistently pressed for arms reduction. Equally important was the fact that Mikhail Gorbachev came to power in Moscow in March 1985 and wanted to reduce the costs of military and foreign commitments in order to advance economic and political reform within the Soviet Union. At roughly the same time, in the summer of 1985, the Reagan administration launched a secret program of arms sales to Iran; and from the autumn of 1986, it would be mired in the public disclosures of the Iran-Contra scandal until Congress issued a report from its joint hearings in November 1987.[21]

The new Soviet leader took the initiative to resume negotiations on INF and strategic arms control in March 1985, and European leaders were pleased when these talks led to the first summit meeting between Reagan and Gorbachev the following November. This Geneva summit failed to produce a breakthrough, but it did open a positive relationship between the leaders of the two superpowers. When progress in the continuing negotiations stalled, Gorbachev proposed an informal summit at Reykjavik to search for solutions. On October 13, 1986, reports from the Reagan-Gorbachev meeting at Reykjavik indicated that the two leaders had agreed on the elimination of all strategic nuclear weapons within ten years but that this unprecedented deal had been broken when Reagan refused to accept the Soviet demand for a ban on the SDI component of testing and possibly basing weapons in space.

Allied leaders in Europe were aghast that such a proposal would be discussed without any senior U.S. military officers present and without any consultation with NATO. They were not reassured that the Reykjavik summit deal had been blocked by the president's insistence on protecting SDI. Less than a month later, on November 4, the news broke that the United States had been selling arms to Iran in violation of its own loudly proclaimed arms embargo and using the profits to fund operations of the contras in Nicaragua, whose U.S. support had been terminated by the Congress.[22]

During the next few months, as the White House staff prepared for multiple investigations of the Iran-Contra affair, those officials at the Defense and State departments who had been marginalized in the Reykjavik negotiations resumed work with Soviet negotiators to try to generate a positive agreement. At the end of February 1987, Gorbachev broke a deadlock by agreeing to consider INF weapons separately from a package linking strategic forces and space weapons in a single proposal. Negotiators focused on INF issues for the rest of the year and signed a treaty on INF weapons on December 8, 1987, eliminating both long- and short-range INF missiles from Europe. The Europeans were pleased to reduce Soviet nuclear weapons on their continent but anxious that the Soviets retained a significant advantage in conventional arms. This anxiety was eased when a year later Gorbachev announced the start of large reductions in conventional forces in central Europe. This was followed in the Bush administration by agreement on the Conventional Forces in Europe Treaty in November 1990 and later by significant cuts in strategic weapons with the signing of START I on July 31, 1991.[23]

Among many ironies in the record of the Reagan administration is the fact that the conservatives who shaped their 1980 foreign policy campaign against arms control and détente had as one of their principal achievements the creation of a strong working relationship with a new Soviet leader that produced a major breakthrough on arms control eliminating two classes of nuclear weapons from Europe. The work of the Reagan team also set the stage for a major success in conventional arms reduction and an important step in cutting the numbers of strategic nuclear weapons.

In its negotiations with Gorbachev over security and arms control, the Reagan administration largely ignored its partners in the strategic triangle. U.S. negotiators did eventually persuade the Soviets to exclude British and French nuclear weapons from consideration in the talks, but officials in London and Paris were not included in shaping policy choices or hammering out compromises with Moscow.[24]

Bush and European Security

Starting in 1989, the administration of George H. W. Bush paid significantly more attention to the interests of its European allies. In the sustained negotiations over German reunification and the withdrawal of Soviet forces from Eastern Europe, Bush and his foreign policy team devoted immense time and energy to getting the German solutions right, and to do so they had to overcome fundamental opposition from both Thatcher and Mitterrand. Ultimately, the triangle functioned. Thatcher reluctantly accepted the German-Soviet deal brokered by Washington, and Mitterrand could not stand against a united front of Bonn-Moscow-Washington. On September 12, 1990, in Moscow, ministers of the two German states and the four occupying powers from World War II signed the treaty setting the terms of German reunification.[25]

As part of its effort to reassure Soviet leaders that the Western powers would not take aggressive advantage of German reunification, the Bush administration took the lead in transforming NATO into an alliance focused on a more political mission of partnership with former adversaries with less emphasis on forward defense and nuclear weapons and with a strengthened Conference on Security and Cooperation in Europe (CSCE). The alliance members accepted these steps at a summit meeting in London in July 1990. This softening of the alliance's goals proved useful in persuading Soviet leaders to accept a reunified Germany within NATO, one of the main objectives of Bush's diplomacy.[26]

With Germany reunified, Brent Scowcroft, Bush's national security adviser, expected competition for the leadership of Europe. He saw Mitterrand as "confident that he could lead the Franco-German entente and through it maintain France's predominant influence" in the European Community (EC) as NATO declined and was replaced by the Western European

Union and the CSCE. Bush administration leaders, however, believed Germany would play a large and constructive role in Europe's future and would insist on a continuing presence for the United States through an active, reformed NATO. U.S. policy for European security in the 1990s would be based upon a partnership with Germany that used the North Atlantic alliance as its principal instrument.[27]

In light of the acknowledged inability of French forces to operate with more modern U.S. units in the Gulf War, some officials in the French Ministry of Defense wanted to explore a return to the military structure of NATO to prevent their possible marginalization in European defense affairs. This led to exploratory talks between Admiral Jacques Lanxade, Mitterrand's defense adviser in the Elysée Palace, and Brent Scowcroft of the NSC in the period November 1990 to February 1991. It became clear that France would consider resuming full participation in the alliance only if there were fundamental changes in the command structure that sharply diminished U.S. domination of the alliance. Inside the Bush administration, Secretary of Defense Dick Cheney and the Joint Chiefs of Staff strongly opposed these changes, and, as it turned out, so did President Mitterrand. This attempted rapprochement ended before it was ever fully articulated. It would be revived by President Jacques Chirac in 1995 but would again collapse over the same objections.[28]

Meanwhile, France also pursued an effort to create an autonomous European defense capability by attempting to revive the WEU as a bridge between the EC and NATO and later to expand the Franco-German brigade into a Eurocorps open to other WEU members. The United States responded forcefully to this challenge with, among other statements, a telegram of February 22, 1991, from Acting Secretary of State Reginald Bartholomew to U.S. diplomats in all NATO member capitals insisting that any new European security entity must not undermine the authority of NATO. The German government found itself caught uncomfortably in the middle of this series of heated exchanges between Paris and Washington. As an NSC official, Robert Hutchings, later stated: "All parts of the administration were basically quite hostile toward the Eurocorps and felt it was a French maneuver to draw Germany away from the United States."

A solution was developed early in 1992 to allow "double hatting" of NATO assigned forces, which would be authorized to participate in WEU missions in which NATO did not choose to participate. This approach, named the European Security and Defense Identity (ESDI), was accepted in principle at the North Atlantic Council meeting in Oslo in June 1992 and further refined at the NATO summit of January 1994 and the Berlin meetings of NATO ministers in June 1996. In reflecting on these events of 1990–92, Hutchings concluded: "In the whole U.S. approach to the new Europe, we had no adequate sensitivity for the need to develop a dialogue on the future of European political union and security activities with the French. This was a significant mistake."[29]

Although U.S. officials had dealt quite successfully with the issues involved in the end of the Cold War, the reunification of Germany, and the breakup of the Soviet Union, they had been much less attentive and ultimately less imaginative in dealing with a series of events that transformed the European Community into an integrated economic union with growing dimensions of political coordination.

Inattentive to European Integration

During the Reagan and Bush years, European leaders made large steps on the road to changing the structure and institutions of the western half of their continent. Yet top U.S. officials, viewing the world through strategic lenses, remained largely unaware and certainly unconcerned with the tectonic shifts occurring across the Atlantic. European foreign ministers and heads of government spent more of their time dealing with economic issues, including European Community affairs, than on security; and by the second half of the 1980s, they were beginning to achieve important success.

In the United States, however, senior Reagan and Bush officials dealing with international affairs devoted very little time to economic questions. International economic policy, including European Community affairs, was the mandate of a separate bureaucracy that involved parts of the Commerce and State departments, the Treasury, the Office of the U.S. Trade Representative, a section of the Federal Reserve, and a small economics staff in the Executive Office of the President. Their work involved the European Community primarily over trade disputes and through preparation for the annual economic summits of the Group of Seven. Issues related to the European Community were seldom on the agenda at Cabinet or NSC meetings, and this lack of attention is reflected in the memoirs of George Shultz and James Baker for their years as secretary of state, covering 1983–88 and 1989–92, respectively. In a volume of 1,138 pages, Shultz has four entries on the European Community, whereas Baker in a shorter volume of 672 pages mentions the European Community thirteen times, with four of these entries dealing with the conflict in Yugoslavia.[30]

In reflecting on the relationship between the Reagan administration and the European Community, Richard Burt made two broad points:

> There are two things going on here. One is that to the extent that anybody worries about the EC, there was a strategic decision taken not to recognize it as a place to do business with the Europeans, because it was just easier and more profitable to work more bilaterally through the major capitals. In a sense we felt why recognize and give that institution status when the United States could more easily succeed in what it was trying to achieve by picking off these countries one by one. Because once you started focusing on the EU and the institutions in Brussels you are in a sense almost granting them character and standing.
>
> The second factor is that frankly it is a matter of lack of understanding and a lack of attention, and I think that most senior decision-makers in Washington (Assistant Secretaries and above) don't pay attention and know what is happening in the EU. [While the EU is] still fragmented and still chaotic and messy, . . . [it is an institution we have to take seriously. Unfortunately] we are always a little behind the power curve in understanding what is happening in terms of Europe.[31]

The objectives of U.S. international economic policy in the 1980s were quite similar to those today. U.S. officials sought to expand trade, open markets, and increase General Agreement on Tariffs and Trade coverage through completion of the Uruguay Round of trade negotiations. With less certainty, they also worked to maintain relative currency stability and an improved fair, transparent rule of law for investment and multinational corporations.

During the Reagan administration, officials in Washington voiced support for European economic integration while continuing to protect U.S. trade and investment interests. Given the preoccupation with arms control negotiations and Iran-Contra hearings, there was little top-level attention devoted to the Single European Act (a set of measures that would create a single internal market among member states by 1992) when it was adopted by the European Community in July 1987.

A good statement of U.S. policy toward the single European market came at a Washington seminar titled "Integration of the European Internal Market: Implications for Europe and the United States" in April 1988. After a description of the goals of the Single European Act and an estimate of its benefits to European economic growth, Paolo Cecchini, former deputy director general for internal market and industrial affairs for the Commission of the European Communities, predicted that the new steps would also benefit foreign companies operating within the European Community and companies outside, which would gain advantages from the simplification of trade regulations. Responding to Cecchini's presentation, James M. Murphy, assistant U.S. trade representative for Europe and the Mediterranean, said that the United States supported the current integration efforts and expected to benefit from increased exports, new access to sectors previously closed such as telecommunications and power-generating equipment, and decreased trade tensions. But Murphy expressed concern about the lack of transparency in European Community rule making, whether there would be new EC-wide quantitative import restrictions, and how the slogan "Europe for the Europeans" would affect U.S. multinationals operating within the European Community. Murphy concluded that the United States would continue to support European economic integration but would remain vigilant to protect American trade and business interests.[32]

The Bush administration brought a positive spirit to its relations with Europe and toward the process of European integration in particular. The president expressed this view well in his May 1989 commencement address at Boston University, where both he and François Mitterrand received honorary degrees. Focusing his remarks on the future of Europe, he discussed the strong historic ties of culture, kinship, and values and spoke warmly of "the promise of a united Europe" in the new century. Bush went on to endorse the creation of a single European market by 1992, while acknowledging that some Americans were apprehensive at this prospect. He then declared: "But whatever others may think, this administration is of one mind. We believe a strong, united Europe means a strong America."[33]

Although there would be problems in joining negotiations with the EC on trade issues and continuing anxiety about the single market fostering protectionism, most Bush administration officials were more supportive of European economic integration than their counterparts in the Reagan years had been. Robert Hutchings of the NSC recalls that some top policymakers believed along with the president that European integration would benefit the United States, and "many others thought that, while European integration might not succeed or possibly could even be detrimental to U.S. interests, we needed to support it in order to increase our influence as a valuable partner at this rapidly evolving period of transatlantic relations."[34]

Some officials in the Bush administration voiced suspicion about certain steps toward European political union, such as the creation of a Common Foreign and Security Policy in the Maastricht Treaty of 1992. But, in general, the focus of the Bush senior policymakers was on the larger issues of German reunification, the breakup of the Soviet Union, and the Gulf War. In dealing with all these problems, the Bush team worked hard and effectively to win the support of its European allies.

The Strategic Triangle

During the Reagan-Bush years, U.S. policy focused primarily on security and defense issues, with missile deployments and arms control negotiations with the Soviet Union being the central theme. Some problems developed in relations with France and Germany, but these largely evaporated as successful missile deployment produced negotiations with the Soviets. The strategic triangle worked in holding France and the United States together to push for Euromissile deployment and in the critical periods of German reunification and the breakup of the Soviet Union. Economic issues played a small role in diplomacy within the strategic triangle, and the Bush administration showed a willingness to put aside concerns about European protectionism in the interests of good transatlantic relations at a time of rapid change.

In Europe, the big story was the decision of the Mitterrand government to tie France to Germany through common economic and security policies and to use Franco-German cooperation to advance European integration. The United States paid little attention to Franco-German security cooperation or to the expansion of EC authority and institutions, and in this way the strategic triangle also functioned well for the two European partners. With the signing of the Treaty on European Union in Maastricht in February 1992, the seeds were sown for increased European independence and a consequent reduction in the usefulness and ultimately the effectiveness of the triangle.

Notes

1. I. M. Destler, "The Evolution of Reagan Foreign Policy," in *The Reagan Presidency: An Early Assessment,* ed. Fred I. Greenstein (Baltimore: Johns Hopkins University Press, 1983), 117–58; Helga Haftendorn, "Toward a Reconstruction of American

From Euromissiles to Maastricht   305

Strength: A New Era in the Claim to Global Leadership?" in *The Reagan Administration: A Reconstruction of American Strength?* ed. Helga Haftendorn and Jakob Schissler (Berlin: Walter de Gruyter, 1988), 3–29.

2. Haftendorn, "Toward a Reconstruction of American Strength," 5–7; Destler, "Evolution of Reagan Foreign Policy," 129–36.

3. James W. Abellera, Roger P. Labrie, and Albert C. Pierce, *The FY 1982–1986 Defense Program: Issues and Trends* (Washington, D.C.: American Enterprise Institute, 1981), 4–9; Samuel F. Wells Jr., "A Question of Priorities: A Comparison of the Carter and Reagan Defense Programs," *Orbis* 27 (Fall 1983): 650–54; Caspar W. Weinberger, *Annual Report to the Congress (FY 1983)* (Washington, D.C.: U.S. Government Printing Office, 1982), I-15–I-16.

4. Wells, "Question of Priorities," 652–66; Haftendorn, "Toward a Reconstruction of American Strength," 11–13, 20–25.

5. Geoffrey Smith, *Reagan and Thatcher* (London: Bodley Head, 1990), 23–48; Samuel F. Wells Jr., "The Mitterrand Challenge, *"Foreign Policy* 44 (Fall 1981): 57–61.

6. Strobe Talbott, *Deadly Gambits: The Reagan Administration and the Stalemate in Nuclear Arms Control* (New York: Alfred A. Knopf, 1984), 56–81.

7. Miles Kahler, "The United States and Western Europe: The Diplomatic Consequences of Mr. Reagan," in *Eagle Resurgent? The Reagan Era in American Foreign Policy,* ed. Kenneth A. Oye et al. (Boston: Little, Brown, 1987), 306–10; Destler, "Reagan Foreign Policy," 141–145; Smith, *Reagan and Thatcher,* 56–58.

8. Raymond L. Garthoff, *The Great Transition: American-Soviet Relations and the End of the Cold War* (Washington, D.C.: Brookings Institution Press, 1994), 546–51; Destler, "Evolution of Reagan Foreign Policy," 146–51; Kahler, "The United States and Western Europe," 310–17; Smith, *Reagan and Thatcher,* 71–75, 95–99; author's interview with Ambassador Richard R. Burt, Washington, May 7, 2001. For a discussion of the Polish crisis with documents from Polish and Soviet archives showing the Soviet Union had no intention of intervening, see "New Evidence on the Polish Crisis, 1980–1981, *"Cold War International History Project Bulletin,* issue 11 ("Cold War Flashpoints") (Winter 1998): 3–133.

9. Smith, *Reagan and Thatcher,* 99–106; Destler, "Evolution of Reagan Foreign Policy," 146–51. For reports of continued threats of extraterritorial sanctions from Richard Perle, see Reginald Dale, "U.S. Threatens Technology Transfer Ban," *Financial Times,* May 17, 1983. While the gas pipeline crisis was still simmering, a huge explosion disrupted the flow of gas during the summer of 1982. Recent publications reveal that this was the result of faulty computer chips supplied to technology the Soviet Union had acquired illegally from Western companies. The plan to provide faulty computer chips was devised by the CIA working on the basis of intelligence shared by French President Mitterrand. See Thomas C. Reed, *At the Abyss: An Insider's History of the Cold War* (New York: Ballantine Books, 2004), 266–70; and David E. Hoffman, "Reagan Approved Plan to Sabotage Soviets," *Washington Post,* February 27, 2004.

10. CIA analysis of the pipeline, August 1982, in *CIA's Analysis of the Soviet Union, 1947–1991,* ed. Gerald K. Haines and Robert E. Leggett (Washington, D.C.: Center for the Study of Intelligence, CIA, 2001), 119–20; Steven Kotkin, "What They Knew, Not! Forty-four Years of CIA Secrets," *New York Times,* March 19, 2001.

11. For a more detailed account of these issues, see Samuel F. Wells Jr., "The United States and European Defence Co-operation," *Survival* (July–August 1985): 158–68.

12. Garthoff, *Great Transition,* 551–53.

13. Josef Joffe, "Stability and Its Discontent: Should NATO Go Conventional?" *Washington Quarterly* 7 (Fall 1984): 146.

14. Walter Schütze, *Prospects for Effective Conventional Defense in Europe: The Case of the Federal Republic of Germany-Problems and Trends*, Working Paper 60 (Washington, D.C.: International Security Studies Program, Woodrow Wilson International Center for Scholars, 1984).

15. Ronald Reagan, Address to the Nation on Defense and National Security, March 23, 1983, *Public Papers of the Presidents of the United States, Ronald Reagan, 1983*, book 1 (Washington, D.C.: U.S. Government Printing Office, 1984), 442–43.

16. Lou Cannon, *President Reagan: The Role of a Lifetime* (New York: Simon & Schuster, 1991), 318–33; Lieutenant General Edward L. Rowny, conversation with the author, May 28, 1985; Robert C. McFarlane with Zofia Smardz, *Special Trust* (New York: Cadell & Davies, 1994), 225–35.

17. Burt interview.

18. Samuel F. Wells Jr., "Mitterrand's International Policies," *Washington Quarterly* 11 (Summer 1988): 65–66; Cannon, *President Reagan*, 333, n. 122 on 862.

19. Wells, "The United States and European Defence Co-operation," 162–64; Kahler, "The United States and Western Europe," 322–24; Samuel F. Wells Jr., "France and European Cooperation: Implications for United States Policy," *Atlantic Community Quarterly* 23 (Winter 1985–86): 382–85.

20. Wells, "The United States and European Defence Co-operation," 166.

21. Quoted in Beth A. Fischer, *The Reagan Reversal: Foreign Policy and the End of the Cold War* (Columbia: University of Missouri Press, 1997), 32–40.

22. Cannon, *President Reagan*, 589–783; Garthoff, *Great Transition*, 551–55; Frances FitzGerald, *Way Out There in the Blue: Reagan, Star Wars and the End of the Cold War* (New York: Simon & Schuster, 2000), 314–69; George P. Shultz, *Turmoil and Triumph: My Years as Secretary of State* (New York: Charles Scribner's Sons, 1993), 597–607, 751–859, 901–24; Strobe Talbott, *The Master of the Game: Paul Nitze and the Nuclear Peace* (New York: Alfred A. Knopf, 1988), 272–88, 314–26; Avis Bohlen, "The Rise and Fall of Arms Control," *Survival* (Autumn 2003): 23–24.

23. Garthoff, *Great Transition*, 555–58; Bohlen, "Rise and Fall of Arms Control," 24–26. In the midst of the Tower Commission investigation of the Iran-Contra affair, National Security Adviser Robert McFarlane attempted suicide on February 9, 1987. Cannon, *President Reagan*, 713.

24. Shultz, *Turmoil and Triumph*, 983–1015.

25. James A. Baker, III with Thomas M. DeFrank, *The Politics of Diplomacy: Revolution, War and Peace, 1989–1992* (New York: G. P. Putnam & Sons, 1995), 84–96, 195–216, 230–59; Philip Zelikow and Condoleezza Rice, *Germany Unified and Europe Transformed* (Cambridge, Mass.: Harvard University Press, 1995); Robert L. Hutchings, *American Diplomacy and the End of the Cold War: An Insider's Account of U.S. Policy in Europe, 1989–1992* (Baltimore: Johns Hopkins University Press; Washington, D.C.: Woodrow Wilson Center Press, 1997); George Bush and Brent Scowcroft, *A World Transformed* (New York: Vintage Books, 1999), 230–99.

26. Bush and Scowcroft, *World Transformed*, 230–35, 292–99.

27. Bush and Scowcroft, *World Transformed*, 301. See also Hutchings, *American Diplomacy and the End of the Cold War*, 272–74.

28. Hutchings, *American Diplomacy and the End of the Cold War*, 274–78. On the 1991 talks, Anand Menon quotes one American official as saying that if "it wasn't for

the French, we might be able to accept the assurances that a new European security entity would be part of a trans-Atlantic partnership, but on this issue, we don't trust the French." Quoted in Anand Menon, *France, NATO and the Limits of Independence: 1981–97: The Politics of Ambivalence* (New York: St. Martin's Press, 2000), 142.

29. Hutchings, *American Diplomacy and the End of the Cold War*, 276–83; quotations from author's telephone interview with Robert Hutchings, August 15, 2001. For the evolution of ESDI, see Jolyon Howorth, "European Integration and Defence: The Ultimate Challenge?" *Chaillot Papers 43* (Paris: Institute for Security Studies of WEU, November 2000), 4.

30. Shultz, *Turmoil and Triumph,* 1150; Baker, *Politics of Diplomacy,* 677.

31. Burt interview.

32. Paolo Cecchini, "Integration of the European Internal Market: Implications for Europe and the United States," unpublished meeting report, Woodrow Wilson International Center for Scholars, May 1988.

33. George Bush, "Remarks at the Boston University Commencement Ceremony in Massachusetts, May 21, 1989," in *Public Papers of the President of the United States, George Bush, 1989,* book 1 (Washington, D.C.: U.S. Government Printing Office, 1990), 583.

34. Hutchings interview.

Chapter 13

Germany and Relaunching Europe

Markus Jachtenfuchs

When trying to grasp the impact of bilateral relationships with France and the United States on Germany's policy toward the European Union, one is immediately faced with the problem of distinguishing between rhetoric and reality. The conventional wisdom is that good relations or even "partnership" with both states have been a strong norm in German foreign policy. In the first decades after World War II, this norm coincided well with Germany's overall interest to regain international influence and standing. In addition, the normative goal of good relations seemed effective because it became institutionalized. This applies in particular to the Franco-German relationship. Stimulated by the Franco-German Treaty of 1963, regular bilateral meetings of a large variety of actors from both countries have taken place—ranging from gatherings of bureaucrats, journalists, parliamentarians, and local politicians to the summits of the French president and the German chancellor.

As a result, common positions of the two countries on matters of major political importance have been elaborated ever more frequently and are often regarded as an indicator of the intensity of the partnership. In the academic literature, France and Germany are frequently mentioned as the most active and most important "actors" of the European Union.[1] However, this institutionalization of strong mutual relationships has developed a considerable dynamic of its own. Much of the academic literature as well as official declarations of political actors are heavily biased in favor of the existence of strong common positions and mutual interaction. The same is said with regard to the United States, although the latter's impact is perceived to be more important with respect to NATO than to the European Union.

A methodological device to move beyond public declarations of mutual friendship is to analyze preferences, which are sets of desired outcomes in specific policy areas independent of concrete decisions. It is precisely this focus on specific or sectoral issues that allows us to distinguish between the rhetoric of friendship and common interests, which usually are expressed on a rather general level, and what governments "really want," because only on this level are concrete costs and benefits involved.

It is increasingly accepted in international relations theory that preferences should be explained by specific causal mechanisms. These mechanisms do not work on the level of the international system, but on the domestic level.[2] Contrary to the materialist bias of some works, international liberalism does not prefer one sort of preferences over another. Apart from economic interests mediated by domestic pressure groups and enterprises, security concerns and fundamental beliefs about political institutions and political community can play a role. The decisive recognition of liberalism for the analysis of German policy in the strategic triangle is that preferences vary depending on the issue area and the configuration of domestic groups and ideas in the respective field. There is no such thing as a "general" German policy toward European integration. Such a general policy orientation may be constructed in retrospect as a generalization from a large number of individual decisions. It also appears in the political discourse as a part of political myths used for strategic reasons.

The following sections analyze Germany's European policy by looking at three major constitutional decisions: the Maastricht Treaty of 1991, the Amsterdam Treaty of 1997, and the 1999 Helsinki summit. Taken together these actions constitute a largely successful effort to relaunch the European project. They can also be seen in the process of widening (enlargement to Central and Eastern European countries) and deepening (mainly in creating common institutions for security and defense policy for the EU). Though the early phase of European integration can now be studied on the basis of solid historical work using primary sources,³ this is much more difficult for the period of the 1990s. One has to rely heavily on soft sources, such as public pronouncements by politicians, newspaper reports, and public documents from the European Commission. While widening and deepening continue, we can give a plausible account of policy development. The main argument is that Germany's European policy has been highly consistent, before as well as after unification.

The Maastricht Process

The negotiations leading up to the treaty adopted at the Maastricht summit in December 1991 were preceded by a long series of bilateral contacts, preparatory meetings and, finally, two month-long parallel intergovernmental conferences on economic and monetary as well as political union. The outcome was a complex treaty that addresses almost all aspects of EU policymaking. Still, an overwhelming part of the literature claims that Maastricht, and in particular Economic and Monetary Union (EMU) would not have happened the way it did without German unification. Helmut Kohl is said to have accepted the abolition of the deutsche mark and the end of Bundesbank autonomy in exchange for Britain's and France's acceptance of Germany's unification. In this interpretation, the Maastricht Treaty was a high-politics deal stuck between political leaders. This view, which seems to be much more popular outside of Germany than inside, is plausible at first glance.

Angst about a unified Germany has frequently been mentioned as a major driving force of French foreign policy, and François Mitterrand's ideas for a pan-European confederation and his joint declaration with Mikhail Gorbachev seem to confirm this interpretation. What really happened at Maastricht is difficult to examine before the governmental archives open. Yet, the broad evidence available considerably weakens the "high-politics bargain" hypothesis.

The French position is easy to explain from a neorealist standpoint.⁴ With respect to EMU, France could not choose between a completely independent monetary policy in the service of the national interest or a submission to the decisions of a European Central Bank (ECB). The real alternative was either a complete loss of control over monetary policy, and de facto control by the German Bundesbank, or at least some French influence in the ECB council and, preferably, by increased monetary decisionmaking in the EU Council of Economic and Finance Ministers (EcoFin). In this situation, the choice was clear: France could only win from EMU. This has been the position of various French governments since the mid-1980s, that is, after the spectacular failure of domestic Keynesianism in 1983. This position was supported by French business elites and remained constant despite the changing composition of governments before and after German unification. Since 1987 at the latest, France has pressed constantly for stronger European monetary coordination.[5]

The German position is more difficult to explain. By agreeing to EMU, Germany seemed to give away something important without getting much in return. Yet, even the German government advocated EMU before 1989. In this case, the constellation of domestic forces explains the German government's position. The major opposition against EMU came from the Bundesbank. This is not surprising, given its institutional self-interest. However, the Bundesbank could not argue itself for the maintenance of its role and power. Instead, its strategy consisted of demanding the emulation of the German central bank model at the European level. It argued that this was the only means to prevent higher inflation rates for German consumers and business, which could have occurred if there had been room for political interference in central bank policy, as the French model stipulated. Already in 1988, in the Delors Report, the central bank governors from the EU member states agreed on a plan that resembled the final provisions of the Maastricht Treaty. As a result, the Bundesbank had reached most of its goals.[6]

Political actors were generally supportive. Former chancellor Helmut Schmidt was a member of the action committee for the monetary unification of Europe,[7] and he strongly supported EMU in order to create a full common market and to reduce transaction costs for German business. Both German coalition parties, the Social Democratic Party and the Free Democratic Party, had advocated EMU in their party programs since the 1970s.[8] Business organizations and trade unions were also supportive.[9] Ideas with regard to the European political structure coincided with domestic economic interests. The German government did not give away the deutsche mark, but it advocated EMU because it corresponded to its political vision of the European Union and at the same time served German business interests.

Nor were the Maastricht provisions for a political union (a synonym for a rather loose set of proposals related to more influence for the European Parliament (EP) and the European Court of Justice and closer cooperation in the field of foreign policy as well as justice and home affairs) the result of a desire of the other member states to bind Germany. As in the case of EMU, German thinking remained unchanged by unification and by the

French position. In this field, French and German preferences were rather far apart.

An old theme of European federalism, the dominant school of thought on the European Union among the German Christian Democrats, has been that European integration must not have an economic bias but be accompanied by "political integration" in order to guarantee popular support. Already in early 1989, Kohl demanded that progress in this field must be parallel to developments in economic and monetary integration. This argument was crucial for calming domestic fears of an omnipotent technocracy in Brussels. Most notably, the Bundestag requested that it not only be given the right of a formal opt-in vote on EMU but also that the EU in general exhibit a more democratic structure by enlarging the powers of the EP. In addition, strengthening the powers of the European Court of Justice (ECJ) and thereby the principle of the rule of law was another core request of the German government.

These views were in full accordance with the prevailing Euro-federalist orientation of most political actors in Germany. The French were much more reluctant concerning a political union. In fact, the issue of how to democratize the European Union has been a major issue of disagreement between Paris and Bonn/Berlin. It is comparatively easy for German political actors to see the EU as another layer in a multitiered federal structure similar to the domestic one. In this layer-cake model, each level of political authority has to be subject to parliamentary control at its own level.

French political theory is largely based on the concept of the "state-nation."[10] In this view, the state represents a particular political community. State institutions such as democracy express the will of that particular community and for this reason cannot simply be transferred to a different institutional level. As a consequence, there is a strong tendency in France to regard the EP with criticism. Although it is a democratically elected assembly, it does not represent the political community. In this view, the European Council as the representative of the European people is the proper institution for democratic control.

As a result, the strengthening of the EP's powers by the co-decision procedure of the Maastricht Treaty was mainly introduced because of German pressure, supported by Belgium and Italy, with France being very reluctant. The strengthening of the EP is a very particular case of voluntary and irrevocable surrender of each member state's control over the European policy process. Powers once given to the EP are lost forever, because it is inconceivable for governmental executives to claim back authorities from a symbol of democratic control, apart from the low probability of ever getting the required unanimity for such a proposal. At the same time, EP behavior is entirely outside member state control when parliamentarians are elected by universal suffrage instead of being appointed. There is no plausible explanation of the German position in terms of material or geopolitical interest. The strong German pressure toward strengthening the EP (and the ECJ) can only be explained by ideological preferences.

In the field of foreign policy as well as in the area of justice and home affairs, the constellation of preferences was similar, with France being reluctant to lose control over what it considered essential parts of its sovereignty, and Germany urging increased majority voting and a more substantial role for both the Commission and ECJ in these fields. The use of joint Franco-German proposals during the negotiations should not obscure the substantive differences between the two countries. Although they showed the vitality of the institutionalization of the Franco-German subsystem within the EU, their common declarations are already compromises.[11] They represented tactical positions but not deeper preferences.

Germany favored an extension of the existing community system with the right for initiatives for the Commission and control by the ECJ in the field of foreign policy, or more precisely what used to be called "European Political Cooperation," as well as in areas such as immigration control, criminal justice, and police cooperation. The last should be carried out by a newly created European Police Office (EUROPOL) which was to be put under the control of both the EP and the ECJ. France, however, was keen not to transfer the supranational community system to these new areas. It proposed instead the three-pillar architecture that was finally adopted at the Maastricht summit.

In the field of defense, Germany advocated a gradual integration of the Western European Union (WEU) into the EU. In this case, the real opposition came from Britain, which regarded any attempt to have the EU instead of NATO deal with defense and military matters as unnecessary and dangerous. Faced with this strong opposition, France aligned with Germany and argued for the medium-term integration of the WEU into the EU.

On the whole, the Maastricht Treaty does not show any sign of a loosening in the German commitment to the EU or even of attempts in big power politics after unification. The popular thesis that German agreement to monetary union had been achieved in exchange for allied support for unification makes sense only if Germany had in fact preferred to continue with the unilateral monetary domination of Western and increasingly Eastern Europe. The available evidence indicates, however, that both French and German politics had converged on a pro-EMU course several years before unification, though for different reasons.

Negotiating the Amsterdam Treaty

At Maastricht, the negotiators had agreed to convene a review conference five years later. This conference started in March 1996 and ended with the signing of the Amsterdam Treaty in June 1997. This conference differed in several respects from the previous ones. First, it was agreed to only after heated and controversial public debates. Whereas the Single European Act had passed largely unnoticed in German public opinion, the Maastricht Treaty had—after a considerable time lag—led to the first major debate on the goals of Germany's European policy since the 1950s. Second, Maastricht was the last time that economic integration played the major role in intergovernmental constitutional conferences. After the completion of the common market and the achievement of monetary union, not much was left in this area to be organized on a European scale. With a much more attentive public, negotiations moved from economics and welfare to internal and external security. In addition, the Amsterdam negotiations were the first round of major constitutional change. Here, one could expect that the new international position of Germany could play a role. If one assumed that changes in the structure of the international system are not immediately and directly effective on national foreign (or European) policies but transmitted through domestic institutions, more than six years should have given German politicians, parties, and interest groups time to adapt.

However, Amsterdam showed a remarkable continuity in the German position (as it did in the French case). As in the case of the Maastricht negotiations, preferences continued to be shaped by domestic factors on an issue-specific basis, such as ideas about a legitimate European political order, predominant policy styles, and concrete problems at the time of the negotiations.

In terms of the basic institutional setup of the EU, Germany continued to press for more parliamentary control at the EU level, aiming at a bicameral system with the Council and EP on equal footing. Under EU decision-making rules, this implied the extension of qualified majority voting to areas that were still under unanimity rule. On the whole, Germany followed its strategy to achieve a uniform institutional system for the EU with the

Commission retaining its monopoly of initiative, the Council and the EP as the two legislative chambers, and the ECJ acting as a constitutional court and administering judicial review. National parliaments were to continue with their task of controlling national governments but not allowed to interfere with EU decisionmaking.

This was in contrast to the French position. France had extended its longstanding attitude of distrust of the EP and had proposed a "High Parliamentary Council" according to an initiative of the Assemblé Nationale.[12] This council was to consist of representatives from national parliaments to introduce democratic feedback, particularly regarding the third pillar (justice and home affairs), where France rejected EP and ECJ controls. In this respect, France and Germany had opposing preferences. This was also revealed by a joint paper by Helmut Kohl and Jacques Chirac during the negotiations that did not state common positions on this field but tried to hide the clash of positions behind a carefully worded compromise.[13]

Similar continuities for each country prevailed for the field of foreign policy. Whereas Germany would have preferred a broad move toward qualified majority voting, reserving unanimity only for cases of major importance, France insisted on unanimity as the key rule and accepted majority voting only for "implementing" decisions. This was the position that found its way into the Amsterdam Treaty. France was also keen to uphold a clear separation between the institutional structure for the Common Foreign and Security Policy (CSFP), the successor of European Political Cooperation introduced by the Maastricht Treaty, and the supranational system of the first pillar, most notably the Commission's sole right of initiative, ECJ control, and parliamentary scrutiny. France's position should not be interpreted as reluctance about CFSP; on the contrary, foreign and security policy were of major importance for France. However, they were to remain intergovernmental and not slowly submerge in a supranational decisionmaking system. The desire to both separate the CFSP from the Community institutions and to give it a high political visibility was the background for the proposal to appoint "Mr. or Mrs. CFSP," a prominent personality with high international reputation elected for several years, which should give the EU's foreign policy a face and a voice—the anecdote of Henry Kissinger asking for Europe's telephone number lurked in the background.

For Germany, this proposal did not seem attractive because it looked like another step of complicating the EU's institutional system even more without necessarily improving its performance. The German government regarded as sufficient the existing system of EU representation by the rotating Council presidency. The outcome was a compromise: The appointment of a secretary general of the Council, also serving as high representative for CFSP, was accepted to avoid establishing a new separate bureaucracy.

Also in the field of security policy, the long-term orientations of France, Germany, and the United Kingdom did not change. Both France and Germany continued to advocate the integration of the WEU into the EU in the medium term, whereas Britain remained opposed. In the meantime, however, an agreement had emerged. The so-called Petersberg tasks neither threatened NATO's prerogatives nor constituted the beginning of a European defense policy.[14] After the change of government in Britain from John Major to Tony Blair, the way was free for their inclusion in the treaty.

Regarding the third pillar (justice and domestic affairs), the German position had been quite ambitious. The government's position stopped short of asking to move the entire issue into the first pillar, because such a proposal did not look very promising. However, the Commission was to receive a right of initiative together with the member states, and the ECJ was to have comprehensive jurisdiction to protect individual rights. Consultation with the EP should be compulsory and majority decisionmaking the rule, particularly regarding the harmonization of asylum and migration policies. In this area, Germany realized that its large share of the total number of refugees was caused by open borders and could only be reduced by common European action—which it hoped to facilitate by the introduction of qualified majority voting. In addition, the transborder movement of criminals should be tackled by EUROPOL, the European police office. EUROPOL should have limited executive competencies. In return, its actions should be subject to ECJ review.

Again, the French position was quite different. France at best accepted a limited right of co-initiative for the Commission, rejected any role of the ECJ, and it proposed a new High Parliamentary Council to guarantee the democratic accountability of third pillar measures. Decisions were to be made by unanimity, and EUROPOL was to remain a purely intergovernmental institution without ECJ interference.

Seen in context, the Amsterdam negotiations show a large degree of continuity in German preferences toward the European Union. Most of the positions taken by the government had not changed since the Maastricht negotiations. They can be traced back to fundamental European policy orientations dating to the 1970s.[15] The only major change in a position was Kohl's refusal to accept majority decisions with respect to a harmonization of asylum policies.[16] Previously, the German government had strongly argued in favor of majority voting.[17] This move, however, does not indicate a fundamental change of preferences, but was a response to domestic concerns.

In Amsterdam as in Maastricht, German preferences differed in substantial points from those of French. Policymakers were aware of these differences and actively sought to come to compromises between the two countries before or during the intergovernmental conferences in order to set the agenda and pave the way for joint decisions that best reflected their interests. The incessant reference to the Franco-German engine and other metaphors should, however, not obscure the fundamental differences. The strategic relationship between the two countries consisted in taking the other's preferences into account for the formulation of one's own policies. It did not lead to changes in preferences.

Helsinki and Beyond

Maastricht, it has been argued, was the last of the classic grand bargains on economic integration among advanced industrial democracies, largely unaffected by the end of the Cold War. The most profound impact of 1989 only slowly began to make itself felt. It was the process of enlargement toward Eastern Europe. It differed in a number of ways from previous enlargements. The mere number of applicant states was higher than ever. About a dozen countries were candidates in a first or a second round. On average, with Poland being the most significant exception, the applicant countries were comparatively small. Under the present system of weighting votes, their admission would lead to a clear advantage of smaller countries at the expense of larger ones with a substantially higher population. Most of the applicants were still going through the double transformation into a market economy and democracy. In short, eastern enlargement implied a profound transformation both of the applicant countries and of the European Union.

At the Copenhagen summit in 1993, the EU adopted a criteria-based approach for enlargement. Every country that fulfilled basic requirements of democratic and economic development would be considered a serious candidate. At regular intervals, the Commission published reports on the applicants' progress on these criteria. This opened up the early possibility of an EU of more than twenty-five member states, not even counting the successor states of the former Yugoslavia. The decision to adopt an open approach toward enlargement presented academic as well as political observers with a puzzle: The conclusion that the net costs of enlargement outweighed the net benefits was hard to escape. Why then did the EU member states unanimously launch such an ambitious project?

Germany was among the first and most vigorous supporters of quick and broad enlargement. This policy was motivated by the desire to create stability on its eastern borders by firmly embedding the transforming states into the web of Western European international institutions. In this strategy, the EU occupied a prominent place because of its unparalleled capacities for action. Only the EU had both the instruments and the power to induce profound economic and political reforms in the candidate countries. In addition, only EU membership offered the possibility of transforming a potential unstable international subsystem in Eastern Europe into one with highly institutionalized and legalized peaceful relations resembling more domestic than international politics. For Germany, the membership of all European countries in international institutions, preferably the EU, was a desirable final status for the European system.

To avoid institutional collapse, the "widening" of the EU had to be accompanied by a process of "deepening." The German concept of European federalism seemed to offer the solution on how to achieve both goals simultaneously: a rigid application of the subsidiarity principle and a catalogue of competencies for each level of government to avoid decision overload and centralization. Increased majority voting would avoid decision-making blockades, and the EP and the ECJ would guarantee democratic control and the rule of law in an enlarged European Union. The German overall strategy of fast and broad widening of the EU seemed to be motivated by an explicit institutional design. It does not prevent long and protracted negotiations and tough positions on individual issues such as agricultural policy, the speed of trade liberalization in individual sectors, or worker migration.[18]

The French strategy toward enlargement was much more cautious, for the country was less concerned with the inflow of migrants because of its geographical distance from Eastern Europe. As a consequence, its political design was less important than concrete interests to protect its domestic producers and to avoid a massive shift of EU redistributive policies. On the whole, France was more concerned with the dangers of enlargement for the stability and functioning of the present EU structure than was Germany. That has to do not only with geographical position but also with different ideas about constitutional design. The German concept of decentralized federalism with an extensive use of majority voting could accommodate a substantially larger membership more easily than the French insistence of intergovernmental control and the maintenance of unanimity.

The only critical issue for Germany's accession strategy was Turkey. The Copenhagen criteria seemed to exclude Turkey's accession for a considerable time because it was highly unlikely that the country could meet the requirements in the foreseeable future. However, the German political class was divided over this issue. For some, the human rights problems, the ongoing civil war against the Kurds, the low degree of economic development (particularly in eastern Turkey), and the prospect of mass labor migration made Turkey hard to swallow for the EU. Others saw in Turkish accession the idea of a closed community of the rich externalizing the real problems and insisted on the primacy of the geopolitical goal of macropolitical stabilization at Europe's eastern borders.

This had also been Washington's position. The United States—unconcerned with serious internal issues such as a reform of the structural funds, labor migration, and human rights in the context of large-scale political change—had long advocated Turkish membership in the EU as a complement to NATO membership in order to bind Turkey, a key regional power, even more tightly into the Western alliance by granting the desire of Turkish governments since the 1960s to became a member of the EU.

The Helsinki summit in December 1999 decided on the EU's accession strategy in terms of concrete countries. It distinguished between two groups of countries: a first contingent consisting of those that were considered ready to enter into specific membership negotiations, which should be completed after 2003; and a second group of countries, which was considered to need more time for economic and political adaptation. Turkey was not included in either list but received an option for future consideration of membership.

This solution looks like a typical EU compromise, in which different preferences about membership were transformed into separate timetables. It is unclear whether the decision on Turkey was a response to American pressure or was motivated by a desire to keep good relations with Turkey without making untenable membership promises. The formula found in Helsinki allows all participants to claim some success and leaves concrete meanings to future negotiations.

The Helsinki summit also made decisions on the deepening of the EU by continuing to establish a European Security and Defense Policy (ESDP), which had gained considerable momentum with the Cologne summit in June 1999. The term "defense" is somewhat misleading, because ESDP does not aim to defend the territorial integrity of EU member states by supplementing or even replacing national defense policies or NATO. In this field, the old controversies among France, Germany, Britain, and the United States still prevailed and prevented meaningful development at the EU level. The new consensus comes from a new opportunity structure that allowed members to set aside the old dissension about NATO and at the same time proceed to develop a genuine European security policy.

The Helsinki decisions on ESDP could easily be discarded as an ex post facto rationalization of what the EU was currently doing in the former Yugoslavia. Although this is certainly a motive, such an interpretation underestimates the dynamic of institutionalization. ESDP's main goal was the stabilization of limited conflicts in the EU's international environment. To achieve this goal, it developed a wide range of instruments, from the deployment of military force and police assistance in maintaining law and order to assistance in establishing functioning legal and administrative systems. In a certain sense, ESDP meant Petersberg tasks writ large. Most important, it established an institutional structure to deal with such operations on a sustainable basis. Two main reasons explain why the preferences of France, Germany, Britain, and the other EU member states converged on ESDP. First, it was the answer to a real problem—violent conflicts at the EU's periphery—that NATO could only solve with U.S. support. Thus, ESDP was an attempt to make a major issue of domestic political debate in most member states less dependent on U.S. decisions. Second, the explicit limitation of its task removed possible competition with NATO, and therefore it did not reopen old wounds.

The Strategic Triangle in Perspective

If one looks at the relations among the partners of the strategic triangle with regard to European integration over time, some fundamental trends can be discerned that transformed relations within the triangle.

In the first place, European integration was increasingly dominated by domestic and economic concerns and less by geopolitical strategies. In the creation of the European Coal and Steel Community, and in particular the attempts to create a European Defense Community in the 1950s, the American desire to stabilize Western Europe and to anchor Germany in the West in the context of an emerging Cold War was an important factor, although a "revisionist" school of historians claims that domestic economic concerns had already at that time outweighed security motives.[19]

Be that as it may, it is clear that fifty years later internal developments in the EU were much less influenced by American policies than was the case after the end of World War II. Many of the issues that were of concern to EU member states at the end of the twentieth century—such as the scope of police cooperation, the possible extension of majority voting, the rights of the EP, or the reweighting of votes in the EU Council—have very few direct consequences for U.S. policy. Whereas the literature is full of accounts of how Washington intervened in the early phases of European institution building, U.S. interference in the 1980s and 1990s is not a theme in later writing. Even an explicit attempt to demonstrate that Europe was still subject to soft hegemonic influence failed to show substantive and concrete cases of intervention.[20]

Second, relations in the economic sphere are now taking place between the United States and the European Union due to the latter's exclusive competency in foreign trade. In this field, the strategic triangle has been "Europeanized" and transatlantic relations have been transformed into a bilateral relationship. Only in the field of security does the old relationship still exist, and it is likely to persist because ESDP does not aim to replace or transform NATO but to complement it.

Finally, fundamental differences in preferences remain between France and Germany. They do not preclude cooperation; on the contrary, harmony would make cooperation unnecessary. The institutionalized norm of cooperation between the two countries makes the realization of joint gains possible. Whereas the role of the United States in the triangle has diminished, the Franco-German relationship is still important for all matters of European policymaking. The strong and institutionalized norm of mutual cooperation has created a subsystem in the EU that allows for the continuous development of common positions on matters of mutual interest.

This highly differentiated and institutionalized system will not lead to a convergence of preferences in the foreseeable future. But it allows for cooperation on the basis of divergent preferences, and the taking into account of the preferences of the other country in shaping political strategies. Joschka Fischer's often-cited Humbold University speech on the future of the EU is a case in point.[21] Though on the one hand fully in the tradition of German Euro-federalism, it makes substantial advances toward the French model with its skepticism about the European Parliament and its insistence on the guiding role of the European Council.

The strong rhetoric of Franco-German friendship and the frequent alarming cries about the perceived worsening of that relationship are important for reproducing it and keeping it alive. In this sense, it is not rhetoric that is to be contrasted with "reality." Instead, Franco-German cooperation is a major part of institutionalized policymaking between the two countries that will continue to be crucial for the future of Europe.

Notes

1. Philippe de Schoutheete, "The European Community and its Sub-Systems," in *The Dynamics of European Integration*, ed. William Wallace (London: Pinter, 1990), 106–24.
2. Andrew Moravcsik, "Taking Preferences Seriously: A Liberal Theory of International Politics," *International Organization* 51 (1977): 513–53.
3. E.g., see Monika Dickhaus, *Die Bundesbank im westeuropäischen Wiederaufbau: Die internationale Währungspolitik der Bundesrepublik Deutschland 1948 bis 1958* (Munich: Oldenbourg, 1996); John Gillingham, *Coal, Steel, and the Rebirth of Europe, 1945–1955: The Germans and the French from the Ruhr Conflict to Economic Community* (Cambridge: Cambridge University Press, 1991); and Klaus Schwabe, "The United States and European Integration, 1947–1955," in *Western Europe and Germany: The Beginnings of European Integration 1945–1960*, ed. Clemens Wurm (Oxford: Berg, 1995), 115–35.
4. Joseph M. Grieco, "The Maastricht Treaty, Economic and Monetary Union and the Neo-Realist Research Programme," *Review of International Studies* 21 (1995): 21–40.
5. Andrew Moravcsik, *The Choice for Europe: Social Purpose and State Power from Messina to Maastricht* (Ithaca, N.Y.: Cornell University Press, 1998), 408–17.
6. Amy Verdun, *European Responses to Globalization and Financial Market Integration: Perceptions of Economic and Monetary Union in Britain, France and Germany* (Basingstoke, U.K.: Macmillan, 2000), 80–82.
7. Association for the Monetary Union of Europe, founded in 1986 by Valéry Giscard d'Estaing and Helmut Schmidt and consisting mainly of bankers and business people; in Moravcsik, *Choice for Europe*, 434; cf. http://www.amue.org.
8. Markus Jachtenfuchs, *Die Konstruktion Europas: Verfassungsideen und institutionelle Entwicklung* (Baden-Baden: Nomos), 179–81, 194–95.
9. Moravcsik, *Choice for Europe*, 391–96.
10. Ulla Holm, "The French Garden Is No Longer What It Used to Be," in *Reflective Approaches to European Governance*, ed. Knud Erik Jørgensen (London: Macmillan, 1996), 128–45; Carlos de Sá Rêgo, *Une nostalgie de grandeur: Essai sur la France Etat-nation* (Paris: Ramsay, 1985).
11. Helmut Kohl and Jacques Chirac, "Schreiben des deutschen Bundeskanzlers und des französischen Staatspräsidenten, Helmut Kohl und Jacques Chirac, an den amtierenden Vorsitzenden des Europäischen Rates, den spanischen Ministerpräsidenten Felipe Gonzáles, veröffentlicht am 6 Dezember 1995 in Bonn und Paris (gekürzt)," *Internationale Politik* (August 1996): 80–81; Helmut Kohl und Jacques Chirac, "Gemeinsamer Brief des deutschen Bundeskanzlers und des französischen Staatspräsidenten, Helmut Kohl und Jacques Chirac, an den amtierenden Vorsitzenden des Europäischen Rates und

Ministerpräsidenten von Irland, John Bruton, 9 Dezember 1996 in Nürnberg (gekürzt)," *Internationale Politik* (March 1997): 82–88; Klaus Kinkel and Hervé de Charette, "Gemeinsamer Beitrag des deutschen und des französischen Außenministers, Klaus Kinkel and Hervé de Charette, für die Tageszeitungen *Le Figaro, Financial Times und die Frankfurter Allgemeine Zeitung*, veröffentlicht am 29 März 1996 in Paris, London und Frankfurt am Main," *Internationale Politik* (August 1996): 108–10; Klaus Kinkel and Hervé de Charette, "Leitlinien zur Gemeinsamen Außen- und Sicherheitspolitik, verabschiedet anläßlich des Seminars der Außenminister Deutschlands und Frankreichs, Klaus Kinkel und Hervé de Charette, am 27 Februar 1996 in Freiburg," *Internationale Politik* (August 1996): 84–86; Klaus Kinkel and Hervé de Charette, "Gemeinsamer Diskussionsbeitrag des deutschen und des französischen Außenministers, Klaus Kinkel and Hervé de Charette, für die Regierungskonferenz zur verstärkten Zusammenarbeit, veröffentlicht am 18 Oktober 1996 in Bonn und Paris," *Internationale Politik* (March 1997): 72–75.

12. Nicole Catala and Nicole Ameline, *Quelles réformes pour l'Europe de demain? Rapport d'information, déposé par la Délégation de l'Assemblée Nationale pour l'Union européenne, sur les réformes institutionelles de l'Union européenne*, Nr. 1939 (Paris: Assemblée Nationale, 1995).

13. Helmut Kohl and Jacques Chirac, "Schreiben des deutschen Bundeskanzlers und des französischen Staatspräsidenten, Helmut Kohl und Jacques Chirac, an den amtierenden Vorsitzenden des Europäischen Rates, den spanischen Ministerpräsidenten Felipe Gonzáles, veröffentlicht am 6. Dezember 1995 in Bonn und Paris (gekürzt)," *Internationale Politik* (August 1996): 81.

14. Ibid.

15. Jachtenfuchs, *Die Konstruktion Europas*.

16. *Agence Europe* no. 6996, June 16/17, 1997, 4; no. 6997, June 18, 1997, 4.

17. E.g., Klaus Kinkel, "Erklärung der Bundesregierung zu aktuellen Fragen der Europa-Politik abgegeben von Bundesaußenminister Klaus Kinkel am 22 Juni 1995 vor dem Deutschen Bundestag in Bonn (Auszug)," *Internationale Politik* (August 1995): 123.

18. Frank Schimmelfennig, "The Community Trap: Liberal Norms, Rhetorical Action, and the Eastern Enlargement of the European Union," *International Organization*, Winter 2001.

19. Alan Milward, *The Reconstruction of Western Europe, 1945–51* (London: Methuen, 1984); Alan Milward, *The European Rescue of the Nation-State* (Berkeley: University of California Press, 1992).

20. Geir Lundestad, *"Empire" by Integration: The United States and European Integration, 1945–1997* (Oxford: Oxford University Press, 1998).

21. Joschka Fischer, "Vom Staatenverbund zur Föderation: Gedanken über die Finalität der europäischen Integration," am 12 Mai 2000 in der Humbold-Universität in Berlin (gekürzt), *Internationale Politik* 55, no. 8 (2000): 100–108.

Part VI

NATO and Post–Cold War Challenges

Chapter 14

Enlarging NATO: The German-American Design for a New Alliance

Stephen F. Szabo

The decision to enlarge NATO made in Madrid in July 1997 represented a fundamental turn in Western policy regarding the European security regime, substantially changing the system that existed during the Cold War. Enlarging and revitalizing an alliance that had been shaped by conditions profoundly altered by the collapse of both the Soviet Union and the Warsaw Pact was not a self-evident result. Only a few years earlier, many in the West were arguing that NATO was finished—its mission accomplished, its adversary vanquished, and its domestic political base eroded. Yet in July 1997, NATO still stood as the centerpiece of a new European security system, while other alternatives that had looked more promising in 1990—the Western European Union and the Organization for Security and Cooperation in Europe—remained as supporting actors on the European stage.

The decision to adapt NATO and expand it eastward was one largely shaped by German and American policymakers, although both the German and the American governments were divided over the policy alternatives and it took at least two years to reach the final decision. The outcome seemed to provide strong evidence for the continued centrality of the German-American partnership. Given the focus of this volume, the strategic triangle—Bonn/Berlin-Paris-Washington—it is a case, much as the Two-plus-Four negotiations—of the German and American legs of that triangle working in a direction that the French government either opposed or about which it had, at the least, serious doubts.

This chapter describes and analyzes the German and American origins of the post–Cold War system, which is still evolving and fragile. The primary sources for this study are interviews with some of the key architects of this policy in Germany and the United States. This analysis is also based on an extensive review of journalistic accounts, speeches, and other public documents as well as the academic literature.

German Unification and the Debate over NATO Enlargement

The story of NATO enlargement really began with the negotiations to unify Germany. An important question concerns what was promised or implied to the Soviets on this topic during the Two-plus-Four negotiations and what we can learn about American thinking about the future European security order at this formative time. Opponents of the policy to enlarge NATO have argued that the United States either implied or explicitly promised that NATO would not expand if the Soviets agreed to allow a unified Germany to remain in the alliance.[1]

Hans Dietrich Genscher, the West German foreign minister during the Two-plus-Four talks, is clear in his memoir that the Germans reassured Mikhail Gorbachev and his team during the negotiations in the Caucasus that NATO structures should not move eastward. The shift in the military balance, in favor of the West and the retreat of Soviet forces, should not be followed by a structurally unchanged eastern expansion of the Western alliance.[2]

The American secretary of state, James Baker, also made similar assurances to the Soviets during his trip to Moscow in February 1990:

> To ease Soviet concerns, Baker used the formula he had picked up from Genscher and, turning Genscher's "no extension of NATO" language into a more lawyerly formulation, promised that if a more united Germany were included in NATO, there would be ironclad guarantees "that

Enlarging NATO 329

NATO's jurisdiction or forces would not move eastward." . . . Baker also pledged that NATO would evolve into a more political and less military-oriented alliance.[3]

Later during his meeting with Gorbachev, Baker repeated the assurances that "there would be no extension of NATO's jurisdiction for forces of NATO one inch to the east."[4] Baker then asked Gorbachev "whether he would rather see an independent Germany outside of NATO, with no U.S. forces on German soil, or a united Germany tied to NATO but with assurances 'that there would be no extension of NATO's current jurisdiction eastward.'" Gorbachev replied that one thing was clear: "Any extension of the zone of NATO is unacceptable." "I agree," Baker replied.[5]

A number of Russian officials have cited these assurances as evidence that the West violated its promises by bringing in former Warsaw Pact states as NATO members. They have received support from Western officials, including the American ambassador to Moscow at the time, Jack Matlock.[6] However, the evidence available does not support these assertions. German and American policymakers were preoccupied with the German unification issue and were focused on settling the military status of the former German Democratic Republic and nothing more. As a German Foreign Office official closely involved in the negotiations with the Soviets put it:

During 2+4, the speed of events overwhelmed everything else; the agreement to keep NATO troops out of the former [German Democratic Republic] did not set a precedent for precluding future NATO expansion; it does show that we did not think of a speedy NATO expansion—it just wasn't on the agenda; however the comments made by Baker to the Soviets on not expanding NATO were probably understood in the broader context; they are not lawyers, they were Russians and they are probably justified in feeling they were misled; however, the speed of 2+4 precluded this as being a first step in a planned phased expansion.

The pressure of events had focused the negotiators exclusively upon cutting a deal on German unification within NATO. The Warsaw Pact still existed, as did the Soviet Union, and Western thinking was concerned with maintaining NATO in the West after German unification. A search of files by both governments uncovered no such commitments.[7]

Gorbachev's acceptance of the Conference on Security and Cooperation in Europe (CSCE) principle that each nation should be free to choose its own alliances also undermines his contention that NATO enlargement was precluded by the deal on German unification. If this principle held for Germany, why should it not also be valid for Poland and the other newly independent democracies of East Central Europe? Furthermore, as Robert Hutchings, a Bush National Security Council (NSC) official, argued, why should Germany preclude the fulfillment of the security aspirations of other states?[8] The inclusion of Germany within NATO, despite Soviet objections, actually stabilized the security situation in Europe and benefited Russia as well. Why should the same not also hold for Poland and other states on the Russian periphery?

NATO drew its own conclusions when, at the London NATO summit, it called for Warsaw Pact states to establish diplomatic liaisons within NATO. This led to the North Atlantic Cooperation Council and the Partnership for Peace.[9]

Adapting German Strategy

The NATO enlargement policy was the product of three clusters of factors: a changing strategic environment, personal ambition, and bureaucratic politics. Unification began a new phase in the adaptation of Germany strategy. Not only did the new post–Cold War security environment require a reorientation, but the Gulf War began almost simultaneously with unification. Adaptation was pushed by a number of factors. First, the Gulf War and the prospect that Israel would suffer chemical or biological attacks with weapons built with German assistance while Germany stood by during the war itself; second, the war in Bosnia and the realization that came from it that military power was needed to protect human rights; third, the instability in the zone between Germany and Russia and the prospect of a reemerging independent German security policy in the region; and fourth, the process of European integration, which led to pressure, especially from France, for Germany to play a larger role in the creation of a European security identity. The creation of the Franco-German corps (later Eurocorps) was part of this adaptation.

Personal ambition and bureaucratic politics reacted to this new strategic environment in a complex interplay, which resulted in the new policy. Volker Rühe became defense minister just as this transition began. Rühe was an ambitious politician who wanted to break free of the constraints of his new job. For most of the history of the Federal Republic, the Defense

Ministry had become a dead end for aspiring politicians, and Rühe wanted to avoid the fate of Gerhard Stoltenberg, Hans Apel, and the many others who had seen their political careers end atop the *Hardthöhe*. He was part of a generation of Christian Democratic Union politicians who had been frustrated by the Free Democratic Party's monopoly of the Foreign Office since 1969. Rühe was looking for a big issue that he could use to wrest foreign policy control away from the Genscher-dominated Foreign Office. A major initiative for alliance reform through outreach to the East was such an issue. The replacement of Genscher on May 16, 1992, by Klaus Kinkel provided Rühe with more opportunities for asserting his views. Kinkel did not have the political clout within the coalition that Genscher carried, and thus a policy vacuum opened that Rühe rushed to fill.[10]

Admiral Ulrich Weisser, head of the Planning Staff, went to Rühe at the beginning of September 1992 and discussed with him ways he could build his political reputation as well as the contribution he could make as defense minister. The constitutional issue regarding Bundeswehr deployments outside the NATO area and the force structure reforms designed to create crisis reaction forces deployable out of the area were discussed, and the defense minister decided to forcefully push these changes through. Weisser also advised Rühe at this time to undertake a major initiative with regard to alliance reform. The link between NATO enlargement and Germany's new "out of area" role was clear. In addition, there was the geopolitical argument made by Weisser:

> We needed to ensure that the Western border was not the Oder-Neisse and to create a favorable strategic position—a *Mittellage* [Middle position] instead of a *Randlage* [Position on the border]. We were now surrounded only by friendly democratic states, but there were some weak ones among them. It was easier to defend Germany in Poland than in Germany and that was also in Poland's interests.[11]

The defense minister was in continual contact with leaders from East Central Europe and was being told clearly of the need for these countries to enter the West once and for all. The Polish foreign minister, Krzysztof Skubiszewski, told him that he wanted to avoid the catastrophic experiences of Polish history. Similar themes were emphasized by Lech Walesa and the Czech leader, Václav Havel. These arguments resonated with Rühe, given his assessment that it was the Polish revolution that set off the revolution in East Germany. Germany should be the last country to oppose Polish interests. There was also a general sense of German gratitude to Hungary for its role in opening the door to Austria for East Germans in the summer of 1989, thus setting in motion the events that led to the collapse of the German Democratic Republic. To Rühe, NATO enlargement was largely about Poland. He had serious reservations about extending NATO to states such as the Baltic republics, which were more peripheral to German interests.

Rühe initially followed the coalition's preference for European as opposed to NATO approaches to the new security situation.[12] The Petersberg Declaration of June 19–22, 1992, of the Western European Union (WEU) was a high point in this German Euro-enthusiasm, as the WEU declared itself willing to take on peacekeeping missions as part of the development of a common European security policy. During this meeting, Rühe made supportive statements about the need for a European identity and stated that the newly formed Eurocorps could intervene under the political authority of the WEU.[13] At the same time, NATO began to enhance its role in peacekeeping, agreeing in late May at the Defense Ministerial meeting to make itself available to act upon CSCE requests for peacekeeping. Though the WEU and the European Community floundered over the growing crisis in Bosnia, NATO began to develop a rapid reaction capability and increasingly became the key player in peacekeeping. By the end of 1992, Rühe had announced the intention to create a new crisis reaction capability for the Bundeswehr and placed the Eurocorps under the supreme allied commander in Europe's command.[14]

Added to these compelling strategic and personal factors were a number of domestic political issues. Public opinion polls in Germany commissioned by the RAND Corporation, the American think tank, began to show declining support for NATO and the U.S. troop presence. A new rationale for NATO had to be found. At the same time, the flow of asylum seekers from the east was having a debilitating effect on the German domestic scene. If something was not done to stabilize the east, right-wing forces fueled by nativism could rise to greater prominence in Germany. If East Central Europe were stabilized through market and democratic reform, then the incentive for emigration would substantially subside.[15]

Although this policy of the creation of a zone of stability in Central Europe was in the German interest, Rühe and many other politicians in Bonn feared that, as one scholar argues, "any distinctly German effort to stabilize the region might antagonize both their western and eastern neighbor. A return to a national *Ostpolitik* outside of multilateral institutions . . . might instigate renewed fears of hegemonic designs."[16]

By the fall of 1992, an interagency debate on expanding the alliance began within the German government and continued into the spring of 1993. The interagency team was headed by Chancellor Helmut Kohl's security adviser, Joachim Bitterlich, and included Weisser from the Defense Ministry and Wolfgang Ischinger from the Foreign Office. During these discussions, the Foreign Office raised its objections to the policy on the grounds that it was premature and could undermine the development of democracy and a Western-oriented foreign policy in Russia. Kinkel wanted to go more slowly. The Foreign Office position was that the enlargement of the European Union and NATO should go hand in hand and that it was not in the interests of the Central Europeans to move quickly to become NATO members first.[17]

The position of the chancellor was ambiguous; at this point, Kohl's style of governing was to let others, in this case Rühe, get out front on a policy initiative and then see what the result was. Kohl clearly knew what his defense minister and party colleague was doing and wanted him to test the waters. Kohl was sensitive to Russian security interests, and as a cautious, consensus-oriented politician, he agreed with Kinkel that EU membership was more important than NATO membership as well as being less destabilizing to the German-Russian relationship. In fact, if there is any one theme, which this pragmatic politician seemed to hold above all others, it was the importance of European integration.

Yet the chancellor recognized that the domestic politics of Western Europe as well as the complex EU accession process meant that EU membership would be much slower in coming than NATO membership and that something had to be done to bridge this gap. In addition, the U.S.-German relationship was another pillar of Kohl's policy, along with the EU and a good relationship with Russia. NATO enlargement would keep the United States in Europe in spite of growing parochial, if not isolationist, tendencies in American politics. The alternative to NATO enlargement would be the bilateralization of German security policy in East Central Europe and thus the danger of unilateralism and competing alliances.

By early 1993, no real policy position had been agreed upon, and Weisser suggested to Rühe that he go public with his views in a speech he was scheduled to give at the International Institute for Strategic Studies (IISS) in London in March 1993. Before the IISS speech, the defense minister had already begun to broach the subject of NATO enlargement, but he was more explicit in his comments in London. These remarks reflected the minister's anxiety that while it was becoming clear that the new democracies of East

Central Europe would become members of the EU, this would leave open the question of their security status. Would they have the protection of NATO without membership in the alliance? If NATO did not open its doors to them, would the WEU then become a competitor with NATO? Finally, and most important from the American perspective, would the United States acquire a backdoor security commitment to these new states without formally offering congressionally sanctioned guarantees? In his speech to the IISS, Rühe questioned whether EU membership should precede NATO membership, in effect challenging the policy of his own government.

Sometime after the IISS speech, Rühe agreed with Weisser's proposal that the RAND Corporation be approached to provide studies and advocacy for the policy of NATO enlargement. Three leading RAND analysts—F. Stephen Larrabee, Richard Kugler, and Ronald Asmus—wrote an influential *Foreign Affairs* article around the time of Rühe's speech,[18] in which they argued that

> geopolitical competition between Germany and Russia along the eastern arc (of crisis) . . . threatens to reactivate old fault lines and dormant historical rivalries. . . . Germany's "strategic emancipation" was a key step in NATO's transformation. . . . Without a strong Germany that fully participates in new security roles, including combat missions, the likelihood of an American withdrawal from Europe increases.[19]

Asmus sent a copy of this article to Ulrich Weisser, and this was the beginning of the intellectual interaction with the German ministry. Rühe's inclination toward the RAND approach was reinforced by his understanding that NATO enlargement would not be decided in Germany alone, and that he needed RAND to make the case in Washington.

The issue of RAND working for the German government was raised with the U.S. undersecretary of defense for policy, Walter Slocombe, who had no objections to the German Defense Ministry approaching RAND so long as RAND shared the results with the Pentagon. In the fall of 1993, RAND's president, James Thomson, agreed that the think tank should take on its first national security contract with a foreign government.[20] This placed RAND in the delicate position of becoming an advocate within the United States debate for a policy being urged by another government, although the thinking of RAND's analysts had been running in the same direction as that of Rühe and Weisser. Asmus, along with Stephen Larrabee and Richard Kugler, became key advocates for the policy within the American and broader

NATO debate.[21] This was also an important sign of the times—that globalization had now begun within the American strategic community and that think tanks consequently could no longer remain national institutions. In this respect, RAND was undergoing the transformation that had already begun within American universities and research institutions.

The RAND team was commissioned to conceptualize a plan for NATO enlargement for the German defense minister, which he subsequently approved. Elements of the ideas from the briefing were later published in *Survival*.[22] The essence of the study was to offer three options for enlargement: one that favored EU enlargement preceding NATO enlargement; one that advocated a "wait and see" attitude; and one (the RAND-Rühe preferred option) labeled Promote Stability, which urged that NATO enlargement precede EU enlargement. Rühe and Weisser were impressed with the briefing, and the minister asked the authors to brief NATO on its contents.

The RAND analysts presented the results of their work to NATO defense ministers, legislators, and others. More than 150 people in all were briefed by RAND. As one Department of State official who was working on the NATO enlargement issue at the time recalled, the RAND briefings were the most direct and effective linkage of policymakers in the U.S. government to the broader ideas behind the policy. As this official put it:

> The only things U.S. [government] policymakers paid attention to were the *New York Times* and the *Washington Post* and the RAND briefers. RAND was effective because it used charts and graphics to concisely make a point and because they could link broader concepts and trends to policy options. The most telling point the RAND briefers made was that enlargement gave NATO a new lease on life.

An important link was also provided by Senator Richard Lugar (R-Ind.). He read the draft of the RAND analysts' *Foreign Affairs* article in the spring of 1993 and called the authors to his office to discuss it. His June National Press Club "Out of Area, Out of Business" speech contained a number of RAND ideas. Rühe was also seeing Lugar often, leading Richard Holbrooke —then the U.S. ambassador in Bonn—to mockingly state that he was "shocked at this back channel."

Within the German government, a major dispute broke out between the Foreign Office and the Ministry of Defense over Rühe's initiative. Foreign Minister Kinkel argued that the rapid-enlargement approach would damage relations with Russia, and Kohl tended to support Kinkel, at least through the end of 1993.[23] The support that Russian president Boris Yeltsin had given to NATO enlargement in August had been suddenly reversed on October 1, followed by the crisis of October 3 through 5, which ended in the storming of the Russian parliament. Kohl at this time called Rühe and pulled him back, urging caution until Yeltsin's position could stabilize.

Richard Holbrooke and the American Debate

The initial official American reaction to Rühe's ideas was reserved and skeptical. A number of prominent former officials were supportive of NATO enlargement, including Zbigniew Brzezinski, Richard Burt, and Henry Kissinger. The German factor was important to all of them. Brzezinski was the most explicit about the need to contain Germany as a principal reason, writing, "involving Germany in a wider framework allows the U.S. to cope with Europe's central security problem of the twentieth century, how to cope with the reality of Germany's power."[24] Kissinger wrote in the summer of 1994 that "further delay (in NATO enlargement) invites Germany and Russia to fill the vacuum between them either unilaterally or bilaterally—a contingency everyone in Europe, Germany above all, seeks to avoid."[25]

To those officials in the Clinton administration who were pushing enlargement, the German factor was also important. As one staff member of the NSC later put it, "Germany still could not be trusted and did not trust itself. The alternative to NATO enlargement was German enlargement." If NATO did not enlarge, Germans might draw the conclusion that NATO was no longer relevant to their central interests and that other alternatives might have to be sought. However, the President's National Security adviser, Anthony Lake, did not believe Germany was central to the decision.

Other administration officials were more reserved about Rühe's ideas, most important Deputy Secretary of State Strobe Talbott and Defense Secretary Les Aspin. Talbott's concerns were well known and centered on his priority for the Russian relationship over approaches to Eastern and Central Europe. The Pentagon was also opposed. As one American analyst deeply involved in the policy debate at the time remembers, "For DOD [the Department of Defense] loose nukes were the issue and NATO enlargement screwed up this Russia agenda. This was really a debate about the Russia agenda and the arms control agenda."

The key figure in shifting American policy toward enlargement was Richard Holbrooke. Although Anthony Lake and others were central to the decision made in Washington, Holbrooke made it happen. One German official called it "Holbrooke's baby," and Stephen Larrabee stated flatly, "It wouldn't have happened if there wasn't Dick Holbrooke." Holbrooke was initially a skeptic when he arrived in Bonn as U.S. ambassador in the spring of 1993. He came to Germany believing that the new post–Cold War German-American relationship would rest on commerce and finance rather than on the old strategic concerns. The centerpiece of his efforts would lie in creating a new German-American business dialogue rather than upon shaping a new NATO. However, as one leading German official put it, "Holbrooke was transformed from Saul to Paul on NATO while he was in Germany."

The subsequent history of American policy on NATO enlargement is best described by James M. Goldgeier. Pressures to do something originated with two prominent leaders, Lech Walesa and Václav Havel, during their meeting with President Clinton during the dedication of the Holocaust Memorial in Washington in April 1993.[26] Lake and his allies in the State Department and the NSC began to gradually push the policy against the opposition of the Pentagon and Talbott.

At about the same time, Lake's efforts to get administration support for NATO enlargement ran into the opposition of Secretary of State Warren Christopher. At a Cabinet meeting on October 18, the administration accepted Talbott's go-slow approach on NATO enlargement, proposing the Partnership for Peace (PfP) as an alternate to membership.[27]

This policy was articulated by Defense Secretary Aspin at the NATO Defense Ministers' meeting in Travemünde on October 20 and 21. In an interview given on the plane trip to Germany, the American defense secretary made it clear that PfP was designed to slow NATO enlargement, not accelerate it. Before the opening of the meeting, Rühe told the press that "this is not about extending the old NATO to the east but is much more about opening membership for new members in a new NATO." He went on to state that the NATO summit in Brussels should "give a clear signal that it will both open the Western security structures while offering a new security partnership with Russia."[28] In his remarks to the meeting on October 20, the German defense minister contrasted his position with that of his American counterpart, urging that there be a consensus on "agreement on the eventual admission of new members to the Western security structures." Although the German defense minister and his advisers came away from Travemünde believing that PfP was designed to slow NATO membership rather than accelerate it, he did not accept this as either final or desirable. In his statements to the press at the conclusion of the meeting, the minister was clear in his interpretation of the results of the meeting:

> My understanding of the U.S. proposal is: We expect and welcome the enlargement of NATO to include the new democracies in the east. The timing and extent of such an enlargement will depend upon the agreement stipulated in Article 10 of the North Atlantic treaty as well as the willingness and ability of each of these states to meet the standards and requirements of membership with consideration given to the security requirements of all CSCE states. *Neither partnership in peace or other North Atlantic Council activities are considered a substitute for NATO membership.* (author's italics)

One German paper labeled Rühe as "the loser in the enlargement debate," although he had brought the issue onto the agenda and had given it respectability.[29] Yet Rühe persisted the following month at a NATO Defense Ministerial in Brussels, stating that membership was a question of "if" rather than "when." Sometime between Travemünde in October and the president's visit to Brussels for the NATO summit and to Prague immediately thereafter, Clinton came around to supporting NATO enlargement.

When Holbrooke arrived in Bonn, he knew that NATO enlargement was a minority view within the administration. When Asmus and Larrabee came to Bonn in the fall of 1993 to brief Rühe on the RAND study, Holbrooke told them: "I am with you but be careful. There is no U.S. government support yet for this and you are in cahoots with Rühe whose position is not compatible with Kohl's. If you get too far out I will have to disown you." He was clearly concerned about getting caught in the middle of a German domestic political war. Yet both Larrabee and Asmus left the meeting believing that the American ambassador supported the direction in which they were going. By May of 1994, Holbrooke was telling Asmus, "Of course I am with you."

Holbrooke had many discussions with key German figures, including Rühe and Weisser. What finally pushed him toward open support was the same combination of ambition and strategic sense that had propelled his generational counterpart, Rühe. That Holbrooke was ambitious was hardly a secret. Hoping for a key position in the new Clinton administration, or at least the ambassadorship to Japan, he had to settle for the Bonn posting as a consolation prize, much as Rühe settled for Defense while still hoping for the Foreign Ministry. Holbrooke needed to ride an issue back to Washington as soon as possible. NATO enlargement and the war in Bosnia, rather than a business and trade dialogue, were two issues that dovetailed and brought Europe back onto the administration's foreign policy agenda. As pressures grew in the United States for the administration to show leadership in foreign policy, especially in Bosnia, Holbrooke became a leading advocate for taking bold action both in Bosnia and with regard to NATO enlargement.

In addition to ambition, Holbrooke became convinced of the strategic necessity of NATO enlargement. What was finally compelling to him was that it was crucial to Germany. He concluded that the policy was in the interests of both Germany and Poland and agreed that either security would be exported or instability would be imported. If Germany became insecure, the classic security dilemma that had plagued Central Europe would reemerge, namely, the competition of Germany and Russia for security and influence in the lands between their borders. These were the same arguments that Brzezinski found persuasive, as did Senator Richard Lugar (R-Ind.) and some NSC staff members, including Stephen Flanagan, an early supporter of NATO's eastern extension.[30]

Finally, Holbrooke drew the conclusion from the war in Bosnia that the United States had to take the lead in Europe. Bosnia was a disaster because Europe had tried unsuccessfully to lead. This should not happen again.[31] Holbrooke was also concerned about the backdoor commitment issue, that allowing EU enlargement to precede NATO enlargement meant that the United States and NATO would be committed to the security of the new members of the EU and WEU without formally deciding that it wanted to make such a commitment. He argued that Russia issues had to be balanced against the issues of a security vacuum in Europe and that the European agenda should not be paralyzed by the long Russian transition.

By the summer of 1994, Holbrooke was called back to Washington to vigorously push the policy. His return, in the words of a key American player, brought a "European voice" to the table:

Even though Strobe [Talbott] was on board, the Administration did not have a European policy; in the late spring of 1994, it was decided to bring Holbrooke back; this gave the European point of view a strong voice in the U.S. [government] and countered Talbott's Russia voice; this led to a balanced policy.

Throughout 1994, the German defense and foreign ministers continued to disagree on priorities, with the chancellor allowing them both to continue their increasingly public conflict. Reports emerged of differences between Kohl and Rühe on enlargement.[32] Yet Kohl stated at the NATO Brussels summit that the alliance had decided to open itself to new members, although he remained vague about the timing and the candidates. This was consistent with Clinton's statement in Prague immediately after the summit that the question was when and how not whether the alliance would take new members. The Bundestag debate, which followed the summit, revealed broad support from both the governing coalition and the opposition Social Democrats for both the concept that the eastern border of the EU and NATO should not be the German-Polish border and the PfP approach.

Rühe began to state that NATO membership would precede EU membership and that Russia could not be a member of either the EU or NATO. He was contradicted by the new American defense secretary, William Perry, who stated that he would not be so categorical as Rühe. The two also differed on the speed with which NATO enlargement would occur.[33] These differences continued through the defense ministers' meeting in Seville, where once again Rühe was out in front of his colleagues in supporting early NATO membership for the Visegrad four (the Czech Republic, Hungary, Poland, and Slovakia). Kinkel criticized Rühe in October for his support of a "rash" and "selective" widening of NATO, which would lead to new bloc building. This produced an angry outburst by Kohl, who stated that "I am absolutely opposed to any minister publicly debating this theme, no matter what his name is."[34]

Following its reelection in October 1994, the new government's coalition agreement took the Kohl-Kinkel line that NATO enlargement should be linked to EU enlargement. The insistence on linking EU and NATO enlargement was based upon Kinkel and Kohl's belief that by embedding NATO enlargement within the EU context, the confrontation between NATO and Russia would be lessened and differing zones of security within the EU would be avoided. What seemed to be at issue between the United States and Germany was not the end goal but the tempo needed to get there.

The final turning point was reached in November following the Republican landslide in the American congressional elections and the German election. The Clinton administration, having decided in the fall to push ahead with enlargement, was now prodded further by the Republican challenge. German press reports, based on Foreign Office sources, and interviews conducted for this study indicate that the German government suddenly felt that it was being pushed by the Clinton administration toward a rapid enlargement of NATO. These sources believed the reasons for the sudden American decision to move beyond PfP to membership for the Visegrad four were to be found in the domestic political pressure mounting on Clinton to provide leadership in foreign policy. Blocked at home, it was argued, the president was seeking a spectacular success in other fields.

The Foreign Office was alarmed by this new urgency in Washington, fearing that it would destabilize the east and alienate Russia. The German ambassador to NATO, Hermann von Richthoven, made some openly critical comments just before the NATO foreign ministers' meeting in Brussels about America's "dangerous policies" on NATO enlargement. He charged that the United States had unilaterally changed its policy without consulting its allies. As one senior official who was at the center of things in the Foreign Office at the time later recalled:

> The policy became Holbrooke's baby, and Kohl came around with reluctance to accepting it. He and Clinton reached an agreement. The deal was that the U.S. would push NATO enlargement and Germany would work to keep Russia from being alienated. By the end of 1994, it was settled in principle, although not the conditions. This was strictly a U.S. policy, and we felt pressured to accept it.

What had happened in Washington between the time Holbrooke was called back in the summer and the push at the end of the year was that Lake and Holbrooke, with the acquiescence of Talbott, had pushed the policy through over the continued resistance of the Department of Defense. Holbrooke became the Clinton administration's "enforcer" of the policy.[35] After a series of sometimes heated meetings between State and Defense, the decision to move ahead with NATO enlargement was finally clear by December of 1994. As Goldgeier concludes,

> By the end of 1994 everyone in the administration finally understood that the president favored NATO's enlargement. But the president had not answered two key questions: when would enlargement take place, and who would be invited to join. He did not answer the first until October 1996, and he did not answer the second until June 1997.[36]

By early December, first at the NATO foreign ministers' meeting in Brussels and then at the CSCE Budapest summit, Kohl, Kinkel, and Rühe were all saying that NATO would enlarge along with the EU and that a partnership with Russia would also have to be formed. Russia would have no veto right, however, and Russia should not be confronted with new alliance members overnight.[37]

The French Factor

France chose to subordinate the NATO enlargement decision to its larger goal of Europeanizing the Atlantic alliance and, consequently, its policy on enlargement must be placed in this larger context.[38] France gave priority to building a European security identity, at first separate from NATO within the EU. In the early 1990s, the government of François Mitterrand opposed any enlargement of the political role of NATO and any monopoly claims for the alliance in the area of security. The French government preferred that the EU and the WEU undertake the political aspects of security policy in Europe. French policy only shifted with the replacement of Mitterrand by Jacques Chirac as president in 1995. By then it had become clear to France that NATO was not going to be displaced by the WEU or the EU, and that the alliance would remain the central security institution for the foreseeable future. As a result, French policy shifted to the objective of building a European security identity within NATO. As one French analyst put it:

> France's change grew out of an observation and was based on a bet. The observation was that Europeans resisted the establishment of a European defense pillar, and that in any case, they were not ready to envision one outside of NATO. The bet was that the development of this pillar would be made easier by French reintegration with NATO, since it could not be built outside the Alliance.[39]

French reluctance to cooperate with NATO began to change with the NATO summit held in Rome in December 1991, when the alliance acknowledged the European Security and Defense Identity. France still resisted the new strategic concept that seemed to broaden the alliance's mission, while at the same time it cooperated with the United States in the Gulf War and with NATO in Bosnia. As NATO began to develop more flexible crisis reaction forces, France pushed for the Eurocorps.

However, as the relationship between NATO and the WEU began to become clearer—and as NATO began to think about a European pillar, flexible forces, and command arrangements such as the Combined Joint Task Force—France became more relaxed about NATO and drew closer to its structures. However, French policymakers insisted that they were Europeanizing NATO rather than reinforcing the military integration of the alliance.[40]

These developments gradually softened French opposition to NATO enlargement. France was concerned about what its leaders considered an eastern orientation of unified Germany both in the EU and in NATO. They only reluctantly accepted the North Atlantic Cooperation Council and did not participate in its first meeting. France saw NATO enlargement as "a threat to its role as the political and geostrategic middle power in Europe,"[41] and the French government feared that the new East Central European members of NATO would be pro-American just as they would be pro-German in the EU. The government of Edouard Balladur preferred PfP and its own stability pact over NATO enlargement.

When the German government had declared by the end of 1994 that EU membership and NATO membership should be seen as parallel processes, France agreed, with Foreign Minister Alain Juppé speaking of "synchronization." Even though Defense Minister Charles Millon threatened in September 1996 to link NATO reform to enlargement, France's options for opposing NATO enlargement were limited. Because President Chirac had advocated EU membership for the Visegrad four and Romania, he could not credibly block NATO membership for these states. He also recognized by then that Germany and the United States had decided on NATO enlargement, and that it was futile for France to resist. France became an advocate for a more ambitious enlargement than that proposed in Bonn and Washington, moving "from a position of reticence on enlargement to one of full support for an expansion that would not be limited either by the American preference for Poland, the Czech Republic and Hungary, or by Germany's desire to stop with its neighbors."[42] France now advocated a southern enlargement, pushing for the inclusion of Romania, while Italy sponsored Slovenian membership, to complement the eastern push of Germany.

The Clinton administration, taking a "Small Is Beautiful plus Robust Open Doors" approach, opposed these French efforts on three grounds. First, it feared that inclusion of Romania and Slovenia would push Baltic membership to the fore; second, there were concerns that the Senate would balk at a larger first wave; and, third and most important, key administration figures wanted to keep open the promise of a second round.[43] Though the French viewed this as hegemonic behavior, the administration simply overrode French objections, although it included language in the summit statement of Madrid mentioning Romania and Slovenia as possible future members. President Clinton also made a special trip to Bucharest to help assuage Romanian concerns. The German government gave lip service to the French position, but it did not make a serious attempt to change the American decision.

Conclusions

Although the saga of NATO enlargement continued through the Madrid summit of July 1997, and Germany played an important role in shaping the Founding Act with Russia, the essentials were decided by the end of 1994. German policymakers had reached a consensus that was broadly accepted by all parties and the public. The contours of the post–Cold War European security structure had been set. NATO, not the WEU or the Organization for Security and Cooperation in Europe (OSCE), was to be the central pillar of European security. What are some of the conclusions that can be drawn from this case?

First, as was the case with the end of the Cold War, the German-American relationship was the central one for this broad European policy outcome. However, in contrast to Two-plus-Four, in this case the Americans pushed the final outcome against a divided and ambivalent German government after being initially provoked by the German Ministry of Defense. The vision of the Bush administration that the United States should remain a European power continued, after initial hesitation, into the Clinton administration. Early preferences in Washington for a more independent European security pillar did not survive Bosnia and NATO enlargement. Germany, when forced to choose between Paris and Washington in the defense area, chose Washington—much as it had done in the early 1960s under Konrad Adenauer. The Eurocorps became subordinated to NATO, which finally took priority over the EU and WEU in terms of security both for the Balkans and for East Central Europe. OSCE became a holding room for states that could not gain entry into NATO.

Germany may have been ambivalent about how quickly it wanted to expand NATO, but there was a consensus that it was in the German interest to do so. This contrasted with French and British diffidence on enlargement. Yet once Bonn and Washington decided, Paris and London followed.

The German factor in the decision was important in a number of ways. American policymakers believed that the Germans wanted NATO enlargement and feared that if they did not get it they would look for alternatives to the alliance for the future. The German government wanted enlargement, but it was divided about the pace and preferred that the United States take the lead. In some ways, the NATO enlargement case repeats the misperceptions that surrounded the decision of the Kennedy administration to push for the Multilateral Force in the 1960s. At that time, many American decisionmakers believed that without this force, Germany might decide to develop its own independent nuclear capability, a concern that was not justified by the political situation in Germany. Again in the late 1970s, the Jimmy Carter administration pushed ahead with the double-track decision, which led to the deployment of Intermediate-Range Nuclear Forces, in large part because of concerns raised by Helmut Schmidt, who then tried to moderate what he saw as an overreaction to his proposal.

Second, the decision was less a major strategic reorientation than an adaptation and extension of the strategic paradigm that prevailed during the Cold War. Certainly the NATO that was being enlarged was different in its missions, but its strategic rationale remained fundamentally unchanged. As one German official interviewed for this study put it, the West, like West Germany in 1990, was faced with the choice of either a major restructuring of institutions and approaches or with transferring what had worked in the West to the East. Like West Germany, NATO chose its version of article 23 rather than calling for a constitutional convention and a new constitution. NATO is still an American-led and -dominated alliance, with the continuing purposes of containing Russian expansion, managing the German problem, and preventing the renationalization of European security policy, although its transformation to something beyond this had begun during this period.

Although many academics and think tank analysts had questioned the rationale for NATO after the collapse of the Soviet Union and the democratization and marketization of the former Warsaw Pact, for policymakers it is much less risky to follow an incrementalist approach and to make discrete and reversible changes to existing institutions than to create new structures in a zero-based approach.

Lessons for the U.S.-German-French Triangle

NATO enlargement was essentially about East Central Europe. The fundamental strategic rationale for the decision was to prevent a vacuum forming between Russia and Germany. Germany was the nation with the most at stake in the policy, while France had little incentive to enlarge an institution about which it had strong reservations by bringing in states more likely to be sympathetic to German and American interests than to those of France.

The Paris-Bonn-Washington triangle seemed to operate on the principle that a close German-American relationship on an issue of key concern to Germany was sufficient to mute French concerns and did not lead to significant tensions between any of the three states. In fact, France was able to make significant progress on its major priority, the Europeanization of European security, in return for acquiescing to a policy in which it had a marginal stake.

The German interest in NATO enlargement was satisfied by the entry of the three key Central European states into NATO. There was less German interest in a further enlargement. The U.S. position, which favored an open door, was followed by the George W. Bush administration, which pursued further enlargement. The French continued to favor enlargement to the south and southeast.

Finally, regarding the Balkans, NATO regional enlargement was spurred in part by the functional expansion into crisis management and peacemaking roles for the alliance. The alliance realized that to survive it had to be able to operate beyond the boundaries of NATO. The hope that the Balkan forest fires would burn out on their own, without spreading to the geographical core of Europe, was a casualty of Bosnia. NATO operations there helped open the door for a greater French role in the alliance as well as transforming the German one and reestablishing an American role in post–Cold War European security. Bosnia also seemed to be at least a setback for a European security identity outside NATO. Kosovo began with the same lessons but may have ended with a quite different conclusion.

Notes

1. See, e.g., Michael R. Gordon, "The Anatomy of a Misunderstanding," *New York Times*, May 25, 1997. Michael Mandelbaum argues that NATO expansion will "violate at least the spirit of Germany unification which implied a bargain between East and West: The Soviet Union had allowed a united Germany to be part of NATO in order to assure its firm anchoring in the West. The West agreed in turn not to bring NATO's military might near the Soviet borders, an agreement that included the territory of the former East Germany." Michael Mandelbaum, *The Dawn of Peace in Europe* (New York: Twentieth Century Fund, 1996), 62–63.

2. Dietrich Genscher, *Erinnerungen* (Berlin: Siedler, 1995), 835; English translation: *Rebuilding a House Divided* (New York: Broadway, 1998).

3. Condoleezza Rice and Philip Zelikow, *Germany Unified* (Cambridge, Mass.: Harvard University Press, 1995), 180.

4. Ibid., 182.

5. Ibid., 183.

6. For examples, see Gordon, "Anatomy of a Misunderstanding," 3.

7. This was confirmed in interviews with a number of officials in both Bonn and Washington. Philip Zelikow, who is intimately familiar with all the documentation of the period stated, according to Michael Gordon's account, that, in Gordon's words, "close scrutiny of the verbal diplomatic exchange does not support Moscow's claim that it was bamboozled. . . . He says that the United States went over the revised proposal (which extended NATO into eastern Germany) on several occasions and the Russians never complained. The diplomatic record also shows that the two sides never discussed the possibility of Poland, Hungary, or other Central European nations joining NATO. If the Soviets took Mr. Baker's pledge as ruling out the alliance's expansion, they failed to nail it down. No Soviet ever said, 'NATO may extend to East Germany but no farther.'" Gordon, "Anatomy of a Misunderstanding," 3.

8. Robert L. Hutchings, *American Diplomacy and the End of the Cold War: An Insider's Account of U.S. Policy in Europe 1989–1992* (Baltimore: Johns Hopkins University Press; and Washington, D.C.: Woodrow Wilson Center Press, 1997), chap. 3.

9. Rice and Zelikow, *Germany Unified,* 322–23. They contend that "The original concept for the diplomatic liaison missions anticipated this development" (fn 78, 466).

10. As one German observer who observed Rühe at close quarters put it, "He saw Kinkel as weak and wanted to take advantage of the situation. He felt Kinkel was too tied down with EU matters and meetings while he never got into EU and European policy. Kohl and Bitterlich [his security adviser] were interested in Europe, not in security policy. He sensed an opportunity left by Kinkel's weakness and, as he always said, it was a win-win situation."

11. Interview with Ulrich Weisser, June 24, 1997.

12. In his inauguration speech to the WEU Council, Rühe stressed that the creation of new cooperation relations "with countries between the Atlantic and the Commonwealth of Independent States" was the consequence of perspectives opened by the Maastricht Treaty, which makes the WEU the defense component of the future European Union, in the framework of a process in which Central European countries have to be included. "WEU Ministers Set Up Consultation Mode with East European States," *Agence Europe,* June 23, 1992. He was consistent with his predecessor's increasing emphasis upon a stronger European security identity. See Gerhard Stoltenberg's remarks to the Wehrkunde conference in February. Werner Stanzl, "Quayle Besteht auf NATO Treu," *Der Standard,* February 10, 1992. Stoltenberg was so pro-European in his remarks that a British general present referred to him as "Monsieur Stoltenberg."

13. Quoted in *Agence Europe,* June 19, 1992.

14. James Goldgeier makes the same point with regard to the concept of separable but not separate forces, which emerged later. "It would also head off any effort by the French to turn the WEU into a competitor to NATO in the European security environment," James M. Goldgeier, *Not Whether But When: The U.S. Decision to Enlarge NATO* (Washington, D.C.: Brookings Institution Press, 1999), 57.

15. Reinhard Wolf, "The Doubtful Mover: Germany and NATO Expansion," in *Will*

NATO Go East? The Debate over Enlarging the Atlantic Alliance, ed. David Haglund (Kingston, Ont.: Centre for International Relations, Queens University, 1996), 197–214.

16. Wolf, "Doubtful Mover," 199.

17. As one senior member of the Foreign Office said later, "We said to the Central Europeans, is it your primary interest to be a member of NATO? The threat is gone so why must it be a priority? Think about the EU first." Behind this reasoning was also a desire for Europe to take the lead and to avoid having the United States remain the leading player in the process. "EU enlargement would be the only game in town and the U.S. role would be lessened. NATO enlargement meant that the Americans were diverting water to their side of the field."

18. Ronald D. Asmus, Richard L. Kugler, and F. Stephen Larrabee, "Building a New NATO," *Foreign Affairs* (September 1993): 28–40.

19. Asmus, Kugler, and Larrabee, "Building a New NATO," 30, 33.

20. This was done apparently in hopes of landing more operationally oriented contracts from other European ministries of defense.

21. The RAND study was described in Focus magazine, with the note that Rühe told the magazine that in the important aspects, his views about a reformed Western defense community were similar to those of the RAND authors. P. Gruber et al., "U.S.A.: Alles haengt von Deutschland ab," *Focus,* August 30, 1993, 158–61.

22. Ronald D. Asmus et al., "NATO Expansion: The Next Steps," *Survival* (Spring 1995): 7–33.

23. Kohl told Polish prime minister Hanna Suchocka in October that while he favored some kind of Western security guarantees, he was not sure that these should occur through membership rather than through simply closer levels of cooperation. See Wolf, "Doubtful Mover," 203.

24. Quoted in Jane Perlez, "Blunt Reasons for Enlarging NATO: Curbs on Germany," New York Times, December 7, 1997. See also Ronald Steel, "Instead of NATO," *New York Review of Books,* January 15, 1998, 21. Steel argues, "But the desire to contain not only Moscow but also, to a lesser degree, Berlin is the simple truth that lies behind all the window dressing about 'incl. U.S. in on' and 'fairness' and 'overcoming Yalta.'"

25. Henry Kissinger, "It's an Alliance, Not a Relic," *New York Times,* August 16, 1994. See also F. Stephen Larrabee, *East European Security after the Cold War* (Santa Monica, Calif.: RAND, 1993), 172–77. For a discussion of the impact of the German factor on American thinking on NATO enlargement, see also Roberto Menotti, "The U.S. Policy of NATO Enlargement: Decsionmaking Process, Political Context, and the Policy Agenda," unpublished draft of paper, Aspen Institute, Rome.

26. See James M. Goldgeier, "NATO Expansion: The Anatomy of a Decision," *Washington Quarterly,* Winter 1998, 86. For an insider's account, see Ronald D. Asmus, *Opening NATO's Door: How the Alliance Remade Itself for a New Era* (New York: Columbia University Press, 2002).

27. See Goldgeier, "NATO Expansion," 90–91; and Goldgeier, *Not Whether But When.*

28. "Einführung des Bundesminisers der Verteidigung, Volker Rühe, in das Pressegespräch am 18 Oktober 1993 vor der Konferenz der Verteidigungsminister der Allianz am 19–21 Oktober in Travemünde."

29. Stefan Kornelius, "Die NATO verordnet sich eine lange Denkpause," *Süddeutsche Zeitung,* October 23, 1993, 4.

30. See Goldgeier, "NATO Expansion, 69–70.
31. In Holbrooke's own words, "When I arrived in Germany in September 1993, I believed that EU membership was more important and would arrive first. What turned me around was the realization that the EU, mired in its own Euro-mess . . . was not going to invite any of these countries in, at the earliest, before 2003." Quoted in Goldgeier, *Not Whether But When,* 69.
32. "Vor dem Gifetreffen des Nordatlantiks-Paktes in Brüssel Kinkel: NATO Erweiterung ein langfristiger Prozess," *Süddeutsche Zeitung,* January 8, 1994. Because it was in Kohl's interest to see this policy realized but not to be seen as pushing it, especially when the Clinton administration seemed not to be on board, he did not wish a clear resolution in the coalition's position.
33. Ewald König, "Deutschlands Vertiedigungsminister glaubt an die AU.S.weitung des Paktes," *Die Presse,* June 17, 1994; "Rühe-Keine NATO and EU Mitgliedschaft Russlands," Reuters German News Service, July 4, 1994; "Perry und Rühe uneins über Verhältnis zu Russland," Reuters German News Service, September 9, 1994; "Rühe-NATO Erweiterung noch vor 2000," Reuters German News Service, September 9, 1994.
34. "Kohl Kristisiert Streit Zwischen Rühe and Kinkel," Reuters German News Service, October 7, 1994; Christian Müller, "Demonstrative Siegeszuversicht Kohls," *Neue Zürcher Zeitung,* October 8, 1994, 1.
35. See Goldgeier, *Not Whether But When,* 73.
36. Ibid., 76.
37. "Kohl-Streit um NATO Erweiterung Lösebar," Reuters German News Service, December 6, 1994; "Kohl Verteidigt bei KSZE Gifel NATO Erweiterung," Reuters, December 5, 1994; "Streit Um NATO Erweiterung Prägt KSZE Gipfel," Reuters, December 5, 1994.
38. For a good summary of the evolution of the French position on NATO enlargement see, Pascal Boniface, "The NATO Debate in France," in *NATO Enlargement: The National Debates over Ratification,* ed. Simon Serfaty and Stephen Cambone (Washington, D.C.: Center for Strategic and International Studies, 1997), 39–54; and Valerie Gurein-Sendelbach, *Frankreich und das vereinigte Deutschland: Interessen und Perzeptionen im Spannungsfeld* (Opladen: Leske and Budrich, 1999), 281–300.
39. Boniface, "NATO Debate in France," 44.
40. See Guerin-Sendelbach, *Frankreich und das vereinigte Deutschland,* 289.
41. Ibid., 297.
42. Boniface, "NATO Debate in France," 49.
43. Goldgeier, *Not Whether But When,* 117–22.

Chapter 15

NATO and the Balkan Challenge: An American Perspective

Kori Schake

The NATO member states, and none more purposefully than the United States, used the Balkan crises as a means to cement their preferred approach to crisis management in Europe. The United States did not consider its interests engaged in the Balkans to the same degree as did its European allies, and only committed its political leverage and military power to the problem in 1995 when it judged that differences over Bosnia were endangering NATO's future. The United States committed its ground forces to peace enforcement efforts to ensure that NATO would survive and retain its primacy in European security; bringing peace to the Balkans was always a secondary motivation.

As of 2000, the divisions of labor in Bosnia, both across the Atlantic and among institutions, represented Washington's preferred equilibrium of effort. Europeans contributed 80 percent and the United States 20 percent of the military effort in Bosnia. NATO was responsible for military implementation, the European Union led on civil reconstruction, the Organization for Security and Cooperation in Europe (OSCE) managed press freedoms and monitored elections, and the United Nations led on issues of justice and human rights. This division of labor supported Europe's ambitions to build an EU defense capability, and it matched the limits of U.S. interests.

These balances have been more difficult to sustain in Kosovo, both because of the disparity in combat power between the United States and its allies, and the unwillingness of Washington to commit that power. The division of labor emerging in Kosovo, in which the United States provides the preponderance of war-fighting forces (and therefore dominates decisions on the use of force) and Europe provides the long-term enforcement forces and civil authority (thereby relieving the United States of responsibility for the ultimate success of the intervention), is unlikely to be satisfactory to either side of the Atlantic. As a result, NATO's intervention in Kosovo may force the United States and Europe to return to basic questions about the divergence of transatlantic interests that called NATO's future into question before the Balkan crises.

Yugoslavia Collapsing: The George H. W. Bush Administration

European governments, especially France and Germany, were strongly motivated to ameliorate the suffering of victims of the conflict and negotiate a peaceful solution to the wars in Yugoslavia. Both France and Germany took leadership roles at different times to precipitate Western involvement in the former Yugoslavia—Germany in the 1992 recognition of Slovenia and Croatia's independence; and France in the establishment of the United Nations Protection Force, the deployment of a Franco-British Rapid Reaction Force, and Prime Minister Jacques Chirac's personal engagement to begin the spring 1994 NATO air campaign enforcing UN mandates.

From the beginning of the Yugoslav wars, the United States sought to limit its involvement. Being geographically farther from the Balkans, Washington did not feel the pressure of immigration and domestic social unrest that shaped European reactions. The George H. W. Bush administration was certainly a foreign policy–oriented presidency, but it did not consider the Balkans a strategic priority for the United States. The top priorities on the administration's agenda were consolidating a unified Germany into NATO Europe, making progress in strategic nuclear arms reduction and stabilization with Russia and the former Soviet states, and constraining Iraq after the Gulf War. There was also very little pressure from the American public for intervention in the Balkans.

Key leaders in the Bush administration were strongly opposed to U.S. involvement in the Balkans. Secretary of State James Baker famously declared in 1991 that "we don't have a dog in that fight."[1] Undersecretary of State Lawrence Eagleburger, a former ambassador to Yugoslavia, believed the state was artificial and could not be sustained.[2] Secretary of Defense Richard Cheney and Chairman of the Joint Chiefs of Staff General Colin Powell did not believe U.S. interests were engaged or that political leaders had identified a military mission achievable within the limits those leaders had set. When presidential candidate Bill Clinton began to get some traction in challenging the Bush administration policy, General Powell (a popular figure from the Gulf War and the foremost American expert on the use of force) publicly defended the administration's unwillingness to intervene.[3]

To the extent that the United States was engaged in events in the Balkans during the Bush administration, it worked through NATO. Consolidating a Europe "whole and free" was the top priority of the Bush foreign policy team, and it viewed adapting NATO to incorporate other political and military functions as the primary means of stabilizing Europe and managing security problems that might emerge.[4]

The Bush administration wanted the widest possible sphere of NATO interest and the fewest limits on its freedom of action, not only for European purposes but also because NATO was considered important to the United States in managing security outside Europe. NATO gave Washington officials an organized, routine engagement with European allies, and the constant interaction provided the means for shaping a common strategic perspective with European states.

NATO was also considered important from a strictly military perspective, and the American military has greater influence over foreign and defense policy than do the military establishments in most other NATO countries. As a leading strategic planner in the U.S. military assessed NATO's value:

Keeping American military forces in Europe and retaining European military forces at levels and standards such that they could contribute to operations in Europe and beyond were two major reasons the American military supported retaining NATO as the traditional threat that engendered the alliance waned.[5]

That is, without NATO, Pentagon officials did not believe that the United States' European allies would maintain military forces of the size and quality to be useful fighting in coalitions with U.S. forces throughout the world. NATO gives Washington the confidence that its European allies can make a real military contribution in a conflict when their interests are also engaged.

The Bush administration's view of a NATO unhindered by regional or functional boundaries was not shared by the major European allies, not even with the suggestion that the United States might employ NATO's new responsibilities in managing crises in Yugoslavia. Instead, America's European allies focused their attention on building the capacity for action in the European Union through the Maastricht Treaty, leading diplomatic recognition of Slovenia and Croatia, initiating negotiations with the parties to the growing conflict in the former Yugoslavia, and delineating the Petersberg tasks for crisis management in the Western European Union. Luxembourg foreign minister Jacques Poos emerged from EU discussions of Yugoslavia in June 1991 to declare triumphally that "this is the hour of Europe. It is not the hour of the Americans."[6]

The United States did make incremental progress in loosening constraints on NATO's ability to manage crises. At the November 1991 Rome Summit, the allies accepted a NATO mission to reach out beyond NATO's membership and territory to shape the European security environment, and in the summer 1992 NATO and Conference on Security and Cooperation in Europe (CSCE) ministerials, the alliance secured the right to conduct peacekeeping operations with a mandate from the UN or CSCE.[7] However, the grudging European acceptance of NATO out-of-area roles reinforced U.S. hesitancy about employing those capabilities in the near future.

Despite having the statutory authority to undertake crisis management missions, NATO itself was not ready to intervene in Yugoslavia, even if the United States had been willing. The alliance's policy options had expanded, but the leaders of the principal military forces did not have a common view of what constituted "peacekeeping." The armed forces of several NATO nations had substantial experience in monitoring an existing peace as part of UN forces, others had experience as constabulary forces working in close cooperation with civilian authority to enforce colonial will, and the United States viewed peacekeeping as a lower-intensity combat mission.[8]

The first involvement by NATO member states in the former Yugoslavia were via the Western European Union maritime monitoring of the UN arms embargo against all parties to the conflict and the UN operation to assist delivery of humanitarian relief in Bosnia and Croatia. The first U.S. involvement in peacekeeping was assisting humanitarian relief in Somalia. As the George H. W. Bush administration departed, none of the allies were prepared to go further.

Yugoslavia Collapsing: The Clinton Administration

President Bill Clinton came into office having supported U.S. participation in the United Nations Protection Force and more active involvement in the Balkans generally.[9] His influential UN ambassador, Madeleine Albright, called for a U.S. strategy of "assertive multilateralism," using international institutions to contribute to, but not dominate, peacekeeping engagements. Secretary of Defense Les Aspin agreed to engage U.S. military forces in airdropping assistance into the former Yugoslavia. Secretary of State Warren Christopher went to Europe in March 1993 to listen to European ideas for managing the Balkans. In general, the Clinton administration's approach was to be less acrimonious and more supportive of European efforts to construct a defense identity within the European Union.

Congressional opposition posed a serious obstacle to a more engaged U.S. policy in the Balkans. Because it is a presidential rather than a parliamentary democracy, the U.S. system of government gives the president authority to command the armed forces in conflict and negotiate treaties; but as a practical matter, Congress largely runs defense and foreign policy.[10] The Clinton administration clearly did not succeed in persuading Congress of the merits of a more active Balkan policy; in the first year of the administration, with a Democratic majority in the House of Representatives, Congress twice nearly approved legislation forcing an end to U.S. enforcement of the UN arms embargo.

Congressional attitudes were frequently characterized, both by Europeans and the Clinton administration, as isolationist. Though there are certainly isolationists in Congress, as an explanation for U.S. actions on the Balkans, isolationism does not do justice to the seriousness of congressional concerns. There were four main strands of congressional opposition to a more active U.S. engagement in the Balkans: (1) members of the Armed Services committees, such as Senator John Warner (R-Va.) and Senator Sam Nunn (D-Ga.), who shared Colin Powell's concern about the lack of an achievable military mission and the overcommitment of American military resources; (2) opponents of an expanded role for the United Nations, including Senator Jesse Helms (R-N.C.); (3) opponents of the arms embargo as a policy choice because it limited the Bosniacs' (i.e., Muslims') ability to defend themselves, including Senate Majority Leader Robert Dole (R-Kan.); and (4) a wide spectrum of legislators, including House Armed Services chair Ron Dellums (D-Calif.) and House Budget Committee member (and later chairman) John Kasich (R-Ohio), who believed the United States had higher priorities, both foreign and domestic.

These formidable congressional opponents would have required the administration to expend an enormous amount of political capital early in the Clinton presidency to build an intervention that Congress might support. And the terms of an intervention that could garner congressional support (lifting the arms embargo, marginalization of the United Nations, strong NATO command and control, openly defending Bosniac positions, minimizing the terms of engagement for U.S. forces) were unlikely to gain support among European allies that remained committed to ameliorating the effects of the violence rather than becoming a party to the conflict.[11]

Finally, the Clinton administration came into office promising to "focus like a laser beam on the economy" and make domestic politics the president's priority. The Balkans simply could not compete with reforming health care, gaining congressional approval of the North American Free Trade Agreement, and balancing the budget, especially when building a program acceptable to both Europeans and Congress would be such an arduous task. So, for different reasons, the Clinton administration turned out to be no more likely to intervene in the Balkans than had the George H. W. Bush administration.

Changing the Calculus: A Growing NATO Role

NATO limped through the first terrible years of ethnic cleansing in the Balkans, fighting within the alliance about the post–Cold War institutional order and providing assistance on the margin to the UN operation.[12] The United States considered French acceptance in 1993 of a NATO role providing close air support to UN Protection Force (UNPROFOR) to be a major victory, especially because France assigned aircraft to the integrated military command (for the first time since 1966) in this first out-of-area NATO operation. To secure this NATO role, Washington agreed to a "dual key" system of UN political control that eviscerated the operational flexibility needed by both NATO air forces and UNPROFOR.

The United States gained another foothold for NATO in the Balkans with planning for implementation of the Vance-Owen peace plan. Because the agreement would have necessitated a peacekeeping force of about 100,000 troops, it was clearly beyond the capacity of any organization except NATO to plan and carry out. Even NATO had substantial challenges in developing processes for adapting alliance procedures to conduct out-of-area operations.[13] France was expected to be a major troop contributor to peace implementation, and therefore NATO had to create leadership posts for French military officers and assuage French concerns about the political control of military operations so that France would have a rationale for participating in NATO defense structures.

UNPROFOR's continuing difficulty and the 1994 mortar attack on Sarajevo provided a clear commonality of interests between France and the United States. Both states acknowledged the limitations of the UN in overseeing "Chapter VII" peace enforcement operations. Both states accepted that NATO would have to organize and run military operations in Bosnia if they were successfully to coerce cooperation from the parties to the conflict. The only remaining problems, from a U.S. perspective, were how to extricate UNPROFOR without humiliating either the UN or the states that had contributed forces to the operation, and how to create terms acceptable to both Congress and the allies whereby the United States would commit ground forces to a NATO operation.

Serbia's major miscalculations in the first stage of the wars of Yugoslav succession were using UNPROFOR troops as human shields during NATO airstrikes in late 1994 and attacking UN "safe areas" in July 1995. These actions coalesced anti-Serb opinion in the West and made UNPROFOR's continuation untenable, sparking a renewed commitment by the international community. The United States colluded in the clandestine arming of the Bosnian army, negotiated a combined effort by Croat and Bosnian military forces, encouraged the Croat offensive that rolled back Bosnian Serb gains on the battlefield and "simplified" the negotiating map, took the lead in negotiating a cease-fire consistent with the new territorial holdings, and committed Washington to participating in a ground enforcement operation.

Evaluating Bosnia

The U.S. intervention was justified to Congress as essential to sustaining NATO and managing security in Europe.[14] American military officers were responsible for negotiating the military annex to the Dayton Peace Accords that restricts NATO missions to imposing order and creating a secure environment. This definition of missions reduced the prospect of military objections to the intervention and made it possible for NATO to succeed in Bosnia whether or not the civil component of the peace took root. These elements, combined with a presidential promise that U.S. forces would remain in the Balkans for only one year, created the basis for congressional and public support of U.S. ground forces being deployed to the Balkans.

The Dayton Accords also established a division of labor among institutions: The UN provided overall political guidance and an international mandate; the OSCE prepared and monitored elections, monitored human rights, and undertook many of the "soft" security roles; the EU provided economic assistance and training in areas of civilian authority and governance; and NATO alone undertook the military missions associated with the accords.[15]

Without NATO's intervention in the Balkans, the alliance could not have pivoted from its Cold War function of organizing Western military establishments for a large-scale, short-warning attack by Warsaw Pact forces from the East to create a new role in managing crises throughout Europe. Had NATO remained confined to Article V missions of collective defense, it would have ceased to be important to either Europe or the United States. Under those conditions, even if NATO had persisted as an institution, it would have lost the political importance that makes worthwhile all the effort of forging consensus and melding together military establishments.

For all the irritation in the transatlantic relationship during the process, the United States achieved its central strategic objectives of establishing NATO's primacy among European security organizations and expanding the range of the alliance's functions. The shrewd use by Washington of the Dayton Peace Accords further served to cement its preferred institutional division of labor for European security. Bosnia also became the way NATO learned to operate "at sixteen" (i.e., with sixteen members including France), creating both a reason for the French to return to participating in NATO defense processes and an acceptable role for France.

President Clinton's promise that the Dayton Accords would rapidly produce the circumstances in which "peace takes on a life and a logic of its own," which would allow the withdrawal of U.S. forces in a year, created less transatlantic disturbance than probably should have been expected.[16] America's European allies understood how slim the margin of congressional approval for deploying U.S. forces had been, and how important continuing U.S. participation was, and they increased the proportion of their own forces in Bosnia and Croatia to permit U.S. reductions important to maintaining congressional support.

Although it was generally believed in Congress that the president had violated his promise, the Republican leadership on Capitol Hill allowed the transition from the Implementation Force (IFOR) to a NATO "Stabilization Force" of 35,000 troops. Whereas the United States had contributed roughly 50 percent of the IFOR contingent, its proportion was only 20 percent in the Stabilization Force.[17] This formula appears to be a sustainable long-term burden-sharing formula for NATO in Bosnia: Congress has continued to fund operations with no threats of invoking the War Powers Resolution restrictions on the president's ability to deploy forces outside the United States, and public support for continuing involvement seems tied to the perceived success of the NATO operations.[18]

Negotiating Kosovo

Serbian repression of the Albanian majority population in Kosovo had been identified as the powder keg of the Balkans since the early 1990s, when Slobodan Milosevic began infringing on the autonomy Kosovars had enjoyed in Yugoslavia since 1974. Serbian policies spurred formation of the Kosovo Liberation Army (KLA) and Kosovar retaliation and guerrilla attacks on Serbian police and military forces, and by early 1998 the spiral of violence was under way. NATO and the United Nations had just extended the NATO mandate in Bosnia for the third time, with no end in sight to those responsibilities.[19]

The circumstances of Kosovo differed in important ways from those of Bosnia. In both Bosnia and Kosovo, the Serb leader Milosevic had precipitated the violence to which NATO was responding, and the alliance viewed its actions as protecting the weak from the strong. However, intervening in Kosovo raised several new issues:

- The NATO countries did not have, nor could they expect to gain, a clear UN Security Council resolution in support of their intervention.
- Whereas the state had collapsed in Bosnia, Kosovo was an acknowledged part of a sovereign state whose actions, however offensive, had protection in much of international law.[20]

- Most Balkan analysts judged that Serbia's historical and religious ties to Kosovo would require imposing by force a settlement granting substantial autonomy or independence to Kosovo.
- The effect on Bosnia's fragile peace and operations of NATO forces there would need to be considered.
- The military requirements for intervening in Kosovo placed a premium on the rapid employment of high-end combat capabilities (mobility, all-weather performance, precision, collection and dissemination of intelligence, stand-off attack), of which American but few other allied forces were capable.

These changed circumstances diminished both U.S. and NATO willingness to intervene in Kosovo. They made political solutions to the conflict even less likely than in Bosnia. They heightened the political cost—especially for Germany—of choosing to support and participate in the intervention. And they depended critically on U.S. leadership and military forces to succeed.

The consuming obligations and slow pace of progress in pacifying Bosnia left little enthusiasm in the United States or NATO for intervening in Kosovo. In the summer of 1998, the allies were willing to do nothing more than threaten the use of force and undertake contingency planning for preventive troop deployments in Albania, air operations against Serbian forces in Kosovo, or deploying NATO ground troops as part of a cease-fire.[21]

The United States was sufficiently concerned by October 1998 to send Ambassador Richard Holbrooke to Belgrade to seek a negotiated end to the crackdown in Kosovo by Serbian military and police forces. Holbrooke's negotiation was constrained both by the unwillingness of the Clinton administration to seek public and congressional support for intervening in Kosovo and the unwillingness of NATO states to consider alliance action without U.S. leadership and a substantial U.S. troop commitment.

Gaining American support for intervening in Kosovo in the fall of 1998 would have been an exceedingly difficult sell by the administration. A cease-fire agreement was unlikely to be reached with Milosevic, requiring NATO to establish a precedent of using military force absent a UN Security Council resolution explicitly authorizing the action and on a slim justification in existing international law. Though the issue of a UN mandate did not pose major difficulties in the United States, which is more accustomed to defending and advancing its interests without benefit of a UN blessing, it could limit or prevent participation of coalition partners. NATO forces would likely have to fight their way into Kosovo along a few unpromising routes, increasing both the numbers of forces engaged and the casualties associated with the intervention. Congress was unlikely to be mollified by promises of short duration or assurances by the administration that Kosovo would be the last war of Balkan secession. Even without the relationship between the President and Congress being poisoned by the impeachment trial, it is unlikely that the Clinton administration could have successfully made the case for "another Bosnia in Kosovo."

It is understandable, then, that the Clinton administration hesitated to commit to using force in Kosovo in the fall of 1998. What is less easily justified is the United States agreeing to place 2,000 unarmed OSCE "verifiers" on the ground in Kosovo as part of the Milosevic-Holbrooke agreement.[22] Such a mission was far beyond the organizational capacity of the OSCE and placed its personnel in danger.[23] Particularly after the use of UMPROFOR troops as hostages and human shields in Bosnia, the OSCE mission negotiated by Ambassador Holbrooke in October of 1998 was irresponsible. A NATO Extraction Force was created to evacuate the OSCE personnel if necessary, but Serbia denied it was part of the agreement and threatened that any use of the Extraction Force would be considered an act of war.[24]

Another aspect of the agreement remained unclear, with even deadlier potential. When General Wesley Clark, NATO's supreme allied commander, and General Klaus Naumann, chairman of the NATO Military Committee, met with Milosevic in late October as part of the follow-up to the Holbrooke agreement. Milosevic claimed that Holbrooke had agreed that the United States and NATO would restrain the KLA from attacks on Serbian troops and police.[25]

The Holbrooke-Milosevic agreement appears to have been a bad deal for all concerned.[26] It did not provide adequate safeguards for Kosovars against the violence of Serb military and police forces. It placed the OSCE and its personnel in jeopardy. It may have created the expectation in Serbia that NATO would restrain the KLA. It engaged NATO once again in threatening airstrikes against Serbia, and withdrawing the threat after ambiguous Serbian compliance. The agreement seems simply to have delayed the conflict, allowing Serbia time to plan the large-scale depopulation of Kosovar Albanians.

That the United States made the agreement suggests one of two strategies; either the Clinton administration was buying time to build a coalition for war against Serbia, or it was stalling for time without knowing what to do. Senior U.S. officials were not engaged in additional planning or preparation for a conflict over Kosovo after the Holbrooke agreement. President Clinton did not consult with members of Congress. Secretary of State Madeleine Albright was not building a coalition of willing states and making a public case for war with Serbia over Kosovo. Secretary of Defense William Cohen was not reassuring non-European allies and explaining how the United States would meet its other security obligations while fighting in Kosovo. In fact, very little was done between the October agreement and the Serb attack on Racak in January 1999. This suggests that the administration was simply stalling, hoping that something would develop to deliver the NATO allies from having to choose from among unpalatable options.

The Contact Group initiated negotiations between Serbia and Kosovar Albanian leaders in February 1999 in an effort to secure autonomy for Kosovo and end the conflict. NATO again threatened airstrikes against Serbia if it prevented agreement (even though the Kosovars also had not yet agreed to the group's terms). The Contract Group's negotiating position essentially faced Serbia with ceding Kosovo by treaty with a NATO peacekeeping force in the province, or fighting to keep it. Given the NATO record of threatening but not using force in the Balkans, it is perhaps not surprising that Milosevic took his chances and continued to haggle over the details at Rambouillet.

It is surprising that the Western democracies did not explore a wider range of negotiating options at Rambouillet, especially given the hesitancy of all the NATO allies to go to war over Kosovo. There is no evidence of alternative negotiating terms that would seek to address Serbian concerns about attacks by the KLA or find alternatives to a NATO force inside Serbia. Instead of searching for an achievable agreement, the momentum of anti-Serbian action picked up substantially in the spring of 1999, even though every NATO government wanted to avoid the conflict.[27]

War over Kosovo

On March 24, 1999, NATO decided that Serbia did not intend to reach a negotiated peace at Rambouillet and commenced an air campaign against Serbia. Serbia responded with a humanitarian nightmare by rapidly making 1.2 million Kosovars into refugees.[28] The air campaign persisted for seventy-eight days, attacking targets in Belgrade and throughout Serbia as well as in Kosovo, until Serbia conceded. NATO deployed 50,000 troops into

Kosovo to enforce the peace and establish a United Nations protectorate for the autonomous but not independent Kosovo.

The central U.S. rationale for going to war in Kosovo was NATO's credibility. Secretary Albright and Secretary Cohen again and again cited the credibility of the alliance as the reason negotiations could not continue.[29] NATO had repeatedly threatened Milosevic, and this had not deterred his actions. Thus, Serbian actions in Kosovo had called into question the central achievement of U.S. strategy in Europe after the Cold War: establishing NATO's primacy in managing European crises. The Clinton administration allowed the need to ensure NATO's credibility to escalate the importance of Kosovo—and the Balkans more generally—up the list of U.S. strategic priorities.

If pacifying Bosnia was a secondary interest for the United States to establishing NATO's post–Cold War primacy, and if there was little likelihood of gaining congressional or public support for another Balkan campaign in Kosovo, why did the administration allow it to dominate the U.S. strategic agenda in 1999 and the dispute to escalate into a peace enforcement operation? There are several possible explanations: increasing unprovoked atrocities by Serbia, applying the lessons of UN involvement in Bosnia to Kosovo, distraction or an inability to prioritize commitments by the Clinton administration, and European pressure of the kind that had convinced Washington to commit ground forces to Bosnia in 1995. None of these are sufficient explanations based on the available data.

The unsatisfying but apparently true explanation for U.S. policy choices is that key decisionmakers in the Clinton administration, principally Secretary of State Albright, Ambassador Holbrooke, and Supreme Allied Commander Europe (SACEUR) General Clark, believed they understood Milosevic and could coerce him to comply with the Rambouillet terms with a very limited bombing campaign.[30] They did not anticipate the large-scale humanitarian crisis Milosevic created. They did not plan for more than five days of NATO bombing. They did not review the impact that defections over time from the NATO coalition could have on Serbia's willingness to continue the war. They did not assess what NATO's options would be if Milosevic did not comply with their expectations.[31]

In short, the United States violated several tenets of the Powell Doctrine on the effective use of force: It had not identified an objective that was achievable within the resource constraints it established; it did not use decisive force overwhelming to its objective; and it did not consider how the use of force might further change the situation.[32] The Clinton administration wanted so much to believe that it could attain its objective at a price that leaders were willing to pay that it lost perspective on the problem.

There are suggestions that this assessment was shared by some in the Clinton administration, notably National Security Adviser Sandy Berger.[33] The demise of Secretary Albright's influence in the Clinton administration is reportedly tied to Berger's anger that Albright failed to leave the president a range of choice when the Rambouillet negotiations failed to produce an agreement.

It is a remarkable achievement that the NATO allies held together throughout the campaign. However, NATO unity is a necessary but not sufficient condition for success. NATO unity is not, in and of itself, a victory in Kosovo. Consensus was eroding in the weeks before Milosevic's surprise capitulation to the point that, as David Fromkin has noted, "it seemed possible that NATO unity might crack before Yugoslav morale did."[34] When the outcome of the war was in doubt, the deficiencies of U.S. strategy for the conflict created serious strains in the alliance.[35]

A related strain on NATO was U.S. unwillingness to seriously consider a ground campaign to take possession of Kosovo if the air campaign did not achieve alliance objectives: "to halt the violence and stop further humanitarian catastrophe."[36] The chairman of NATO's Military Committee admitted that "we cannot stop such a thing entirely from the air," but allied planners never seriously considered a ground campaign that more closely matched means to objectives.[37] NATO never considered it, because the United States had ruled out ground forces.[38] Even when bipartisan defense leaders like Senator John McCain and General Colin Powell offered President Clinton protective cover from Republican criticism, there is no sign that the administration was willing to commit to a ground campaign.[39] The U.S. aversion to risking its ground forces has continued into the Kosovo force implementation.[40]

The U.S. unwillingness to risk its ground forces came just as European allies were reminded of both the dominance of American military power for high-intensity combat operations and the military consequences of making war by committee in full public view. The Dutch defense expert Rob de Wijk has argued that the central lesson from Kosovo is that

> warfare requires a *lead nation* which dominates both political and military decision-making during the operation. Fighting a war the democratic way, with nineteen member states involved in the decision-making process, undermines the effectiveness of the operation.[41]

If other Europeans ascribe to this view, then Kosovo will likely further Washington's principal post–Cold War objective of establishing NATO primacy. However, a more likely conclusion is that Kosovo will cause European allies to question whether NATO is the appropriate instrument for managing crises, given American predominance in NATO decisionmaking, the U.S. hesitancy to commit its powerful military, and shortcomings in devising strategies that capitalize on its strengths. It is also plausible that NATO's experience in Kosovo will cause both Europeans and Americans to conclude that policymakers can no longer assume a confluence of interests in the transatlantic relationship.

Conclusion

The violent collapse of Yugoslavia is the seminal event in understanding why NATO survived the end of the Cold War. Without the forcing function of needing to act in the Balkans, the United States and its Western European allies would not have reached a consensus on a post–Cold War rationale for the alliance. Germany, France, and the United States all used the Balkan wars as a means to establish their preferred approach to crisis management by the community of Western democracies. Germany had a strong preference for concerted diplomatic and economic actions by "interlocking" multinational institutions unconnected to the coercive use of force. France had a strong preference for establishing the autonomy of Europe in using force and the subordination of NATO to other multinational institutions. And the United States had a strong preference for adapting NATO to manage security problems throughout Europe.

Although other nations had a major impact on the course of diplomacy and the use of force in the Balkans—most notably Britain—Germany, France, and the United States were the states that had to make fundamental choices. For the NATO allies to manage the crises in the Balkans, Germany, France, and the United States had to create a common approach to the use of coercive force, the role of various international institutions, and a long-term plan for pacifying a failed state in which ethnic identity had become the paramount political factor. Each had to make major concessions in their preferred approaches to manage the problem: Germany had to accept the use of coercive force integral to foreign policy, France had to accept that NATO was necessary to bring the military firepower and constructive U.S. engagement to the task of peacemaking in the Balkans, and the United

States had to accept the commitment of its ground forces to ensure American leadership and NATO's institutional primacy. For the alliance to meet this new challenge, the members of the Strategic Triangle had to develop a new consensus.

NATO plans for implementing the 1995 Dayton Peace Accords codify this intra-alliance agreement: NATO had sole responsibility for implementing the military annexes of the accords.[42] Subsequently, the European-American division of labor in maintaining peace in Bosnia seems to have stabilized at a mutually acceptable 80 percent European NATO effort and 20 percent American contribution.[43] If the Balkan challenge had ended with Bosnia, the United States would likely have succeeded in cementing NATO's post–Cold War role in managing crises throughout Europe. Washington would also likely have succeeded in keeping European aspirations for a European Security and Defense Policy within the context of "separable but not separate" from NATO.

Managing the second stage of the Balkan challenge—Serbia's repression in Kosovo—raised again in a new context the same issues that had been resolved inside NATO with the 1995 deployment of NATO ground forces to Bosnia and Croatia. Even with the differing circumstances of Kosovo, the policies of both Germany and France demonstrate continuity with the basic agreements of 1995: Germany accepting participation in the coercive use of force, and France accepting that NATO would organize and execute the military campaign. The United States, however, broke from the 1995 bargain in refusing a ground campaign to achieve NATO's objectives in Kosovo.

Although America did contribute 80 percent of the combat power during the Kosovo air campaign, its unwillingness to consider a ground campaign reminded Europeans again in 1999 that U.S. interest in managing the Balkan challenge was substantially less than the commitment of its European allies. The ramifications of this U.S. choice are still echoing throughout the alliance, but its effects are already evident in the greater momentum behind and broadening support for an autonomous European Security and Defense Policy, concerns about U.S. unilateralism in the arms control arena, and U.S. irritation at Europe's unwillingness to spend more on defense.

In both the 1995 NATO enforcement of the Dayton Peace Accords and the 1999 NATO air campaign in Kosovo, the United States agreed to undertake the preponderance of war-fighting tasks and the Europeans agreed to take the greatest share of the burden for long-term peace enforcement. However, the difference in political terms under which that burden-sharing arrangement was adopted made the 1995 deal a stabilizing equilibrium for

NATO, whereas the 1999 deal seems unstable. NATO's management of the Kosovo crisis appears to return the alliance to the pre-Dayton concern that American interests were no longer sufficiently compatible with European interests for the alliance to be a meaningful tool for managing security. In effect, Kosovo has returned NATO to the pre-Balkans debate about the value and future of the alliance. The consensus shaped over Bosnia within the Strategic Triangle is once again fundamentally in question.

Notes

1. James Baker, quoted in "Atrocity and Outrage," *Time,* August 17, 1992.
2. Edward Mortimer and Lionel Barber, "Crisis in Yugoslavia," *Financial Times,* July 4, 1991; see also David Binder, "Europeans Warn on Yugoslav Split: U.S. Deplores Moves," *New York Times,* June 26, 1991.
3. Colin L. Powell, "Why Generals Get Nervous," *New York Times,* October 8, 1992. Eliot Cohen and some other scholars of civil-military relations believe General Powell did a disservice to military professionalism by engaging in the public debate about intervening in Kosovo. However, because Powell was making his case in the first instance prior to a political decision, and subsequently supported an established policy by the political leadership, it seems within bounds for an active-duty military officer.
4. Speech by Secretary of State James Baker, Berlin Press Club, December 12, 1989. Robert Zoellick, a key Baker aide, considers the Baker speeches the best public record of U.S. policy. Personal interview.
5. General George L. Butler, former director for strategic plans and policy, U.S. Joint Chiefs of Staff, personal interview, September 9, 1997.
6. Jacques Poos, quoted in Alan Riding, "Conflict in Yugoslavia: Europeans Send High-Level Team," *New York Times,* June 29, 1991.
7. North Atlantic Council (Heads of State and Government), *Rome Summit Declaration,* November 9–10, 1991; North Atlantic Council (Ministerial Meeting), *Final Communiqué,* Oslo, June 4, 1992.
8. Rob de Wijk, *NATO on the Brink of the New Millennium* (London: Brassey's, 1997), 59–63.
9. For examples of this position, see comments by Clinton quoted in Doyle McManus, "Column One: After Cold War What Is Security?" *Los Angeles Times,* October 17, 1992; Rupter Cornwall, "The US Presidential Elections," *Independent,* October 13, 1992; and analysis of the Clinton views by Leslie H. Gelb, "Foreign Affairs: No More Hawks and Doves," *New York Times,* October 8, 1992.
10. The Constitution reserves to the Congress "the right to raise armies and maintain a navy," and because most defense policy choices are long-term spending choices, congressional control of the purse strings predominates over executive authority. In foreign policy, congressional control over treaty ratification establishes the limits of presidential action.
11. For an examination of differing U.S. and European approaches, see David Gompert, "How to Defeat Serbia," *Foreign Affairs* (July–August 1994): 30–47.

12. Before 1993, this assistance included providing intelligence information to the UN for monitoring Bosnia-Herzegovina airspace and agreement to provide support in carrying out future Security Council resolutions. See United Nations Secretary General Boutros Boutros-Ghali, Letter to NATO Secretary General Manfred Woerner, December 14, 1992.

13. Vice Admiral Norm Ray, assistant secretary general for defense support at NATO, personal interview, October 20, 1997.

14. Briefing by Deputy Assistant Secretary of Defense Joe Kruzel to members of Congress, November 1995.

15. North Atlantic Treaty Organization, "IFOR Fact Sheet" (NATO Integrated Data System), February 16, 1996; U.S. Department of State, "Summary of Dayton Peace Agreement," November 21, 1995.

16. William J. Clinton, "Address to the Nation on Implementation of the Peace Agreement in Bosnia-Herzegovina," November 27, 1995, in *Public Papers of the Presidents, William Jefferson Clinton* (Washington, D.C.: U.S. Government Printing Office, 1995), vol. 2, 1786.

17. NATO International Staff, "Fact Sheet on North American and European Allies' Military Efforts—1999," April 2000.

18. Steve Kull, "Public Opinion and U.S. Engagement in the Balkans," Program on International Policy Attitudes, March 2000.

19. S/RES/1174 (1998), June 15, 1998.

20. For an excellent discussion of the legal issues associated with the mandate issue, see Catherine Guicherd, "International Law and the War in Kosovo," *Survival* (Summer 1999): 19–34.

21. Dick A. Leurdijk, "NATO as a Subcontractor to the United Nations: The Cases of Bosnia and Kosovo," in *NATO after Kosovo,* ed. Rob de Wijk, Bram Boxhoorn, and Niklaas Hoekstra (Breda: Royal Netherlands Military Academy, 2000), 130.

22. The October 1998 agreement also established a NATO "air verification mission" using noncombat reconnaissance planes to provide information on compliance with UN resolutions.

23. The Federal Republic of Yugoslavia guaranteed the safety of the OSCE personnel as part of the agreement. "Agreement on the OSCE Kosovo Verification Mission," para. 6.

24. *International Herald Tribune,* December 11, 1998.

25. General Klaus Naumann, former chairman of the NATO Military Committee, personal interview, February 16, 2000.

26. World Vision associate director Serge Duss called the deal "the worst possible news." Quoted in Mary McGrory, "Truces and Cease Fires," *Washington Post,* October 15, 1998.

27. Clinton Statement on Kosovo, White House Press Release, February 23, 1999; "U.S. Steps Up Pressure on Serbs and Kosovo Albanians," *Financial Times,* February 22, 1999; "U.S. Turns up Heat on Stalled Kosovo Talks," *Scotsman,* February 14, 1999.

28. The most commonly accepted figures are: 800,000 deported from Kosovo and 600,000 internally displaced persons.

29. Testimony by Secretary Cohen and General Hugh Shelton to the House Armed Services Committee, March 15, 1999.

30. Based on discussions with the authors, this is also the explanation to be offered by Ivo Daalder and Michael O'Hanlon in their forthcoming book on Kosovo.

31. For detailed discussions of NATO and U.S. planning, see Craig R. Whitney, "Conflict in the Balkans: Military Analysis," *New York Times,* March 24, 1999; and Dana Priest, "Soldering On in a War of Constraints," *Washington Post,* May 30, 1999.

32. For an excellent discussion of this and several other mistakes made in the Kosovo campaign, see Ivo H. Daalder and Michael E. O'Hanlon, "Unlearning the Lessons of Kosovo," *Foreign Policy* (Fall 1999): 128–40.

33. John Lancaster, "Albright's Influence Waning at Foggy Bottom," *Washington Post,* March 28, 2000.

34. David Fromkin, *Kosovo Crossing: American Ideals Meet Reality on the Balkan Battlefields* (New York: Free Press, 1999), 2.

35. I examine this issue in greater detail in "NATO as a Crisis Management Organization," a forthcoming Institut Français des Relations Internationales note.

36. NATO secretary general Javier Solana, NATO Press Release (1999)041, March 25, 1999.

37. General Klaus Naumann, chairman of the NATO Military Committee, press conference, NATO Information Service, Brussels, May 4, 1999.

38. British officials attempted to suggest during the air campaign that the United States had secretly agreed to a ground campaign because Washington agreed to allow the SACEUR latitude to plan for such a campaign. Such planning occurs on the premise that no nation is bound to support an actual operation. The British leak is detailed in Patrick Wintour and Peter Beaumont, "Revealed: The Secret Plan to Invade Kosovo," *London Sunday Observer,* July 18, 1999.

39. The White House responded to a letter from a bipartisan group of Congress members advising a ground campaign, and "there's still no intention" of a ground campaign on 10 April. See Mark Matthews and Jonathan Weisman, "Clinton Advised to Plan for Kosovo Ground War," *Baltimore Sun,* April 10, 1999. For comments by Senator John McCain, see Jessica Lee, "Some Republicans Turn Up Volume of Criticisms," *USA Today,* April 5, 1999; Powell's views are reflected in "A Common Purpose: Europe Should Unite Over Kosovo," *Guardian,* May 18, 1999.

40. E.g., concern about force protection had led U.S. forces not to live in the community or engage in the kind of "community policing" approach to peacekeeping that British forces have successfully used. R. Jeffrey Smith, "A G.I.'s Home Is His Fortress," *Washington Post,* October 5, 1999.

41. Rob de Wijk, "What Is NATO?" in *NATO after Kosovo,* ed. de Wijk, Boxhoorn, and Hoekstra, 3.

42. Summary of the Dayton Peace Agreement, U.S. Department of State, November 21, 1995.

43. The figures refer to military forces committed to the NATO Stabilization Force in Bosnia; they do not include military support outside the Balkan theater or nonmilitary contributions, such as the European Union's Stability Pact or national commitments of civilians to United Nations efforts. European NATO members contribute about 60 percent of the force, non-NATO European states and Canada contribute about 20 percent. NATO, *Fact Sheet on North American and European Allies' Military Efforts* (Brussels: NATO International Staff, 2000).

Epilogue: A New Geometry?

The crisis over Iraq, which exploded in the summer of 2002 during the German election campaign and then deepened in January 2003 with the French and German opposition to a second UN Security Council resolution, marked a major departure in German foreign policy. The failure to reach a new partnership on Iraq in the years after the fall of Saddam Hussein was evidence that a new era in transatlantic relations had opened.

As the cases studied in this volume indicate, before the fall of 2002, the German leadership always preferred being between Washington and Paris, and it made every effort to avoid a choice between the two. This position allowed Germany to play the role of broker and maximized its flexibility and influence. It also reflected the importance of two of the three key pillars or circles in German foreign policy, the Atlantic and the European (with the eastern circle being the third).[1] However, the crisis over Iraq was to change all of this. For the first time, Germany clearly sided with one of its key partners against the other and helped to organize a coalition against its major ally on an issue that was seen as vital to the American administration.

Even more, a new entente cordiale was formed between Paris, Berlin, and Moscow, ushering in a new fluidity in the European political and diplomatic arena. This remarkable situation resulted in what as experienced an observer as Henry Kissinger called "the gravest crisis in the Atlantic Alliance since its creation five decades ago."[2]

The End of the Triangle? An American Perspective

Stephen F. Szabo and Samuel F. Wells Jr.

From the perspective of senior George W. Bush administration officials, the policies of the German and French governments went beyond dissent to an active attempt to build a countervailing coalition against the United States. They believed the open disunity that this produced not only split Europe but also may have given Saddam Hussein and his leadership the impression that if they only held out the West would crack, perhaps resulting in a miscalculation of the seriousness of the threats Iraq faced.

The administration's reaction to the Franco-German–led countercoalition was to encourage those in Europe who valued the transatlantic link over the European Union to undercut the efforts of Paris and Berlin. There is clear evidence that the Bush administration was not only aware of the efforts of Tony Blair and Jose-Maria Aznar as well as of the Vilnius Eleven to publicly oppose Jacques Chirac and Gerhard Schröder, but actively encouraged these efforts.[3] The division of Europe into "old" and "new" by U.S. defense secretary Donald Rumsfeld and the development of a new military basing scheme for Europe (which will shift U.S. forces from Germany to Poland, Bulgaria, and Romania, as well as back to the United States), while in the planning stage for many years, was not unrelated to this effort to favor new allies while punishing older, less compliant ones.

This all leads to broader questions concerning whether the United States is reassessing its support for European unity and has concluded, instead, that a unified Europe led by Paris and Berlin might be less desirable than a looser and broader Europe that included Britain, Italy, Spain, and Poland.

American policy toward Europe in the twentieth century was based on one key vital interest: the prevention of the domination of the continent by a hegemonic power. With the demise of the Soviet Union and the subsequent weakness of Russia, there is no real prospect of a new hegemon arising in Europe. The European Union and NATO provide a stable framework

Epilogue: A New Geometry?   373

for containing the nationalism of the member states while channeling their diversity. In short, from the U.S. perspective, the European Problem, like the German Problem, has been solved in the twenty-first century. Now the United States must decide whether an ever more unified Europe, perhaps under French and German leadership, is really in its long-term interest. Certainly there is abundant evidence that the George W. Bush administration has pursued a divide-and-conquer strategy regarding Europe. It explicitly stated in its *National Security Strategy* document of September 2002 that it would brook no competitors and that it would do all that it could to maintain American preeminence.[4]

Of all the world's major regions, only Europe has the resources, economies, population base, and leadership to pose as a "friendly balancer" to the power of the United States. A key question now facing American policymakers is whether to regard a unifying Europe as a desirable precondition for a more effective transatlantic partnership, or whether this type of Europe should be opposed as a possible "peer competitor."

The American public's view of France and Germany also deteriorated during the Iraq crisis. Press coverage of French and German opposition to the war became overwhelmingly negative in January 2003 and especially after the beginning of the war, although France remained a larger target for populist discontent than Germany.[5] The strategy of the Bush administration at the end of the war was concisely summarized by the president's national security adviser as being one of "punish France, ignore Germany and forgive Russia."[6]

Whatever the longer-term consequences, it seems clear that the German-American relationship was fundamentally altered by the events of 2002 and 2003. Bush and Schröder were catalysts for a deeper change, which had been building between the two 9/11s—November 9, 1989, when the Berlin Wall fell; and September 11, 2001, when the United States was attacked by terrorists.

This strategic shift reflects even more fundamental ones in American foreign policy under the George W. Bush administration. The divergence of approaches between Washington and Berlin could not be greater. The strategic glue that held the two countries together during the Cold War and the division of Germany is clearly much weaker, and the common threat posed by the Soviet Union has not been replaced by that of international terrorism. Though specific terrorist groups pose a common threat, a "war on terrorism" has not produced a common threat assessment. More important, the U.S.-German relationship is not as central to either party as it was during the Cold War. It is also less emotional or special to the generations that are now leading both countries and do not have the memories or ties shaped by confronting a major common threat.

The result is likely to be a much looser coalition, which will shift from issue to issue. The two sides will have to learn to live with disagreements without being disagreeable. Common interests will continue to provide a basis for a realistic cooperation, but American attempts to divide Europe and to play old Europe against new Europe could further erode the transatlantic sides of the triangle and replace it with a new and more complex one. The Germany of Schröder and Angela Merkel will not simply agree to follow the American lead if it is not consulted and treated as a partner. It will not dissolve its national interest within either the European Union or NATO. Much of the language used by the Schröder government reflected a strong desire to be taken seriously as a partner and an aversion to being treated as a "satellite," or to "clicking its heels" when the United States demanded support. Following the Iraq experience, the Bush administration has lost a great deal of credibility in Berlin, and if the U.S. government does not alter both its leadership style and its assessment of Germany's strategic and political culture, a more serious and long-term split cannot be ruled out.

At the same time, the United States' relationship with France seems to have crystallized an American view of France as an adversary more than a partner, yet an adversary with little real political or economic weight of its own. As the American march toward war grew in 2002, Europe was split into two responses. One was that of France, led by Chirac, and of Schröder's Germany, who followed the approach of challenging the American administration from the outside and creating a counter to the unipolar world approach of the neoconservatives and their allies, while, "the Blair perspective has Europe influencing U.S. policy from within."[7] Both Chirac and Blair had hoped to enmesh American power within a broader multilateral context, and both failed.

American political leaders, both Republican and Democratic, were deeply offended at the sight of French foreign minister Dominique de Villepin touring Africa in early 2003 seeking votes against a draft U.S.-U.K. resolution in the UN Security Council giving a clear authorization to use force against Iraq. Chirac continues to offend U.S. officials by his niggling objections to Washington's proposals for French forces to train Iraqi police within Iraq and his conditions for NATO operation in Afghanistan. Any future French proposals for EU-NATO security cooperation or EU use of NATO assets will likely generate an icy response from Washington.

As many of the cases in this study have shown, the United States was much less inclined to see a strategic triangle than were the European states. America has gone its own way in the past and is likely to do so with increasing frequency in the future. As Europe has faded in strategic importance and other regions have risen as threats and problems for U.S. national security policy, there has been a tendency for American policymakers to devalue ties to Paris and Berlin. On the European side, America has declined in its importance to European security and has begun to emerge as a problem rather than a solution for the future European and global systems. The triangle seems to have been replaced with a new European and transatlantic geometry that will have to be shaped by the next generation of leaders.

A French Perspective

Georges-Henri Soutou

At the time of writing this epilogue, the transatlantic strategic triangle is evidently out of kilter. The only present evidence of the existence of some sort of triangle is the fact that its demise has been the result of converging, trilateral efforts by the three concerned countries to destroy it. As for the French, there has recently been a sea change in their worldview: they no longer see their interest in the triangle (even warped and isosceles, with Paris standing at the apex, as explained in the introduction to this volume). The present French foreign policy is in that respect of course a development of the Gaullist policy of national independence, but it goes much further; for de Gaulle himself, even after 1963, there was still some sort of triangle. And the present French foreign policy in that respect is even different from that which Chirac, already president of the French Republic, tried to achieve in 1995–96. To be convinced of that, it is sufficient to click on the very good Web site of the Quai d'Orsay, where all official pronouncements and foreign policy speeches by the president and the minister for foreign affairs since 1990 are listed, with the possibility to search for particular words or expressions.[8] For instance, at the end of July 2003 the word "multipolaire" had appeared in 152 speeches or declarations by Chirac since 1995.

The concept of "multipolarity" is thus a mantra that goes to the heart of the matter. In the bipolar world, in the French view, there were two "blocs"; France refused to belong to either one, but it was aligned with the West. France recognized that the United States was essential to maintain the bipolar balance and peace, and it was quite happy nurturing its own interests in two major ways: with the triangle, as already explained; and with a kind of tacit reinsurance in Moscow to balance discreetly both the United States and Germany. But now there is no longer any bipolar world order, and in the French view the United States itself has changed: It has become unilateralist if not outright imperialist, and it is no longer interested in, and even has turned against, the three major institutions it promoted after 1945: the United Nations, NATO, and a unified Europe. (The irony of the fact that Paris at times was no strong supporter of at least the first two of those institutions does not escape some commentators).[9]

Moreover, France sees current American foreign policy as dangerous, because it leads to a "clash of cultures" and to instability. This policy then has to be resisted, in the framework of a "multipolar world" where there will be several major partners and partnerships: a European Union with a foreign policy identity, under the guidance of the Franco-German partnership (strongly revived since the autumn of 2002); a Paris-Berlin-Moscow axis; China; India; and a strong link between France (and Europe) and Africa. It should be stressed that despite some superficial convergence, this vision is very different from the one suggested by Henry Kissinger of a new world system of interlocking regional balances where the United States would in all regions play a cooperative but central role.[10] For the French, "multipolarity" is not meant to modify or to enhance the world role of the United States in the new situation but to reduce it, because it is seen today as excessive and unbalanced.

Of course, the present transatlantic crisis (which is not only but first of all a French-American one, the German-American one coming as a close second) is not the first. And the previous crises were sooner or later solved and the triangle (because those crises always went to the heart of the triangle, as does the present one) was repaired, usually tolerably quickly. It might also be the same thing this time, but there are good reasons to doubt it, because both the international environment and French policy have changed deeply in recent years.

Some historical distance might be useful here. After 1962, Franco-American relations entered a state of permanent crisis. In 1969–70, President Georges Pompidou could largely repair them, without renouncing the basic tenet of Gaullist foreign policy: national independence. But his worldview and his foreign policy agenda did not collide directly with the American ones, and inside his political constituency there was an important Atlanticist core, which he had to assuage (apart from his own convictions).

Once again, in 1973–74, the Franco-American relationship turned sour, although Pompidou managed to keep the new rift within manageable limits. And his successor, Valéry Giscard d'Estaing, reestablished strong links to Washington and to the Atlantic alliance. Once again, the relationship deteriorated toward the end of President Giscard d'Estaing's term. It has never fully revived since then, even if at times (but only at times) it became better under François Mitterrand. And in 2002–3 it took a very negative turn, although President Chirac had suggested, in 1995–96, a solution that would have put Franco-American and transatlantic relations on a much better, permanent footing: France getting fully back into NATO, which would in turn recognize the existence within the alliance of a European identity (as recognized by the Atlantic Council in Berlin in June 1996). But as we know, that tentative Franco-American agreement ultimately failed.[11] One could speak of three breaks, but only two reconciliations.

Is the current crisis a conjectural accident, only linked to a major difference of views about the way to handle the Iraq question? Or does it go deeper, as indicated by the fact that it has actually been simmering for years? One would tend to lean toward the second view, for three sets of reasons.

The first set of reasons concerns *geopolitics*. French geopolitical interests and aims have remained basically the same since de Gaulle: through a strong Franco-German link, take the leadership of Europe and thus, so to say by proxy, retain global influence, political but also economic and cultural. But the end of the Cold War, German reunification, the evolution of Germany and of Russia, and the perceived change in American foreign policy have modified the French game, or at least, if not the goal of the game, its rules—the United States is no longer considered to be a useful ally or at least a sort of reinsurance of last resort, but the main obstacle to the achievement of French goals: the achievement of a European defense and foreign policy identity, of a strong relationship with Russia (eventually in the form of a Paris-Berlin-Moscow axis), and of powerful links with North Africa, both to keep an eye on the evolution there and to give more weight to France at the international level. Thus *the triangle has lost its previous positive importance for France;* Paris still wishes to remain at the apex, but not of such a configuration. The triangle, for that school of thought, is no longer useful to further the French agenda, but actually detrimental.

The second set of reasons concerns *ideology*. De Gaulle, Pompidou, and Giscard d'Estaing alike never felt or expressed a different view of basic values as understood on both sides of the Atlantic. This is no longer the case; the French consider themselves and Europe at large to represent another worldview and indeed another culture compared with the "Anglo-Saxons." It goes beyond the well-known disputes about the death penalty, the environment, and the international court. This has much to do with the perceived need to defend a French model (which is under attack within the country itself through the tendency toward communitarization linked, largely but not only, with the heavy immigration since the beginning of the 1970s) against the disruptive forces of "globalization" and "communitarization," which are seen as the self-serving agenda of "Anglo-Saxon" powers.[12]

The third set of reasons concerns *politics*. Under Pompidou and Giscard d'Estaing, there was a strong constituency for good Franco-American relations, expressed in the spectrum of political parties. One of the reasons for de Gaulle's failure to win the referendum of April 1969, which led to his resignation, was the opposition of important parts of French society and political elites to his American and NATO policies. And both Pompidou and Giscard d'Estaing (even leaving aside, once again, their own views) needed the right-of-center Atlanticists to retain a majority in Parliament.[13]

But this Atlanticist constituency no longer exists, or at best is too widely dispersed. From polls and through inquiries, one could guess that approximately one-third of French political elites do not wish a permanent tension with Washington. But on the right, since a majority of Union pour la Démocratie Française leaders joined the new Union pour un Mouvement Populaire, which is basically the Gaullist party, they have little leverage on major issues of foreign affairs; having burned their own boat, they cannot leave the one they now sit in. As for the moderate Socialists, which are by no means anti-American (even if the current American administration has, generally speaking, few supporters in France), they cannot hope to regain power without allying themselves with the Communists, the Greens, and the Ultra-Left, all groups opposed to America as a matter of principle. There is, as of now, no possible political combination, either on the left or on the right, for a real revitalization of Franco-American and Franco-Atlantic relations. This has to do with the evolution of French politics, as we have seen above, but also of French society (where a long period of high unemployment has destroyed the recent acceptance of liberalism, which lasted for a few years around 1990) and even of French population through immigration. The Franco-American rift has probably become a structural problem.

Yet it is very doubtful whether the French will achieve much success along their present line. Germany does not have the same agenda; it wishes certainly to redress the balance inside the alliance, but not to create a new imbalance for the benefit of the French. Moscow will play its own game and will not unduly antagonize Washington. It might be possible that the realization of the lack of results induces a change of mind, although the current policy can go on for a long time without achieving many tangible results; in any case, it serves a useful internal goal of rebuilding national unity.

A new French orientation will depend, in the long term, on three things: a change of public spirit when the present period of economic troubles, social turbulence, and difficult and much disputed reforms abates; a renewed capacity in Washington to express a view of the world both workable and convincing for the French elites; and an effort by those elites to realize where exactly the present course of transatlantic tension might lead all of us. In the short term, of course, much will depend on the evolution of the Iraq crisis; a complete American failure would not reinforce those who wish in France to repair the relationship with Washington, but a sort of stabilization allowing Europe in general and France in particular to play a larger, or a perceived larger, role in Iraq could help.

If such developments occurred, provided they coincided with parallel ones in Germany, the triangle could possibly be revived. Berlin, having been more prudent than Paris in the recent confrontation, could eventually play the role of honest broker between Paris and Washington, which would not be for the first time. But the triangle would no longer be the same vital framework for the West. Franco-German reconciliation is now a historical fact and has no need to be nurtured by Washington; and the Soviet threat, which was a major prop of the triangle, no longer exists. And France and Germany together can no longer control the European Union, which disposes of a major reason for Washington to be on good terms with them. In the West, there are now just too many players for the triangle to regain its former importance.

A German Perspective

Helga Haftendorn

The controversies generated by the Iraq conflict have dealt a severe blow to the strategic triangle. Washington, supported by London, saw itself confronted with a Berlin-Paris-Moscow axis. The other European states found themselves in a dilemma: either losing American protection and support, or endangering the European project. Though weary of French-German hegemony in Europe, they tried to avoid choosing sides; and when this was not possible, they chose to side with the United States.[14] Germany, instead in being in a position to influence international affairs, found itself in a very disagreeable position: sacrificing close relations with the United States, losing its leadership role in Europe, and finding itself dependent on France. This situation could not last. But before recounting why Germany had left its position of a balancer between Paris and Washington, and what impact this change of attitude had on the triangle, we need to look at the forces that produced this situation.

The changes in the global structures manifesting themselves since 1990 became fully visible with the terrorist attacks of September 11, 2001. For Americans, the world had changed—or at least their perception of the world. But for the Europeans, it was America that was changing. The repercussions of the attacks on the American psyche, a hitherto unknown feeling of immediate threat, were difficult to appreciate abroad. Americans were shocked to realize that their enormous capability for global power projection could not prevent attacks from small, nonstate terrorist groups.

Reacting to the events of 9/11, the George W. Bush administration declared war on the global terrorist movement. From its right of self-defense, the administration deduced that the war on terrorism gave it an authority for unilateral action and for forming "coalitions of the willing" according to its own need instead of seeking assistance from multilateral institutions such as the United Nations or NATO. In fighting the terrorists and those states that provided a safe haven for them, the United States was prepared to use military force, if necessary in a preemptive mode. The administration felt that it should meet the criticism of its allies by demonstrating forceful leadership, assuming that its partners around the world would then automatically fall into line.

Not surprisingly, the Europeans who had manifested their solidarity with the United States after the 9/11 attacks responded with irritation to America's unilateralism. Still, they supported the American intervention in Afghanistan, because its connection with the 9/11 terrorist attacks was evident and it was backed by the United Nations. But they criticized the United States for proceeding unilaterally according to the motto "We'll call if we need you." The Europeans, for their part, preferred to fight terrorism and further democratic institution building primarily by political means though backed by military power. Germany—just like France—thus has contributed significantly to both the stabilization effort in Afghanistan and to rebuilding the Afghan state.

In contrast to the Afghanistan war, the attack against Iraq in March 2003 lacked a UN mandate, an explicit linkage with international terrorism, and the presence of weapons of mass destruction—despite American and British assertions to the contrary. Therefore, France and Germany had good reasons to vigorously criticize the Anglo-American operation and to decline to participate in it.

Concerning the conflict with Iraq, substantive considerations in the West meshed closely with structural and tactical arguments. France challenged the American claim to set the global agenda unilaterally, and it argued, as did Britain, in favor of UN involvement before intervening militarily. Without the pressure from Prime Minister Tony Blair, President Bush might not have gone to the United Nations on September 12, 2002; and without French diplomatic assistance, UN Security Council Resolution 1441 of November 8, 2002, would not have passed. This resolution threatened Iraq with serious consequences if it did not cooperate with the United Nations and comply with its arms control inspectors. To beef up this demand, the United States moved substantial military units to the Persian Gulf and deployed them at Iraq's borders. This scenario of threat, however, developed a dynamic of its own as the UN inspectors had resumed their work in Iraq, but were unable to discover any proof that Saddam Hussein's regime had operational weapons of mass destruction at its disposal, as the U.S. administration argued. Under these conditions, the United States and its partners failed to get approval for a new UN resolution sanctioning military intervention in Iraq. Though now without a concrete mandate, the United States together with Britain and a number of other nations attacked Iraq on March 16, 2003.

In unison with the French government, Berlin opposed military intervention in Iraq. But whereas Paris had shown its diplomatic skills in bringing about Security Council Resolution 1441, the German chancellor used a campaign speech on August 5, 2002, in Hanover to declare that Germany under no circumstances would participate in a military adventure in Iraq, not even if intervention were mandated by the United Nations.[15] With this statement, he did not respond to the international challenges but rather tried—in the end successfully—to turn the ongoing federal election campaign in his favor. The proclamation of a "proper German way" signified, however, a threefold breach with German traditions: first, domestic considerations took precedence over international ones; second, negating the UN authority for peacekeeping was a break with Germany's traditional principle of multilateralism; and third, Berlin risked an open conflict with the United States.

In effect, the Iraq war caused a threefold defeat for the Federal Republic: Berlin could not prevent the war; it risked international isolation; and, to overcome this isolation, it succumbed to dependence on France, especially in European affairs. The Federal Republic's government had intended to demonstrate its power and its autonomy; instead, the government incurred serious losses in its international room for maneuvering. Paris now was able, together with Berlin and Moscow, to wage a fierce opposition against the United States.

The transatlantic relationship was especially hurt when the German government turned the conflict with the United States from one over methods to one over values. Its "no" to the Iraq war—justified on political grounds—was turned into a claim of moral and cultural superiority, according to the motto: "peace-loving Europeans" versus "trigger-happy Americans." The United States, however, turned the game around. Secretary of Defense Donald Rumsfeld now distinguished between "old Europe," whose days had passed, and a "new Europe," which was up to the challenges of the time and prepared to meet current and future problems alongside the United States.[16] Both formulations made a bad transatlantic debate worse.

As soon as the Iraq war had passed its climax, it was evident that states in a globalized world depended on each other and needed their partners' assistance. This was also true for the world's only superpower, the United States. In postwar Iraq, the limits of American power became only too visible. The United States with its superior military force could win the war, but not gain the peace and build democratic structures. As a result, Washington asked for international support in the pacification of Iraq, especially for financial assistance and additional capabilities—without, however, agreeing to the European request to cede full responsibilities to the United Nations.

Irrespective of events in Iraq, the United States remains the dominant global player setting the international order and operating as a gatekeeper in the global economy. To advance its own goals, Berlin must work on improving its relations with Washington and also ease its dependency on Paris, which has been a consequence of its policy of denial during the Iraq war. A greater reliance on London was no alternative during this conflict because London—against much domestic protest—had closely allied itself with Washington, displaying little sympathy for the German-French position. After the war, France also realized that it could not stay aloof if it wanted to participate in the global game.

Germany is no superpower, but it is a state with a global political outlook and with worldwide economic interests. It has to pursue its interests above all through multilateral institutions. International institutions give it equality compared with more powerful states, and they correspond to its interest in embedding its policies in a legal framework. An improved state of relations with Washington is also necessary because of Berlin's interests in European integration, for many EU member states have resented the German-French course in the Iraq case. Progress in the direction of European political union can only be achieved together with Britain, Italy, Spain, and the smaller countries of Western and Central Europe. Berlin has thus quickly tried to get out of the box that its opposition to the Iraq intervention had put it in. In the course of 2003, the German government tried to improve relations with Washington, although with limited success. The chagrin about having been deserted by a onetime close ally went too deep inside the beltway. To balance its dependency on France, Germany also tried to bring Britain closer again to the two continental powers.

Things did change with the advent of the George W. Bush administration in January 2005 and the coming to power of a red-green coalition in Germany ten months later. In Washington, the new secretary of state, Condoleezza Rice, introduced a new style in transatlantic relations without changing very much of the substance of American policy. One of the president's first visits after his inauguration led him to Europe where he not only attended a meeting of the NATO Council but also a summit of the European Council. After this gesture, relations with France and Germany warmed.

In Germany, Angela Merkel, the leader of the Christian Democratic Union / Christian Social Union, ran on a platform that called for restoring a constructive transatlantic relationship as one of Germany's prime foreign policy goals. Having won by a very thin margin in the elections, her conservative party group had to form a coalition with the Social Democrats, which got their fair share of government posts. Schröder's old chief of staff, Frank-Walter Steinmeier, became foreign minister, and in his new job he loyally supported Merkel's course in transatlantic relations.[17] The new government successfully shed the image of remaining a loyal vassal of French president Chirac—or Russian president Vladimir Putin—without straining relations with these two important foreign policy partners.

It may appear that the strategic triangle has survived the terrorist attacks and the Iraq war undamaged. This is, however, not the case. Although Germany continues to take advantage of the trilateral relationship, major changes have taken place. The United States no longer needs support from Europe, especially not from Germany—it can do without it. Further, the NATO alliance lacks cohesion in the absence of a common threat. The campaigns against international terrorism and the spread of weapons of mass destruction do not provide as strong a glue as anticommunism did. The American concept of functional alliances, of coalitions of the willing, relies on transient cooperation with states that in specific situations offer what the United States needs most: territory, forces, financial resources, or regional political clout. These are things that Germany, as a rule, cannot offer. This is not to minimize the German contribution to the stabilization and democratization of Afghanistan and its logistic services, which facilitated the Anglo-American campaign in the Gulf. These were welcome, and were applauded by Washington, but—as the case of Turkey has proven—the United States could have done without them.

A return to the happy times of the strategic triangle is highly unlikely. The international environment in which the United States, France, and Germany operate has changed significantly; so have the American and the European roles in it. They each have gained in power internationally, but their domestic responses have been different. Because of the 9/11 attacks, for the United States the highest priority now is safeguarding homeland security by using its global power in an unrestricted way, and if necessary disregarding its partners' concerns. For Germany, since unification, international issues have also been relegated to a secondary role.

Being a "normal country"—as many have asserted Germany has become since reunification[18]—has the effect that its foreign policy is now primarily driven by domestic concerns. But it is true for both Berlin and Washington that "there is no central . . . interest which can be realized without the cooperation with other states."[19]

From "Strategic Triangle" to "Euro-American Ellipse"

Because it wants to be relevant in international affairs, Germany has a strong interest in a cooperative relationship with the United States based on mutual respect and consideration for each other's interests. A Europe that strengthens its cohesiveness and unity without becoming a competitor with the United States will be listened to in Washington. Only by being unified and by creating consensus positions can Europe act as a potent political actor on the international stage. France shares Germany's interest in the European project. The strategic triangle may be evolving into a Euro-American ellipse, for example, an integrated structure in which independent states assemble around two nuclei, a European and a North American one, but cooperate closely with each other as issues and resources dictate.

In building the Euro-American ellipse, Britain offers itself as an essential ally. Given its special relationship with Washington, London should know how to develop this project without raising Washington's concerns that the old continent is ganging up against America. Britain also has an interest in strengthening its European connection. It wants neither to appear as "America's poodle"[20] nor forgo the opportunity to profit from European economies of scale.

To make the European project compatible with the Atlantic relationship, British prime minister Blair met a couple of times with his French and German counterparts. In a change from its previous position, Britain now supports the idea of an effective European military capability, able to act autonomously. The British support adds credibility to the European Security and Defense Policy (ESDP), and hence is a sine qua non for its effectiveness. After prolonged negotiations, an agreement has been reached between NATO and the EU ("Berlin Plus") regarding the resources (especially planning and command capabilities) on which the ESDP can rely for its missions if NATO decides it does not want be involved in a specific operation.

All partners must join in the global transformation process, which has been led by the United States. For this purpose, all in the ellipse have to agree on which tasks they want to undertake and can jointly tackle. Early issues for cooperative action have been the initiatives of the "EU-3"—the foreign ministers from France, Germany, and Britain—toward Iran to dissuade Tehran from developing nuclear capacities for military purposes as well as the joint support of the EU, Americans, Russians, and the United Nations for the road map to the Arab-Israeli conflict. Future tasks include rebuilding Afghanistan and Iraq as well as jointly coping with future crises.

Although Germany is comfortable with a transatlantic ellipse, the basic question is whether the United States, France, and Britain are interested in such a structure of cooperation. France has for a long time sought to strengthen Europe's capability for action, but the French conception is fundamentally different from that of Germany. Paris wants to develop the European Union into a counterweight to the United States, whereas Berlin assumes that a strong Europe should be a reliable partner of Washington. Germany wants to retain the Atlantic alliance as a transatlantic framework for action and as an instrument for crisis management and peace enforcement. But an ellipse might provide a more suitable structure because NATO is limited in membership and purpose.

The American position toward Europe is, however, marked by ambivalence. Washington requests a larger European contribution in meeting global problems, but it is apprehensive about the evolution of a European competitor. To safeguard its position, Washington frequently uses NATO to bring its European partners into line. Each time it notices indications for the evolution of a European nucleus—as when leaders of four European states meeting in Tervuren decided to develop a common European defense planning and operational unit—it tries to divide the Europeans among themselves and prevent the development of an autonomous and credible ESDP.

The biggest stumbling block for a larger European role is—as the failure to ratify the constitutional treaty by two major EU countries has shown—both a lack of a consensus regarding the future political order on the continent and a lack of will to muster the necessary resources. Only with credible capabilities will the Europeans have a chance to be listened to in the world. They therefore need to strengthen their potential for common action, especially by further developing the Common Foreign and Security Policy and the ESDP. If the Europeans try to form a counterweight against the United States, they will necessarily fail, for at least two reasons. First, the protagonists of such a position cannot count on the support of a majority of European states; second, the United States will prevent building such a counterweight. But Europe is not America's vassal. The Americans, for their part, have now realized that not even a superpower can lift the world's burdens all by itself, and that it needs allies. Europe should offer itself as a partner for these tasks.[21] The ellipse can be the framework for such cooperation.

Notes

1. See Christian Hacke, "Deutschland, Europa und der Irankonflikt," *Aus Politik und Zeitgeschichte* B24–25 (June 10, 2003): 8–16; and Robert Graham and Haig Simonian, *Prospects for the Franco-German Relationship: The Elysee Treaty and After,* AICGS Policy Report 4 (Washington, D.C.: American Institute for Contemporary German Studies, 2003). On the concept of the circles of German foreign policy, see David P. Calleo, *The German Problem Reconsidered: Germany and the World Order, 1870 to the Present* (Cambridge: Cambridge University Press, 1978); and Calleo, *Rethinking Europe's Future* (Princeton, N.J.: Princeton University Press, 2001).

2. Henry A. Kissinger, "Role Reversal and Alliance Realities," *Washington Post,* February 10, 2003. See also Ivo H. Daalder, "The End of Atlanticism," *Survival* (Summer 2003): 147.

3. "The Rift Turns Nasty: The Plot That Split Old and New Europe Asunder," *Financial Times,* May 28, 2003.
4. The National Security Strategy (Washington, D.C.: White House, 2002). For an account of the political and intellectual origins of this policy, see James Mann, *The Rise of the Vulcans: The History of Bush's War Cabinet* (New York: Viking Press, 2004).
5. For a good description of anti-Europeanism in the United States during this period, see Timothy Garton Ash, "Anti-Europeanism in America," *New York Review of Books,* February 13, 2003, 33. For an example of leftish anti-Americanism in Europe, see Will Hutton, *The World We're In* (London: Little, Brown, 2002).
6. Jim Hoagland, "Three Miscreants," *Washington Post,* April 13, 2003.
7. Philip Stephens, *Tony Blair: The Making of A World Leader* (New York: Viking Press, 2004), 227.
8. See http://www.doc.diplomatie.fr.
9. See, e.g., Jean-Claude Casanova, "De Charles de Gaulle à Jacques Chirac," *Le Monde,* July 25, 2003.
10. Henry A. Kissinger, *Does America Need a Foreign Policy? Toward a Diplomacy for the 21st Century* (New York: Simon & Schuster, 2001).
11. Gilles Delafon and Thomas Sancton, *Dear Jacques, cher Bill* (Paris: Plon, 1999).
12. Georges-Henri Soutou, "France, Nations and Empires from the Nineteenth Century to the Present Day: Between Jacobin Tradition, European Balance of Power and European Integration," in *Governance, Globalization and the European Union: Which Europe for Tomorrow?* ed. Henry Cavanna (Dublin: Four Courts Press, 2002).
13. In the case of Pompidou, see *Un politique: Georges Pompidou,* ed. Jean-Paul Cointet, Bernard Lachaise, Gilles Le Béguec, and Jean-Marie Mayeur (Paris, PUF, 2001).
14. See "Letter of Eight," *The Times,* January 30, 2003. Signatories were Tony Blair (Britain), Jose-Maria Aznar (Spain), Jose Manuel Durao Barroso (Portugal), Silvio Belusconi (Italy), Václav Havel (Czech Republic), Peter Medgyessy (Hungary), Leszek Miller (Poland), and Anders Fogh Rasmussen (Denmark).
15. Rede des Bundeskanzlers zum SPD-Wahlkampfauftakt, Hannover, August 5, 2002, http://www.wahlkampf 2002.net/redendokumente.phg.
16. See "Empörung in Berlin und Paris über Washington: Rumsfeld rügt das 'alte Europa,'" *Frankfurter Allgemeine Zeitung,* January 24, 2003.
17. See "Germany's Foreign and Security Policy in the Face of Global Challenges," Chancellor Angela Merkel's speech at the Forty-Second Munich Security Conference, http://www.securityconference.de/konferenzen/rede.php?menu_2006&menu_konfer...; and in comparison, Gerhard Schröder's speech on the same occasion a year earlier, http://www. www.securityconference.de/konferenzen/rede/php?menu_2.
18. See Gunther Hellmann, "Nationale Normalität als Zukunft? Zur Außenpolitik der Berliner Republik," *Blätter für Deutsche und Internationale Politik,* no. 7 (1999): 837–47.
19. See Karl Kaiser, *Deutschlands außenpolitische Verantwortung in einer interdependenten Welt* (Stuttgart: Robert Bosch Stiftung, 2000), 28.
20. Flora Lewis, "The Same Old French–U.S. Row," *International Herald Tribune,* December 13, 1996.
21. See Joseph S. Nye, *The Paradox of American Power: Why the World's Only Superpower Can't Go It Alone* (New York: Oxford University Press, 2002).

Contributors

William H. Becker is professor of history and international affairs at George Washington University. He was a visiting professor at L'École des Hautes Études en Sciences Sociales, Paris, in January 2004, and a public policy fellow at the Woodrow Wilson International Center for Scholars in summer 1998. During 1998 he was also a visiting professor at the National University of Singapore, and in 1996 at the Johns Hopkins University. His research and teaching interests focus on American business history and the history of the international economic system. He has authored or collaborated in writing six books and was the editor of a nine-volume encyclopedia of American business history.

Frédéric Bozo is professor of contemporary history at the Sorbonne (University of Paris III, Department of European Studies). Previously he was professor at the University of Nantes and associate professor at the University of Marne-la-Vallée He was a senior fellow at the Norwegian Nobel Institute in 2002, to which he will return in 2007. His focus is on French foreign and security policy, transatlantic relations, and Cold War history. His most recent publications include: *Mitterrand, la fin de la guerre froide et l'unification allemande: De Yalta à Maastricht* (Paris: Odile Jacob, 2005, Engl. transl. forthcoming); *Two Strategies for Europe: De Gaulle, the United States and the Atlantic Alliance* (Rowman & Littlefield, 2001); and *Etats-Unis-Europe: Réinventer l'Alliance,* co-edited with Jacques Beltran (Paris: Ifri, 2001).

Eric Bussière is professor (Chaire Jean Monnet) of contemporary European history at the Sorbonne (University of Paris IV), where he teaches the history of European integration. He is a member of the scientific advisory council of Comité pour l'histoire économique et financière de la France (CHEFF) and president of the advisory council of the Association Georges Pompidou. His research interests include banking history and European integration, especially in the field of economics. Among his most recent publications are: *Georges Pompidou face à la mutation économique de l'Occident, 1969–1974,* editor (Paris: PUF, 2003); and *London and Paris as International Financial Centres in the Twentieth Century,* coeditor with Youssef Cassis (Oxford University Press, 2005).

Desmond Dinan is Jean Monnet Professor of Public Policy at George Mason University and a visiting professor at the College of Europe, Natolin, Poland. His publications include *Europe Recast: A History of European Union* (Lynne Rienner, 2004); *Ever Closer Union: An Introduction to European Integration,* third edition (Lynne Rienner, 2005); and an edited volume, *Origins and Evolution of the European Union* (Oxford University Press, 2006).

Helga Haftendorn is Professor Emerita at the Free University of Berlin, and until 2000 was director of its Center on Transatlantic Foreign and Security Policy Studies. She previously taught at the University of Hamburg and at the Military University, also in Hamburg. She has been a visiting professor at Georgetown University, Stanford University, and the European University Institute in Florence; in 1988 and 1998, she was a visiting fellow at the Weatherhead Center for International Affairs at Harvard University. Currently she is serving as a consultant to various German government agencies. She has published widely on German foreign policy and on international affairs. Her latest book is *Coming of Age: German Foreign Policy since 1945* (Rowman & Littlefield, 2006).

Markus Jachtenfuchs is professor of European and international governance at the Hertie School of Governance in Berlin. He has served in various positions at the Mannheim University, Greifswald University, and International University, Bremen. His research interests are in the fields of European integration and the transformation of the state.

Martin Koopmann is in charge of the Franco-German Program of the German Council on Foreign Relations in Berlin. From 1998 to 2002 he was a research fellow at the Institute of Contemporary History, charged with editing the documents on German foreign policy, Auswärtiges Amt (Bonn/Berlin). His publications include *Partner oder Beitrittskandidaten? Die Nachbarschaftspolitik der Europäischen Union auf dem Prüfstand*, with Christian Lequesne (Nomos, 2006) and *Das schwierige Bündnis: Die deutsch-französischen Beziehungen und die Außenpolitik der Bundesrepublik Deutschland 1958–1965* (Nomos, 2000).

Michael Kreile is professor of international politics at Humboldt University, Berlin. From 1982 to 1992, he was professor of international politics, University of Constance. During the years 1974–82, he was an assistant professor at the Institute of Political Science, University of Heidelberg. He also was a Visiting Konrad Adenauer Professor, Georgetown University, Washington, D.C., in 1980–81.

Gale A. Mattox is chair and professor of the Political Science Department, U.S. Naval Academy, and chair of chairs. She is former president of Women in International Security, and has served at the Department of State, Policy Planning Staff, working on nonproliferation issues and Europe. As a Council on Foreign Relations Fellow, she worked at the Department of State Office of Strategic and Theater Nuclear Policy, as well as at the Congressional Research Service. She has published books on Germany and European defense, including *Enlarging NATO: The National Debates*, co-editor with Arthur Rachwald (Lynne Rienner, 2001).

Kori Schake is a research fellow at the Hoover Institution and Bradley Professor of International Security Studies at the United States Military Academy at West Point. Previously she was the director for Defense Strategy and Requirements on the National Security Council. She has held policy jobs in the Office of the Secretary of Defense and the Joint Staff, and was on the faculties of the Paul H. Nitze School of Advanced International Studies at the

Johns Hopkins University; the University of Maryland's graduate school of public affairs; and the National Defense University's Institute for National Strategic Studies.

Thomas A. Schwartz is professor of history at Vanderbilt University, and previously taught at Harvard University. His publications include *America's Germany: John McCloy and the Federal Republic of Germany* (Harvard University Press, 1991), and *Lyndon Johnson and Europe: In the Shadow of Vietnam* (Harvard University Press, 2003).

Georges-Henri Soutou is professor of contemporary history at the Sorbonne (University of Paris IV). He is vice chairman of the Commission de Publication des Archives du Ministère des Affaires Étrangères, in charge of the 1944–54 period. His field is the history of international relations in the twentieth century. His publications, among others, include *L'Alliance incertaine: Les rapports politico-strategiques franco-allemands, 1954–1996* (Fayard, 1996).

Stephen F. Szabo is professor of European studies at the Paul H. Nitze School of Advanced International Studies at the Johns Hopkins University and visiting professor at the Hertie School of Governance in Berlin. Previously, he was associate dean for academic affairs and then interim Dean of the Nitze School. From 1982 to 1990, he was associate dean and professor of national security affairs at the National Defense University. He was a Bosch Public Policy Fellow at the American Academy in Berlin in the fall of 2002 and held a fellowship with the Woodrow Wilson International Center for Scholars in 1988. He is the author of *Parting Ways: The Crisis in German-American Relations* (Brookings Institution Press, 2004), and other books.

Samuel F. Wells Jr. is associate director of the Woodrow Wilson International Center for Scholars in Washington, D.C., where he has worked in various capacities on issues of international security and European affairs since 1976. He has taught at Wellesley College and the University of North Carolina. He is the author of *The Challenges of Power: American Diplomacy, 1900–1921* (University Press of America, 1990), as well as studies of the Carter and Reagan defense programs, European reactions to the Strategic Defense Initiative, and the international policies of France during the presidency of François Mitterrand.

Index

Acheson, Dean, 113, 135, 136, 139
Adenauer, Konrad
   agricultural policy dispute, 38–39
   and Britain's EC membership discussions, 41, 45–46
   de Gaulle relationship generally, 44–45
   and EC economic proposals, 36
   Elysée Treaty, 2, 8, 48–49
   force planning negotiations, 134
   Fouchet Plans, 65–66, 68–69
   and France-U.S. relations, 9
   in free trade negotiations, 33, 34
   Rambouillet summit period, 58–63
Afghanistan, 15, 89, 272, 276, 380, 2374
agricultural policy disputes, 37, 38–40, 41–42, 46–47, 48, 66, 213
Ailleret, Charles, 112, 114–15
Albright, Madeleine, 355, 362, 363, 364

Allardt, Helmut, 214
Amsterdam Treaty, 315–18
Angola, 265
Ansiaux, Hubert, 177
arms control negotiations
   Helsinki Agreement, 278, 284–85n37, 285n44, 320–21
   INF missiles, 273, 279, 290–91, 293–94, 297–98
   Non-Proliferation Treaty, 82, 84
   SALT agreements, 192, 238, 239, 243, 246, 266–72, 283n19, 290
   Strategic Arms Reduction Treaty, 295, 298
   Strategic Defense Initiative, 295–96, 298
   Test Ban Treaty, 82, 84
   See also détente *entries;* NATO *entries*
Articles of Agreement, IMF, 155

Asmus, Ronald, 334–35, 338
Aspin, Les, 336, 337, 355
Austria, 163
Aznar, Jose-Maria, 372

Bahr, Egon, 212, 213, 214–15, 216, 219, 220, 237, 249
Baker, James, 301–2, 328–29, 353
balance of payments problem, 140, 150, 151, 161, 162, 164–65, 199–200
See also international monetary policy
Balkan conflicts
  Bosnia, 330, 338–39, 342, 351–52, 354, 357–60, 363, 366, 367n10
  G. H. W. Bush administration approach, 352–55
  Clinton administration approach, 355–67
  Kosovo, 11, 352, 359–65, 366, 367n3, 369nn38–39, n43
  and NATO enlargement debate, 346
  overviews, 351–52, 365–67
Ball, George
  European Community development, 38–39, 40–41, 43, 46–47, 48, 49
  NATO crisis, 113, 130, 133, 134–35
Banque de France, 173, 174–75, 182, 183, 184–85
Barber, Anthony, 160
Barre, Raymond, 174, 179, 184, 185
Bartholomew, Reginald, 300
Barzel, Rainer, 241, 242
Basic Treaty, 217–18, 219
Bator, Francis, 131–33, 135, 136, 137–38, 140, 167n10
Becker, William
  biographical highlights, 389
  chapter by, 189–206
  comments on, 23
Belgium
  détente policies, 83, 94
  in European Community development, 43, 44, 69
  international monetary policy, 162, 176, 177–78, 179

nuclear freeze movement, 273
Bell and Howell Company, 197
Berger, Sandy, 364
Berlin, in *Ostpolitik* negotiations, 214, 215, 218, 219–20
Berlin Agreement, 221, 242–43
Bitterlich, Joachim, 333, 347n10
Blair, Tony, 2, 372, 374, 381, 385
Blankenhorn, Herbert, 61, 67
Blessing letter, 140, 152, 167n10
Bohlen, Charles, 48, 105, 111, 133, 143n27
Bonn Declaration, 64
borders, in *Ostpolitik* negotiations, 214–15, 235, 248, 263
border tax, Nixon administration, 201, 202
Bosnia, 330, 338–39, 342, 351–52, 354, 357–60, 363, 366, 367n10
Bozo, Frédéric
  biographical highlights, 389–90
  chapter by, 103–26
  comments on, 23
Brandon, Henry, 128
Brandt, Karl, 39
Brandt, Willy
  European Security conference, 221
  foreign minister appointment, 138
  international monetary policy, 158, 181, 184
  NATO crisis, 94, 98, 117
  Ostpolitik policy, 211, 212–13, 216, 217, 218, 249
Brentano, Heinrich von, 59, 60, 67
Bretton Woods system, overview of collapse factors, 149–55
See also international monetary policy
Brezhnev, Leonid
  and Carter administration, 265–66, 269–70, 275
  de Gaulle discussions, 232
  and Nixon administration, 222
  Pompidou discussions, 235, 241, 245, 247
Britain
  Amsterdam Treaty negotiations, 317

and Elysée Treaty, 2
European Community membership,
   31, 40, 41–48, 64–65, 72n28
exchange rate negotiations, 157, 158,
   160, 163
Fouchet Plans, 66
France relations, 31–32, 33–34, 40,
   42–44, 47
free trade area proposals, 30, 31–37
Kosovo conflict, 368n22
in Maastricht process, 314
in NATO crisis, 84, 87, 89, 90–91,
   118, 137, 140
nuclear freeze movement, 273
and *Ostpolitik* policy, 213, 216, 219,
   220–21
and Pompidou's détente policy, 230
pound crisis, 159, 171
Britain-U.S. relations
and G. H. W. Bush administration, 299
during G. W. Bush administration,
   372, 374, 381, 382
during Reagan administration, 288,
   289–90, 292, 296, 299
and strategic triangle future, 385
traditional, 19
Britain-U.S. relations, and European
   Community development
Britain's membership discussions, 31,
   41–42, 46, 64–65, 72n28
and free trade negotiations, 30, 33, 34,
   35–36
Kennedy's Grand Alliance vision, 37–38
Nassau Agreement, 47–48, 78
Brosio, Manlio, 95
Bruce, David, 131
Brzezinski, Zbigniew, 336, 339
Budapest Declaration, 211
budgets, military
in NATO crisis, 81, 84, 89–90,
   137–38, 140, 144n50
Reagan administration, 289, 296
Bulgaria, 372
Bundesbank, 152, 157, 159, 165,
   167n10, 175, 182, 311, 312

Bundestag, Elysée Treaty resolution, 49,
   109
Bundy, McGeorge, 105, 128, 129–30,
   131–32, 143n27
Burns, Arthur, 195
Burt, Richard, 290, 291, 292, 295–96,
   297, 302, 336
Bush, George H. W. (and
   administration), 298, 299–302,
   303–4, 352–55
Bush, George W. (and administration),
   371–74, 380–81, 383–84
Bussière, Eric
   biographical highlights, 390
   chapter by, 171–87
   comments on, 23

Camps, Miriam, 34
Canada, European Security conference,
   221, 222
Cannon, Lou, 295
CAP (Common Agricultural Policy), 37,
   38–40, 41–42, 46–47, 48, 66, 213
Carstens, Karl, 67, 211
Carter, Jimmy (and administration),
   164–65, 265–72, 275, 279, 345
Cecchini, Paolo, 303
CFSP (Common Foreign and Security
   Policy), 5, 316–17
Chaban-Delmas, Jacques, 108
Charter 77 group, 277, 285n44
Cheney, Dick, 300, 353
Chicken War, 40
   See also Common Agricultural Policy
   (CAP)
China, 192, 232, 243, 244
Chirac, Jacques
   Amsterdam Treaty negotiations, 316
   Balkan crises, 352
   and France's NATO membership, 16,
      300, 377
   Iraq conflict, 372, 374
   NATO enlargement debate, 342, 343
Christian Democratic Union (CDU), 211,
   241, 313, 331

Christian Democratic Union/Christian
  Social Union (CDU/CSU), 61, 79,
  98, 138, 211, 383
Christopher, Warren, 355
Church, Frank, 271
CIA report, on Soviet Union, 292–93
civil rights movement, 193
Clappier, Bernard, 177, 178, 182
Clark, Wesley, 361, 363
Clark, William P., 291
Cleveland, Harlan, 136
Clinton, Bill (and administration),
  336–42, 343–44, 353, 355–67,
  368n22
Cohen, Eliot, 367n3
Cohen, Warren, 143n27
Cohen, William, 362, 363
Committee of Governors, 174–77, 182
Committee of Twenty, 153–54, 160–61
Common Agricultural Policy (CAP), 37,
  38–40, 41–42, 46–47, 48, 66, 213
Common Foreign and Security Policy
  (CFSP), 5, 316–17
Conference on Security and Cooperation
  in Europe (CSCE)
  Balkan crises, 354
  and German reunification, 299
  and human rights, 274–76, 278
  NATO enlargement debate, 329–30
  Nixon administration approach, 222
  and Pompidou's détente policies, 243,
    245–47, 248
  Review Conference conflicts, 274–77
confidence problem, in Bretton Woods
  collapse, 150, 151–52, 153, 189–90,
  199–200
Congress, U.S.
  Balkan crises, 355–56, 357–59, 364
  defense spending generally, 367n10
  and NATO force planning, 90, 118,
    137
Connally, John, 158, 194, 196–97,
  199–201, 203
conventional forces. *See* force planning,
  in NATO crisis; Mutual and
  Balanced Force Reductions (MBFR)

Conventional Forces in Europe Treaty,
  298
Copenhagen criteria, EU membership,
  318–19, 320
Costigliola, Frank, 143n29
Council for International Economic
  Policy, 197
Couve de Murville, Maurice, 61, 67, 111,
  117, 122n35
credibility problem, in NATO crisis,
  106–7, 118–19
Croatia, 352, 354
CSCE. *See* Conference on Security and
  Cooperation in Europe (CSCE)
Cuba, 265, 271
currency crises. *See* international
  monetary policy
Czechoslovakia, 84, 211, 215, 217, 278,
  285n44
Czech Republic, 340

Dallek, Robert, 128
Davis, Lynn E., 282n10
Dayton Peace Accords, 358, 366–67
Debré, Michel, 38
Defense Department, U.S.
  and France's NATO withdrawal, 113,
    130–31
  and INF negotiations, 290–91
  NATO enlargement debate, 336,
    337–38, 341
  Reagan administration policy
    approach, 289, 295–96, 298
Defense Ministry, Germany, 330–34,
  335, 339–40
Defense Planning Committee, NATO's,
  115, 117
deficits, in Bretton Woods collapse. *See*
  international monetary policy
de Gaulle, Charles
  franc valuation, 152–53, 157
  on Lyndon Johnson, 128
  Pompidou views compared, 230,
    231–32, 233–34, 235–36
  resignation factors, 378
  Soviet relations, 231–32

and strategic triangle generally, 12–13, 14, 20
de Gaulle, Charles (and European Community development)
　agricultural policy dispute, 38
　Bonn Declaration, 64
　Elysée Treaty, 8
　Fouchet Plans, 43–45, 53n45, 65, 68–69
　free trade area negotiations, 32, 33–34
　Rambouillet summit period, 59–60, 61, 63–64, 71n9
　and U.S. Grand Alliance vision, 37–38
　U.S. relations generally, 49–50
　veto of Britain's membership, 31, 40, 47–48, 50
de Gaulle, Charles (in NATO crisis)
　diplomacy stages, 108–10
　Harmel Report, 119
　military cooperation after withdrawal, 112, 115
　nuclear defense policies, 81, 99n5
　policy goals, 78–79, 104–5, 110, 112
　Soviet relations, 79, 83, 105–6, 109–10, 121n8
　withdrawal announcement and activity, 90, 97, 99n6, 110–12
Deguen, Daniel, 174
Dellums, Ron, 356
Delors, Jacques, 185
Democratic Party (U.S.), 192–93
Denmark, 83, 163
d'Estaing, Giscard
　monetary policy, 161, 163–64, 173, 178–79, 180, 184
　and strategic triangle generally, 12, 14–15
　U.S. relations generally, 244, 377–78
détente policies
　Carter administration, 266–72
　and German reunification question, 83, 94, 101n24, 236–37
　Johnson approach, 129–30, 138–39
　Nixon's goals, 191–92
　overviews, 230, 261–65, 277–82

　Reagan administration, 272–73, 274–77, 292
　See also Ostpolitik policy
détente policies, and NATO crisis
　de Gaulle's approach, 79, 83, 105–6, 109–10
　Harmel Report, 93–97, 119–20
　legitimacy factor, 107
　U.S.-Soviet Union negotiations, 82–83
détente policies, Pompidou's approach
　and Ostpolitik policy, 213, 236–38
　philosophy summarized, 229–33, 251–53
　Soviet Union discussions, 234–36, 240–48
　U.S. relations, 243–44, 250
Deutsch, Karl, 5
deutsche mark. See international monetary policy
devaluation arguments. See international monetary policy
Diebold, William, 39
Dillon, Douglas, 32–33, 34, 35, 36, 38
Dillon Round, GATT, 42
Dinan, Desmond
　biographical highlights, 390
　chapter by, 29–53
　comments on, 22
Dole, Robert, 356
dollar standard
　confidence factor, 189–90, 199–201
　convertibility policies, 167n10, 181, 190
　gold termination decision, 150, 155
　liquidity problem, 150–51
　and NATO force planning, 140, 141
　oil pricing effects, 154–55, 202
　See also exchange mechanisms
drawing rights, 152, 174–75
Duckwitz, Ferdinand, 216
Dulles, John Foster, 104

Eagleburger, Lawrence, 353
East-West relations. See détente entries; Ostpolitik policy; Soviet Union entries

ECB (European Central Bank), 312
ECJ (European Court of Justice), 312–17
ECMF (European monetary cooperation fund), 182
Economic and Monetary Union (EMU), 162–63
economic relations, Reagan and G. H. W. Bush administrations, 301–3
See also budgets, military; European Community development; international monetary policy
Economics Ministry, Germany, 58
Eden, Anthony, 136
EFTA (European Free Trade Association), 34–35
Eisenhower, Dwight D. (and administration), 36, 40, 63, 108, 190
El Salvador, 288, 289
Elysée Treaty, 2, 8–9, 14, 48–49, 109
émigrés, in *Ostpolitik* negotiations, 217
Emminger, Otmar, 160, 175, 177–78, 182
EMS (European Monetary System), 15, 163–64, 202–3, 311–13
EMU (Economic and Monetary Union), 162–63
enhanced radiation weapons (ERW), 283n13
EP (European Parliament), 66, 67, 312–17
Erhard, Ludwig
 Britain's EC membership, 45–46
 chancellorship assumption, 49
 de Gaulle's political union initiative, 58
 free trade negotiations, 34, 35, 36
 Johnson relationship, 129
 in NATO crisis, 84, 135–36, 138
 and strategic triangle generally, 98
Ermarth, Fritz, 293
ERW (enhanced radiation weapons), 283n13
ESC (European Security conference), 211–12, 220, 221–22, 231, 234, 241–42
See also Conference on Security and Cooperation in Europe (CSCE)

ESDI (European Security and Defense Identity), 300–301
ESDP (European Security and Defense Policy), 10–11, 320–21, 385
Eurêka program, 296, 297
Eurocorps proposal, 300–301, 330, 332, 342, 344
eurodollar market, 206n39
European Central Bank (ECB), 312
European Community development
 agricultural policy dispute, 37, 38–40
 Bonn Declaration, 64
 Britain's membership, 31, 40, 41–42, 45–48, 64–65
 and Elysée Treaty, 48–49
 Fouchet Plans, 65–69
 and free trade area negotiations, 31–37
 overviews, 29–31, 49–51, 55–58, 69–70
 Rambouillet summit period, 58–63, 68–69, 362
 and U.S. Grand Alliance vision, 37–38, 40–45
See also international monetary policy; NATO *entries*
European Council, 313, 315–17
European Court of Justice (ECJ), 312–17
European Free Trade Association (EFTA), 34–35
European monetary cooperation fund (ECMF), 182
European Monetary System (EMS), 15, 163–64, 202–3, 311–13
European Parliament (EP), 66, 67, 312–17
European Police Office (EUROPOL), 314, 317
European Political Union. *See* European Community development
European Security and Defense Identity (ESDI), 300–301
European Security and Defense Policy (ESDP), 10–11, 320–21, 385
European Security conference (ESC), 211–12, 220, 221–22, 231, 234, 241–42

See also Conference on Security and Cooperation in Europe (CSCE)
EUROPOL (European Police Office), 314, 317
exchange mechanisms
  under Bretton Woods system, 149–53, 155–57
  overview of transition, 171–73, 189–91, 201–3
  reform negotiations, 152–54, 155, 157–61, 177–85
  regional cooperation incentives, 162–65, 201–3
  Smithsonian Agreement effects, 153
  See also international monetary policy
export statistics, 198
Extraction Force, NATO, 361

Falin, Valentin, 215
Federal Reserve Board, U.S., 195
Finance Ministry, France, 173, 174–76
Finland, 22, 221
fixed exchange rate. *See* exchange mechanisms
Flanagan, Stephen, 339
flexible exchange rate. *See* exchange mechanisms
Flexible Response strategy
  adoption of, 87, 89, 97, 117, 118–19, 141
  proposal and negotiations, 78, 80, 86–87, 107
  reform arguments, 269, 294
Force d'Action Rapide, 294
force planning, in NATO crisis
  budget factors, 81, 84, 89–90, 118, 137–38, 144n50
  Lisbon gap, 88, 101n29
  negotiations, 88–91, 102n30, 116–17, 134–40
  and nuclear defense policies, 85–88, 141
  overview, 80–81, 118–19, 131
Ford, Gerald (and administration), 263, 268, 284n35

Foreign Office, Germany
  de Gaulle's political union initiative, 58–59
  Fouchet Plans, 65–67, 69
  NATO enlargement debate, 331, 333, 335–36, 339–40, 341
Fouchet, Christian, 43
Fouchet Plans, 14, 43–45, 53n45, 62–69
franc. *See* international monetary policy
France
  and Afghanistan, 380
  Balkan conflicts, 352, 356–57, 365
  international monetary policy generally, 171–76, 185–86
  NATO enlargement perspectives generally, 342–44, 346
  nuclear freeze movement, 273
  See also NATO crisis (1966–67); *additional* France *entries*
France, in strategic triangle (overview)
  dynamic challenges, 2–5, 9, 11–19, 375–79
  future requirements, 384–86
  importance of, 1–2, 377
  national identity issues, 5–8
France-Britain relations
  EC membership discussions, 31, 40, 42–44, 47
  free trade area negotiations, 31–32, 33–34
  and strategic triangle generally, 2, 3
France-Germany relations
  Amsterdam Treaty, 315–18
  and détente generally, 281–82
  EU enlargement policy, 318–20
  Helsinki summit, 320–21
  Maastricht process, 310–15
  Mitterrand period, 287–88, 293–94, 296–97
  and NATO enlargement debate, 343–44, 346
  and *Ostpolitik* policy, 212, 216, 220–24, 236–38, 248–49
  and Pompidou's détente policy, 235, 236–38, 241, 242–43, 248–49

France-Germany relations, and European
    Community development
  Bonn Declaration, 64
  Elysée Treaty, 2, 8, 48–49, 109
  Fouchet Plans, 65–69
  in free trade negotiations, 33, 34, 35,
    36–37
  overviews, 29–31, 44–45, 50–51,
    55–58, 69–70
  Rambouillet summit period, 58–64
France-Germany relations, and NATO
    crisis
  détente policies, 82, 94, 95
  and force planning negotiations, 90,
    117, 134–36
  nuclear defense policies, 81, 99n5,
    122n31
  overviews, 79–80, 82, 97–99, 108–9,
    120–21
  September Memorandum, 122n22
France-Germany relations, international
    monetary policy
  currency valuation arguments, 152–53,
    157
  exchange mechanism negotiations,
    157–59, 160–61, 175–76, 177–80,
    182–85
  overview, 161–62, 171–72
  regional cooperation incentives,
    163–65
France-Soviet Union relations
  de Gaulle period, 79, 105–6
  and détente generally, 281–82
  Mitterrand period, 15–16, 290
  Pompidou period, 231–38, 240–48,
    249–52
France-U.S. relations
  during Balkan crises, 356–57, 358,
    365–67
  during G. H. W. Bush administration,
    299–301, 306–7n28
  during G. W. Bush administration,
    372–73, 374–76, 381
  and détente generally, 281–82
  international monetary policy, 151–52,
    161, 172–73, 180, 181–82, 190

during Johnson administration, 128,
    129, 130–32, 143n28
  and NATO enlargement debate, 343
  and *Ostpolitik* policy, 223–24, 239
  Pompidou period, 230–31, 232–33,
    235, 238–40, 243–45, 249–53,
    376–78
  during Reagan administration, 287–88,
    290, 291, 292, 294, 296–97, 299
  and Vietnam War, 82, 129, 233
France-U.S. relations, and European
    Community development
  agricultural policy dispute, 37, 38, 39
  in Bonn Declaration, 64
  Britain's membership, 42–43, 46
  Fouchet plans, 44
  and free trade area negotiations, 35, 36
  Kennedy's Grand Alliance vision,
    37–38
  and Nassau agreement, 47–48, 78
  overviews, 30–31, 49–50, 55–58,
    69–70
  Rambouillet summit period, 63, 72n22
France-U.S. relations, and NATO crisis
  background, 130–32
  de Gaulle's diplomatic overtures, 108,
    109–10, 111
  nuclear defense policies, 99n5, 107, 111
  overviews, 78–80, 82, 97–99, 104–5,
    120–21
  in post-withdrawal military
    negotiations, 115–16, 124n58, 134
  at withdrawal announcement, 109,
    111, 112–14, 122n35, 132–34
Franco-British Rapid Reaction Force,
    352
Franco-German Treaty (1963), 90
Free Democratic Party (Germany), 79,
    153, 312, 331
Freedman, Lawrence, 86
Freeman, Orville, 39
free trade area (FTA), proposals, 30,
    31–37
Fromkin, David, 364
frontiers, in *Ostpolitik* negotiations,
    214–15, 216–17, 235, 248, 263

FTA (free trade area), proposals, 30, 31–37

Garthoff, Raymond, 293
gas pipeline controversy, 273–74, 291–93, 305n9
General Agreement on Tariffs and Trade (GATT), 35, 40, 42, 155, 302
Genscher, Hans Dietrich, 276, 328, 331
German Democratic Republic, in *Ostpolitik* negotiations, 214, 215, 217–19, 220–21
See also German reunification
German-German Traffic Treaty, 218
German reunification
  and G. H. W. Bush administration, 299
  de Gaulle's views, 232
  and détente policies, 83, 94, 101n24, 280–81
  and Maastricht process, 314–15
  and NATO enlargement debate, 235–36, 328–30, 346n1
  and *Ostpolitik* negotiations, 215, 216
  Pompidou views, 235–37
Germany
  and Afghanistan, 380
  Balkan crises, 352, 360, 365
  export statistics, 198
  nuclear freeze movement, 273
  See also additional Germany *entries*
Germany, in strategic triangle (overview)
  dynamics challenges, 2–5, 8–11, 379–84
  future requirements, 384–86
  importance of, 1–2
  national identity issues, 5–6, 7–8
Germany, international monetary policy
  balance of payments problem, 156–57
  under Bretton Woods system, 149–50, 155–56
  currency revaluation pressures, 152–53, 157, 200
  dollar holdings, 152, 200
  exchange mechanism negotiations, 157–61, 177, 178–85
  overview of transition, 149–50, 165–66
  regional cooperation incentives, 161–65
  U.S. relations, 149–50, 158, 161, 164–65, 167n10
Germany, NATO enlargement policy
  international context, 330
  overviews, 345–46
  public opinion factor, 332
  RAND study, 334–36
  and reunification process, 328–30
  Rühe's role, 330–34, 337–38, 339–40
  U.S. relations, 327–28, 333, 334–35, 336–41, 344–46
Germany, *Ostpolitik* policy
  European Security conference, 221–22
  France relations, 212, 216, 220–24, 236–38, 248–49
  negotiations, 214–21
  overviews, 209–14, 222–24
  U.S. relations, 212–13, 216, 219, 220–21, 223–24, 225nn12–13
Germany-France relations
  Amsterdam Treaty, 315–18
  and détente generally, 281–82
  EU enlargement policy, 318–20
  Helsinki summit, 320–21
  Kohl period, 293–94, 296–97
  Maastricht process, 310–15
  Mitterrand period, 287–88, 293–94, 296–97
  and NATO enlargement debate, 343–44, 346
  and *Ostpolitik* policy, 212, 216, 220–24, 236–38, 248–49
  and Pompidou's détente policy, 230–32, 235–38, 241, 242–43, 248–49
  Schmidt period, 293–94
Germany-France relations, and European Community development
  Bonn Declaration, 64
  Elysée Treaty, 2, 8, 48–49, 109
  Fouchet Plans, 65–69
  in free trade negotiations, 33, 34, 35, 36

Germany-France relations, and European Community development (*continued*)
  overviews, 29–31, 44–45, 50–51, 55–58, 69–70
  Rambouillet summit period, 58–64
Germany-France relations, and NATO crisis
  détente policies, 82, 94, 95
  and force planning negotiations, 90, 117, 134–36
  nuclear defense policies, 81, 99n5, 122n31
  overviews, 79–80, 82, 97–99, 108–9, 120–21
  September Memorandum, 122n22
Germany-France relations, international monetary policy
  currency valuation arguments, 152–53, 157
  exchange mechanism negotiations, 157–59, 160–61, 175–76, 177–80, 182–85
  overview, 161–62, 171–72
  regional cooperation incentives, 163–65
Germany-Soviet Union relations
  NATO enlargement debate, 328, 330, 333, 334, 335–36, 340, 341–42, 346n1
  Ostpolitik policy, 2, 209–16, 220–22
Germany-U.S. relations
  Balkan crises, 365–67
  G. H. W. Bush administration, 299–301
  G. W. Bush administration, 371–75, 379–84
  and détente generally, 279–81
  European Security conference, 221, 222
  international monetary policy, 149–50, 158, 161, 164–65, 167n10
  Kohl period, 293–94
  NATO enlargement debate, 327–28, 333, 334–35, 336–41, 344–46
  Reagan administration, 290, 293–97
  SALT agreements, 266–68, 283n19
  and Vietnam War, 82, 101n20

Germany-U.S. relations, and European Community development
  agricultural policy dispute, 37, 38–39
  in Bonn Declaration, 64
  and Britain's EC membership application, 44–45
  Elysée Treaty, 48–49
  and free trade area negotiations, 35
  overviews, 30–31, 55–58
  Rambouillet summit period, 61, 62–63
Germany-U.S. relations, and NATO crisis
  background, 131
  détente policies, 82–83, 139
  force planning negotiations, 85–91, 134–36, 137–38, 139–40
  at France withdrawal announcement, 113, 123n49, n54, 133–34
  nuclear defense policies, 81, 85–88, 92–93, 141
  overviews, 79–80, 82, 97–99, 109, 141–42
GLCM missiles, 269
Glenn, John, 271, 284n27
G-10 meetings, 157
gold. *See* dollar standard
Goldgeier, James M., 337, 341, 347n14
Goldman, Eric, 127–28
Goldwater, Barry, 130
Gomułka, Władysław, 217
Gorbachev, Mikhail, 291, 297–98, 328–30
Gordon, Michael, 347n7
Gould, Lewis L., 127
Grand Alliance vision, 37–38, 40–45
Grechko, Marshall, 256n67
Gromyko, Andrej, 214–15, 216, 233, 240–41, 243
Gronchi, Giovanni, 58
ground campaign arguments, Kosovo conflict, 364–65, 369nn38 & 39
Gulf War, 330, 342

Haftendorn, Helga
  biographical highlights, 390–91

chapters and section by, 77–102,
209–27, 379–84
comments on, 23, 24, 106, 141
Haig, Alexander, 291–92
Haines, Gerald K., 292
Haldeman, H. R., 199
Hallstein doctrine, 210
Harmel, Pierre, 93–94
Harmel Report, 93–97, 119
Havel, Václav, 285n44, 331, 337
Helms, Jesse, 356
Helsinki summit and agreement, 278,
284–85n37, 285n44, 320–21
Henning, Randall, 161–62
Herter, Christian, 35
Hoffmann, Stanley, 77
Holbrooke, Richard, 335, 336–42,
348n2, 360, 361, 363, 368n22
hostage crisis, Iranian, 271
humanitarian relief, Bosnian, 354–55
human rights, 274–75, 277
Hungary, 340
Hutchings, Robert, 300, 301, 303, 330
Hyland, William G., 283n23

IMF (International Monetary Fund),
153–55, 160–61
Implementation Force (IFOR), 359
import statistics, 198
inflation control, Nixon administration,
195–96, 204n14
See also exchange mechanisms
INF (intermediate-range nuclear forces)
missiles, 273, 279, 290, 293–94,
297–98
International Energy Agency, 5
International Monetary Fund (IMF),
153–55, 160–61
international monetary policy
under Bretton Woods system, 149–53
European cooperation incentives,
161–65, 172, 174–76, 201–3
exchange mechanism negotiations,
152–54, 155, 157–61, 177–80
and Maastricht process, 311–12
oil pricing effects, 154–55, 202

overviews of transition, 149–50,
165–66, 171–73, 185–86, 189–91
and Pompidou's détente policy, 239–40
U.S. domestic context, 191–201,
204n14
Iran, 271, 297, 298, 385
Iraq conflict, 371–72, 373, 379–82
Ireland, 160, 163
Ischinger, Wolfgang, 333
Italy
détente policies, 83, 163
France's security/political proposals,
58, 69
international monetary policy, 158,
160, 162, 163, 177–78, 182
nuclear freeze movement, 273

Jachtenfuchs, Markus
biographical highlights, 391
chapter by, 309–24
comments on, 24
Jamaica Agreement, 155, 161
James, Harold, 154
Japan, 158, 165, 198, 202
Jobert, Michel, 157–58, 180, 243, 247,
249, 250–51
Joffe, Josef, 294
Johnson, Lyndon (and administration)
de Gaulle relationship, 136, 143n27
détente policies, 83–84, 129–30, 138–39
domestic programs, 194–95
economic conditions, 194
exchange rate actions, 190
France relations generally, 128, 129,
130–32, 143n28
Germany relations, 90, 134–41
NATO crisis, 112–14, 123n49, n54,
133–37
overview, 127–29, 141–42
Soviet Union relations, 81–84, 92–93,
130, 132, 137
Vietnam War factor, 82–83
Juppé, Alain, 343

Kaiser, Rolf, 159
Kampelman, Max, 277

Kaplan, Fred M., 283n13
Kaplan, Lawrence, 136, 145n73
Kasich, John, 356
Kastl, Joerg, 275–76
Kennedy, John F. (and administration)
  and Britain's EC application, 41–42, 46, 64
  de Gaulle relations, 49, 104, 109, 122n35
  economic conditions, 194
  exchange rate actions, 190
  Grand Alliance vision, 37–38, 40–45
  missile gap description, 285n40
  NATO enlargement debate comparison, 345
  Soviet relations, 105
Kennedy Round, GATT, 42, 50
Kiesinger, Kurt, 95, 138, 139, 157, 211
Kinkel, Klaus, 331, 333, 335–36, 340, 341–42, 347n10
Kissinger, Henry
  détente goals, 263, 282n7
  European policy goals, 192
  and gold standard change, 201, 203
  NATO enlargement debate, 336
  and *Ostpolitik* policy, 213, 218, 220, 222, 225nn12–13
  and Pompidou's détente policy, 243–44, 251
  and SALT II agreement, 270
Klasen, Karl, 181, 185
Kohl, Helmut
  Amsterdam Treaty, 316, 317
  INF missiles, 294
  Maastricht process, 311, 313
  NATO enlargement debate, 333, 335–36, 340, 341–42, 348n23, 349n32
Kohl, Michael, 218
Koopmann, Martin
  biographical highlights, 391
  chapter by, 55–73
  comments on, 22–23
Kosovo, 11, 352, 359–65, 366, 367n3, 369nn38, 39, & 43

Kosygin, Alexei, 216
Kreile, Michael
  biographical highlights, 391
  chapter by, 149–69
  comments on, 23
Krone, Heinrich, 61
Kugler, Richard, 334–35

Lake, Anthony, 336–37, 341
Lanxade, Jacques, 300
Larosiére, Jacques de, 161
Larrabee, Stephen, 334–35, 337, 338
Larre, René, 174, 176, 178
leadership problem, in NATO crisis, 106, 108, 118
Leggett, Robert E., 292
legitimacy problem, in NATO crisis, 107, 119–20
Lemnitzer, Lyman, 112, 114–15
Lennep, Émile van, 175
Lewis, Flora, 9
liquidity problem, in Bretton Woods collapse, 150–51, 152–53, 189–90, 200
Lisbon gap, 88, 101n29, 102n30
Louis, Victor, 256n67
Lugar, Richard, 335, 339
Luxembourg, 175–76

Maastricht Treaty, 16, 310–15, 318
MacEachin, Douglas, 293
Macmillan, Harold, 33, 34, 36, 47
Mandelbaum, Michael, 346n1
Mansfield, Mike, 90, 118, 137
Matlock, Jack, 329
Mattox, Gale
  biographical highlights, 391–92
  chapter by, 261–85
  comments on, 24
MBFR (Mutual and Balanced Force Reductions), 221, 222, 238, 239, 241, 246–47, 248
McCain, John, 364
McCloy, John, 90, 113, 118, 123n49, 135, 140
McCracken, Paul, 195

McFarlane, Robert, 295
McGhee, George, 131, 134
McNamara, Robert, 78, 88, 113, 130–31, 134–35, 138, 144*n*50
membership enlargement policy, European Union, 318–21, 333–34, 335, 340, 343, 349*n*31
See also NATO enlargement debate
Menon, Anand, 306–7*n*28
Merkel, Angela, 374, 383
Millon, Charles, 343
Milosevic, Slobodan, 359–63
Mitterrand, François
  foreign policy goals generally, 311
  NATO enlargement debate, 342
  and Reagan administration, 290, 291, 296, 299, 301
  security dialogue proposal, 293
  and strategic triangle generally, 12, 15–16
MLF (Multilateral Force), 81, 92–93, 130, 137
Monetary Committee, 174–78, 180–81, 182, 183
  See also international monetary policy
Monnet, Jean, 13–14, 43, 53*n*45
Moscow Treaty, 215–16, 220
Multilateral Force (MLF), 81, 92–93, 130, 137
multipolarity, French perspective, 56–57, 375–76
Murphy, James M., 303
Mutual and Balanced Force Reductions (MBFR), 221, 222, 238, 239, 241, 246–47, 248

Nassau Agreement, 47–48, 78
national identity, and strategic triangle generally, 5–8
National Security Council, pipeline controversy, 291–92
National Technical Means (NTM), 271
NATO
  and ESDP resources agreement, 385
  and European Community development, 33–34, 36, 57, 59–61, 62–63, 66
  and European Security conference, 220, 221
  and French-German joint maneuvers, 296–97
  and German reunification, 299
  and Helsinki summit, 321
  Pompidou's policy approach, 234–35
  and SS-20 missile threat, 269, 279, 283*nn*23 & 25, 289
  and Turkey's potential EU membership, 320
  and WEU discussions, 299–301
NATO, Balkan conflicts
  air campaign, 356
  and G. H. W. Bush administration, 353–54
  and Clinton administration, 357–59
  early involvement, 354
  Kosovo conflict, 359–65, 368*n*22, 369*n*43
  overviews, 351–52, 365–67
  peacekeeping forces, 357
  and UN, 368*n*12
NATO crisis (1966–67)
  background, 78–80, 130–32
  budget factor, 81, 84, 89–90, 137–38, 140, 144*n*50
  causes, 80–85, 104–10
  détente policy approaches, 93–97, 119–20, 136–37
  nuclear defense policies, 81, 85–88, 91–93, 119, 122*n*31, 141
  overviews, 77, 97–99, 106–7, 118–21
  and strategic triangle generally, 4–5, 9, 10, 14, 97–99
  and structural reform, 97, 118–20, 122*n*35
  See also force planning, in NATO crisis
NATO crisis (1966–67), and France
  de Gaulle's policy goals, 78–79, 83, 104–6, 108–10, 112
  post-withdrawal military negotiations, 112, 114–16, 124*n*58, *n*61, *n*63, *n*70

NATO crisis (*continued*)
  September Memorandum, 122*n*22
  withdrawal announcement and activity, 90, 97, 99*nn*5–6, 110–14, 123*n*49, *n*54
NATO enlargement debate
  France viewpoints, 342–44
  and German reunification, 328–30, 346*n*1
  Germany's policy approaches, 330–34, 337–38, 344–45
  international context, 330
  overviews, 327–28, 344–46
  U.S. perspectives, 336–42
Naumann, Klaus, 361
Netherlands
  in European Community development, 43, 44, 66, 69
  international monetary policy, 162, 175, 177, 182, 183
  nuclear freeze movement, 273
neutron bomb, 266–67
Nicaragua, 288, 289, 298
Nixon, Richard (and administration)
  on détente, 264
  dollar crises, 199–201
  economic conditions, 194–97, 204*n*14
  Europe visits, 192, 211, 220
  exchange mechanism negotiations, 158–59, 181, 201–3
  gold standard change, 150, 190–91, 197, 201, 203
  and *Ostpolitik* policy, 211, 220
  policy advisor perspectives, 197–99
  policy goals generally, 191–93, 264–65
  Pompidou period, 238–40, 243–45
  Soviet Union relations, 222, 263
  Watergate impact, 264, 268
nonproliferation negotiations. *See* arms control negotiations; détente *entries*
Non-Proliferation Treaty (NPT), 82, 84
Norstad, Lauris, 63
North Atlantic Cooperation Council, 330, 343
North Atlantic Council, 115
Norway, 163

NTM (National Technical Means), 271
nuclear defense policies
  Carter administration, 266–69
  Nixon administration, 283*n*13, *n*19
  Rambouillet summit period, 63
  Reagan administration, 272–73, 289, 290–91, 293, 294–97
  See also arms control negotiations; détente *entries*
nuclear defense policies, in NATO crisis
  and force goals, 85–88, 141
  France actions, 99*n*5, 111
  MLF negotiations, 91–93
  overview, 78–79, 80–82
nuclear freeze movement, 273, 279, 288, 290
Nuclear Planning Group (NPG), 87, 93, 97, 117, 130, 141
Nunn, Sam, 355

OECD (Organization for Economic Cooperation and Development), 35–36
OEEC (Organization for European Economic Cooperation), 31–32, 34, 35
oil prices, 154–55, 202, 250
OPEC (Organization of the Petroleum Exporting Countries), 154, 202, 250
Organization for Economic Cooperation and Development (OECD), 35–36
Organization for European Economic Cooperation (OEEC), 31–32, 34, 35
Organization for Security and Cooperation in Europe (OSCE), 344, 351–52, 358
Organization of the Petroleum Exporting Countries (OPEC), 154, 202, 250
OSCE (Organization for Security and Cooperation in Europe), 344, 351–52, 358
Ossola, Rinaldo, 178
Ostpolitik policy
  European Security conference, 221–22
  negotiations, 214–21
  overviews, 209–12, 222–24, 230

and Pompidou's détente policy,
    236–38, 241, 242–43, 252
and strategic triangle generally,
    222–24
and Western allies, 212–14, 216, 217,
    219
Outline of Reform, 153–54, 154–55
overflight rights, and NATO crisis, 114

Partnership for Peace (PfP), 330, 337–38
Pentagon. *See* Defense Department, U.S.
Perle, Richard, 290
Perry, William, 340
Pershing II missiles, 269, 294
Petersburg Declaration, 317, 321, 332
Peterson, Peter, 197–99, 205n21
PfP (Partnership for Peace), 330, 337–38
Pierre-Brossollette, Claude, 180–81,
    183–84
pipeline controversy, 273–74, 291–93,
    305n9
pluralistic security community, premise
    of, 4–5
Poehl, Karl-Otto, 183
Poland
    martial law crisis, 274, 275, 276, 291
    NATO enlargement debate, 331–32,
        339, 340
    and *Ostpolitik* policies, 215, 216–17
    and U.S. force deployments, 372
Polaris missile agreement, 47–48, 49
Pompidou, Georges
    détente views generally, 229–33,
        251–53
    exchange mechanism negotiations,
        158–59, 176, 179–81, 184
    monetary policy generally, 173, 176,
        179–80
    and *Ostpolitik* policy, 213, 236–38
    Soviet Union relations, 234–36,
        240–48
    and strategic triangle generally, 12,
        14–15
    U.S. relations, 243–44, 250, 376–77
Poos, Jacques, 354
Potsdam Accord, 215, 217, 219

poultry dispute, 40
pound crisis, 159
Powell, Colin, 353, 364, 367n3
Prague Treaty, 217
preferences, as analytical tool, 310
    See also Amsterdam Treaty; Helsinki
        summit and Agreement; Maastricht
        Treaty
price and wage controls, Nixon
    administration, 196–97, 201

Quai d'Orsay, 67, 234, 240, 375

Raimond, Jean-Bernard, 236, 248, 250
Rambouillet summit period, 58–63,
    68–69, 71n9, 362
RAND Corporation, 334–35, 348n17
Reagan, Ronald (and administration),
    270, 272–77, 287–97, 301–3
Republican Party (U.S.), 191, 192–93,
    195
revaluation arguments. *See* Germany,
    international monetary policy
"Reykjavik Signal," 96
Rice, Condoleezza, 383
Richthoven, Hermann von, 341
Risse, Thomas, 5
Robin, Gabriel, 256n67
Romania, 343–44, 372
Rome Treaty, 29, 31, 38, 53n45
Rowny, Edward L., 295
Rühe, Volker, 330–34, 335–36, 337–38,
    340, 341–42, 347nn10 & 12
Rumsfeld, Donald, 372, 382
Rusk, Dean, 44, 48, 113, 122n35, 131,
    133, 134–35
Russia, 336, 339, 341–42, 378–79
    See also Soviet Union *entries*

Saint Malo initiative, 3
SALT agreements, 192, 238, 239, 243,
    246, 266–72, 283n19, 290
Schake, Kori
    biographical highlights, 392
    chapter by, 351–69
    comments on, 24

Scheel, Walter, 98, 216, 249
Schiller, Karl, 157, 159, 178–79, 180
Schmidt, Helmut
  and Mitterrand's security dialogue proposal, 293
  monetary policy, 15, 159, 161, 163–64, 312
  and Reagan administration, 290
  SALT negotiations, 266, 267–68, 283n19
Schröder, Gerhard, 46, 66–67, 135, 372, 373, 374
Schuman, Robert, 13–14
Schumann, Maurice, 240
Schütze, Walter, 294
Schwartz, Thomas
  biographical highlights, 392
  chapter by, 127–45
  comments on, 23, 114
Scowcroft, Brent, 299–300
security concepts, strategic triangle generally, 4–7
  See also Conference on Security and Cooperation in Europe (CSCE); NATO *entries*
September 11 attacks, 380
Serbia, 357, 359–65
Seydoux, Roger, 234, 240
Shultz, George, 194, 195, 292, 301–2
Single European Act, 302–3, 315
Skubiszewski, Krzysztof, 331
Slocombe, Walter, 334
Slovakia, 340
Slovenia, 343, 352
Smithsonian Agreement, 153, 158–59, 163, 184, 202
Social Democratic Party (Germany), 79, 98, 153, 165, 211, 215, 312
Somalia, 355
Soustelle, Jacques, 33–34
Soutou, Georges-Henri
  biographical highlights, 392
  chapter and section by, 229–57, 375–79
  comments on, 24, 222–23
Soutou, Jean-Marie, 67
Soviet Union
  and CSCE Review Conference, 274–77
  dollar holdings, 206n39
  See also Russia
Soviet Union–France relations
  de Gaulle period, 79, 105–6, 121n8
  and détente generally, 281–82
  Mitterrand period, 15–16
  Pompidou period, 231–38, 240–48, 249–52
Soviet Union–Germany relations
  NATO enlargement debate, 328, 330, 333, 334, 335–36, 340, 341–42, 346n1
  Ostpolitik policy, 2, 209–16, 220–22
Soviet Union–U.S. relations
  Carter administration, 265–72, 275
  and CSCE Review Conference, 284n35
  Johnson administration, 81–84, 92–93, 130, 132, 137
  Kennedy administration, 105
  NATO enlargement debate, 328–30, 339, 346n1, 347n7
  Nixon administration, 192, 222, 249–50, 263
  and *Ostpolitik* policy, 2
  overviews, 261–65, 277–82
  pipeline controversy, 273–74, 291–93, 305n9
  and Pompidou's détente policy, 236–38, 243–44, 246
  Reagan administration, 272–77, 288–89, 290–91, 292–93, 297–99
  See also détente *entries;* Russia
Spaak, Paul-Henri, 43, 94
Special Drawing Rights (SDRs), 152
SS-20 missiles, 266, 269, 270, 279, 283nn21, 23, & 25, 288, 289
Stabilization Force, NATO, 359, 369n43
stagflation, during Nixon administration, 195
START negotiations, 295, 298
State Department, U.S.
  Balkan crises, 353
  and France's NATO withdrawal, 113, 130–31, 133
  and free trade area negotiations, 35
  gas pipeline controversy, 291–92
  and INF negotiations, 290

NATO enlargement debate, 336, 337, 341
Steinmeier, Frank-Walter, 383
Stikker, Dirk, 88
Stoph, Willi, 218
Strange, Susan, 156
Strategic Arms Limitations agreements, 192, 238, 239, 243, 246, 266–72, 283n19, 290
Strategic Arms Reduction Treaty negotiations, 295, 298
Strategic Defense Initiative (SDI), 295–96, 298
strategic triangle, overview
　dynamic nature, 2–5, 321–23
　French perspectives summarized, 11–19, 375–79
　future requirements, 384–86
　German perspectives summarized, 8–11, 379–86
　importance of, 1–2
　national identity issues, 5–8
　U.S. perspectives summarized, 19–22, 372–75
　See also specific topics, e.g., Germany entries; international monetary policy; NATO *entries*
Strauss, Franz Josef, 134, 139
Strycker, Cécil de, 178
Suchocka, Hanna, 348n23
surcharge, Nixon administration, 150, 158, 181
Sweden, 163
Switzerland, 158, 222
Szabo, Stephen
　biographical highlights, 392–93
　chapter and section by, 327–50, 372–74
　comments on, 24

Talbott, Strobe, 295, 336, 337, 339, 341
tariffs
　and European Community development, 31–32, 36, 40, 42
　Nixon's approach, 150, 158, 181, 198–99
TEA (Trade Expansion Act), 39, 42
terrorism era, 11, 373, 380

Test Ban Treaty, 82, 84
Thatcher, Margaret, 288, 289, 292, 296, 299
Thomson, James, 334
Tobin, James, 150
Tokyo Round, 155
Trachtenberg, Marc, 106
Trade Expansion Act (TEA), 39, 42
trade relations. *See* common agricultural policy (CAP)
Triffin dilemma, defined, 151
troop levels. *See* force planning, in NATO crisis
Turkey, 320

Ulbricht, Walter, 218
unemployment, Nixon administration, 195–96, 199, 204n14
United Kingdom. *See* Britain
United Nations
　Afghanistan war, 380
　Balkan conflicts, 352, 354, 355–57, 358, 368n12
　Iraq conflict, 374, 381
United States
　gas pipeline controversy, 273–74, 291–93, 305n9
　and Turkey's potential EU membership, 320
　See also additional United States *entries*
United States, and European Community development
　agricultural policy dispute, 37, 38–40
　Britain's membership, 31, 40, 41–42, 46, 64–65, 72n28
　and free trade negotiations, 30, 33, 34, 35–36
　Grand Alliance vision, 37–38, 40–45
　Nassau Agreement, 47–48, 78
　support of, 32–33, 35, 36–37
United States, Balkan conflicts
　during G.H.W. Bush administration, 352–55
　during Clinton administration, 355–67, 369nn38–40
　overviews, 351–52, 365–67

United States, in strategic triangle (overview)
dynamics challenges, 2–5, 9, 19–22, 372–75
future requirements, 384–86
importance of, 1–2
national identity issues, 5–6, 7–8
United States, international monetary policy
dollar crises, 199–201
domestic context, 191–99, 204n14
exchange mechanism negotiations, 201–3
France relations, 151–52, 161, 172–73, 180, 181–82, 190
Germany relations, 149–50, 152, 158, 161, 164–65, 167n10
overview of transition, 189–91, 203
United States–Britain relations
and G. H. W. Bush administration, 299
during G. W. Bush administration, 372, 374, 381, 382
during Reagan administration, 288, 289–90, 292, 296, 299
and strategic triangle future, 385
traditional, 19
United States–Britain relations, and European Community development
Britain's membership discussions, 31, 41–42, 46, 64–65, 72n28
and free trade negotiations, 30, 33, 34, 35–36
Kennedy's Grand Alliance vision, 37–38
Nassau Agreement, 47–48, 78
United States–France relations
during Balkan crises, 356–57, 358, 365–67
during G. H. W. Bush administration, 299–301, 306–7n28
during G. W. Bush administration, 372–73, 374–76, 381
and détente generally, 281–82
international monetary policy, 151–52, 161, 172–73, 180, 181–82, 190

during Johnson administration, 128, 129, 130–32, 143n28
and NATO enlargement debate, 343
and *Ostpolitik* policy, 223–24, 239
Pompidou period, 230–31, 232–33, 235, 238–40, 243–45, 249–53, 376–78
during Reagan administration, 287–88, 290, 291, 292, 294, 296–97, 299
United States–France relations, and European Community development
agricultural policy dispute, 37, 38, 39
in Bonn Declaration, 64
Britain's EC membership, 42–43, 46
Fouchet plans, 44
and free trade area negotiations, 35, 36
Kennedy's Grand Alliance vision, 37–38
and Nassau agreement, 47–48, 78
overviews, 30–31, 49–50, 55–58, 69–70
Rambouillet summit period, 63, 72n22
United States–France relations, and NATO crisis
background, 130–32
de Gaulle's diplomatic overtures, 108, 109–10, 111
nuclear defense policies, 99n5, 107, 111
overviews, 78–80, 82, 97–99, 104–5, 120–21
in post-withdrawal military negotiations, 115–16, 124n58, 134
at withdrawal announcement, 109, 111, 112–14, 122n35, 123nn49 & 54, 132–34
United States–Germany relations
Balkan conflicts, 365–67
G. H. W. Bush administration, 299–301
G. W. Bush administration, 371–75, 379–84
and détente generally, 279–81
European Security conference, 221, 222
international monetary policy, 149–50, 152, 158, 161, 164–65, 167n10

during Johnson administration, 129, 130
Kohl period, 293–94
NATO enlargement debate, 327–28, 333, 334–35, 336–41, 344–46
and *Ostpolitik* policy, 212–13, 216, 219, 220–21, 223–24, 225nn12 & 13
Reagan administration, 290, 293–97
SALT agreements, 266–68, 283n19
and Vietnam War, 82, 101n20
United States–Germany relations, and European Community development
  agricultural policy dispute, 37, 38–39
  in Bonn Declaration, 64
  and Britain's EC membership application, 44–46
  Elysée Treaty, 48–49
  and free trade area negotiations, 35
  overviews, 30–31, 55–58, 69–70
  Rambouillet summit period, 61, 62–63
United States–Germany relations, and NATO crisis
  background, 131
  détente policies, 82–83, 139
  force planning negotiations, 85–91, 134–36, 137–38, 139–40
  at France withdrawal announcement, 113, 123nn49 & 54, 133–34
  nuclear defense policies, 81, 85–88, 92–93, 141
  overviews, 79–80, 82, 97–99, 109, 141–42
United States–Soviet Union relations
  Carter administration, 265–72, 275
  and CSCE Review Conference, 284n35
  Johnson administration, 81–84, 92–93, 130, 132, 137
  Kennedy administration, 105
  NATO enlargement debate, 328–30, 339, 346n1, 347n7
  Nixon administration, 192, 222, 249–50, 263
  and *Ostpolitik* policy, 2
  overviews, 261–65, 277–82
  pipeline controversy, 273–74, 291–93, 305n9

and Pompidou's détente policy, 236–38, 243–44, 246
Reagan administration, 272–73, 275–77, 288–89, 290–91, 292–93, 297–99
See also détente *entries*
UN Protection Force (UNPROFOR), 356–57

verification factor, SALT II agreement, 270–71
Vietnam War, 82–83, 101n20, 107, 129, 193, 233, 263, 268
Villepin, Dominique de, 374
Volcker, Paul, 159, 200, 204–5n18

wage and price controls, Nixon administration, 196–97, 201
Walesa, Lech, 331, 337
Warner, John, 355
Warsaw Treaty, 215–16, 220
Watergate impact, 264, 268
Weinberger, Caspar, 289, 296
Weisser, Ulrich, 331, 333, 334, 335
Wells, Samuel
  biographical highlights, 393
  chapter and section by, 287–307, 372–74
  comments on, 24
Werner Report, 162, 177
Western European Union (WEU), 249, 293–94, 296, 299–301, 314, 317, 332, 347n12, 354
Wijk, Rob de, 364
Winiewcz, Józef, 216
Witteveen, Johannes, 179
Wormser, Olivier, 174–75, 177, 180, 185

Yamal pipeline controversy, 273–74, 291–93, 305n9
Yeltsin, Boris, 336
Yeo, Edwin, 161
Yom Kippur War, 250
Yugoslav wars. *See* Balkan conflicts

Zelikow, Philip, 347n7